MYSTERIOUS WISDOM

The Life and Work of Samuel Palmer

Rachel Campbell-Johnston

B L O O M S B U R Y

LONDON · BERLIN · NEW YORK · SYDNEY

First published in Great Britain 2011

This paperback edition published 2012

Copyright © by Rachel Campbell-Johnston 2011

The moral right of the author has been asserted

Bloomsbury Publishing Plc
50 Bedford Square
London WC1B 3DP

www.bloomsbury.com

Bloomsbury Publishing, London, New York, Berlin and Sydney
A CIP catalogue record for this book is available from the British Library

ISBN 978 1 4088 2222 7

10 9 8 7 6 5 4 3 2 1

Typeset by Hewer Text UK Ltd, Edinburgh

Printed in Great Britain by Clays Ltd, St Ives plc

MIX
Paper from
responsible sources
FSC® C018072

For Will whom I love and for Sebastian whom I have lost.

'The painter's and the poet's struggles are solitary and patient, silent and sublime'

from an 1881 letter from Samuel Palmer to his son

Contents

Preface

The young man in the picture looks straight out at the viewer. But he is also at the same time staring into himself. His gaze is so distant that it seems almost drugged. What is he thinking? The spectator can't help but wonder about the world that lies beyond that broad, high brow.

Samuel Palmer was barely out of his teens when he drew his defining self-portrait. It's hardly the image you would expect from an upcoming artist at that time. He does not strike the pose of the ambitious young professional; make a bid for new clients by parading palette and brush. He hasn't bothered to shave or to straighten his collar; no comb has been run through his thick tousled hair. This is not a picture that presents a public persona. It is a portrait that asks you to look into a mind.

How can he conjure the visions that move through his entranced imagination, speak of the feelings that swell like an organ fugue in the heart? These are the problems that Palmer faced all his life as a painter. To try to understand them is to enter the head of the dreamer who stares out from this picture, to know why his image, a longstanding favourite of Ashmolean Museum visitors, is also among the most evocative of its Romantic age.

Palmer's life leads its followers into a world that has been transformed by a visionary imagination, into the landscapes that lie beyond earthly veils. It is a place in which the magical shines through the material, in which nature and heaven are intertwined, in which God in all his mildness blesses man's harvests and the darkness of night can be innocent and day. This is not the haunt of any workaday painter. It is the home of the artist as mystic and seer and poet.

The Palmer Family

O! blessed biography which has embalmed a few of the
graces of so many great and good people
from *The Letters of Samuel Palmer*

To stand on the Old Kent Road amid the fumes of the traffic crawling in from the suburbs and the thunder of lorries rumbling off to the coast is to feel an awfully long way from the land of Samuel Palmer; from his slumbering shepherds and his tumbling blossoms, his mystical corn-fields and bright sickle moons. But take a turn down a side street, beside the betting shop where cigarette butts scatter the pavement and oppo-site the fuel pumps of a garage forecourt, and within a matter of paces you will find yourself stepping into what could almost be another world. The noise of cars fades to a dull background grumble, the fumes leak away amid rustling plane leaves. You might even spot a songbird flitting into a garden as you slip between the posts that prevent the passage of vehicles and enter the peaceful enclave of south London's Surrey Square.

To the right, behind a row of ornamental iron railings, runs a hand-some terrace of houses. They are Georgian. Each has an elegant three-bay façade with a smartly symmetrical pattern of sash windows, a panelled door with brass knocker and a pretty fanlight; a few are distin-guished by an old-fashioned lamp bracket arching over the steps that lead up from the street. It is one of these – now number 42 – that is marked out with a homemade English Heritage-style plaque. And it is here that the story of Samuel Palmer starts.

Life is always a lottery, but the odds were not good at the beginning of the nineteenth century. Almost a quarter of all babies would have been bundled into their graves before they reached their first birthday, a fraction that rose to more than a third among the urban poor. Palmer would one day learn the pain of loss only too well. But for now he was lucky: he was born into a middle-class family whose comfortable financial circumstances could cushion a few of the world's harsher blows.

The surname of Palmer is not an uncommon one. It derives from the medieval nickname for pilgrims who, returning from their long, faithful tramps to the Holy Land, brought home with them palm fronds which they displayed as proof. But the branch of the Palmer family to which Samuel belonged boasted gentlemanly origins. Its members bore arms, tracing their ancestry back to the fourteenth-century Henry Chicheley who, as Archbishop of Canterbury, had been immortalised by Shakespeare in *Henry V*. In the play, he is the favourite who first urges the King to lay claim to France and, in real life, to atone for his role in disastrous French wars, he founded the Oxford college of All Souls.

Palmer, however, would relate rather more closely to a later Anglican lineage which included the sixteenth-century theologian Richard Hooker and the eighteenth-century Archbishop of Canterbury William Wake. The family also claimed kinship with the Whig politician Charles James Fox who, having filled a number of senior government posts including that of Britain's first foreign secretary, was still in office when Samuel was born, though he died the following year. 'My Father used to say that his brother . . . made out their relationship to Charles James Fox in two minutes, beginning with the words "Sir Stephen Fox married so and so",'[1] Samuel would recall towards the end of his life, though the only evidence he could offer of this connection was the story of a Mr Barry who, standing in the same relation to Fox as Palmer's father, had upon application been endowed with a valuable government appointment for life. As for the Palmers' much-vaunted relationship to the Church of England's principal primate, it was no closer than that effected through a marriage to an archiepiscopal niece.

The family descended more directly from a line of rather humbler Anglican clergy. Palmer's great-great-grandfather, Samuel, had left Ireland in the early eighteenth century and, having made an advantageous match with the aforementioned niece, was offered the living of Wylye in Wiltshire where his memorial slab can still be found inset in the church wall. His son, Edward, had followed in his clerical footsteps, becoming the rector of Ringmer in East Sussex. But towards the end of the century the family had moved into business as the rector's son, Christopher, set himself up as a hatter, becoming a partner in the firm of Moxon, Palmer and Norman based in Cannon Street on the fringes of the City of London.

Hat-making in England at this time was a lucrative business. In 1795, in order to raise money to fund a war against France, the government had imposed a tax on hair powder with the result that, almost immediately, the modishly puffed coiffeurs of the era had gone out of fashion to be replaced by a taste for millinery. Soon the British 'topper' would be reaching a foot in height. The unfortunate beavers whose pelts were required for these towering adornments did not prosper – the animal was rendered all but extinct – but members of the Worshipful Company of Feltmakers, the city livery company to which hatters belonged, flourished. Palmer's paternal grandfather, Christopher, was of this thriving breed. He married the daughter of one of his business partners and, setting a precedent for the longevity which his son and his grandson would later enjoy, lived until the ripe old age of eighty-two. He had a 'most excellent natural constitution', Palmer later recorded, adding with what was to become an obsessive interest in digestive functions, that 'he would have seen a hundred if he had minded his bowels'.[2]

Christopher Palmer had five children: three sons, Edward, Nathanial and Samuel, and two daughters, Sarah and Mary. Little is known of the girls. The eldest son, Edward, owned property in Ireland which, after he was killed in 1830 by an overturning hackney carriage, was sold out of the family. The second boy, Nathanial, became a corn factor at a time when a corn factor was a force to be reckoned with, for first the Napoleonic Wars had prevented cereals from being brought in from the continent and then, when foreign trade was finally resumed, the newly passed Corn Laws would place punitive tariffs on imported grain. The price of Britain's staple food soared, not least in the wake of an appalling 1816 harvest. There were riots and, at the heart of the fray, stood the profiteering factor: the intermediary without whom no business could be carried out. The third son Samuel, Palmer's father, would not prove so shrewd. Too squeamish to follow the surgeon's career which he had initially contemplated, he had embarked on a career in the family hatting firm, purchasing his Freedom of the City of London as a feltmaker before, realising that he far preferred folios to animal furs, he had decided to set himself up as a bookseller instead. His family, considering trade a grave slur on its gentlemanly credentials, had tried to discourage him but he was of stubborn disposition and had remained resolute. Palmer's father was always to put personal fulfilment above fiscal ambition or social status.

———

Palmer was proud of his paternal heritage. As a young man he liked to seal letters with his armorial crest: a bowed arm grasping a spear. But when it came to more practical matters – particularly monetary ones – his mother's half of the family played the more important role.

Palmer was descended on the maternal side from the Yorkshire-born William Giles who, having travelled extensively in his youth and visited China, had returned to London to work briefly as a hatter before taking up stockbroking instead, a career in which he would find great success, boasting friendships with such esteemed figures in the field as Sir William Forbes, the pioneering founder of a private banking firm.

Giles's interests, however, extended beyond the financial. He was a committed member of the Baptist Church – a congregation which, finding its roots in post-Reformation Europe had, until the eighteenth century, been much persecuted. By Giles's day it was rapidly expanding, however, not least in Britain where ordinary people were growing increasingly critical of the corruption and complacency of the Established Church. The name Baptist, originally coined as a term of mockery for the initiatory rite involving total immersion in water, was eventually adopted by members of the faith themselves. They were also in the nineteenth century commonly known as 'dissenters' or 'Nonconformists'. The Church of England, the dissenters argued, had moved much too far from its original forms; pomp and ceremony had come to play too large a part; it was to the Bible and not the bishop that the faithful should turn; the Church should be constituted of true believers not of just anyone born into a parish and these believers should be free to follow their hearts.

In 1773, Giles married Martha Covell, a fellow Nonconformist. Martha was born in Margate, the daughter of one of the town's first dissenters, a Mary Covell who, initiated at the age of almost sixty, had, despite the jeers of a husband who nicknamed her 'Nanny Baptist', remained steadfast in her loyalty to her new creed. The pair established themselves in a comfortable home on the fringes of south London, looking over leafy gardens towards far-off Dulwich slopes. Here Giles could pursue not only his business dealings but his cultural ambitions, entertaining such eminent contemporaries as Thomas Stothard and Thomas Uwins, the most sought-after society painters of the day, and indulging his talents as a writer, producing several books which, though now entirely forgotten, had that tone of didactic piety which particularly appealed to the religious sensibilities of his times. Such titles as *The Refuge, The Victim, Thoughts on the Sufferings of Christ* or *A Guide to Domestic Happiness* went through several editions and the last was included in a collection of English classics. Giles also compiled a volume of British poetry, composed music, particularly psalmodies (one of which made its way into a Wesleyan hymn book) and tried his hand at humorous sketches, claiming authorship of one of *Mrs Caudle's Curtain Lectures,* a popular series of comic monologues published in *Punch* which purported to be the outpourings of a poor henpecked shopkeeper who, unable to sleep after the death of his wife, lay in bed nightly recalling her protracted rants. Unlike this browbeaten fellow, however, Giles was a man of overbearing character. His word was law to a wife who meekly obeyed him and, revering his literary talents, would refer to him deferentially as 'The Author'. She bore him four children: William, Martha, Thomas and Mary. It was the second of

these, Martha, who, born on 3 November 1778, was to fall in love with
the bookish youngest son of the mercantile Palmer family.

———

Palmer's father was twenty-eight years old when, in October 1803, he
took Martha as his wife. He had joined her Baptist faith but, since law
at that time required all marriages to be conducted in church, the ceremony took place at St Mary's in the parish of Newington in which the
young couple were to live. They could have walked home afterwards to
their new house in Surrey Square; it would have made a pleasant stroll.
The area was still semi-rural, a place of lush gardens in which day-
trippers could wander, of fields and orchards, flower nurseries and
vegetable plots. Newington Butts, now part of the traffic clot of the
Elephant and Castle, was famous in those days for cultivating luxury
fruits. The pineapples, grapes and nectarines which furnished grand
London tables were nurtured in the conservatories of a parish that
could boast its very own exotic species: the Newington peach made a
sweet, summer treat when it ripened around Bartholomewtide.

In 1801, the year of the first London census, there were 14,847
people recorded as living in the south London parish of Newington,
but suburbia was already beginning its inexorable creep. Thirty years
later that number had almost trebled; by the end of the century the
parish's pleasurable green acres would be all but completely buried
beneath sprawling brick. This was the sort of development that Palmer
was to come to detest; and yet his first home was a herald of its approach.

Surrey Square had been the first of several housing projects to be
undertaken by the architect Michael Searles. Its construction had been
quick. Within two years of the first stone being laid in 1792, all the
houses had been occupied. They had appealed to a well-off sector of
mercantile society which, keen to keep up with fashion, had liked
Searles's cut-price copies of current architectural tastes.

Surrey Square was never actually a square. It was a terrace of houses
with an elegantly laid out communal garden to the front. Each residence, with two principal rooms on each floor, a kitchen tucked away
in the basement and a long narrow garden running out at the back, was

possessed of exactly that air of gentrified respectability that its residents would have desired. It must have suited the newlywed Samuel and Martha: small but smart and just around the corner from the bride's old family home. Maybe Martha's father had helped them to choose it. He had probably paid. Certainly, the dowry that he settled on his daughter provided the couple with a modest independence and, as they set out on their married future, their lives bore little sign of any troubles to come.

Early Years

The gate into the world of vision
from Samuel Palmer's 1824 sketchbook

Samuel Palmer was born on 27 January 1805. It was a wintry night. The weather all over England had been bad all week. In the country thick snowfalls had left villages stranded. The stones of the cities were encrusted with ice. And in the capital, on the corner of Adam Street, *The Times* reported, the house of a tallow chandler had caught on fire, forcing a terrified serving girl to leap for her safety from a second-floor window only to break both her legs on the cobbles below.

Apart from this mildly sensational episode, nothing considered of public note had troubled the peace. But in one quietly respectable Surrey Square dwelling, the residents would not have slept that night. A small upper room – lit by the glow of the visiting doctor's lantern, warmed by the flicker of a sea-coal fire, disturbed by the bustle of a midwife with her kettles of hot water – must have been the scene of much anxious fluster as a fragile young woman went into her first labour. At five o'clock on Sunday morning she finally gave birth. She would have been pleased to discover that her first-born was a son.

The world into which Palmer arrived was a world at war. In 1789 the storming of the Bastille by an enraged Parisian mob had raised the curtain on a revolutionary drama, the repercussions of which were to affect the entire century in which he lived.

Many in Britain had at first welcomed this rebellion. France's *ancien regime* had been greedy, cruel and corrupt and it was hoped that something more like a parliamentary system might replace it, that over-gorged empires and rotten dynasties would be followed by a fairer, more democratic form of rule. But optimism soon faded as aristocratic heads rolled. Political panic flared. Would France's revolutionary fervour prove contagious? The British Establishment felt under grave threat.

In 1793, France declared war on Britain and Holland. It was the first salvo of a conflict that would not only prove very long – it would continue pretty much unbroken for the next two decades – but would also be fought on a gigantic scale. Mobilising the first ever citizen army, France sent it marching across the European map. The emergence in 1796 of Napoleon Bonaparte only further exacerbated the situation. Britain found itself facing the most powerful military leader that it had ever known. As Nelson and Wellington battled doggedly to defend their nation and its most valued institutions, a patriotic spirit of crusading conservatism ruled the day.

A peace signed briefly at Amiens in 1802 lasted just a few months. By 1803 hostilities had opened again. The baby Samuel was born into a country at real risk of invasion. It was only eight months later that, with Nelson's victory at Trafalgar in October 1805, Napoleonic ambitions to occupy Britain were decisively thwarted – not that the conflict would end with that. By 1807, having defeated Russia and occupied Berlin, the by-then self-crowned Emperor decided that the most effective way to get the better of his English enemies would be to attack their already war-weakened economy and close European ports off from all British trade. This, the first major example of economic warfare, was to prove highly effective. In Britain, as taxes soared to foot military bills, markets plummeted and bankruptcies loomed. The populace, faced with food shortages, grew increasingly desperate. Social unrest and rioting followed. But the country managed to pull through in large part because Napoleon, affected by his own trading bans, was forced to relax them and finally, in 1815, with the Battle of Waterloo, twenty-two years of almost unbroken warfare in Europe

drew to its close. Britain was the only nation involved in this cata-
clysm to emerge with traditional structures of monarchy, aristocracy
and parliament intact.

Samuel Palmer's birth was registered at Dr Williams's Library in Red
Cross Street, an institution which, originally set up to house a collection of Nonconformist literature, had come to be treated as a place of
safekeeping for the baptismal records of dissenters. Dr William
Williams, a descendant of the library's founder, was a friend of Palmer's
father, a relationship which this new birth would further cement. Two
men who already had books and beliefs in common now also had boys
of about the same age. Years later, Palmer would still continue his
acquaintanceship with this family of old friends.

Palmer was called Sam at home. He was a delicate child and from an
early age showed signs of the respiratory problems that would trouble
him throughout his life. He was only a few months old when his
anxious mother first took him to stay with her family in Margate in the
hope that the fresh air might do him some good. Margate, with its
sandy beaches and its sea-bathing hospital, had by then been transformed from a humble fishing town to an elegant Georgian resort and
this was the first of many holidays that Samuel was to spend there. He
would always love its wide, windy views. The skies over Thanet were the
loveliest in all Europe, believed the great Romantic landscapist Joseph
Mallord William Turner, who remained all his life a regular visitor and
took his Margate landlady as a long-standing mistress. The same marine
vistas that enchanted this painter sank down through the depths of
Palmer's baby stare as his mother, busily fussing over little muslin
bonnets, dabbing at dribble and adjusting shawls, carried him in her
arms along the sea front.

Palmer's lasting interest in the supernatural would be nurtured in
Margate. As a child, he would listen, wide-eyed, to the town's many
ghost stories, especially to the one that involved an ancient brick house
in the high street from the window of which his own grandmother,
spooked by some vaporous apparition, had once leapt. 'It is reported

that the people who *now* live there leave it every Saturday and inhabit elsewhere,' Palmer informed a friend more than fifty years later. 'Only think of a restless spirit wandering about *one* house for nearly a century!'[1] Palmer was always to harbour a lurid fascination for ghosts. Psychic sensibilities, he suspected, ran in his mother's family and one of the stories that he would later tell involved another relation, one Sarah Covell, who claimed to have been paid a call by a friend who, even as she appeared to be making her sociable visit, was in fact in her own home several miles away.

Palmer's mother, Martha, however, showed no paranormal propensities. An affectionate and devoted parent, she was the product of that enlightened generation which, influenced by John Locke's groundbreaking treatise on education, had all but invented the idea of childhood. No longer were infants expected to behave like miniature adults. Unlaced from tight costumes and suffocating conventions, they were encouraged to play. They were part of a family that for the first time in English history had begun to define itself less as an economic entity than as an affectionate group. Palmer grew up amid tenderness, encouragement and love. 'Sorry to say our dear boy's Cough has prevented his bathing,' his mother reported back from Margate to a husband who had had to remain working in London. 'He is a lovely child.'[2]

Sam's sickly constitution began to improve once a nurse, Mary Ward, was engaged. She prepared solid food for the infant instead of insipid pap. On the day that she first gave him a plate of smoked salmon, he stretched out starfish hands in greedy excitement – an early sign of the hearty appetite he would later enjoy. Samuel had a peacefully uneventful life. There are no recorded disasters beyond that of the day when his chair toppled over and his mother, screaming with fright, dashed to apply 'Riga ointment' to the bump. This sharp-smelling juniper salve would no doubt have had to be used fairly frequently for, as Palmer remembered, he had a particular trick of tumbling upstairs. He was probably tripping on the hems of the petticoats in which all young children, regardless of gender, were at that time dressed. It was not until the age of six or seven that the moment for 'breeching' finally arrived and a boy, in what came to be viewed as an important rite of passage, was dressed in his first pair of trousers. No promotion in later life could ever quite match it, Palmer suspected, and yet he was not a boisterous child, preferring sedentary pleasures to more active pastimes, pop-guns and kite-flying to running races or piggy-back rides. The only game of which he was ever to grow fond was backgammon.

Though he would have encountered other children in Surrey Square's communal garden, companions scarcely feature in accounts of his youth. There are very few mentions of his cousins in Clapham and barely a reference to his younger brother William who, born in 1810, was the only one of the many babies whom his mother conceived to survive. Palmer remembered her intermittent periods of confinement well. 'They used to be golden days,' he wrote. 'Boy-like I knew the closet where all the diet-bread and cakes and cold boil'd chickens were kept, and I took care to be as much confined to that spot as my Mother was to her room, except when the nurse pushed me out.'³ But Palmer did not long for siblings to play with. He was a solitary child with a grave disposition and a propensity for daydreaming. He delighted in music – few people could love it more than he did, he said – and books offered a pleasure that would never pall. 'What a wonderful thing is a good book,' he would later write: 'next to a clear conscience, the most precious thing life has to offer.'⁴ His father, delighted to find that his first-born shared his literary enthusiasms, would bring home volume after volume from his stall and Palmer discovered a world that entranced him between their leather bindings. Curled up by the parlour fire or huddled behind the curtains with a glass of syrupy cordial, a pocket of ginger nuts and his purring pet cat, Watch, snuggled up on his lap, he would work his way through the treasures of literature. If we were placed in this world 'merely to please ourselves then I think that reading at all events *would* be worth living for', he wrote.⁵

Beyond Surrey Square lay the crowded jumble of a vast metropolis: 'No! Not the city but the nation of London,'⁶ as Thomas de Quincey, an amazed first-time visitor to the capital in 1800, had exclaimed. Palmer, putting down his books and scrambling out on to the roof, would have been able to gaze out over that great city, that 'colossal emporium of men, wealth, arts and intellectual power',[7] which de Quincey described. Keeping close to his mother, he would have jostled through the market crowds or visited the Southwark leather-binders' workshops with his father, or the chapel on East Street where the famous Welsh divine, Dr Joseph Jenkins, would preach to his impassioned congregation of Particular Baptists, an exclusive sect which believed in the redemption of only a predetermined elect and to which Palmer's father, with the exaggerated fervour of a convert, would for a time belong.

It was only a mile or so from Surrey Square to the Old London Bridge, the main thoroughfare into the city from the south. Samuel would often have gone there, jumping to safety from the fast-dashing carriages; pushing past overburdened pedestrians or beating a path through bleating flocks of sheep. The cries of the drovers, the shouts of the pedlars, the songs of the flower sellers, the pleas of the beggars, the curses of the boatmen: all would have been familiar to Sam's attentive ear. Below, on the river, the mists drifted gloomily over the water; fires glowed sullenly from craft moored off dark wharves. The putrid stench rising from the leather-tanners' pits of urine and faeces mingled with the rich pungency of brewing hops. This was an area that was famous for beer. By 1810, the Anchor Brewery in Park Street was turning out so many barrels a day that Charles Dickens's Pickwickian character Count Smorltork put it on his itinerary of unmissable tourist sites.

Dickens, whose novels Palmer was to come to enjoy, knew this part of London very well. He spent several months of his childhood in Southwark when his father, imprisoned as a debtor, was sent to Marshalsea. Later, in *Oliver Twist*, he would describe the riverside, east of St Saviour's dock, in an area that came to be known as Jacob Island: 'Crazy wooden galleries common to the back of half a dozen houses, with holes to look upon the slime beneath; windows, broken and patched, with poles thrust out, on which to dry linen that is never there; rooms so small, so filthy, so confined, that the air would seem too tainted even for the dirt and squalor which they shelter; wooden chambers thrusting themselves out above the mud, and threatening to fall into it – as some have done; dirt-besmeared walls and decaying foundations; every repulsive lineament of poverty, every loathsome indication of filth, rot and garbage.'

Dickens campaigned against the social evils of his day, against the poor laws that condemned honest people to the miseries of the workhouse and the long hours of child labour that stole young lives away. But then he came from a family which knew only too well what poverty meant. Such social injustices did not impinge upon the life of the privileged young Palmer. He may well have bestowed the odd charitable coin on some soldier invalided out of the Army or left jobless by peace, but the rough world of the slums which sprawled along the southern banks of the Thames did not appear to have troubled his conscience. Nor did he refer to any of the momentous local happenings: the whale which in 1809 was carried on a barge, its tail projecting four yards over the stern, to London Bridge where it was sold in vast chunks at a shilling a customer, creating excellent business despite the intolerable stench; or the frost fair of 1813 when market stalls were erected on the frozen Thames, when carriages were driven right across the river and ox roasts and dances carried out on the ice; or the Bankside mustard mills fire of 1814, one of many conflagrations that flared in the overcrowded slum courtyards and which created a particularly spectacular sight. The whole heterogeneous medley of urban existence lay less than half an hour's walk from his childhood home, but Palmer from the start turned his back on it, preferring the fertile domestic landscapes and sylvan villages that lay to London's south.

Given the delicate condition of his lungs this is not surprising. The capital was growing increasingly polluted; its air thickened by coal smuts and dank river-borne fogs. 'It is difficult to form an idea of any kind of winter days in London,' an American visitor recorded in 1810: 'the smoke . . . forms an atmosphere perceivable for many miles.' Towers, domes and steeples poked skywards through a smothering pall. London was a sorry place to bring up a child, Palmer reflected. Muriatic acid pervaded the air, corroding the very stone, and 'what will peel a stone wall is not likely to put flesh on a baby . . . Then there is the case of the filthy gas . . . and the typhus steaming up through the drain vents in the streets.' Not even a 'horse breeder or dog trainer would consent to rear his whelps or fillies in such a medium', Palmer later wrote, and yet we strive to 'rear the tenderest infancy' in such vile spots.[8]

––––––––––

Following paths that led out through an unregulated straggle of development, past smoking brick kilns and pens of muddy hogs, by piles of stinking refuse and the discarded corpses of dogs, Palmer and his father would head off in search of rural pleasures. Sometimes they would go eastwards, following the river as it broadened between banks of smelly mud towards the village of Greenwich where a gentle chalky slope had once provided a picturesque setting for Henry VIII's palace (long since demolished and replaced by Wren's seamen's hospital) and a steep hill rising above offered a fashionable perch for the home of some Palmer relations on whom father and son would occasionally pay a call. At other times they would wander southwards across the fields to Peckham, then still a quiet country spot, though at night timid villagers would not have risked the walk home for fear of footpads. It was in these very fields that, some fifty years earlier, the great visionary William Blake had been witness to heavenly apparitions. He had seen bright-feathered angels roosting in branches and, gazing out across hayfields, had spotted glorious seraphim. But for Palmer it was Dulwich rather than Peckham that was to become what he later, under Blake's intoxicating influence, would describe as the 'gate into the world of vision',[9] and Dulwich lay a little further on.

One way to walk there was along the ridge of Herne Hill, passing under chestnut boughs and between billowing lilac bushes before descending downwards into lush meadowlands. The village itself was then still prettily rustic with cows and sheep ambling down its grass-lined streets. A few fine houses were scattered along the lanes and upon the gentler slopes. There was a common where gypsies camped with their donkeys, where the butchers grazed their cattle and old women chivvied their flocks of flat-footed geese. There was a village pond with a mill and a couple of public houses to which young men would ride

out. Families would enjoy pleasant day trips in picturesque surroundings. And it was here, to this village, that Dickens imagined the amiable
Mr Pickwick retiring.

The River Effra, now flowing for the most part underground, wound
through it, a slender rivulet, its plaiting currents crisscrossed by little
wooden bridges leading up to the cottages which nestled among sheltering laburnums and hawthorns. The young Sam, like the critic John
Ruskin – whom he was later to know – learnt much of his love of
nature here, sharing the same sort of boyish pleasures that Ruskin
describes: squatting down by the waters, poring over the tadpoles that
squiggled in pools, stuffing himself with blackberries from the overspilling hedges, collecting bunches of cowslips and gathering the wild
dill from which the village – *Dilwihs* or *Dylways* meaning 'the damp
meadow where dill grows' – takes its name. And later, also like Ruskin,
Palmer would bitterly lament the development, that 'foul and unnatural enlargement of London',[10] which would lead to the destruction of
this enchanted spot. He was always to treasure it, a rural idyll in his
memory. 'Remember the Dulwich sentiment at very late twilight time,'
he would note, 'with the rising dews . . . like a delicious dream.'[11]

The relationship which Sam and his father now forged set a pattern
for the strong male friendships that Palmer was always to foster. The
pair must have presented a companionable picture, walking side by
side along country lanes, the elder striding along in a flapping overcoat, the younger bobbing beside him in short jacket and cap making
periodic forays into hedgerows and fields to fetch birds' nests or flint
stones, mushrooms or beech nuts. There were treasures to be hoarded
and Sam, having emerged in one bound 'from short petticoats . . .
into trousers and . . . O rapture! – into *pockets*',[12] had found just the
place. Amid the lucky-dip of delights – 'gingerbread nuts, story
books, toffy, squirts and pop guns'[13] – which his bulging pockets
harboured, he would always keep his most prized gift of a knife. One
day he had asked his father to file its blade even sharper and it had
had to be explained to him that if an edge was too finely honed it

would do nothing but shave because, if put to any other purpose, it would turn. Palmer would discover in this advice a metaphorical lesson: the human mind, also, could become too acute. 'Whatever sharpens narrows,'[14] as the philosopher Francis Bacon, whom he would frequently cite, had once said.

Palmer's own education was broad. Considered too fragile for school, the foundations of his learning were laid at home. The Bible was a bedrock. Sam was made to learn a passage from it daily. But his father, on very rare occasions with the aid of a rod, also taught him good Latin and the rudiments of Greek. He was allowed to graze freely in the pastures of literature with only the vaguest of programmes to guide him. Volumes discovered in solitude were to become matchless companions. 'There is nothing like books,' as he would later say: 'of all things sold incomparably the cheapest, of all pleasures the least palling, they take up little room, keep quiet when they are not wanted and, when taken up, bring us face to face with the choicest men who ever lived, at their choicest moments.'[15] The lessons of these men were to form the weft of his life. He would never forget, for example, his first reading of Pope's *Essay on Criticism*, a didactic composition which pursues a discussion as to whether poetry should be 'natural' or written according to set classical rules. Pope resolves the problem by arguing that classical rules are natural. It was an idea that Palmer was later to explore in his painting. Joseph Glanville's *Sadducimus Triumphatus*, which decried scepticism about witchcraft, was, with its lurid illustrations and its tales of drumming spirits, a particularly favoured volume according with his boyish tastes but also, in its more serious aspects – its reconciliation of the rise of science with supernatural powers – serving to validate his faith in metaphysical possibilities, preparing him for his meeting with Blake, who believed ardently in magic.

Palmer's father added to his knowledge on their rambles through the country, talking and reciting and reading to him as they walked from one of the little vellum-bound notebooks which he always kept tucked into a waistcoat pocket. These books were stuffed with a haphazard assortment of observations, quotations and facts which had been harvested randomly from whatever he happened to be reading. Ranging

from the scribbled solution to an algebraic problem, through a few
lines of poetry to the religious pronouncements of some admired
divine, their ideas would, one by one, be slipped into the formative
mind of young Sam.

Palmer's father, in many ways, was not a good role model. An
unworldly dreamer, he could be carefully methodical in small things;
but when it came to matters of more serious import – not least, financial provision for his family – he was prepared to act upon improvident
whim. Even when it became obvious that he was misguided, he would
continue stubbornly on. Once, finding the gate to a bridge over a river
locked, he had without hesitation waded straight out into the flow.
And yet, he was as lenient as he could be obstinate and Palmer was
always to remember the day when, due for a birching, he had pleaded
with his parent to turn his mind to other more pleasant matters and so
been let off.

Many years later, Palmer would look back with gratitude on the
upbringing that an affectionate and enthusiastic father, a man who had
'loved knowledge for its own sake',[16] had offered him. He would always
value the kindness and, even more importantly, 'the liberality'[17] with
which he had been allowed to pursue his interests when a more worldly
parent, eager to be rid of financial encumbrance, would have pushed
his son into trade.

Around 1814 the Palmer family left Surrey Square, moving to
Houndsditch on the eastern border of the City of London. This road
is now a steep gulley of glass, all but deserted outside business hours,
but then it was part of a labyrinth of narrow, crowded streets, overlooked by ramshackle houses and blocked by horse-drawn-traffic
jams. The move was probably made for financial reasons. Two young
sons were not cheap to support and the bookselling business, it was
hoped, would be brisker in this part of the capital where a stallholder,
setting out his wares on the pavement, could attract the custom of
walkers returning from work in the City to the residential West End.
To the country-loving Sam, however, the change would have felt

bleak. Houndsditch was rough, surrounded by the notorious rooker-
ies of the Jewish Quarter and famous for its rag fair: a 'mass of old
clothes, grease, patches, tatters and remnants of decayed prosperity
and splendour'.[18] It was said that a silk handkerchief could be bought
back here within hours of its having being stolen. It was certainly not
a salubrious area and Palmer would later recall with disgust the sight
of a dead man's brains lying in the middle of Ludgate Hill with only
a little hastily scattered sawdust to cover them.

Worse was to come. In May 1817, Sam was sent away to school.
Merchant Taylors' was chosen: an institution founded in 1561 by the
City livery company of that name. Now located outside London, in
Palmer's day it was established in some bare old buildings in Suffolk
Lane in the shadow of St Paul's. The school motto, *Concordia Parvae
Res Crescunt* – 'small things grow in harmony' – could almost have
served as a professional maxim for the painter that Palmer was to
become, but it far from reflected his experiences at the time. A
cosseted child with a tendency to shed 'delicious tears at performances on the organ'[19] did not cope well with the coarse rough and
tumble of school life.

The diminutive twelve-year-old with his thick russet hair, his pale
complexion and his asthmatic's cough, gazed with misgiving at the
boisterous creatures around him. 'I . . . thought they resembled
baboons,' he later wrote. He was always to disdain the public school
system in which 'the fag crawls to be kicked, and, in his turn, kicks the
fag who crawls to him', even as he sardonically acknowledged that the
system 'perfectly represents and so admirably prepares for the requirements of public life' for 'what is statesmanship but successful crawling
and kicking?'[20]

The timid young Palmer sought, as ever, a safe haven in books and it
may well have been around this time that his particular affection for the
work of William Cowper was nurtured. Cowper, then, was one of the
nation's most popular poets. His homely vision was deeply to move
Palmer. He saw his mother as the living counterpart of the domestic
paragons of Cowper's verse and 'Tirocinium' – a poem in which Cowper
urges a clerical friend not to send his sons off to boarding school but to

opt for private tuition instead – contained painful resonances for the unhappy little boy.

> *Why hire a lodging in a house unknown*
> *For one whose tenderest thoughts all hover round your own?*
> *This second weaning, needless as it is,*
> *How does it lacerate both your heart and his!*

Maybe Palmer followed the same pleading tack. By the time autumn came, his parents had brought him home. The Merchant Taylors' experiment had lasted barely six months.

———

Palmer was delighted to be back in familiar surroundings from which, like the protagonist of Cowper's most famous work, 'The Task', he could peep at the world through 'the loop holes of retreat'; watch 'the stir/ of the Great Babel', but not 'feel the crowd'. Seclusion was always to suit him and most of all when it was shared with a small companionable group. 'SNUG', he was later to write: 'how much lies in that little word . . . Did you never put up your feet on the fender and . . . wish you could *roll* yourself up like a dormouse? . . . a cosy corner is the thing to sit down in.'[21]

His nurse, Mary Ward, was a cherished member of his homely circle. More than just a hired help, she became a much-loved part of the family with which she would remain for the rest of her life. She was clearly an unusual woman for, at a time when most servants would have been illiterate, she had read deeply from her two most treasured volumes: the Bible and a popular copy of Milton's verse. It was to Mary, Palmer said, that he owed his first true poetic experience, one that would shape his vision for the rest of his life.

Palmer had not yet turned four at the time and had still been living in Surrey Square where, tucked up in bed on a winter night, he remembered lying wakefully, watching the moon rising through the bare elm branches, floating away into a deep violet dusk. Its silvery light flooded into his room. Palmer gazed at the shadows that were cast by the trees, at their shapes fiddling and tangling upon painted walls. But it was Mary, he said, who gave meaning to these ephemeral patterns, fixing a picture of them forever in his head. 'Well do I remember,' he recalled many years later, 'while the long shadows of moonlight were stealing over an ancient room, her repeating from Dr Young: "Fond man, the vision of a moment made,/ Dream of a dream, and shadow of a shade!"'[22] This couplet – Edward Young's poetic echo of the philosophical allegory in which Plato imagines that mankind is imprisoned in a cave, perceiving reality only in the form of its shadows as they are cast by a fire upon surrounding walls – entranced the youthful Palmer. Shadows for him accrued a soulful new resonance from then on, conjuring not just an awareness of life's fragile mysteries but also a wistful yearning for a greater reality beyond. Again and again, as an artist, he would paint crepuscular scenes. 'Of all creatures the owls and I love twilight best,'[23] he would say.

Mary Ward also instilled a deep reverence for the poetry of Milton. She would have known the great poet's work from her youth when it had been very much part of popular culture, its epic dramas inspiring the era's leading artists or conjured up for the masses in the Eidophusikon, an entertainment palace in London's Leicester Square in which, by means of complicated systems of mirrors and pulleys, huge theatrical paintings of Miltonic scenes were made to appear to move. Mary had a Tonson's pocket Milton, an illustrated collection of his poems which, first published by Jacob Tonson in 1688, was to run into more than sixty editions between 1770 and 1825. This was the volume, seldom far from her side, from which Mary would recite to Sam as a child and which she would bequeath him upon her death. It was a legacy he would always treasure, along with her pair of simple, roughly worked spectacles and the tin ear-trumpet which she used in old age. Binding the book with brass corners, he would carry it in his pocket for more than twenty years. He came to know most of it by heart. Its images stocked his artistic imagination; its sonorous rhythms stirred the depths of his soul. 'I am never in a "lull" about Milton,' he would write more than fifty years later; '. . . nor can tell how many times I have read his poems . . . He never tires.'[24] 'I do believe his stanzas will be read in heaven.'[25]

Mary Ward became almost a second mother to Palmer. She had to be for, on 18 January 1818, his real mother suddenly died. She was not yet forty. Sam was almost thirteen and was visiting his grandfather when an uncle arrived to break the tragic news. 'It was like a sharp sword sent through the length of me,'[26] he wrote.

Portrait of Sam Palmer 1819 by Henry Walter. This likeness of Palmer taken by his childhood friend presents a solemn fourteen year old at the very beginning of his artistic career.

The Beginnings of an Artist

Oh that I had had the human bones broken about my stupid head
from *The Letters of Samuel Palmer*

The death of a devoted mother would fall heavily on any young boy, but for the home-loving Sam it was particularly painful. He struggled to cope with a confusion of feelings and even many years later the wounds had not healed. He would sit and weep softly over Cowper's *On the Receipt of My Mother's Picture*, a work which, recalling the poet's own bereavement, would always move Palmer to tears.

My mother! when I learn'd that thou wast dead,
Say, wast thou conscious of the tears I shed?
Hover'd thy spirit o'er thy sorrowing son,
Wretch even then, life's journey just begun?
Perhaps thou gav'st me, though unseen, a kiss;
Perhaps a tear, if souls can weep in bliss . . .

It was, he thought, the most affecting poem in the English language.

The more practical consequence of the loss, however, was to set people thinking about the direction which thirteen-year-old Sam's life should take. An artistic path, it was decided, would suit his proclivities. Attitudes to painters had altered greatly over the course of the previous fifty years. Where formerly they had been considered mere craftsman, by the end of the eighteenth century they had acquired professional respect. Immanuel Kant had effected what he had himself claimed to be the equivalent of a Copernican revolution in philosophy: where Enlightenment thinkers had sought to describe a strictly objective world, he had argued that reality could only be interpreted from the unique viewpoint of each individual and in so doing he had paved the way for Romanticism. He had set the creative spirit free to soar up to imaginative pinnacles, to a place where the dreamer could commune with a higher reality and the visionary discover truths in the solitude of his soul.

Palmer, as a boy, had dreamt of becoming an author like his grand-father. He had attempted verse from early youth, but as a poet he was never to advance beyond an ornately self-conscious style:

> Methinks the lingring, dying ray
> Of twilight time, doth seem more fair,
> And lights the soul up more than day,
> When wide-spread, sultry sunshines are.
> Yet all is right and all most fair,
> For Thou, dear God, hast formed all;
> Thou deckest ev'ry little flower
> Thou guidest ev'ry planet ball
> And mark'st when sparrows fall.[1]

In prose, however, Palmer was to discover a more authentic voice. His letters reveal a descriptive verve, a stylistic flair and freshness of perception that suggest that, had he shed a lecturing tone of long-winded and sometimes pious pomposity, he might have made something of the writer's calling. He speaks of 'our earthly hopes' being 'shed like shirt buttons';[2] he describes a damaged etching plate as being 'bent up like an earwig disturbed in an egg-plum';[3] he explains that 'to stuff the mind with a legion of little facts makes it stupid and heavy as a bed is made heavy by its fullness of light feathers';[4] he describes the tortured flourishes of modern operas as running 'up and down, backwards and forward, and round and round, like a squirrel in his cage'.[5]

'Attention [is] the daughter of Curiosity who seldom can be prevailed

upon to go anywhere without her mother,'[6] Palmer wrote; or 'in the
North when there happens to be a dull summer – nothing but grey grey
grey – the poor mind begins to feel as if it were going to bed with cold
feet'.[7] His images are resonant and his relish for language can almost be
tasted on the tongue when he describes a cup of cocoa with its 'oleagi-
nous globosities bobbing about as you stir it like porpoises of the deep'[8]
or discusses the 'sapid hotch potch' of Southey, in which he has been
'routing like a hungry hog',[9] or rails against 'all this gaseous rhodomon-
tade about the Ideal'.[10]

However for all the vigour of the copious letters that Palmer would
write throughout the course of his life, his literary ambitions, remained
those of the 'true bookworm'. 'Some place their bliss in action,' he
wrote to his boyhood friend Walter Williams in 1839, effortlessly slipping in a line from Pope, but on 'a dull, pattering, gusty December
day, which forbids our wishes to rove beyond the tops of the chimney-
pots', what he would most want would be 'a good register stove; a sofa
strewed with books; a reading friend, and above all, a locked door
forbidding impertinent intrusions'. A day like this, he wrote, punctuated by 'a light dinner about one o'clock', 'a little prosy chat (not
too argumentative), just to help digestion; then books again, till
blessed green-tea-time winds us up for *Macbeth* or *Hamlet*',[11] was his
idea of ecstasy.

As far as a profession was concerned, however, it was decided that
Palmer should apply himself to the visual arts. Looking back, he considered the choice misguided. 'It is too commonly the case,' he observed,
that when a young man 'prefers scribbling over paper to his Latin and
Greek, he is supposed to have a "taste for painting"'.[12] He had liked
music and architecture more, he said. His earliest known picture – a
tiny watercolour done when he was seven of a windmill, with a man
fishing in the pond in front of it – though dated and proudly preserved
by his mother (and then kept by him for his 'dear Mother's'[13] sake),
reveals no especial talent although its small size and rural subject matter
might be considered prescient.

It is possible that his family had pushed him towards painting
because they felt they were pursuing a deceased mother's wish. Martha

had always encouraged her son's creative efforts. In an 1814 letter from Margate she told her husband that Sam had been sketching the local church for a cousin and that now this same relative wanted a picture of a mackerel too. This letter, however, also hinted at the source of the misunderstanding regarding his choice of career. His earliest artistic forays, he much later explained, stemmed not from an inborn attraction to painting but from a 'passionate love' – and the expression was not too strong, he assured his correspondent – 'for the traditions and monuments of the Church; its cloistered abbeys, cathedrals and minsters', which he was always imagining and trying to draw; 'spoiling much paper with pencils, crayons and watercolours'.[14]

Palmer had grown up steeped in the Baptist faith. His parents' shared beliefs created a powerful marital bond. On Sundays they would attend a succession of religious services and the content of sermons would be much discussed. And yet Sam, from first youth, showed a particular fascination for Anglican traditions. In his earliest surviving letter he reports to his father on the Margate vicar and though, at the age of nine, he is rather more riveted by a mighty blow dealt by the choirmaster to a boy in the organ gallery than anything more conventionally clerical (and is soon diverted to telling how he has written the name of his cat on the sands of the beach), it was an ecclesiastical interest that was to gather rapid pace.

The church would, quite literally, have served as a beacon in the young Sam's life. As he crossed London Bridge the shadows of its twin sentinels, the tower of St Saviour's and the steeple of St Magnus's, would have fallen across his path. The scattered pinnacles of the City's churches would have poked up through the smog. The great dome of St Paul's would have been a prominent landmark and, as a miserable schoolboy, he often found solace in its echoing spaces, frequently visiting on Sunday afternoons. 'Gazing upwards into the sublime obscurity', he would listen to sacred music: music which he came to 'prefer to all other of every kind'. The way that it brought together 'sublimity fullness and power with the most luscious sweetness and last delicacies of sound',[15] he said, could allay all nagging anxieties and feverishness of mind and many years later he was to rail against the (never-to-be-accomplished) plan to tile the 'dim and solemn' cupola of Wren's majestic cathedral with 'metallic reflectors' to make it 'gay'. 'There is a kind of craziness which neither raves nor mopes: – it rummages,' he protested. 'Whatever it encounters it desires to change into something else; to reverse to pervert.'[16] 'Fancy putting frescoes into the dome to give it light, when its essence is gloom and mystery!'[17]

For Palmer, the sacred calm of the city's stone temples felt akin to that peace which he discovered in the countryside. Religion and nature, first beginning to mingle in his mind as his father read to him from the Bible among meadows and woods, continued to blend in his thoughts. Moved by strange mystic feelings, he applied himself to drawing pictures of the church buildings that bred them. His parents, eager to help but misunderstanding his motives, took this as evidence that he wanted to be an artist and so supplied him with architectural drawings, botanical engravings and art historical prints of famous canvases and frescoes to copy.

After the death of his mother, a drawing master was engaged for Sam, a minor artist who would have fallen through a hole in art history if it were not for the passing role that he was to play in Palmer's life. William Wate was a landscapist of unostentatious ability: a competent painter of pleasant topographical views. Not for him the passionate extremes of a Romantic aesthetic; Wates leant safely towards the mildest form of 'the picturesque'.

In 1782, the clergyman, author and artist, the Reverend William Gilpin, had introduced the idea of the picturesque to cultural debate. Looking for 'that kind of beauty which is agreeable in a picture',[18] he had toured the country, squinting upwards at rocks from vertiginous angles, framing foregrounds with trees and sprinkling distances with ruins as he had sought to present a new painterly ideal. He had found much room for improvement in nature's sense of composition and a colourful peasant or misplaced hovel could easily be added to or subtracted from a scene. Ruined castles and abbeys were objects of particular 'consequence' and a low viewpoint which tended to emphasise the sublime was always preferable to a higher prospect.

Soon, the picturesque as Gilpin had defined it was considered the very apogee of cultural fashion. With the continent closed off by conflict, there was hardly a beauty spot to be discovered in Britain without finding also an amateur artist in its midst. Equipped with their easels and a portable clutter of artistic knick-knacks, they surveyed the landscape in their dark-tinted 'Claude' glasses – small, convex mirrors which, by isolating a fragment of the natural scenery and unifying its tones, created a hazily atmospheric composition of the sort which the seventeenth-century master Claude Lorrain had made highly popular. The wild places of Britain were treated like hunting trophies: they were taken to be mounted on drawing-room walls.

The more clear-sighted were sceptical, even scathing, of the pictur-esque's formulaic rules. In Jane Austen's *Northanger Abbey*, drafted and written in the 1790s (though only posthumously published in 1817), Catherine Morland, the naïve heroine, while out on a walk, is given such an effective crash course on the subject, on foregrounds and distances and second distances, that by the time she and her teacher, Edward Tilney, have reached the top of Beechen Cliff she has 'voluntarily rejected the whole city of Bath, as unworthy to make part of a landscape'. And, in 1809, the comic writer William Combe, working in collaboration with the cartoonist Thomas Rowlandson, dispatched a satirical character, an impoverished schoolmaster called Dr Syntax, off on a tour of Europe atop his grey mare Grizzle in search of fashionable prospects the recording of which, he hopes, will make him 'a real mint'. 'I'll *prose* it here, I'll *verse* it there,/ And *picturesque* it every where', Syntax informs his wife in the opening canto. The ensuing narrative with its accompanying illustrations, published in monthly instalments between 1809 and 1811 in the *Poetical Magazine* and subsequently turned into a book that ran into several editions, proved an immense success. But such satire did little to shift popular tastes. By the time Palmer was learning to paint, Gilpin's principles had become as narrowly prescriptive as a painting-by-numbers chart. Any bravely original thinker would by then have abandoned them; but Wate was no flaringly talented Turner, no stubbornly rebellious John Constable: he followed a peaceably commercial path and it was along its obedient course that Palmer was now led.

Only two of his early sketchbooks survive. The earliest – a slim rectangle, about the size of a cheque book, bound in soft battered leather and fastened by a brass clasp – is now in the custodianship of the British Museum. The visitor who makes an appointment at the Department of Prints and Drawings and leafs through its pages with white art-handler's gloves can wander off on a sketching trip with the fourteen-year-old Palmer, stroll alongside him through his south London haunts, rambling upriver from Greenwich to Battersea, visiting rural Chiswick or Richmond's lush meadows or embarking on forays to Bedfordshire or Kent.

The sketchbook is dated 1819. King George III – 'old, mad, blind, despised, and dying' as Percy Bysshe Shelley describes him in his passionately radical political sonnet *England in 1819* – was entering the last year of his reign. His son, who for almost a decade had already presided as regent, was on the verge of ascending to the throne. A foppish and dissolute figure, he was hardly likely to fulfil Shelley's hopes of a 'glorious Phantom' to 'illumine our tempestuous day'. It was he who, in the aftermath of the infamous 1819 Peterloo massacre – in which the cavalry had charged a crowd of demonstrators in Manchester, peacefully campaigning for parliamentary reform – had issued royal congratulations to the cutlass-wielding hussars.

The Napoleonic wars were over but the political problems of Britain were still far from resolved as the second generation of Romantics emerged, Keats publishing in 1819 two of his most famous works, *La Belle Dame Sans Merci*, a ballad of a knight who falls under the fatal enchantment of an ethereal temptress, and *The Eve of Saint Agnes*, a passionately charged poem which tells of the elopement of two lovers, and Byron producing the first cantos of his satirical epic *Don Juan* in the same year. Meanwhile Constable, though still unrecognised by the painterly establishment, was embarking on the unique six-foot sketches of local Suffolk scenes which were to represent his great breakthrough and mark him out as a modern, while Turner, inspired by a trip to Italy, by the classical lineaments of the buildings and the clarity of the light, was learning to unite atmosphere and architecture, past and present, art and history, in his work. In 1819 he showed his largest canvas ever: a landscape painted on Richmond Hill, a picture of a real England made ideal, and he was about to begin another canvas which, like some imaginative verso, would present an ideal Rome made real.

This was the cultural milieu into which Palmer was setting out, but his first sketchbook reveals quite how far he had to go. Occasionally it offers intimate glimpses of the developing artist. A special feeling for trees is revealed by a particularly attentive pencil sketch – 'the willow behind the cottage was thin and playful' he noted – or a still unformed personality is found trying out different versions of his signature: the name 'Sam Palmer' is followed by the more grown-up 'S Palmer' and then – as he contemplates posterity – a date is added as well. But for the most part this book consists of a series of unremarkable topographical studies by a young man who is learning basic skills.

Wate would have introduced him to the elementary drawing lessons of the popular tutors of the day: to the eighteenth-century Alexander Cozens who wrote four major treatises on 'practical aesthetics', setting out to fix the basic forms – 'shape, skeleton and foliage' – of thirty-two species of tree, or producing nineteen plates that purported to define the 'principles of beauty relative to the human head'; or to Rudolph Ackermann's books, including his 1811 study of watercolour which was to become one of the most influential manuals of its day. Illustrated by David Cox (though he was not actually credited), it had the unforeseen effect of training a whole generation of artists to adopt Cox's style – albeit that of his earlier more picturesque landscapes rather than of the later atmospheric works for which he is now more admired. In 1808, Cox had settled in Dulwich. His subject matter – gypsy encampments on the common, kite-flying children, grazing donkeys and rustic cottages – would certainly have been familiar to Palmer and, in his 1819 sketchbook, he follows Cox's instructions for the capturing of atmospheric effects as he carefully records the sepia gradations of twilight or studies the Margate pier by the glow of the setting sun. But later he would come to dismiss him: 'Cox is pretty – is sweet, but not grand, not profound,' he wrote after a day out in Dulwich. 'Carefully avoid getting into that style which is elegant and beautiful but too light and superficial.'[19]

Palmer had by then found a master to inspire him. In 1819 he had gone for the first time to a Royal Academy summer exhibition. This annual art show was a major event. The Royal Academy was a prestigious institution. Election to its charmed circle was a coveted honour for, established in 1768 under the patronage of George III, it had been founded to raise the professional standing of artists by providing not just a school which could guarantee a sound classical training but a public forum in which to display new work. The Academy conferred status and with status came commissions and wealth.

At that time, an art show was a novelty in England. The Academy's summer exhibition, a higgledy-piggledy parade of densely packed paintings, sculptures, drawings and prints, was among the great spectacles of Georgian and Regency London: a glorious bear garden which every ambitious artist would have aspired to be part of and no gossiping socialite would have wanted to miss. This was the stage upon which the triumphs and the tragedies, the scandals and sensations, the celebrations and controversies of the British art world were played out. It was here, upon the canvases of the most fashionable painters, that the public could meet aristocrats, dignitaries and stars; come face to face with Thomas Lawrence's Prince Regent in all his flamboyance, see Thomas Gainsborough's Georgiana in her rakishly tilted hat or admire Joshua Reynolds's Sarah Siddons in full theatrical flight. It was here that artists would introduce their most eye-catching ideas; that, in 1771, Benjamin West would challenge the traditions of history-painting by clothing the figures in his tableau of a dying General Wolfe in contemporary rather than classical dress; that, in 1781, Henry Fuseli would assure himself of a lasting reputation by revelling in the sensual eroticism of a woman abandoned to nightmarish sleep or that, in 1812, Turner would show off the sheer audacity of his vision, whipping up a great vortex of a snowstorm in his *Hannibal and his Army Crossing the Alps*.

Success at the summer exhibition was crucial and competition was fierce. Only a fraction of the works submitted could be selected. The jury was far from impartial; and even having been chosen, an artist still had to hope that the hanging committee would accord his works an honourable spot. In 1784, Gainsborough withdrew his contributions in a huff because he felt that they had not been treated with the dignity they deserved and, in 1809, the placing of Benjamin Haydon's *Dentatus* in an insignificant side chamber ignited a quarrel with the Academy which was never to be soothed. Everyone aspired to have their work hung in the Great Room (rather than in one of the cramped subsidiary spaces) and 'on the line' which now means roughly eye-level but, at that time, had a quite literal connotation for in the Academy's galleries, first at Trafalgar Square and then in Somerset House, a dado rail ran around the room about eight feet above the ground. A picture was 'on the line' when its frame rested almost upon it. Large works were almost invariably placed above the line and, if they were higher up, tilted slightly forwards; smaller pieces, distributed like space fillers among them, would often be all but impossible to appreciate, even though spectators would bring spyglasses or even telescopes.

As artists competed for attention, jealous rivalries broke out. In 1781, Fuseli and Reynolds went head to head. The former, having spotted Reynolds at work on his *Death of Dido*, decided to challenge him by painting his own version of the subject. This was the sort of stunt which could make a name known. The combative Turner was certainly not above such behaviour. In 1832, he made his usual visit to the summer exhibition on 'varnishing day'. This was a day just before the public opening which had originally been allocated so that artists who had submitted freshly painted canvases could apply a protective gloss to their works; but for many years it had been used instead to make last-minute alterations. Turner, fond of parading his daunting technical skills, was particularly famous for putting this extra time to good use: he would submit half-painted canvases and then, on varnishing day, proceed to complete the entire picture right in front of his fellows in just a few hours. When, in 1832, he found his muted seascape *Helvoetsluys* hung alongside a festively coloured Constable canvas, *The Opening of Waterloo Bridge*, he thought it looked drab and so added a small red buoy to his composition: a bright dab of scarlet to give it a new life while, just as importantly, making the work of his rival look gaudy. 'Turner has been here and fired a gun,' Constable remarked in dismay when, at the grand opening, he saw what had been done. A canvas that had taken him almost a decade to complete had been suddenly diminished by his competitor's stunt.

The more sharply the artists elbowed for attention, the more eagerly the public crowded to see, pushing and shoving to gawp at the most gossiped-about pictures. Parasols, umbrellas and walking sticks had to be banned and in 1806 when David Wilkie, then still an unknown Scottish teenager, made a debut with his *Village Politicians*, a realistic portrayal of rustics arguing in their local inn, a subject of such mundanity that no previous artist had ever aspired to paint it, crush barriers had to be erected to contain the chaotic throng. Everyone wanted to look at this most extraordinary image of completely ordinary life.

For emerging artists, the summer exhibition was a formative experience. The first that Palmer attended was to be fixed in his mind forever by Turner's 1819 *Entrance of the Meuse: Orange Merchant at the Bar, going to pieces*. Even to the modern-day viewer familiar with this master's late canvases, in which light and colour dissolve in tempestuous flurries and sublime passions are whipped up by the sheer power of paint, this cloudscape feels stirring. The young Palmer was rooted to the spot. Here was a freedom he had never before encountered. He was, as he put it, 'by nature a lover of smudginess'.[20] He could find a painting lesson, he said, in the sediment at the bottom of a coffee cup. A lifelong admiration for Turner was instilled. 'I have revelled in him from that day to this,'[21] Palmer recorded more than fifty years later. The finest artists, he came to believe, could combine both precise visual description and hazy vagueness of mood but, of these two, he considered the indefinite part to be the most difficult as well as the most desirable. 'When I think of a pocket sketch-book of soft printer's paper, a piece of charcoal, or very soft chalk, and a finger to blend it about, I think of improvement,' he wrote.[22] Turner led the young artist away from mere description towards a pursuit of the 'effects' that he was to fight to capture all his life. He began to experiment with a new vigour, even trying out blustery Turneresque scenes, attempting to convey the glower of a rainstorm as it sweeps its sullen shadow across a bay's glittering expanses. And yet, for all the gusty freshness of the gales that, over the course of his life, he would find himself dashing down, his landscapes would tend to owe more to the peaceably nostalgic views of Dutch painters than to Turner's dramatic visions.

Little in Palmer's early work heralded his distinctive talent, though future subjects can be spotted – the softly domed hills that enfold humble dwellings, the church towers that speak of higher spiritual truths, the cattle that will wander off to re-emerge as sheep (the more conventional denizens of the pastoral dream) – and themes that will later be developed emerge. Palmer followed Turner to the riverside vantage point from which he had painted his 1819 *Richmond Hill on the Prince Regent's Birthday*. This impressive view, its vistas stretching away down lush green slopes across the ancient Petersham meadows and beyond to the broad curve of the Thames, was already famous as the landscape that had inspired Henry Purcell to compose and tempted Thomas Gainsborough away from his portraits and, retiring in old age to Richmond, James Thomson, the author of the words to *Rule Britannia*, would describe it as the very quintessence of 'happy Britannia'.

At a time when painters were first turning away from the tenets of antiquity and, with an affection nurtured by fear of invasion, starting to associate native scenery with Britishness, it is significant that Palmer should have tackled so emblematic a view. 'Landscape is of little value,' as he was later to put it, 'but as it hints or expresses the haunts and doings of man.'[23] In painting his local countryside, he was also speaking of a quintessentially British way of life.

The young artist also made several studies of his beloved churches which, from the soaring cathedral to the humblest grey turret, seemed to him as a Christian 'the most charming points of our English landscape – gems of sentiment for which our woods, and green slopes, and hedgerow elms are the lovely and appropriate setting'. Take away the churches, he said, 'where for centuries the pure word of God has been read to the poor in their mother tongue . . . and you have a frightful kind of Paradise left – a Paradise without a God'.[24] For

Palmer, the English countryside embraced the lives of its people like the walls of a church surrounding its congregation. It seems no accident that one of the few overtly religious subjects that he tackled was that of the Old Testament wrestling match between Jacob and the Angel. Palmer's work grappled with the spiritual world in much the same way. He struggled to give it a physical presence, to bring it back down to the earth. Slowly but ineluctably a sense of landscape, Church and nation drew together in his imagination. It is not hard to see why, after much time spent 'in controversial reading which ought to have been given to painting',[25] he moved towards the Establishment faith. He became a committed member of the Church of England and considered even those he most loved – his father and his dear old nurse – to be misled. One cannot help wondering what his hero, John Milton, an almost heretical freethinker and a 'surly republican',[26] would have thought.

Palmer enjoyed a modest early success. In 1819 he exhibited two oil paintings at the British Institution, a club which, founded in 1805 by private subscription to promote national talent, had provided an important alternative to the Academy at a time when an open market for art was fast developing and the number of practitioners escalating apace. One of his pictures found a buyer much to Palmer's delight. The scrappy little note that he got from the keeper informing him of a sale made to a Mr Wilkinson of Marylebone was discovered among his papers at the end of his life.

Mr Wilkinson suggested that Palmer should pay him a visit. He may have been a little surprised at the youth of the artist who arrived on his doorstep. Palmer, having just turned fourteen, had not embarked upon his career at an uncommonly early age but, judging by the drawing which his friend Henry Walter did of him at this time, he looked little more than a child and, for all that he has trussed himself up in wing-collar and cravat for the portrait, was possessed of a child's earnest innocence to boot. It was an impression that Palmer was often to give for, small and pink-cheeked, he had a high piping voice which, though imbued with a richness that made him a fine tenor, was always to keep the clear timbre of youth.

Palmer was hopeful. His career was showing promise – not least when compared with that of his father who, supported by an annuity from his brother, Nathanial, was in the process of uprooting himself again. He was moving his home, his sons, his loyal family retainer (on whom, without his wife to tell him to put on fresh small clothes, he was more than ever dependent) and his bookshop to 10, Broad Street in Bloomsbury. It was a dingy house, disturbed by the rattle of incessant traffic, but the social cachet of the area was on the way up. 'You must not confound us with London in general, my dear sir,' insists Jane Austen's haughty Isabella Knightley of her house in the locality. 'The neighbourhood . . . is so very different from all the rest. We are so very airy!'

Airiness would have suited the asthmatic Palmer but his father's new home was rather closer to the cramped tenements of the run-down Covent Garden than the Regency terraces that Miss Knightley extols, and his health started to decline around this time, causing him to miss appointments and deadlines. Nonetheless, the move fitted his career. He was now just around the corner from Charlotte Street which, as the upper classes decamped to the fashionable West End, was increasingly colonised by painters and so became known as the new artists' quarter, while the British Museum, the capital's richest repository of books and antiquities, was only a short walk away. It was here that Palmer would later spend a lot of time drawing.

The young painter also benefited from the help of his grandfather's friends. Thomas Stothard offered advice and encouragement and would occasionally present the young artist with tickets to Academy lectures at which he would hear such celebrated figures as the sculptor John Flaxman, then the single most influential artistic practitioner of his day, enjoining his students to search out the ideal lineaments that lay hidden within nature, to look to such great home-grown talents as Milton, to appreciate the beauties of a lost medieval aesthetic and respect the simple purity of line. 'Sentiment is the life and soul of fine art!' Flaxman said. 'Without it all is a dead letter.'[27] Such ideas lodged themselves firmly in Palmer's mind.

Palmer was also forging his first artistic friendships. George Cooke, a line engraver, often used to call in at Broad Street for rousing discussions. He encouraged the young artist to keep looking at Turner for whom he and his brother, from 1811 to 1826 (when they fell out with the artist), did many engravings. They possessed a magnificent collection of Turner prints which 'formed part of the pabulum of my admiration', Palmer wrote.[28] A watercolourist, Francis Oliver Finch, three years older than Palmer and at the time of their first meeting studying under the renowned drawing master John Varley, joined Henry Walter as an artistic ally. Palmer was also to remain friendly with Wate and when his old teacher succumbed to cholera a decade or so later leaving his widow with nothing but a few sticks of furniture, Palmer went to some effort to secure her an annuity from a beneficence fund.

In 1820, Palmer had a picture accepted by the Royal Academy and the next year another while the British Institution took two. The year after that, despite having none at the Academy, there were three at the British Institution, one of which was singled out (along with Constable's *Haywain*) by the critic of *The Examiner* who praised it for 'touches at once so spontaneous and true, and light so unostentatiously lustrous'.[29] Prospective buyers were beginning to make appointments. And yet, despite these tokens of public success, Palmer was floundering. He lacked the confident grounding of a classical training. He had not learnt the rudiments of anatomy. 'O that I had had the human bones broken about my stupid head thirty years ago,'[30] he was later to lament, wishing that he had been 'well flogged when somewhat younger'[31] and so forced to adopt a less dilettantish approach. He came deeply to regret the 'years wasted any one of which would have given a first grounding in anatomy – indispensable anatomy'. 'The bones are the master key,' he would say. 'Power seems to depend upon knowledge of structure.'[32]

At the time, however, it was not his lack of formal learning that dismayed him so much as a sense that his poetic impulses were fading. He felt that he was losing touch with those dreams which the countryside had once stirred, with those visions of shadowy enchantment that his nurse had first fixed. Later, looking back on what he called 'his soul's journey',[33] he wrote: 'By the time I had practiced for about five years I entirely lost all feeling for art . . . so that I not only learnt nothing . . . but I was nearly disqualified from ever learning to paint.'[34] It was just at this moment that John Linnell arrived in his life.

John Linnell

Time was misused until my introduction to Mr Linnell
from *The Life and Letters of Samuel Palmer*

Linnell was thirty and Palmer was seventeen when, in September 1822, they first entered each other's lives. For the next sixty years, their courses would run closely together, at first easily interweaving, but increasingly tangling to create intractable knots.

Linnell, born in 1792 into a London family of respectable but far from wealthy craftsmen, had had a very different upbringing from the cosseted Palmer. Brought up in the dismal backstreets of Bloomsbury, he had been forced to understand from an early age that success, if it came, would be a hard-fought commodity, for his father, having completed an apprenticeship as a carver and gilder, had tried to set up his own business and failed. Facing ruin, he had panicked and fled home, leaving his wife and three children – including four-year-old John – to fend as best they could. He had enlisted as a soldier in the service of the East India Company and would have vanished abroad forever had a cousin not managed to save the situation just in time by dashing down to Plymouth and purchasing his release from the military at the cost of £40.

Returning, Linnell's father had found employment once more as a gilder and regained his mental balance. But for his eldest son the memory would always remain. Linnell would, for the rest of his life, be meticulous about financial matters. He would keep the most precise accounts, recording every transaction in a leather-bound ledger down

to the five shillings that he had once bestowed upon a gypsy who had
happened to be in his garden as she gave birth. He would clarify the
exact terms of any business agreement and, often at risk of offence,
insist upon prompt payment from clients.

Linnell, from an early age, loved reading and would devour anything
he could lay his hands on – from Dr Johnson's dictionary to the four
large folio volumes of Roman history which the family owned and which
thrilled him with their battles and their big illustrative plates. But it was
his artistic rather than his intellectual talent that first came usefully to the
fore. A skilled draughtsman who, as a child, had often decorated kites for
his friends, he would frequently trot along to Christie's auction rooms to
sketch the sale paintings. His father, spotting a commercial opportunity,
set him to copying populist pictures to sell. Linnell was happy to oblige.
Even in church, when his hands should have been piously folded, he
would be drawing, scratching portraits of the congregation onto the pews
with a nail. He would even sketch with his fingers on the empty air. It
taught him to see forms in his mind's eye, he later said, fostering the
remarkable visual memory which, along with fierce powers of observation, would serve him well as a portraitist.

One day, while furtively sketching a Girtin watercolour at an auction
house, he was spotted by the connoisseur William Varley who, struck
by the boy's skill, dispatched him promptly to see his brother, John, a
landscape painter, who, though his placid vision has long since fallen
from fashion, earned a niche in art history as one of his era's most
sought-after drawing masters. John Varley, impressed by Linnell's
talent, encouraged the adolescent prodigy to go on working as widely
and from as many different subjects as he could, and most particularly
to draw from nature. He invited him to visit his studio whenever he
wanted. It was the beginning of a lasting friendship between Linnell
and this ebullient master who would not only put in a fourteen-hour
day at the easel but, by way of a break, don a pair of boxing gloves and
go a few rounds with his pupils, or, tiring of that, divide his protégés
into teams and get them to toss him back and forth between them
across a table. This last was to become an increasingly onerous challenge; always a big man, Varley was eventually to top seventeen stone.

Varley was financially hopeless but, resolutely Micawberish, he was generous to a fault and refused to see anything but the bright side of life. He was imprisoned several times for debt; his house was burnt down; he had an 'idiot son'; but, as he told Linnell, 'all these troubles are necessary to me. If it were not for my troubles I would burst with joy.'[1] Linnell would, over the years, have to come to Varley's aid with increasing frequency, but he never resented it nor forgot the debt that he owed him – not just for help offered in childhood but for continuing support for, when Linnell was first trying to set up himself up as a professional artist, Varley would recommend him to the sort of aristocratic clients who could afford to pay generously to have their portraits done.

With his visits to Varley's house, Linnell found himself moving into artistic circles. He made friends with William Henry Hunt who had only recently signed up as one of Varley's pupils and with whom the ten-year-old Linnell, 'wondering if I should ever be able to accomplish as much as he had attained to – he was so far in advance of me in general knowledge of Art',[2] would go on sketching expeditions. He also took an immediate liking to William Mulready, an Irishman six years his senior who, while studying at the Royal Academy, had been fêted as one of its most promising pupils. When Linnell first met him, he was embarking on a career as a landscapist, although later, turning to genre scenes, depictions of everyday domestic realities, the romanticised twist that he could give to ordinary life would prove very popular to Victorian tastes. Mulready was a complicated character: genial, irascible, sentimental and extravagantly Romantic, he was a professional success but a failure in his private life. At eighteen he married Varley's elder sister, Elizabeth, but after seven years and four sons the relationship ended in separation – he blaming her for unspecified bad conduct; she accusing him of cruelty, pederastic inclinations and unfaithfulness.

Mulready and Linnell became inseparable companions. They would burn up their youthful energy in enthusiastic bouts of boxing, go sculling on the Thames or take off on escapades that could last for several days. Once, returning in the small hours to find themselves locked out, they had had to clamber up the back wall of their lodgings much to the consternation of Mulready's drunken landlady whose habitual mala-propisms were a frequent subject of mirth among the two friends. (She called Linnell 'Cotton' because she thought his real name was Linen and frequently spoke of their fellows as 'Acadaminions'.) But, most importantly, Linnell and Mulready painted together, the younger learning much from his older companion.

Another visitor to Varley's house, the miniaturist Andrew Robertson, offered Linnell an introduction to the President of the Royal Academy, the American-born Benjamin West, and from then on Linnell would visit West in his Newman Street studio once or twice a week, showing him the drawings that he made from casts and watching him work on his grand historical tableaux. This kindly American was always support-ive: it was he who had famously tried to encourage a dismayed Constable after one of his pictures had been rejected for exhibition – 'Don't be disheartened, young man, we shall hear of you again,' he had said. 'You must have loved nature very much before you could have painted this.' Many years later, in 1818, he would still remember Linnell, writing a recommendation for him when he applied for permission to copy a Holbein painting at Windsor Castle, praising him in the letter as 'an ingenious young artist'. It was not the last time a president of the Academy was to help Linnell out. In 1822, he sent up a picture to the summer exhibition which was slightly too small to be hung on the line. Thomas Lawrence, seeing the problem, promptly dispatched the work to his own frame maker so that it could be made bigger and hence hung in the best spot.

On the strength of Linnell's talent, Varley managed to persuade his father to put a stop to the picture copying and let his son come to live in as a pupil instead. It would affect the family's finances in the short run, Varley explained, but in the long term it would prove an investment. He was evidently convincing: Linnell's father even produced £100 in fees. 'Go to nature for everything',[3] was Varley's motto. His pupils wandered the parks and meadows of London with rectangles of millboard and boxes of paints. Linnell applied himself to sketching outdoors with such dedication that, as a naturalist, he could rival Constable.

When his year with Varley was over, Linnell applied to enter the

Royal Academy as a probationer and, at the end of 1805, was admitted to the life-drawing class. The youngest pupil, at just thirteen years old, he was affectionately nicknamed 'the giant' by the diminutive and famously foul-mouthed Henry Fuseli, Keeper of Schools. In 1807 he was awarded the Academy's life-drawing medal, Mulready having won it the previous year. In 1809, exhibiting at the British Institution, he went on to win a fifty-guinea prize. His versatility was extraordinary. In the Academy's annual competition between sculptors and painters, in which each was challenged to tackle the other's discipline, Linnell took first place.

At the Academy, he was tutored in art theory. He attended Turner's last lecture on perspective and was there for the first by Flaxman on sculpture. He pored over the art of the past, studying the brawny designs of Michelangelo in which the physical and spiritual meet with a muscular force, as well as the subtler harmonies of Raphael which he knew from the copperplate reproductions of Giulio di Antonio Bonasone, a fine selection of whose engravings he would one day own. He was deeply indebted to these masters of the Italian Renaissance, but it was the work of their German contemporary, Albrecht Dürer, which he most loved, admiring its unique combination of precision and excess: an appreciation that one day he would pass on to Palmer.

Sometimes, in the evenings, after his day at the Academy was over, he would go to visit Dr John Monro, the physician who had attended George III in his madness. Monro would pay him one shilling and sixpence an hour to make copies from his fine collection of drawings, reproductions which Linnell suspected would sometimes get sold on as originals. He enjoyed the companionship of his fellow students, figures such as David Wilkie and Benjamin Haydon, both of whom were to go on to make names for themselves, but who then were still lads, lunching together on the heavily marinated stews of London beef houses or, when there was no money to spare, larking about in the streets. Sometimes, in summer, they would go down to Millbank to swim in the Thames; or make their way to the house of the hospitable Varley to dine on eggs, bread and butter all washed down with porter and to argue with each other late into the night. And all the time Linnell was reading. He devoured endless volumes: Paley's *Moral Philosophy* and *Natural Theology*, Francis Bacon's essays, Milton's *Paradise Lost*, Homer's *Odyssey* and the Bible along with a profusion of Baptist tracts pressed upon him by Cornelius Varley (one of John's brothers) who by way of supporting argument also persuaded him to go and listen to John Martin, an impassioned but plain-spoken old Baptist pastor. Linnell was impressed by his unflinching conviction and liked to tell the story of how once this old preacher, invited to a grand dinner, had found himself confronted by an array of rich delicacies. 'There is nothing here that I can eat,' he had informed his hosts who had immediately made enquiries as to what further choice morsels might be brought. 'Bring me,' Martin had said, 'an onion and a pot of porter.'

In 1812, Linnell was received into the Baptist faith. From then on, his religious beliefs would infiltrate every aspect of his life. Stringent to the point of severity, he set himself to learning Hebrew and Greek. He did not trust the authorised version of the Bible and, convinced that meanings and truths were getting lost in translation, was determined to read it in its original form.

By then Linnell was giving a few drawing lessons of his own. In 1814 he was elected a member of the Society of Painters in Oil and Watercolour, a professional organisation which would help to promote him as an artist. Through his Baptist connections his first important portrait commissions began to come in, including one of the crumple-faced Martin who had converted him. It was also in chapel circles that he met Charles Heathcote Tatham, an architect who had studied in Italy and acquired a substantial reputation. Tatham began introducing Linnell into aristocratic society where he would pick up the sort of commissions that would launch his career.

Linnell needed to make money. He had fallen in love with Mary Palmer, the daughter of his chapel treasurer (but no relation to Samuel). He was hoping to marry her and yet to do so he would have to be capable of supporting a family. With characteristic resolution, he made a plan and then proceeded to achieve it. He went on a sketching tour of Wales, took on several portrait commissions, repaired pictures for his father, painted the figures in Varley's landscapes and did illustrations for books: some for the commercial artist Augustus Charles Pugin (father of the Gothic architect), others for a new edition of *The Compleat Angler*. Sometimes his life felt hard. He was often alone on his journeys. 'One day I was compelled to talk to my self to counteract the painful impression of solitariness,'[4] recorded the city-bred young man. But whatever he was doing and wherever he was travelling he made the most of it, sketching landscapes for the purposes of future pictures or experimenting successfully with his first portrait miniatures on ivory. His efforts began to pay off. A commission for one member of a family soon led to the next and Linnell's financial future began to look secure. One problem still remained, however, before he could take his wife. Civil marriages were not legal in England and, with typical obstinacy, Linnell refused to undergo what he described as the 'degrading' and 'blasphemous' ceremony of the Anglican Church.[5] He was only twenty-five, but his principles were fixed and now they led to a long, hard and extremely uncomfortable journey to Scotland where a pair of Nonconformists could be legally conjoined without Church involvement. Linnell, jolting along on the outside of the coach, pulled out his sketchbook whenever they stopped; his fiancée Mary, meanwhile, felt horribly travel sick.

In July 1817, in front of a magistrate, the pair were finally married and set off for a honeymoon-come-sketching-trip in the Highlands. It was hardly luxurious. One day they got lost and, before passing a night in a cow shed, dined on a trout begged from a passing fisherman. Linnell wouldn't have worried. He always remained true to his humble roots. He lived simply and was never afraid of menial tasks. He would walk everywhere, carry pictures to clients and hang them himself; he would often tell the story of the time that he had taken a lift in a pig cart to visit a patron, only alighting a short way from the grand country house of his destination lest his hosts mistake him for a ripe-smelling hog.

The first of Linnell's offspring was born in 1818 and his family grew rapidly from then on. He was eventually to have nine children. Meanwhile, ever resourceful and undaunted by such temporary setbacks as being thrown out of lodgings, he worked busily to expand his practice. His prices went up and he kept back a little from every sale that he made. A successful artist had once complained to him that it was impossible to save anything on an income of just £2,000 a year, but Linnell had replied that, even had his income been only £20 a year, he would still have put at least a shilling aside. In business matters, he remained unbudgeable and pioneered the now standard arrangement whereby a deposit is paid down before delivery. When payment was due he was no respecter of rank and once greatly embarrassed the Duke of Argyll by button-holing him in public, loudly demanding settlement of an old debt. Yet, for all his penny-pinching, Linnell could also be generous. The very same account books that record his hoardings show him making loans to his father, Mulready and Varley.

From 1821 his career gained rapid momentum. For a while he wondered if he might even be made a court painter. Twice he was commissioned to execute a portrait of Princess Sophia Matilda, the sister of George IV, but his unfailing regard for truth lost him further commissions. 'I ventured to make my pictures to look really like . . . and I calculate it was on that account I had no more from that connection,' he later said. 'I asked Lady Torrens at the time what would be the consequence in her opinion if, in the event of my being employed to paint George IV, the King, I made a faithful likeness. "It would be your ruin," she said. "I cannot help it," I replied. "So I shall do if I get the commission." Which I did not. And a good thing for me, too, that I did not.'[6]

Linnell was never elected to the Royal Academy. He supposed it was because he was a dissenter who nurtured republican leanings; but professional jealousies and personal antipathies also played a part, not least those of Constable who, hearing rumours that Linnell had engaged in sharp financial practices, preferred to pass on the gossip than check whether it was true. But Linnell's lack of social graces would not have recommended him in elevated circles: a friend once advised him that he should dress more carefully, pointing out a large stain on the front of his coat. From 1821 to 1841, he applied year after year for Academy admission, going through the prescribed motions of setting down his name as a candidate for an associateship (an initial form of half-membership, hopefully transmuted with time to full academician's status). Finally, after twenty years in which he had been consistently passed over in favour of often far inferior men, he gave up. 'The Academy can make me an RA but it can't make a fool of me,' he said and, even when subsequently entreated to revoke his opinion, he remained steadfast. 'Let them keep the RA for men who can't sell their pictures without it. I can,'[7] he told Edwin Lawrence, who had been deputed to try to persuade him. The once-coveted badge of honour had come to seem a mere bauble to Linnell by then.

In the early 1820s, Linnell moved his wife and their by then three offspring to a rented cottage in Hampstead where the air was much healthier and the children, who were often ferociously quarrelsome, could run free. His family remained always at the top of his priorities. At weekends he would spend time with them, making bread, brewing beer, keeping hens and digging wells, but the weekdays were passed in his Cirencester Place studio where he would work on six or seven canvases at once. His was a punishing schedule; often he would start at half past six in the morning and still be standing at his easel well after midnight, a timetable which took its toll on his health. For a while he would buy bottles of oxygen, or 'vital air', which he would inhale to increase his energy. It became a compulsive habit and at one point his consumption rose to twelve bottles a day as he struggled to overcome what he described as a weakness in the limbs. He blamed this debilitation on his having overtaxed his strength in boxing matches with the boisterous Mulready, but, more probably, he was suffering the lingering effects of some viral infection.

Linnell battled his ill health. He kept himself fit, often walking home to Hampstead after a full day's labour, sometimes, when his family had been up to visit, with one of his daughters perched on his shoulders. One day on this journey he came face to face with an infuriated bull thundering down the road towards him, head lowered and horns sharp. Linnell's wife, Mary, enjoyed telling the story of how her husband had stood his ground until the last minute when, whipping off his cloak and flourishing it like a matador, he had let the animal take it. As it had galloped away, the cloth wildly flapping, he had vaulted for safety over the nearest stile.

It is easy to see why the wavering Palmer would have been fascinated. Linnell was a man of many facets. A gentle father who at one moment might be playing with his golden-haired daughters was a tyrant the next, delivering strident opinions that brooked no dissent. He could turn from elaborating the daintiest of ivory portrait miniatures to kneading the bread dough with his huge strong thumbs. He would stay up late into the night, drinking and discussing abstruse theories with Cornelius Varley, and then be away the next morning, tramping through the predawn darkness to his latest painting job. He could turn from the labour of love which his own engravings represented to receive some distinguished sitter and then shift focus again to give a lesson to a pupil for whom drawing had to be included in a plethora of fashionable accomplishments. But, for all his many aspects, Linnell never lost his sense of purpose, never abandoned his professional focus or his religious quest.

Palmer was impressed. But then Linnell, for all that he was small in stature – he was only five foot five – had a powerful presence. He had a firm mouth, a penetrating stare and a loud and unexpectedly raucous voice that commanded the attention of those who met him. To shake him by the hand was to be assured of his strength. He had the hard, bony grip of a labourer. This was the grip that he kept on his life. It was precisely what the aimless Palmer was looking for.

The Sketchbook of 1824

A good angel from Heaven to pluck me from the pit of modern art
from *The Life and Letters of Samuel Palmer*

Few works remain from the period when Palmer and Linnell first met, but it was a pivotal moment for the younger artist as his only surviving self-portrait, which most likely dates to around this time, suggests. Drawn in black and white chalks on a piece of cardboard coloured paper, it may at first glance seem a fairly scrappy memento, smudgily finished and carelessly splashed. But there is no mistaking the unflinching intensity of his look as, bringing his eyes, nose and mouth into sudden sharp focus, picking out each eyelash and the adolescent moustache that dusts his upper lip, Palmer searches his face for signs of the future, even as he captures his mood of introspective retreat. This is an image that speaks of profound self-exploration. It presents a Romantic spirit at the moment of awakening.

Feeling the sudden fresh influx of his new teacher's energy like a numbed limb feels the rush of returning blood, Palmer filled notebook after notebook with his ideas, busily recording, as his father had taught him, everything that he considered to be worth remembering: lines from poems, passages from essays, lists of unusual words, columns of accounts. Even his problems were punctiliously listed because, in so doing, he often found that a solution would suggest itself.

Only one of these metal-clasped pocket books survives: the sketchbook of 1824. Its pages, cut out and mounted, can now be seen in the British Museum. They are the first record of Palmer's visionary future.

Gone is the meek obedience to the picturesque manuals. Here is a vivid new strength of design. Palmer credited Linnell for the change. He had fallen into a pit, he said, and entirely lost all taste and feeling. 'I not only learnt nothing . . . but I was nearly disqualified from ever learning to paint.' But then 'it pleased God to send Mr Linnell . . . a good angel from Heaven to pluck me from the pit of modern art'.[1]

What Palmer thought of as 'the pit of modern art' was on display annually at the Royal Academy's summer show, for, though in theory this institution had been set up to inculcate classical principles, to instruct developing artists in a rigorous academic style, the stern discipline which Reynolds had promoted in his seminal *Discourses* was, by the early nineteenth century, beginning to look outmoded. The 'History Painting' – grand renditions of battles, Bible stories and mythological dramas – that he had championed as the noblest genre, had fallen from favour. Reynolds might have hoped that by offering the British public access to the best works of art the Academy would elevate the nation's taste, but fewer and fewer people were prepared to pay for some vast military picture. Portraits were far more desirable: they added a personal touch to the drawing room and showed off the frills and the furbelows of high society tastes. Even Reynolds had earned his bread and butter by painting them.

Landscape was also growing increasingly popular. The history of this genre dates back many hundreds of years. Its skies and its mountains, its pastures and trees can be admired in anything from ancient Greek murals through the manuscript illuminations of the medieval era to the glowing oil canvases of the High Renaissance. But in these earlier images, landscape remained merely a background, the setting for some mythical encounter or biblical event. It was only in the seventeenth century in the hands of such masters as Nicolas Poussin and Claude Lorrain that it found its beginnings as a genre to be appreciated in its own right. It was to the example of such forebears, and most especially to Claude – almost half of whose entire oeuvre of almost three hundred paintings would by the early nineteenth century have passed into British collections – that Turner and Constable had started to look.

Turner had proved a consummate master. He had managed to turn his pictures into talking points. This mattered. Painting was still a fairly precarious profession and most practitioners were presented with two basic choices: either they became popular, commercial entertainers or they had to face impoverished obscurity. Most chose the former, but competition was fierce. First impressions were vital, however superficial: the louder, the brighter, the more audacious the picture, the better; it would increase its chances of attracting a buyer.

Palmer's contemporary, the author Edward Bulwer Lytton, satirised the art scene of the era through the persona of his Mr Gloss Crimson. This character 'ekes out his talk from Sir Joshua Reynolds' discourse . . . is intensely jealous, and more exclusive than a second-rate countess; he laments the decay of patronage in the country; he believes everything in art depends upon lords; he bows to the ground when he sees an earl'. But 'his colours are as bright and gaudy as a Dutchman's flower-garden for they are put on with an eye to the Exhibition where everything goes by glare'.[2]

Turner, applying his own competitive dab of gloss crimson to his exhibition canvas, would have recognised the truth of this description. His rival, Constable, certainly did. In an 1802 letter to his East Bergholt friend, the plumber John Dunthorne, he put his finger on the problem: 'The great vice of the present is *bravura*,' he said; 'an attempt to do something beyond the truth . . . *Fashion* always had, & will have its day – but *Truth* (in all things) only will last.'[3]

Constable eventually proved his point. His 'truth' in the long run was acknowledged; but he had had to wait many years. Meanwhile, in the marketplace, a crowd of diverse styles and manners and idioms all jostled for attention. Palmer was setting out into a confusing world. Cash counted for more than aesthetic acumen as rich manufacturers replaced perceptive connoisseurs. Flashy techniques supplanted spiritual feeling. 'The low and the mercantile creep over the national character,' declared Bulwer Lytton, who created another character called Snap, a minor academic who, having studied Locke at Cambridge, laughed down his sleeve if he heard the word 'soul'.

Palmer was not tempted by the 'flashy distracted present'.[4] 'The modern English art is all bustle – surprise – excitement,' he said, which did not seem to him a 'legitimate aim'.[5] 'How superior is Mr Linnell's style and colouring to that of any other modern landscape painter,' he observed, even if 'not half so captivating to an ignorant eye'.[6] He confidently placed his career under the auspices of the older man who set him to concentrating on the rigours of line: to discovering its strength and its subtlety, its gentleness and severity, its pliability and its discipline. He encouraged Palmer to look anew at his artistic heritage, to study the crisp detail of early Flemish masters, to admire the fluid tenacity of Dürer's designs.

Linnell, as a student, would have spent hour upon hour in the Academy's cast room where plaster replicas of the world's most famous sculptures posed and sprawled and reared and pranced. The Uffizi Mercury, the Callipygian Venus or the Furietti centaurs would be rolled on castors across ample spaces to catch the changing light, while shelves of busts, racks of limbs and whole libraries of frieze-fragments lined the walls. Palmer, however, had to rely upon the nearby British Museum. There, under the watchful eye of an old German warder, he joined a body of students – among them a young man, George Richmond, who was to become one of his closest friends – drawing from the antiquities in the Elgin and Townley Galleries.

'The time of trifling . . . is passed forever,'[7] declared Palmer. He set fervently to work, but with no one to instruct him he found himself floundering. His 'sedulous efforts to render the marbles exactly, even to their granulation', led him, he said, 'too much aside from the study of organisation and structure'.[8] He could not see the wood for the trees. Linnell's great friend Mulready was encouraging. A painter could not take a step without anatomy, he said, but having learnt that he had then to go on to 'investigate its most subtle inflections and textures, for if he has not learnt to perceive all that is before him, how can he select?' All the best artists had begun with 'niggling', he explained.[9]

The freshly heartened Palmer would return to the fray. 'I shall not be easy,' he noted in one of his sketchbooks, 'until I have drawn one Antique statue *most severely*.'[10] Hunched over his pad, he would pass entire days in the galleries, only finally uprooted from his little wooden sketching stool when the patrolling warder called out that it was time to close.

Occasionally Palmer could delight in moments of 'delicious vision',[11] and it was in the museum's Townley Gallery that he encountered one of his earliest loves: a recumbent Graeco-Roman shepherd lad carved in the late second century AD. Palmer was enchanted by this perfect slumberer, this Endymion 'who ever sleeps but ever lives and ever dreams in marble'. He was always to remember him and his 'hard-to-be-defined but most delicious quality of perfection',[12] and thirty years later, picking him up as a parent might pick up a sleeping child, he would carry him from Mount Latmos to lay him down softly in a watercolour painting, in the sunlit doorway of a Kentish barn. This 'peerless shepherd', an ageing but still ardent Palmer would write, evoked 'the tenderest pastoral' and offered a 'sure test of our imaginative faculties'. 'Bend over it,' he enjoined his friend Leonard Rowe Valpy in 1864. 'Look at those delicate eyelids; that mouth a little open. He is dreaming. Dream on, marble shepherd; few will disturb your slumber.'[13] The words, tender as a lover's, are almost erotic in tone.

Linnell encouraged Palmer to try outdoor oil sketching and together they visited many old Dulwich haunts. Palmer, ingratiatingly attentive to his new teacher, took down long lists of 'fine things to be seen', but he was no longer looking through the lens of the picturesque painter; he was seeking a more direct vision, an honesty of a sort that 'would have pleased men in early ages when poetry was at its acme and yet men still lived in a simple pastoral way'.[14] His progress, however, was far from straightforward. His vision had been so occluded by 'slime from the pit', he declared, that it had taken him a year and a half just to clear enough away to see quite what a miserable state he had got himself into. 'I feel ten minutes a day, the most ardent love of art, and spend the rest of my time in stupid apathy, negligence, ignorance, and restless despondency,'[15] he noted. 'The least bit of natural scenery reflected from one of my spectacle glasses laughs me to scorn, and hisses at me.'[16] 'Sometimes for weeks and months together, a kindly severe spirit says to me on waking . . . the name of some great painter and distresses me with the fear of shortcoming,' he recorded in one sketchbook.

He persevered, encouraged on his way not only by Linnell but by the eccentric Mulready who, as well as instructing him in artistic technique, kept his 'Mulreadian cabinet of anecdotes' well stocked. Almost sixty years later Palmer was still drawing from this store, enjoying his memories of the Irishman's gift for mimicry, recalling how he could send his friends into such convulsions of laughter that, rendered completely incapable, they would roll about helplessly on the floor. Palmer would willingly have been dragged about in a sack if it meant he would get a sight of one of Mulready's 'wrought and polished gems', he said.[17] He admired him enormously and for the rest of his life would quote his opinions on pretty much anything, from the complexities of flesh painting to the folly of imbibing too much liquid in a day. Certainly, as a young man, determining to 'make my conversation with all clever men . . . a process of pumping – or sucking their brains', he resolved to 'get as much knowledge out of him'[18] as he could. Linnell, on at least one occasion, had his nose so put out of joint that Palmer had earnestly to reassure him: 'I hope when I put those questions to Mr Mulready you did not think that it meant the least distrust of your own judgement,' he wrote in a postscript to an 1835 letter. 'If I could have one man's opinion I would sincerely rather have your's than anybody's.'[19]

It was Mulready rather than Linnell, however, who gave Palmer the lesson that he counted among the most important of his life. Mulready had been looking through a portfolio of studies by young artists of great promise when a fellow Academician, also leafing through them, had cried: 'Why can't we begin again?' Mulready's reply had been quick. 'I *do* begin again!' he had said, with a sharp emphasis on the 'do'.[20] Palmer owned a book of aphorisms. 'Who can act or perform as if each work or action were the first, the last, and only in his life, is great in his sphere,' was one he particularly remembered.[21] He considered Mulready to be among the few who actually realised this piece of advice. For all his outward joviality he took his art very seriously. 'I have drawn all my life as if I were drawing for a prize,'[22] he would, as an old man, declare.

Palmer tried hard to follow his example. He would begin over and over again, struggling and failing and picking himself up, starting each new sketchbook with renewed hope and humility, a fresh resolution to find the language of feeling, to be a better artist, and a better person to boot. 'Now it is twenty months since you began to draw,' he reminded himself in a scribbled memorandum. 'Your second trial begins. Make a new experiment. Draw near to Christ and see what is to be done with him to back you. Your indolent moments rise up, each as a devil and as a thorn at the quick. Keep company the friends of publicans and sinners, and see if, in such society, you are not ashamed to be idle.'[23] Palmer was not just pursuing an artistic training, he was also following a spiritual path.

———————

The sketchbook of 1824 opens a window into a young man's mind. The conventional topographies of earlier works have been abandoned. Instead, searching for simplified shapes, trying out textural effects, exploring patterns and designs, Palmer feels his way towards a unique graphic style. Drawing with pencils, pen and ink and occasionally a fine brush, he experiments with anything from the flicks of a nib which can capture a form at a stroke, to that sharpness of focus which can pick out a chin's unshaven bristles or the individual hob nails in the sole of a boot.

His vision is far from mature. In a notebook which ranges from landscapes to portraits, from botanical studies to extravagant fantasies, from the fair copies of poems to a recipe for laxatives, his attention can drift from a single frail seed head to an entire heavenly vision. At one moment he may be planning an elaborate polyptych – 'a grand subject for a series of pictures', he decides, would be 'the springing of man from God & the fellowship of God & man in the patriarchal ages'[24] – but on the very same page that he announces this monumental project he makes minutely detailed studies of an ash tree's pinnate fronds.

To flip through the pages is to embark on one of the journeys that the young painter would make with his pet bulldog, Trimmer, an ebullient creature which, when not whining and kicking in its sleep, wearing out the carpet with its convulsive friction, would bark at passing horses, chase sheep and even, one day, get run over by a goods van until, after five years, Palmer felt compelled to confess himself to be 'so UnEnglish' as to prefer his pocket Milton as a walking companion to a dog.[25] Palmer starts in the capital, looking back across the river towards Westminster Abbey, its tower luminous as mother-of-pearl in the 'mild glimmering poetical light of eventide', before, in a progression that becomes typical, moving from close observation to a technical analysis of how appearances might be captured in line, shading and tint: 'perhaps we should oppose a brilliant coloured warmth to a brilliant coloured cool (as ultramarine)', he suggests, 'though an elaborate building with strongly marked shadows would through a neutral tint bear out against a flat mass of the most vivid colour'.[26] But then Palmer leaves London behind him. By the next page of the sketchbook he is in the countryside, wandering through gently rounded hills and across newly ploughed fields, past slopes of ripe corn and girls picking apples, under shady chestnut boughs and along the edges of woods to pretty thatched villages that nestle in the shadow of churches. It is here, in 'cottage gardens of sweet herbs and flowers', that the painter drowses, forgetting the 'wretched moderns and their spiders webs and their feasts on empty wind'.[27]

His progress is fitful. He may start punctiliously enough with little framed landscapes and neatly penned notes, but before long he has been swept up by plans for grand cycles of paintings. He leaps enthusiastically forward in a sudden flurry of sketches before, abruptly confronted by his own limitations, he brings his attention back down to the facts. He practises figures, studying the anatomical masses of muscle, the patterns of drapery falling over a body, the classical stances of *contrapposto* – that asymmetrical counterpoise in which the weight of the body is shifted onto one leg. 'To prevent meagreness of composition from single limbs might it not be useful sometimes where there are several figures to cluster together several limbs in one full mass?' he wonders.[28] He brings his attention to bear on the ridge of a knuckle, the bend of a knee or a foreshortened foot. He tries out the expressive possibilities of line, his emblematic early pictures giving way increasingly to more impetuous sketches. He explores surface textures, learning to capture their various qualities with cross-hatching or stipples, with flicks, loops or spiralling coils. He experiments with perspectives and shifting viewpoints, sketching the approach to a village twice: once from a way off, and then again from up closer as he finds out what difference a few yards can make. He plays with scale. As he lies down among meadow grasses – the 'sun shines through each blade making masses of the most splendid green; inimitably green and yet inimitably warm so warm that we can only liken it to yellow & yet most vivid green'[29] – he enters a microscopic world in which fescues grow tall as the distant church steeple or the furthest horizon is formed by warped thistles and dandelion clocks. 'These round ones go down to the utmost littleness,'[30] he notes as he picks out each speck of a clover's tripartite leaf. But in other pictures he gazes as if through a telescope at some far-off landscape, rendering trees, houses and flocks with a precision that the foreground lacks.

Encouraged by Linnell, Palmer pays particular attention to trees. He notices how foliage clusters into masses, how sunrays stream through leaves and stars glister through gaps in a canopy of ancient elms. He looks at their distinctive shapes and silhouettes, at their trunks, gnarled, knotted or smooth, twined with clambering ivy, embossed with burly excrescences or silvery supple as a sapling birch. Each tree, he observes, has its own unique character: sometimes they seem almost human, he says: 'I saw one, a princess walking stately and with a majestic train.'[31] He stares with the concentration of a naturalist at anything from the creviced face of a rock through the patterns of ploughed furrows to the circles of light that surround Saturn's planetary orb. He looks at the bristle-backed hogs in their pens, at his pet cat sleeping, its paws softly curled, at a bony-faced sheep that confronts him head on.

He studies the old masters as Linnell has directed him, admiring the variety of Raphael's textures ('hard enamel face, soft silky hair and hard jewels on the cape'),[32] or noting how Michelangelo, when working on the Sistine ceiling, would scratch in his outlines with a sharp point and fill the grooves with pitch.[33] 'Outlines cannot be got too black,'[34] he observes. He remembers his mentor's injunction – 'delightful in the performance'[35] – to look at Dürer and, like this great draughtsman, he sets out to describe entire landscapes with line alone. Linnell has also introduced him to the works of the sixteenth-century Bolognese engraver, Giulio Bonasone. 'To copy precisely in pen and ink some limb of Bonasone's,' Palmer notes, is to 'understand shadow in its poetic sleep'.[36]

Palmer learns also from his peers. He takes a note of Finch's suggestion of using a 'dark cool stem'[37] as a framing device and, trying to keep up with Richmond, his former British Museum companion who is now a student at the Royal Academy, he transcribes part of a lecture by Fuseli. Clearly struck by the work of this histrionic painter, Palmer makes sketches of the 'wicked thief' on the cross; he shows the crucified criminal, head flung violently back, mouth gaping, eyes rolling, as he tugs out his nails amid cartoonish showers of blood. But Palmer, unlike Richmond, does not have the notoriously caustic Fuseli to scold him for his mistakes. He has to be his own master. 'Place your memorandums . . . more neatly you dirty blackguard,'[38] he admonishes himself in a note.

In the end, however, it is an individual vision that Palmer must discover. This is what he reaches for, most importantly, in his 1824 sketchbook. Scattering stars like a child scatters glitter, casting crinkle-winged bats out upon the twilight, hanging moons like shining lanterns and igniting vast glowing suns, he speaks of the marvels that for him can transform the mundane. His world becomes a magical one in which natural phenomena are personified, where the sky is 'low in tone', as if 'preparing to receive the still and solemn night'[39] and the rising moon stands 'on tiptoe on a green hill top to see if the day be going & if the time of her vice regency be come'.[40] A donkey is transformed into a spindle-legged, bristle-backed, armour-plated monster; the feathers of a bird's wing can lend an angel flight.

Palmer still likes to draw the ecclesiastical architecture that first inspired him, its steeples and arches and traceries and vaults, but more and more frequently his churches are found merging with the landscapes that enfold them. 'These leaves were a Gothic arch,'[41] Palmer notes as fronds rise in a trefoil that frames a distant tower. Trees grow in groves with church spires. A peasant woman soars solid and columnar as a cathedral pillar. A rustic shepherd becomes a Christ figure. A cornfield takes on a sacramental glow. 'The earth is full of thy richness': Palmer puts a quote from the psalms on the cover of the Bible that he places unopened in the hands of a recumbent figure who, pondering this wisdom, gazes dreamily out across a far-reaching rural view.

Leaf by leaf, Palmer draws his vision together in his sketchbook of 1824. Here in black and white – with a rare wash of pigment when the prism of a rainbow or the sudden radiance of the sun demands it – is a vivid picture of the young artist's soul. Linnell has sharpened the young man's perceptions. He has shown him how to look. But now Palmer yearns not just to look, but truly to see. He is ready for his meeting with the visionary William Blake.

William Blake

The Maker, the Inventor; one of the few in any age
from *The Letters of Samuel Palmer*

William Blake, born the son of a London hosier in 1757, was reared amid nightcaps and stockings, garters and gloves. He could almost have been some star child or changeling, suggests Peter Ackroyd, his most vivid biographer, for right from the beginning he found himself living in a world that was inhabited also by heavenly hosts. He saw seraphim roosting in the trees of Peckham and angels wandering amid the haymakers as they mowed the summer grass. As a boy, his mother had once beaten him for saying that he had just seen the prophet Ezekiel, but it would have taken far more than a mere thrashing to convince him that he was wrong. 'When the Sun rises do you not see a round Disk of fire somewhat like a Guinea? . . . Oh no no I see an Innumerable company of the Heavenly host crying Holy Holy Holy is the Lord God Almighty,' Blake declared.[1] His soaring imagination slipped free from all earthly restraints, his childhood perceptions of alternative realities unfurling and elaborating over the course of his life into the vast, fantastically complicated and almost incomprehensible mythic system of his books.

'Blake be an artist & nothing else. In this there is felicity.'[2] A divine messenger had instructed the boy as to what path he should take and so, at the age of ten, having proved hopeless behind the shop counter, Blake was sent off to Henry Par's Drawing School in the Strand, a respected institution which offered the sort of academic training which

Palmer was always to wish that he had also had. Blake had long nurtured an interest in art. His indulgent father had got into the habit of buying him prints that, considered dull or unfashionable at that time, could be picked up for mere pennies. These laid the foundations of what was to grow into a valuable collection, the piecemeal sale of which would help to stave off penury in later life. But Blake was also a talented draughts-man and, at the age of fourteen, having completed his first training, he was indentured to the engraver James Basire.

Basire was his second choice. Blake had originally been destined to work with William Ryland but, on meeting him, had refused. 'Father,' he had said, on leaving the studio, 'I do not like the man's face: *it looks as if he will live to be hanged.*'[3] His premonition had turned out to be true. Ten years later, charged with the forgery of notes, Ryland would swing from the gallows at Tyburn. Basire, however, was to prove a kind and thorough master. Old-fashioned and peaceable, he instilled in his often-impetuous pupil the virtues of precision and patience. He taught him a carefulness to temper his arrogance. He was embarking on a time-honoured profes-sion, he told him, for the art of engraving went back to the Hebrews and their Chaldean forbears and beyond them, via Zoroaster, maybe even to God who had engraved the tablets of stone which Moses had brought down from the mountain.[4] The hopeful young apprentice could hardly have guessed what a long, arduous, backbreaking, sight-blurring, spirit-battering future his craft held in store for him.

In 1779, Blake enrolled for six years as a student of engraving at the Royal Academy. He was an assiduous learner, though he loathed the life room. What good was the slavish copying from nature, he wondered. Life drawing smelt of mortality. Modern man stripped of his clothing was but a corpse. He was equally revolted by what he saw as the bland urbanity and faux humility of the, by then, grand old man of the Academy, Sir Joshua Reynolds. He detested his ponderous lectures on the virtues of 'general beauty' and the pursuit of 'general truth'. 'General Knowledges are those Knowledges that Idiots possess,'[5] Blake raged, scoring the margins of Reynolds's *Discourses* with furious annotations. 'Damn the Fool'. 'This Man was Hired to Depress Art' he inked in black letters on the title page.

Blake refused to follow Reynolds's classically influenced course, far preferring the art of what he saw as a profoundly spiritual age: the monuments of Gothic antiquity and the effigies of the medieval church. He was not alone in his tastes. A small community of fellow artists shared his predilection for the Middle Ages, among them Thomas Stothard who, when he had first met Blake, had been working on a set of illustrations to the *Poems of Ossian*. This Gaelic epic, purporting to record the songs of the blind bard Ossian about the battles of Fingal the warrior, had caused a literary sensation when it was published by James Macpherson in 1773, though subsequently it was condemned as fake. Stothard and Blake became artistic allies but, where the former went on to become an art world grandee, the latter never rose to be more than a jobbing engraver: a craftsman with undoubted skills but some decidedly unconventional views. Blake's choice of a bride did not help. In the aftermath of a failed courtship, he had met a sympathetic but probably illiterate gardener's daughter, Catherine. 'Do you pity me?' he asked her. 'Yes indeed I do,' she said. 'Then I love you,'[6] he replied and shortly afterwards they married. She signed the register with a cross. It was not a liaison that would bring access to society or membership of an Academy which valued social status. Nor did Blake show the sort of financial acumen that a rising artist needed. Detesting 'the merchant's thin/ Sinewy deception',[7] he refused to engage in a scrabble for wealth and, though Catherine learnt increasingly to help him, he was always to find it difficult to make ends meet.

The fundamental cause of his worldly problems, however, was the fact that he was considered quite mad. Blake was living in the 'Age of Reason'. René Descartes had set the agenda in the seventeenth century with his mechanistic model of the universe and, ever since, mathematics had been taken as the template of knowledge and science had put nature to stern empirical test. Blake openly professed his loathing for this logical world. He detested Newton with all his 'wheels and orbits . . . particles, points and lines'.[8] These wheels were to him the cruel 'cogs tyrannic' which ground up human freedom, destroying 'harmony and peace'.[9] He hated the empiricism of Francis Bacon and John Locke. It blotted out the light of divinity, he thought. Instead,

Blake believed in his visions. A chat in his Lambeth study with the Archangel Gabriel or an impromptu visit from the ghost of a flea – 'his eager tongue whisking out of his mouth, a cup in his hands to hold the blood and covered with a scaly skin of gold and green'[10] – were to him far more real than any scientific abstract. 'I do not believe the world is round. I believe it quite flat,' he declared. He had it on good authority: 'I have conversed with the Spiritual Son,' he explained: 'I saw him on Primrose Hill.'[11]

When discreet inquiries were made as to Blake's eligibility to become an Academician, such fixations were to prove far from helpful. Even Fuseli, a fellow eccentric and, as Blake described him: 'The only man that e'er I knew/ Who did not almost make me spew',[12] thought that his friend had 'something of madness about him'.[13] Blake was never to be elected to the Academy. And yet there was clearly something compelling about this small man with his impassioned points of view. 'Another eccentric little artist', recorded Lady Charlotte Bury in her diary after meeting him at a dinner in 1818. But if on first encounter she had assumed him merely to be an amusing curiosity, she soon found her mind changing. 'He looks care worn and subdued; but his countenance radiated as he spoke,' she wrote and, though his views were peculiar, they were 'exalted above the common level of received opinion'. He was 'full of beautiful imaginations and genius. Every word he uttered spoke the perfect simplicity of his mind and his total ignorance of all worldly matters.'[14]

Blake's closest friends certainly recognised his incorruptible talent. Flaxman and Fuseli believed that the time would come when his art would be as esteemed as highly as Michelangelo's; furthermore, he was 'damned good to steal from',[15] Fuseli said. He and Stothard both collaborated with Blake. Flaxman, too, remained a supporter and together with George Cumberland, an amateur artist and connoisseur of early Italian prints who, like Blake, believed in 'the inestimable value of the chaste outline',[16] would introduce him to clients. But Blake was uncompromising. His fantasies were too powerful for the tastes of the period. Stothard blamed Fuseli. He had 'misled' Blake 'to extravagance'[17] he said, though, in fact, even this most melodramatic of artists had urged Blake to tone down his more unruly outpourings.

For some twenty years, the visionary genius relied almost entirely for his living upon the patronage of a government servant, Captain Thomas Butts, who, having accrued a modest fortune as the chief clerk in the office of the muster master general, became a steady buyer. Purchasing works at a rate of up to a drawing a week, he gradually transformed his Fitzroy Square house into a private gallery of miracles. For many years, Palmer was later to claim, Butts was the only man who stood 'between the greatest designer in England and the workhouse'.[18]

'He who has few Things to desire cannot have many to fear,'[19] Blake declared. He did not crave luxuries. He could have made his life easier by being a little more malleable, but he treasured his freedom far more highly than any hoard of worldly goods. 'I know of no other Christianity and no other Gospel than the liberty both of body & mind to exercise the Divine Arts of the Imagination,'[20] he said. Sometimes his untameable enthusiasms could be alarming, as his wife knew only too well. Throughout their long marriage, Blake made frequent, sometimes bizarre and occasionally frightening, sexual demands on her. Such unbridled urges, he believed, were an essential life force. His forcible opinions could be whipped into a fury. Cumberland, ever eager to help, had once introduced him to a clergyman who had commissioned four watercolours, the initial pair of which was to represent malevolence and benevolence. As soon as the cleric saw the first of these images the commission was cancelled. It looked unreal, he thought: it was difficult to understand. Blake's pride was violently roused. 'What is Grand is necessarily obscure to Weak men,' he declared. 'That which can be made Explicit to the Idiot is not worth my care.'[21] This was just one of a number of enraged quarrels which, over the course of Blake's life, left friendships in ruins. As poverty, neglect and the utter failure of an 1809 exhibition held in his brother's hosiery shop caused him mounting frustration, Blake picked bitter arguments with his erstwhile supporters. He turned on Flaxman with accusations of hypocrisy; he successfully alienated the peaceable Stothard and, by 1810, had even managed to fall out with the 'Dear Friend of My Angels', the benevolent Butts. There were no more commissions forthcoming. 'I found them blind and taught them how to see/ and now they know neither themselves or me,'[22] wrote the despairing poet.

'The Maker, the Inventor, one of the few in any age'[23] was how Palmer would describe him, yet Blake in his lifetime suffered a heartbreaking neglect. His first book of poems, the only one to be published, had been printed in 1783. His last piece of work, a set of illustrations to Dante, would still be incomplete at the time of his death. In between the visions of a rhapsodic imagination would pour forth like a torrent – anything from the simplest songs of childhood to the most elaborate apocalyptic scenes – and yet, by the time he was entering his sixties, Blake would be reduced to engraving pictures of crockery sets for the Wedgwood sample book. 'The great author of Eternity was obliged to illustrate egg cups, tureens, candlesticks and coffee pots,' wrote Ackroyd.[24] Little wonder that over the course of his life he devoted more than seventy engravings to the story of that most embattled of biblical characters, Job. And yet, even as his spirits were flagging, his imagination would flare. 'I laugh and sing,' he would cry: 'for if on earth neglected I am in heaven a Prince among Princes.'[25] He lived all his life in the bright lands of the spirit. 'I have very little of Mr Blake's company,' his wife once informed an inquirer: 'He is always in Paradise.'[26]

Blake was at a low ebb when, in June 1818, John Linnell, having been introduced by George Cumberland, the son of the great collector and connoisseur, first visited his home. Linnell was twenty-six and his career was just beginning to gain momentum. He had met his first major patron, Lady Torrens, and within a year or two would be introduced (by the ever-generous Varley) to the even more influential Lady Stafford who, charmed by his portrait-miniatures, would offer him the run of her aristocratic connections which would mean that he could start putting his prices up. His prospects could hardly have been further from those of the sixty-one-year-old Blake. Nor were their artistic ideas alike. Varley had taught Linnell to 'go to nature for everything' but to Blake nature was merely a mass of mundane material. He far preferred the spirits of his visionary life. And yet the two men had much in common. They were both religious dissenters and political radicals; they shared a reverence for the scriptures and had both learned Hebrew and Greek; they admired the art of Michelangelo, Dürer and Van Eyck and, both the sons of tradesmen, they preferred simple manners to a smart social life. Their friendship was to span the last decade of Blake's life. They would visit each other's studios, go to plays together, dine with mutual acquaintances and gaze at pictures side by side, including quite possibly, in the 1821 Academy summer show, an early landscape by Palmer whom, at that time, Linnell did not yet know.

Linnell, the down-to-earth businessmen, was determined to advance the career of the other-worldly Blake who had by then sold his 'pension', his collection of prints. He introduced the old artist to a variety of possible patrons and, though none of the grand aristocrats wanted to commission him, the family doctor who had recently attended the birth of Linnell's first child, Hannah, offered Blake an engraving job. Dr Robert John Thornton, besides practising medicine, was an amateur botanist, a classical scholar and an enthusiastic pedagogue who at that time was interested in discovering which Latin classics would best serve as school books. Thornton did not believe in assisting children with direct translation and was preparing an edition of Virgilian pastorals in which the original text would be accompanied only by a simplified imitation of the first eclogue by the eighteenth-century poet Ambrose Philips. Now, encouraged by Linnell, he commissioned Blake to elucidate Virgil's work further with a series of small illustrative designs.

The engravers greeted Blake's first attempts with derision; the publishers wanted to abandon the project; but Blake, thanks to Linnell's behind-the-scenes persuasions, was allowed to continue. He worked on in the face of considerable difficulty for, to meet the needs of the printers, he had to remake his images as woodcuts and this was a technique which he had never before tried. The result was a series of small but daringly idiosyncratic pastorals that glitter with light.

Linnell also commissioned Blake: an act of benevolence and respect which was later to involve him in hurtful controversy with the artist's widow who, befuddled and frightened after her husband's death, would accuse him of taking advantage of Blake's impoverished circumstances. In fact, Linnell had saved the proud visionary from penury (and the added indignity of a job doing pictures of poultry and pigs) by commissioning him first to engrave copies of his watercolour illustrations to the *Book of Job* and then, when the old man was in his mid-seventies, to illustrate Dante's *Divine Comedy* (Blake set himself to learning Italian so that he could fulfil this commission) originally with a series of watercolours and then with engravings for which he would pay him on weekly account. This allowance was all that stood between the Blakes and starvation. 'I do not know how I shall ever repay you,' Linnell recalled Blake saying. 'I do not want you to repay me,' Linnell replied. 'I am only too glad to be able to serve.'[27]

Palmer Meets Blake

More attractive than the threshold of princes
from *The Letters of Samuel Palmer*

Palmer's 'never-to-be-forgotten first interview'[1] with Blake took place on 9 October 1824 when he and Linnell called round at Fountain Court, a tall, plain and rather morose red-brick building on the Strand, on the first floor of which the sixty-seven-year-old visionary lived with his wife, seldom venturing out for anything more pressing than to fetch a jug of porter.

Palmer crossed the reception room, its walls plastered with pictures, to reach a second chamber beyond, a space which served as workshop, bedroom, kitchen and study all at once. It was crowded, but it felt far from squalid, Palmer reported. Everything was clean and orderly; everything was in its place, from the cooking utensils to the engraving implements which were laid out ready on a table in the corner, a print of Dürer's *Melancholia* pinned onto the wall above. Blake was in his bed by the window, from which he could just glimpse the Thames shining like a bar of gold beyond. He was unable to walk, having badly scalded his foot, and so was sitting propped up on pillows 'like one of the Antique patriarchs or a dying Michelangelo', Palmer recalled, surrounded by open volumes and drawing the 'sublimest designs'[2] in the pages of a great book.

The awed nineteen-year-old gazed into Blake's face, its high forehead, snub nose and stubborn jaw now familiar from the life mask that was cast around this time by a neighbour, a keen amateur phrenologist who had wanted to record the cranial protrusions that spelt out an advanced imaginative faculty. Blake's eye, Palmer said, was the finest he ever saw: 'brilliant, but not roving, clear and intent, yet susceptible'. It could flash with genius, he said, or melt with tenderness. And it could be terrible, too. 'Cunning and falsehood quailed under it,' he wrote, 'but it pierced them and turned away.'[3] This was the eye that Blake turned upon Palmer at that first meeting. 'Do you work with fear and trembling?' he asked. 'Yes indeed,' came the reply. '"Then," said he, "you'll do."'[4]

A copperplate was lying on the table and Palmer took a peep. It was an illustration to the *Book of Job*. 'How lovely it looked by lamplight strained through the tissue paper,' Palmer remembered. But then, through the veil of this man's vision, the whole world could be transformed. 'The millionaire's upholsterer,' Palmer said, could 'furnish no enrichments like Blake's enchanted rooms. He ennobled poverty and . . . by the influence of his genius, made two small rooms in Fountain Court more attractive than the threshold of princes.'[5]

———

Palmer was a dandy in those days. Growing up in the Regency, he liked to cut a dash and despite his small stature and pronounced tendency to corpulence, would deck himself out in white duck trousers, waistcoat and cravat and walk with a swagger, swinging his slender cane. Blake's clothes, in contrast, were threadbare. 'His grey trousers had worn black and shiny in front, like a mechanic's,'[6] Palmer said. Yet he saw in the shabby impoverished figure not a misfit or a madman but a noble and dignified mentor.

On their first meeting, Palmer ventured to show Blake a few of his drawings. The old man's kindly response – 'for Christ blessed little children'[7] – left Palmer grateful but not self-satisfied. Blake 'was energy itself': he 'shed around him a kindling influence; an atmosphere of life, full of the ideal',[8] he said. And Blake in his turn recognised some special gift in Palmer. The two, who had many things in common, from their Nonconformist backgrounds to their affection for cats, grew increasingly close. Palmer from then on would often call round at Fountain

Court, Blake rising to greet him with a smile as he arrived with his bundles of sketches and his burgeoning ideas.

They would pore for quiet hours over books of prints. Blake was 'anything but sectarian or exclusive', Palmer said, and 'found sources of delight through the whole range of art'.[9] 'He did not look out for the works of the purest ages, but for the purest work of every age and country.'[10] Dwelling with particular affection on the rare and perfect talent of Fra Angelico, Blake nurtured Palmer's interest in sacred art and helped to deepen his understanding of the medieval era as well as of Michelangelo and Albrecht Dürer, although the reverential Palmer was taken aback when the old visionary, studying the designs of the latter, suddenly grew angry with the acclaimed German master and scolded him for neglecting some area of detail. 'No authority or popular consent could influence [Blake] against his deliberate judgement,' Palmer observed.[11] This was a man who would converse over dinner of the follies of Plato or the mistakes of Jesus Christ.

Sometimes Palmer and Blake would visit exhibitions together. Palmer was always to remember one particular trip when Blake was standing in the Royal Academy praising a picture by Thomas Griffiths Wainewright, a painter who was later to be tried and condemned as a murdering poisoner. There was Blake, he recalled 'in his plain black suit and *rather* broad-brimmed, but not quakerish hat, standing so quietly among all the dressed-up, rustling, swelling people, and myself thinking "How little you know *who* is among you!"'[12]

———

Blake's health was declining rapidly at this time. He was all 'bones and sinews . . . strings and bobbins, like a weaver's loom',[13] said a friend. In the spring and summer of 1825 he suffered terrible shivering fits that confined him to bed. It may have been gallstones causing an inflamed bladder, modern doctors suggest. Bile was mixing with the blood, declared the medics of the day. Blake simply called it 'this abominable ague'. He felt frail 'as a young lark with no feathers'.[14] Linnell was concerned. He offered Blake and his wife free lodging in his London house and, in 1826, suggested that they should move northwards to be near him in Hampstead in a cottage for which he would pay. Both offers were declined. Blake, who suffered from terrible bowel problems, was reluctant to travel. Just reading Wordsworth's *The Excursion* was enough to set off an intestinal tumult. Besides, he had always considered the north to be malefic, if not positively devilish. He certainly did not want to take up residence there.

When in good health, however, he still liked to make day trips to the Hampstead home that the Linnells first rented in the summer of 1823. It was a part of Collins Farm, a rambling red-roofed dwelling on the west side of the heath, looking out towards gorse slopes on one side and meadows in which the children could romp freely on the other. The move had proved a happy experiment and Linnell's growing family had thrived. The following year he had taken over the rent of the whole building and, though he still spent the working week in his studio, it is there at Collins Farm that the modern-day visitor can find the English Heritage plaque that commemorates not only his residence but also the fact that Blake was his frequent house guest.

Blake liked to visit on Sundays and often, passing Palmer's Broad Street home, he would pick him up on the way. They always went on foot – the alternative, a bumpy cabriolet ride, being considered by Blake 'a rumble I fear I could not go through'.[15] Not that Palmer would have minded. Walking with Blake, he said, was like walking with the prophet Isaiah. He kindled the imagination, transforming even London's 'charter'd streets'[16] into a bejewelled City of God.

The conversation of these walking companions might be guessed at. Perhaps Blake told Palmer about the 1780 Gordon Riots when, after Parliament had drafted a bill lifting restrictions from Roman Catholics, cries of 'No Popery!' had rung through the capital. A pitched battle between mob and militia had taken place in Broad Street where Palmer now lived. Blake, as a young man strolling home, had been swept up by the rabble, borne on its tide towards Newgate where rioters with sledge-hammers and torches had set the prison on fire. He never forgot the flickering leap of the flames and the shrieks of trapped felons; the images of conflagration and chaos that pervade his poetry may in part, Ackroyd has suggested, spring from this harrowing memory.

The two would have doubtless spent much time discussing artistic matters. They might well have talked about Cowper, whose works they both loved: Palmer because they reminded him of his dead mother; Blake because Cowper who, suffering from manic religious fits had spent months in an asylum, seemed to him the very type of the mad poet most to be pitied and celebrated. They would have dwelt on Milton, for Blake recognised in this stubborn rebel an artistic forerunner who shared not just a sacred vision but a poetic mission to arouse England from spiritual slumber and return it to the state of ancient grace which it had enjoyed in the times when (as Milton put it) the 'Druids created the cathedral of philosophy'.[17] And maybe Blake described to Palmer the hallucinatory visits he had received from this long-deceased English poet who had appeared to him both in the guise of a youth and an old, grey-bearded man.

Following the meandering course of the River Fleet, the pair left London behind for the fresh air of the open fields. To walk with Blake in the country was 'to perceive the soul of beauty through the forms of matter',[18] Palmer wrote. They would pause to rest on their way up Haverstock Hill, the dome of St Paul's behind them and, on clear days, the towers of Westminster Abbey also visible beyond. Blake may have told Palmer, whose reverence for England's ecclesiastical architecture he shared, how this abbey had been the home of 'his earliest and most sacred recollections'.[19] Blake had been sent there by Basire to make drawings of its tombs and had spent many solitary hours alone among its bright splendours, amid the coloured waxworks and painted funeral effigies, the marbles and mosaics, the stained glass and gilded decorations from which his rich sense of colour may have first arisen. Memories of the old cathedral enchanted him all his life and he would often recall the wondrous moment when he saw the spirits which dwelt amid its Gothic vaults; when its 'aisles and galleries . . . suddenly filled with a great procession of monks and priests, choristers and censer-bearers, and his entranced ear heard the chant of plain-song and chorale, while the vaulted room trembled to the sound of organ music'.[20] Blake often talked of his visions: when he said 'my visions', the journalist Henry Crabb Robinson recalled, 'it was in the ordinary unemphatic tone in which we speak of trivial matters that everyone understands'.[21]

The Linnell children would watch for their father's two friends as they crested the brow of the hill, their coat tails flapping, their pockets stuffed to bulging with pencils and scraps of paper and volumes of poetry, and sometimes also a book brought along as a present for Mrs Linnell. At a wave of greeting from Blake, the lively troupe would come rushing: Hannah at the fore, her gold ringlets flying, her plump cheeks flushed pink. Children loved Blake, Palmer recalled, for he had not 'the least taint of affectation about him',[22] and Blake in his turn loved them back. He liked to listen to them playing in the courtyard below his flat, their laughter echoing round the brick. One visitor remembered once being led to the window and Blake, leaning out, pointing at the little ones beneath. 'That is heaven,' he had said. 'He thought that no one could be truly great who had not humbled himself "even as a little child",' Palmer recalled.[23]

The Linnell children remembered Blake as 'a grave and sedate gentleman, with white hair, a lofty brow, large lambent eyes [and] . . . a kind and gentle manner',[24] whose gaze would fill with tears when their mother, Mary, sat at the pianoforte to play one of his favourite Scottish songs. Blake was easily moved to tears and Palmer recalled the time when, dwelling upon the beauty of the parable of the prodigal son, he had begun to read it but at the words 'when he was yet a great way off his father saw him' had found himself unable to go further. Blake also liked to sing and would choose his own poems or some simple popular melody while Palmer with his rich tenor and the high-piping children would join in.

Sometimes Hannah would bring her pet cat in a big furry armful. Blake shared Palmer's opinion of these creatures: 'so much more quiet in her expressions of attachment than a dog'.[25] Once Blake showed them a book of pictures he had done as a boy of fourteen, including a drawing of a grasshopper that they had all particularly liked. Occasionally he would take out his pencils to sketch. Three delicate drawings of a baby survive. Blake would tell the children stories. He could make his listeners laugh with such tales as that of the time that he had been sent a flask of walnut oil to try out as a solvent for his paints. Blake had tasted it and then gone on tasting it until the whole lot had been drunk. The artistic experiment had never taken place.

Constable may also have visited. He had lodgings just across the heath and knew the Linnells, although the only conversation recorded between him and Blake was that which took place as the old visionary leafed through one of his sketchbooks. 'Why, this is not a drawing, but *inspiration*,' he had said as he had admired a picture of Hampstead trees; whereupon Constable had replied: 'I never knew it before; I meant it for a drawing.'[26]

As the evenings drew in, Blake liked to stand at the door, enjoying the mild summer air. He would gaze out in tranquil reverie at the hills or, sitting peacefully in the arbour at the end of the garden, would ruminate with the cows that chewed the cud on the far side of the fence. Sometimes Varley would arrive along with Mulready or other guests and they would sit down to dinners that lasted late into the night, starting with intense artistic discussions and ending with arguments and laughter and jokes. Linnell shared Mulready's knack for mimicry and could imitate their foul-mouthed professor, Fuseli, so well that it may have been one of his impersonations that led the Academician to remark: 'It is very good; it is better than I could have done myself.' A sketch by Linnell shows Varley and Blake conversing after dinner. Varley, caught in the middle of animated conversation, is probably trying to convince Blake of the truth of his astrological theories. He was riveted by horoscopes and, upon meeting a new person, would immediately ask them their date of birth, whereupon he would start unstuffing his huge sail pockets of their cargo of almanacs. He believed firmly in his forecasts. One day, calculating that Uranus was about to exert a malign influence on his life which would reach its peak at midday, he took the precaution of remaining in bed. As the clock struck twelve there came a cry of 'Fire!' and Varley, rushing out, discovered that his house was in flames. He was so delighted to have predicted the disaster that the damage to his home didn't bother him at all. Varley believed in Blake's spiritual visitants as ardently as Blake himself and, in 1819, they had held a series of seances during which, between nine in the evening and three in the morning, Blake would keep open studio to any heavenly caller. Herod, Socrates, Mahomet, Owen Glendower and Voltaire were among the more notable figures that dropped in and Blake, sitting with his sketchpad, took all their portraits.

Darkness would long since have fallen when Mary Linnell bundled Blake warmly up in a shawl and sent a servant with a lantern to guide him and Palmer back across the heath. From there, the two would walk slowly homewards under the stars. The mythological stories of the glittering constellations felt far more real to Blake than the scientific discoveries of his day and Palmer was always to remember him, roused irritably from his silence, when talk at a friend's house had turned to the vastness of space: 'It is false!' he had declared. 'I walked the other evening to the end of the earth, and touched the sky with my finger.'[27]

8

The Oxford Sepias

A mystic and dreamy glimmer as penetrates and kindles the inmost soul
from *The Life and Letters of Samuel Palmer*

Palmer was in awe of Blake. Leafing through his portfolios, he would marvel at their vitality, at the 'spectral pigmies, rolling, flying, leaping among the letters; the ripe bloom of quiet corners, the living light and bursts of flame'. The pages seemed almost to tremble under his touch. 'As a picture has been said to be something between a thing and a thought, so in some of the type books over which Blake had long brooded, with his brooding of fire, the very paper seems to come to life,' Palmer said. When he had finished, he would lay the portfolio as tenderly back down on the table as if he 'had been handling something which was alive'.[1]

Blake flung open the windows of Palmer's youthful imagination; through them he could see further than he had ever seen before. He began to work in new ways. Already in his 1824 sketchbook he had begun dashing down his drawings with an impulsive energy. By the autumn of 1825 he had written to a Mr Bennett who had commissioned him just a few months previously, to warn him that he might be surprised by his new style. At first, he promised to take back any which displeased their new owner and listen to suggestions as to how they might then be improved, but a few weeks later he thought better of this offer. 'I will no more, by God's grace, seek to moderate for the sake of pleasing men,' he wrote. 'The artist who knows propriety will not cringe or apologise when the eye of judgement is fixed upon his work.'[2]

Palmer took his cue from the uncompromising Blake whose ideas from this point on pervaded his development – from his loftiest ambitions to some technical aide-memoire: remember 'that most excellent remark of Mr B's . . . how a tint equivalent to a shadow is made by the outlines of many little forms in one mass'.[3] If Palmer did not completely lose his own trajectory it was in large part because he never really understood his new mentor.

Palmer's approach to nature was quintessentially Romantic. The philosophers of the Enlightenment era had, broadly speaking, regarded the human and the natural as two opposing poles; but in the latter half of the eighteenth century ideas had started to undergo an important shift in their course. Where the Age of Reason had argued, along with Thomas Hobbes, that man in a 'state of nature' has no notion of goodness and is vicious because he knows nothing of virtue, in the Romantic era Jean-Jacques Rousseau posited that, on the contrary, 'uncorrupted morals' prevail in natural man. Though his belief in the 'noble savage' (an oxymoron that was, in fact, first introduced not by him but by the British poet John Dryden in his 1672 play *The Conquest of Granada*) has been greatly exaggerated by subsequent history – Rousseau never actually suggested that human beings in a state of nature behave morally – he did argue that morality was not essentially a construct of society. Rather, he considered it to be 'natural' in the sense that it was innate in so far as it was a product of man's instinctive reluctance to bear witness to suffering; whereas civilisation, as Rousseau saw it, was essentially artificial and bred inequality, envy, and unnatural desires.

By the time Rousseau's final book, his 1782 *Reveries of a Solitary Walker*, was published, Europe had become a far safer place to travel. Its citizens felt freer to journey for the purpose of pleasure alone. The heights of the mountains, the depths of the woods, the dramas of the thunderstorm were no longer merely hazards to be overcome, but awesome experiences to be enjoyed and pondered, to be appreciated almost as aesthetic performances. Nature had come to be seen as a source of the sensations that would arouse the emotions that provoked imaginative visions which, opening man's perceptions to divine powers, could act as a morally improving force.

Blake's work, however, for all that it is full of references to animal and plant life, did not stem from naturalistic observation. His creatures played a purely symbolic role. His lamb or his tiger, his stately raven or sinister worm, were emblems. They embodied the states of the human soul: the good and the evil, the innocence or experience. Nature, in all its profusion and variety, was just so much obfuscating material as far as he was concerned. It was 'the work of the devil', he even once said.[4]

The young Palmer would have been confused. He saw spiritual meanings shining forth from material beauties and was becoming, if anything, more attentive to the natural world. He particularly admired Blake's landscapes, delightedly perusing his Virgil woodcuts. They were 'visions of little dells and nooks, and corners of Paradise', he said: 'models of the exquisitest pitch of intense poetry'.[5] Several drawings in Palmer's 1824 sketchbook show similar views, sweeping valleys and looping rivers, peaceful shepherds and floating clouds, but it was not so much the scenery as the mood which pervaded it that captivated Palmer. He was entranced by the 'sentiment' which Blake, through his contrast of solemn depth and vivid brilliancy, managed to conjure; by a quality quite 'unlike the gaudy daylight of this world', which seemed to him to offer a precious glimpse of that which 'all the most holy, studious saints and sages' have enjoyed: that 'rest which remaineth to the people of God'. It was this numinous atmosphere that he too wanted to capture: 'a mystic and dreamy glimmer as penetrates and kindles the inmost soul'.[6] Before he met Blake, Palmer had been planning a landscape in which the hills of David and the hills of Dulwich would be as one, but now it would no longer be enough merely to 'unite scattered recollections' into 'a Dulwich-looking whole'. He must evoke that diaphanous half-light which speaks of divine presence; which would make these same hills promise that 'the country beyond them is Paradise'.[7]

A set of six sepia drawings survive from this period. Palmer was proud of them: they are all signed; all but one has been dated '1825'. He kept them among his possessions almost until the end of his life. Now in the collection of the Ashmolean Museum, and known as the Oxford Sepias, they present a series of peaceful rural scenes: a smocked

ploughman harnessing his curly-polled bullock, a hare loping its solitary way through the woods, a recumbent man reading amid a ripening
cornfield, a pipe-playing shepherd with his gathered flock. Three of the
drawings describe the delicate clarity of daybreak, three the gentle
closing in of the dusk. Palmer captures the glimmering magic of these
transitional moments to perfection. He sees the first paling of the sky
in the earliest morning; notices the long shadows cast by a just risen
sun; observes the way that the darkness is drawn into the folds of a
landscape; delights in the sprinkled brightness of a crescent moon.

Palmer used a sepia ink, extracted from cuttlefish, and applied it in
washes so that some parts of the picture surface were left unpainted
(the moon shines with the white of the underlying paper); others were
built upon layer by layer, lines fattened and thickened by a viscous
pigment made, as Blake would have taught him, by mixing the sepia
with gum arabic. Slowly he would assemble the images in obsessive
detail, from the tiniest figure perched on the furthest horizon, to the
little horned molluscs that probe a foreground. As he elaborated,
observing the courtship of a pair of song thrushes, the translucent fungi
that sprout in the damp, the individual shape of every different tree
leaf, the characteristic texture of every trunk, he moved towards an
oddly magnified view of the world in which every detail assumes a
significance, becomes part of a patchwork of myriad patterns which
draws their many elements into a harmonious whole.

The varnish was also made of gum, again applied layer by layer, each
coat given time to dry between applications and in a very uneven
manner so that where there was more pigment it became an impasto
– a layer so thick it is textured – and where there was no paint it formed
an all-but-transparent veil. Palmer would have known that the black
sepia would fade with time to rich brown and the gum slowly darken
to an amber tone. He would have foreseen the golden glow that these
works now possess. And it was this luminosity that he most wanted to
capture. His landscapes are consecrated by a beneficent light.

9

The Primitive

A pure quaint crinkle-crankle goth

from *The Letters of Samuel Palmer*

Blake was obsessed with the idea of a lapsed spiritual age. All his life he would look for what he called 'lost originals',[1] peering back through the layers of successive civilisations, through the veils of history and the confusions of belief, to discover the purified lineaments of some fundamental truth. It was in Westminster Abbey that he had first glimpsed it, he told Palmer. It was there that, with 'his mind simplified by Gothic forms & his Fancy imbued with the livid twilight of past days', he had found what he knew to be 'a true Art'.[2] The abbey's Gothic memorials had revealed a 'simple and plain road to a style . . . unentangled in the intricate windings of modern practice'. They had taught him how, by working within native traditions, he could recapture the unsullied virtues of the artists he most admired: the sanctified purity of Fra Angelico's frescos, the linear chastity of Mantegna's designs, the innocent perfection of Raphael's paintings, the hieratic clarity of Dürer's woodcuts. 'Everything connected with Gothic art and churches, and their builders, was a *passion* to him,'[3] Palmer recalled.

Blake was not alone in his preoccupation with the past. In the eighteenth century, inspired by a growing fascination with the researches of such historical figures as John Aubrey, who had made haphazard investigations into anything from pre-Catholic rituals in the lives of the peasantry to circular depressions in the ground at Stonehenge, or William Stukeley, who had published recondite studies of druidical cultures and giant geomantic 'worms', the people of England began popularly to indulge a passion for antiquarianism. It developed into a sort of national hobby and by the time that Blake was growing up the country was crawling with amateurs hunting for evidence of ancient tombs or heathen temples, shamanistic totems or the lost city of Atlantis; Blake was certainly not the only person to believe that the British Isles might be the last surviving remnant of this legendary antediluvian empire. What might in retrospect look like a cranky predilection for esoterica was very much a product of the cultural fashions of the period.

Blake encouraged his ardent young protégé to look back to primitive beginnings, to try to recover the dreams of an earlier age. Often what might now in Palmer's work appear most forward-looking – the simplifications of shape to the point of abstraction or the distortions of scale – was paradoxically intended to be facing in the opposite direction: to be gazing backwards towards the beauties of a long bygone age.

————

Palmer's feeling for Gothic art forms, for the soaring grandeur and spiritual grace of a vernacular British aesthetic, accorded well with the wider mood of his era. In 1815, with the battle of Waterloo, the Napoleonic wars had come at last to an end. A society which had battened down its hatches through decades of conflict had suddenly been flung open. Change had flooded in and with it all sorts of problems. Hundreds of thousands of demobilised servicemen were now looking for civilian work. There was mass unemployment in the towns and cities and, in the farms and villages from which the soldiers had first come, prospects were not hopeful. Harvests were bad for several years in succession. Britain was entering a prolonged period of agricultural depression.

The five years following 1815 were to bring Britain closer to complete social breakdown than any others in its history. Radical voices which, for so long, had been stifled by an atmosphere of resolute patriotism now rang out. England became a theatre for mass rallies and marches and uprisings. What was subsequently to become known as the industrial revolution had dawned. Manual labour was giving way to the machine; coal and steam power were starting to fuel huge increases in production; and with the creation of improved turnpike roads and the construction of railways and canals, manufactured goods could be transported more efficiently around the country. Trade underwent a tremendous expansion as consumerist appetites steadily swelled.

A sudden dramatic increase in the country's population was a powerful driving force, propelling it ever faster towards change. Couples began marrying younger and so producing more children who could be nurtured better as the economy grew. Agricultural methods improved and a public health system slowly emerged. Average life expectancy, which had not risen above thirty-seven for the previous century, now lengthened: by 1820 it had reached forty-one. Census returns show that between 1801 and 1821 the population expanded from 8.9 million to 12 million, an increase of 35 per cent. It would continue to grow rapidly from then on. A rural economy could never be expected to support this flourishing population. People left the countryside to try to make a living in the towns as thriving new industries offered better hope of employment and the prospect of higher wages. At the beginning of the century only about a quarter of the population would have been urban; by 1881 this proportion had risen to 80 per cent.

Great behemoths of cities grew and grew, engorged by an influx of job seekers. The population of Birmingham more than doubled in the first three decades of the century. Manchester and Liverpool, Bristol and Sheffield expanded apace. But infrastructures were not strong enough to cope. Systems creaked and then cracked under the strain. The industries that were breeding so much wealth were also spawning human misery. People needed housing and, as suburbia swallowed up fields and pastures, the poor were increasingly corralled into squalid urban tenements from which there was less and less chance of escape. Huge, stinking slums spread unsanitary ghettos which developers ignored. An entire urban underclass was being created, its members grist to the economic mill.

Small wonder, then, that those who could afford the luxury of such fantasies, began to look back nostalgically along the ways that they felt were being lost: to imagine the life of the peasant as a pastoral idyll, to see the countryside as a haven of Arcadian peace. It was a pleasing dream. Primitive man, Rousseau had postulated in the preceding century, was in some ways superior to the denizens of a modern age for, however raw his existence, however basic his lifestyle, a proper sense of mutual responsibility had at least prevailed. Archaic society, he had argued, had been built on foundations of comradeship and sharing and had not given itself over to the greedy arrogation of wealth. Such visions had done much to nurture the idealists of the French Revolution and their plans for establishing a mutually beneficial republic. By Palmer's day, that particular fantasy, betrayed by Napoleon and his imperial ambitions, had turned horribly sour and so, in the hope of discovering an alternative idyll, people were beginning to look back towards the Middle Ages instead. Medieval society could be more safely admired. Here was a spiritual antidote to contemporary materialism; here was an era in which, it was wistfully imagined, the values which modernity was destroying could be rediscovered again. The towers of England's Gothic churches stood like stone guardians amid its patchwork landscapes, stalwart survivors of a lost age of belief. They rose like reminders of the glories of faith, of the grandeur of God and of man's highest aspirations and the fact that the Gothic style was widely believed to have been British in origin made such ideals feel appropriately patriotic to boot.

Artists were in a quandary. It was all very well to admire the simple grace of the Gothic, but what about the hard-fought advances of their professional practice? For generations painters had striven for the skills of life-like representation, studying anatomy, poring over perspective, learning to render the light and shadow which could lend three-dimensionality to form, testing out a variety of atmospheric effects, striving to present the figure in motion, to capture the variety of facial expression, to manifest the drama and vibrancy of life. By the nineteenth century, an ability to imitate naturalistically had become a benchmark of talent. Such mimesis could not simply be abandoned without finding some other great achievement to elevate in its place. A group of German artists presented one solution. Coming together in Vienna in 1809 with Johann Friedrich Overbeck, the son of a Protestant pastor, at their centre, they formed a cooperative similar to that of a medieval guild. Members of the Brotherhood of St Luke – named after the patron saint of artists – believed in hard work and holy living. Forswearing the painting techniques of the present, eschewing the antique as pagan, the Renaissance as false, they looked instead to the art of the Middle Ages, aiming for a style which would combine nobility of intention with precision of outline and scholastic composition and to which light, shade and colour could be added, not for sensual allurement, but for further clarification of their sacred message.

In 1810 the group travelled to Italy and, moving into the abandoned monastery of St Isidoro in Rome, formed the core of a loose commune of fellow believers who, wearing biblical robes, rough beards and long uncut locks, would garden or do household chores in the morning before coming together to collaborate on artistic projects, including, most prominently, religious fresco painting, until the end of the day. This group became known as the Nazarenes, a name that had originally been coined as a term of mockery but which, with time, would become adopted as a badge of pride. The Nazarenes, even as they pursued the Christ-like affectations which their critics derided, rejected at the same time all that was easy or familiar. Refusing to fall in line with the academy system of teaching, spurning the naturalistic conventions of their day and hence also, symbolically, the materialism of modernity, their practice slowly accrued what was seen as an innate moral power.

The Nazarenes' paintings look rather less impressive from a historical perspective than they did to their contemporaries. Their compositions are stilted, their subject matter is derivative and their colours lack energy. But, in their day, these images proved eye-catching if only because they were also so odd. Their style had 'little or nothing to do with reality', declared Charles Eastlake, a painter of historic and biblical subjects who was to go on, in 1843, to become the first Keeper of the National Gallery and the President of the Royal Academy. 'To censure it for being destitute of colour, light and shade, would be ridiculous,' he wrote in a review, for 'such merits would, in fact, destroy its character . . . they have dignified their style by depriving the specta-tor of the power of criticising the execution.'[4]

By eschewing the parameters by which painting was normally judged, the Nazarenes had ducked under the barriers of critical conven-tion and discovered what for a while felt like an exhilarating new freedom. By the time that Palmer was looking for a fresh way forward, they were already internationally renowned. A major 1816 fresco commission in Rome, devoted to the story of Joseph in Egypt and painted on the walls of the Palazzo Zuccari (it is now in the Alte Nationalgalerie in Berlin) had, even before the project was completed, opened up two further important fresco commissions: the Dante, Tasso and Ariosto rooms at the Casino Massimo and the Gallerie Chiarimonti frescoes in the Vatican. These, capturing the attention of the many trav-ellers to Italy who, with the end of the Napoleonic wars, had started flooding back to the continent, brought celebrity to their makers. Grand tourists would return with descriptions of paintings which, even as they showed off modern fresco techniques, wilfully spurned any superficial virtuosity. They would gossip about the odd commune of artists who had created them, about their peculiar monastic habits and their odd priestly robes. Their desire to return to the celestial origins of art, to cleanse painting of its earthly tarnish and revive its spiritual purpose, struck a resounding chord.

The eighteenth century had looked to classical style because it had wanted to express a universal ideal. When Reynolds in his *Discourses* extolled 'general beauty' and 'general truth', he had been encouraging a quest for some perfected template that lay beyond the natural world. This ideal was not so far from that which the Nazarenes sought, it is just that Reynolds's slow, methodical progress, leading step by step back-wards towards ancient Greek models, was not nearly as appealing to a new generation as the thrilling illogical leaps that the Romantic imagi-nation could make. 'Mere enthusiasm will take you but a little way,' Reynolds had admonished; but Blake was speaking for many when he scribbled indignantly: 'Damn the fool, mere enthusiasm is all.' By 1830, the Nazarenes had disbanded, all but Overbeck returning to

Germany, several to become teachers in the very academies which they
had once spurned. But for a while, they had set an inspiring precedent.
They were 'one of the chief renovators of Christian art', George Eliot
wrote of them some fifty years later, for they had 'not only revived but
expanded that grand conception of supreme events as mysteries at
which successive ages were spectators, and in relation to which the great
souls of all periods become contemporaries'.[5]

———

In 1824, Linnell introduced Palmer to a German collector, Charles
Aders. His Euston Square home was to become almost a place of
pilgrimage to the eager young painter who sought an art of vision not
of mere verisimilitude. Aders was a wealthy merchant and insurance
broker. His wife, Eliza, the daughter of the portraitist John Raphael
Smith, was a gifted artist in her own right. A friend of the poet August
Schlegel (brother to the more famous philosopher) and of the novelist,
critic and founding father of the Romantic movement, Ludwig Tieck,
Aders was steeped in the spirit of German Romanticism and had come,
through this, to develop a discerning admiration for the art of the
northern primitives. During the upheavals of the Napoleonic wars, he
had managed to purchase many works which, routed from the religious
institutions for which they had been painted, came on to the market at
very low prices. Scattered throughout the rooms and up the staircases
of his London home, were works by such masters as Jan Van Eyck,
Hans Memling, Rogier Van der Weyden and Albrecht Dürer.

By the mid-1820s, when an interest in German literature and northern art were at the height of their vogue in Britain, invitations to Aders's
various residences were highly sought. The English actor Charles Mayne
Young describes a visit to his castle in Godesberg on the Rhine during
which he met Coleridge, Wordsworth and Schlegel, and in Euston
Square the merchant kept open house to anyone from Charles Lamb
through Flaxman to Crabb Robinson. Linnell brought Blake along in
the hope that he might find a new patron and Aders obliged, buying,
among other works, copies of both the *Songs of Innocence* and *Songs of
Experience*. The nineteen-year-old Palmer was also invited and it was

probably there that he met Jacob Götzenberger, a pupil of Peter Cornelius, a leading figure among the Nazarenes.

Palmer was not completely uncritical of what he saw. He had the outspoken opinions of youth. The faces in many of the paintings, he complained in an 1828 letter to Linnell, though exquisitely drawn, were too much like portraits and the purity of naked form was too frequently 'thwarted with fringes and belts and trappings' as the artists focused disproportionately on textiles and drapes. But for the most part it was through the work of these 'primitive' northern masters, through paintings which 'our modern addlepates grin at for Gothick and barbarous',[6] that he encountered a style which to him felt completely authentic. It was not the pictures that were barbarous, the young man decided, but the ignorant onlookers who dismissed them as such.

Linnell was equally enthusiastic. He had spent many patient hours engraving a minutely rendered copy of a panel by Van Eyck. Look for Van Leydenish qualities in the landscape, he instructed his eager pupil. He did not find the stylisations of this artist's primitive aesthetic in the least inimical to naturalistic study; rather, as far as he was concerned, medieval art aimed at a direct, unprejudiced description of the world and a careful rendition of creation's wonders amounted to a proof of the presence of God. This was not an uncommon belief. Among the most popular books of that period (it was to remain one of the most influential texts in Britain right up until the Victorian era and even Darwin would be required to read it as a student at Cambridge) was the *Natural Theology* of the cleric William Paley, best known for his use of the 'watchmaker analogy': a teleological argument for the existence of God which posited that, just as the complex mechanism of a watch requires an intelligent designer to make it, so the entire world must also have been designed by some omnipresent creator and must still be kept ticking by this potentate. Linnell saw the accurate rendition of nature as an acknowledgement of and homage to this divine presence. By paying meticulous attention to detail, the painter raised his labours to the plane of prayer.

But Palmer aimed at more than a literal transcription of God's creation. He wanted nothing less than 'the much hoped and prayed for revival of art'.[7] The way to achieve this, he decided, was not simply to go onwards, polishing techniques that could capture the physical world precisely; it was to evoke the transcendent atmosphere that pervaded the world. And to do this, he believed, he would have to double back, to recover the richness of an era of true faith. He determined to become once more 'a pure quaint crinkle-crankle goth'.[8]

10

The Ancients

Brothers in art, brothers in love
from Samuel Calvert, *A Memoir of Edward Calvert*

Palmer would have met several fellow pilgrims on his backward-looking path and by the beginning of 1824 a group of nine companions, with Palmer at their centre, had begun regularly gathering. By summer that year they were referring to themselves as the Ancients. Most of them were practising artists. Palmer's friends Francis Finch, Henry Walter and George Richmond were among the number, as well as an engraver Welby Sherman, a sculptor Frederick Tatham and Edward Calvert, an accomplished miniaturist. But Palmer's cousin John Giles, a stockbroker's clerk with strong religious convictions, and Tatham's brother Arthur, a Cambridge student, were also part of the brother-hood. Blake and Linnell were never actually members though the former was to become something between a mentor and a mascot while the latter, at least at the beginning, played host to their gatherings and was a trusted confidant.

Artistic fellowships, sprouting like weeds in the soil turned up by the French Revolution, would soon start playing an important role in European culture. The excluded had discovered a new way to make their presence felt. By banding together in the face of opposition they could find a new strength. The idea of 'the movement' gathered pace as the century progressed and, from the mid-1850s, group after group emerged: the Pre-Raphaelites, the Impressionists, the Post-Impressionists, the Expressionists, the Cubists, the Futurists, the Surrealists. The baton would be passed with increasing rapidity down the decades as each new set of convictions found its followers and flourished, their ideas and improvisations driving Modernism forwards. But, when the Ancients were gathering, the idea of such groups still felt new. A couple of break-away cabals had sprung up briefly on the continent. Paris, at the end of the eighteenth century, had nurtured *Les Barbus* ('the bearded ones'): quarrelsome outcasts from the studio of Jacques-Louis David who, rejecting the three-dimensional dramas advocated by their neo-classical master, looked to the simple linear motifs of Greek vase painting instead. And then there had been the Nazarenes. But the brotherhood of the Ancients was the first of such congregations to grow up in Britain and had, in consequence, a somewhat tentative, un-selfconfident feel. Members did not publish a resounding manifesto, establish a strict code of practice or follow a defined style. In fact, most of them were only part-timers. But they were bound broadly together by their spirituality, their shared belief in the purity of archaic culture and the deep sense of affection which they had for one another. 'We were brothers in art, brothers in love, and brothers in that for which art and love subsist – the Ideal – the Kingdom within,'[1] as Calvert would say.

———

Palmer's closest and most loyal friend among the Ancients was the artist George Richmond (1809–96). Barely fifteen when the group was founded, he was small, almost squat, with big hands and feet and long waving brown hair which, judging by a youthful self-portrait, he would have been constantly sweeping back from his high, clear brow. The son of a painter of miniatures, Richmond had right from the beginning, when he and Palmer first met in front of the marbles at the British Museum, an artistic facility which his friend, with his obsessive tendency to niggle, lacked. Richmond had gone on to enrol at the Royal Academy where the passions of the histrionic Fuseli would have prepared him for the erratic tempests of Blake, a figure whom, like all his fellow Ancients, he was to come deeply to admire. 'Never have I known an artist so spiritual, so devoted, so single-minded or so full of vivid imagination,'[2] he would tell the poet's future biographer Alexander

Gilchrist; yet, at the same time, Gilchrist reported, he would also make so bold as to argue back against Blake.

Palmer and Richmond shared a genial disposition, a pleasure in debate and a delight in the ridiculous. They would often visit exhibitions together and, stumping up the shilling entrance fee, could frequently be found standing side by side in front of a canvas at Somerset House, or studying canvases in the 'enchanted school'[3] of the National Gallery which, from the moment of its foundation in 1824, was to become one of their favourite points of call. They both exulted in music and one of Richmond's earliest memories was of being crushed in the pit listening to Paganini play in a concert in which the audience had been roused to such a fever pitch of frenzy that they had risen almost as one to shake their fists in each other's face. Years later, Richmond would also hear Chopin play in Paris, in a concert for which the great maestro of Romance, wrapped in blankets and sweating in the last stages of consumption, had had to be carried to his piano stool; but as soon as he had touched the keys, Richmond remembered, his inspiration had returned.

Richmond, with his boyish vivacity, his conviviality and his wicked talent for mimicry, made a sympathetic and amusing companion. John Ruskin noted the kindness of his soft brown gaze while another friend described how, when part of a gathering, 'he drew out those around him with the tenderest skill [and] . . . never allowed the humblest company to feel left out'. 'Where others might see blemishes, Mr Richmond always saw beauties,'[4] he said. But Richmond was also the most ambitious of the Ancients. While his fellows wasted time dithering about exactly which path to take, he was travelling in France trying to broaden an education which, if the impossible handwriting of letters littered with spelling mistakes is anything to go on, had been at best informal. While his friends were debating a communion of saints, he was in Calais exchanging pinches of snuff with the exiled Beau Brummell and, while they were living in rural retirement, he was building up a society portraitist's clientele. He never indulged the eccentricities that could jeopardise a career.

Edward Calvert (1799–1883) was to be another lifelong companion to
Palmer. He was a committed fellow visionary as well as a faithful friend.
The son of a naval officer, reared on England's rugged south-western
coasts, he had been only six years old when wandering at sunset in his
grandmother's garden he had had his first mystic experience, being
suddenly possessed by a feeling which, as his son would later describe
it, was 'as of a loving spirit taking up his abode within him, and seating
himself beside his own soul'.⁵ And yet Calvert was not some fey dreamer.
He was a robust country lad who, at the age of seven, had rowed out
alone to visit a fishing fleet trawling several miles from the shore and,
at the age of fifteen, when his fellow Ancients were first picking up
palette and brush, he had enlisted in the Navy to serve as a midship-
man. He was wounded in 1816 during the bombardment of Algiers
– the spectacular climax of a punitive British campaign intended to put
a stop to piracy in the Mediterranean and prevent a thriving trade in
European slaves – but though Calvert soon recovered and more than a
thousand Christian captives were liberated, his closest friend, hit by a
cannonball, was killed.

The harsher realities of a career which until that moment had
seemed more like an exciting adventure were brought home. From
then on the man of action faded and the thinker came to the fore.
With several years still to go before he could obtain his certificate of
release, Calvert found what must have seemed to his shipmates an
eccentric way of filling them. He set about learning to draw, filling
page after page with his sketches as, in the confines of his midship-
man's cabin, he practised his draughtsman's skills by the lurching
lamplight. Soon he was relishing a journey through the Aegean not
for its seafaring opportunities but for the chance it afforded him to
study the rocky landscapes of myth. Calvert had been presented with
a copy of Virgil on his baptism and it had filled his mind with vivid
imaginings of a pantheistic world. This voyage through the islands
now brought them to fresh life. Pagan enthusiasms – or 'naughty
disobedient heresies'⁶ as Palmer would call them – would always

compete with the Christian commitments of the man who would later build an altar to Pan at the bottom of his London garden.

As soon as Calvert had secured his release from the Navy – to the consternation of a family who feared he was abandoning a sound career – he started to study under an art teacher in Plymouth and, within a year or two, was producing accomplished miniatures. He met the ringleted Mary Bennell, a Londoner, on a visit to her family in the West Country, and after a brief courtship involving a great deal of poetic recitation, they married and moved to the capital in 1824. Calvert was admitted to the Royal Academy the next year. He had simply shown Fuseli his drawings and Fuseli had said: 'That will do, we want more of this.'

One of the first people whom Calvert had met in London was Palmer's cousin, John Giles, with whom, in the course of negotiating the sale of some shares, he had discovered a mutual fascination for the art of antiquity. The two had quickly made friends and it was probably Giles who had told Calvert about Palmer and Richmond. He had certainly spoken of the sailor-turned-artist to these two and when Calvert spotted Richmond in the Somerset House Library he had come immediately across and, holding out a hand, said: 'You must be Richmond,' to which Richmond replied: 'And you Mr Calvert whom I have wished to see.'

Squarely built, with a broad forehead and an expression more contemplative than observant, Calvert had looked on first acquaintance, Palmer later remembered, like 'a prosperous stalwart country gentleman . . . redolent of the sea and in white trousers'.[7] Linnell thought that he resembled an Old Testament prophet and the young Ancients seem rather to have regarded him as such. One of Calvert's sons (he was to father six children, one of whom died in infancy) captured a sense of the role that he played in their circle: 'His voice was subdued and impressive as his manner was dignified and unassuming, while his countenance, fair and almost unfurrowed, glowed with interest and simplicity. He would listen attentively to whoever was speaking, after which, when disposed to reply there would be noticed a slight movement in his features – an indication that he was about to say something – and those around would withhold further remark.'[8]

Calvert's home in Brixton, where he moved in 1826, became a meeting place for the Ancients. They 'unceremoniously dropped in as impulse or convenience prompted', his son remembered, 'reading . . . or comparing notes, aflame with earnest spiritual faith'.⁹ William Blake particularly liked him, Palmer said, for he had, 'in no small degree' that 'innocence and humility of heart'¹⁰ which Blake most loved to find. But purity of heart, as Calvert's family came to understand only too well, does not lead necessarily to fiscal profit and, for all that he was possessed of a modest private income, they often found themselves suffering for his art. 'Oh Edward, you will never do anything to make yourself famous,' his frustrated wife had once cried after he had turned down an offer from the precociously successful animal painter Edwin Landseer to complete one of his equestrian portraits. Calvert's belief was that: 'Painting must be a resource not a profession.'¹¹

Palmer, Richmond and Calvert formed the core of the Ancients; but four other artist members were also involved. Francis Oliver Finch (1802–62), Palmer's earliest friend, had been brought up in severely straitened circumstances by a widowed mother. He had been a sickly boy until, handed into the care of a grandmother who lived in Aylesbury, he had begun to thrive on such rural pastimes as swimming and rowing. Finch had a natural love of learning and by the time he was in his teens his imagination was steeped in the great works of literature, in *Paradise Lost* and Spenser's *Faerie Queene*, in Ovid and Virgil, Bunyan and Shakespeare. He had also started painting despite the advice of a neighbour who had confidently informed him: 'There's no good in making pictures little Finchy, you'd better be a parson and make sermons instead.'¹²

By the time Palmer met Finch, by then a student of Varley, he was a principled young man possessed of the highest religious standards which, though he found them difficult to capture in poetry or painting, he did his best to express in everyday life. He made a calm, kindly and most loveable companion who played an influential part in guiding Palmer towards a way of working that could integrate his faith and his art. They shared a love of music, Finch being a pianist and a singer with a fine contralto voice and a taste for old English songs: anything from *Stilly Night* to Handel's *Messiah* would ring out round their rooms. They also shared their affection for cats and many a hungry stray would find safe harbour in Finch's home.

By the time the Ancients were founded, Finch had had some success with Romantic pictures inspired by the *Poems of Ossian*. He had first exhibited at the Academy in 1817 and been elected an associate of the Old Watercolour Society at the age of nineteen, becoming a full member in 1827. 'He had imagination,' Palmer said, 'that inner sense which receives impressions of beauty as simply and surely as we smell the sweetness of rose and woodbine.'[13] He particularly loved the Keatsian image of 'embalmed darkness' which, appearing in *Ode to a Nightingale*, had been composed in 1819 in the garden of the Spaniard's Inn in Hampstead, a stone's throw from where Linnell would rent a rural home. Finch, of all the Ancients, was the one who at that time believed most passionately in Blake's spiritual course. In the late 1820s he was to convert to Swedenborgianism, a bizarre visionary cult developed from the writings of its eponymous eighteenth-century founder, a theologian who claimed to have had visions in which scriptural truths were revealed. It was a cult with which Blake for some years had also been fascinated, though he had eventually rejected it in favour of the even more radical doctrines of Paracelsus, the late fifteenth-century physician whose fundamental premise was that 'the imagination is like the sun',[14] and Jacob Boehme, a cobbler who, born a century later, famously pronounced that 'he to whom time is the same as eternity, and eternity the same as time, is free of all adversity'.[15]

The other artist members of the Ancients have been all but overlooked by history. Henry Walter (*c.*1799–1847), whose sketch of the fourteen-year-old Palmer embarking fresh-faced upon his new profession is the earliest known portrait of the artist, appears to have been included among the Ancients purely on the strength of old friendship because his pictures – watercolour portraits and paintings of animals – have nothing to do with the spiritual aesthetic of the group. He added

gaiety to their gatherings, however, was a witty caricaturist and, as far
as the artists' children were concerned, put his skills as an animal painter
to most impressive use, making a wolf mask for a Christmas party
which they would always remember for its bright glass eyes, jagged
teeth and lolling tongue of red cloth.

Welby Sherman, a draughtsman and engraver, was to prove an
untrustworthy addition to the group – not that the other-worldly
Palmer noticed. He continued to offer him every encouragement,
trying to drum up support for him when his prospects were poor, stubbornly disregarding the warnings of his more far-sighted friends.

Next there was Frederick Tatham (1805–78), an indifferent sculptor and miniaturist whose stiff early portraits produced under the
auspices of the Ancients soon gave way to a more conventional, if
utterly unremarkable, style. He was, however, a generous-hearted
man; sympathetic, tolerant and attentive with a caring disposition as
his frequent acts of charity to the villagers among whom he would
live showed.

Tatham was the son of Charles Heathcote Tatham, the architect who
had done so much to help Linnell by introducing him into society, and
the brother of Arthur Tatham, one of the pair of non-artist members of
the group. Arthur, when he joined the Ancients, was still a Cambridge
undergraduate, but he was soon to take holy orders becoming, as
Palmer who was with him on the eve of his ordination would inimically
put it, a servant at 'that glorious altar, that Holy of Holies within the
rent veil'. May he 'long live to minister oblations of acceptable praise to
God and good gifts to men', Palmer wrote, hoping that in 'the fiery
trial' which he believed to be coming to purify the Church, he would
stand undaunted or die a martyr.[16] Tatham went on to become
Prebendary of Exeter.

Last in this list of members, though most certainly not the least for
it may well have been he who first brought the Ancients together, was
Palmer's first cousin, John Giles. He was the youngest of the gathering
and embarking upon the career as a stockbroker in which he would
remain for the rest of his life. Yet, despite his prosaic profession, he was
steeped in poetry and would long remain a lynchpin of the group. Giles

was one of the very few to whom Palmer would dare show his more idiosyncratic pieces. He is 'a great favourite both with Richmond and me', he later told Linnell, for besides his 'unflexible and unblemished integrity', he 'has so much knowledge of books and general information – with such sincerity, good humour and real kindness of heart that I have passed no hours of relaxation with more pleasure than in his society'.[17] Giles and Palmer regarded it a 'sacred custom'[18] to spend Christmas day in each other's company, talking about literature, leafing through manuscripts and communing with their favourite 'feathered friend'[19] – one of the fat greasy geese upon which Palmer loved to feast. Giles exercised 'a great influence . . . of love hardly to be exaggerated',[20] Richmond's son would say.

The burly Giles would have cut a substantial figure among the diminutive Ancients on the grounds of his stature alone; but he was also a man of powerful conviction who, having come from an austere Nonconformist background and converted later to the Anglican faith, nurtured a profound reverence for the superior wisdom and spiritual purity of the medieval age. In the simplicity of ancient man had lain a grandeur and a glory to be emulated, he believed, and, deploring the brash innovations of modernity, he imparted his vision to his companions whenever he could: a vision which, as Calvert was wistfully to describe it, felt 'so remote, so near, simple, peaceful, settled in golden innocence, secured in the recesses of its blessedness'.[21] Giles was so enamoured of this lost age that he affected to speak in what he thought was an archaic way, putting an accent on the final syllable of such words as furrēd or averrēd. At their Christmas gatherings, he and Palmer would eat mincēd pies.

Giles was an unquestioning patron of the poet whom he called 'the divine Blake' and whom he stoutly believed to have 'seen God, sir, and talked with angels'.[22] On one memorable occasion, he discovered and secured for a bargain price the original engraving plate for his *Canterbury Pilgrims*. He was a lifelong friend to Richmond to one of whose sons (Harry Inglis) he taught Latin, drumming in the grammar with great shouts rather than blows. A mistake was a cause for a roar which would have staggered a stranger; correct repetitions were rewarded with gifts of oranges.

Giles never married. A lifelong and increasingly eccentric bachelor, he would lighten the monotonous piety of Sundays at the Richmonds by calling round and reading to the children (one of whom, Willie, was a godson) from his beloved John Bunyan. He must have relished the company. Living all his life on Albion Street, working on the stock exchange (where he was nicknamed John Bull), spending his free time browsing through bookshops, he must often have felt lonely. Not that he would have complained; there were others far worse off. 'Think of the martyrs who boiled in hot oil,' he once boomed at his godson when the boy complained that he was being bullied at school.

———

At first, this motley brotherhood would meet under the auspices of John and Mary Linnell. Over brimming mugs of home-brewed beer, they would discuss books and art, argue over religion and test out new philosophies, play music and sing until late, sometimes too late, into the evening, as a note from the Tathams' father suggests. 'While fully confident and very grateful to you for your friendship and kind offices to my dear Frederick,' he wrote to Linnell, 'I was last night kept up till half past 11 o'clock in *anxious suspense*' awaiting his return. He asked his friend to try to prevent this happening in future. 'As I grow older I am not less nervous,' he explained in a letter which serves as a reminder of quite how young these Ancients actually were when they met.

It was Blake, however, who provided the focal point of the group. As far as its members were concerned, heaven beat in the blood of this pale old man. Where the uninitiated saw only a shabby engraver in the grip of wild fantasies, they saw a prophet crying out in the wilderness. 'Centuries could not separate him in spirit from the artists who went about our land, pitching their tents by the morass or the forest side, to build those sanctuaries that now lie ruined amidst the fertility which they called into being,'[23] Palmer said. They called him 'The Interpreter' after the character in *Pilgrim's Progress* who explains spiritual enigmas to Christian, and his Fountain Court flat became the goal of their pilgrimages. As they approached, Calvert said, they would 'gaze up at that divine window where the blessed man did his work' and, like acolytes attendant on some High Church altar, they would kiss the bell-pull, perhaps giggling a little self-consciously at the action for they were often playful, although at the same time profoundly serious in their intent.

Among themselves they referred to Blake affectionately as 'dear old William' or 'Michelangelo Blake', but to his face he was always respect-fully addressed as 'Mr Blake'. After years of neglect and mockery and scorn, the old man must have relished such esteem. He would rise from his table with a smile of welcome and the Ancients would spend long hours in his rooms, sharing a simple mutton dinner, perhaps, or sending out for pots of foaming porter before settling down to long hours of discussion, of dogmatic assertion and contradiction and counter-argument. It must have been rare for Blake to feel that his listeners were not remotely sceptical. The Ancients encouraged him to unfurl his vision in full and when Palmer asked him if he would like to paint his design of *The Sons of God Shouting for Joy* on the great West Window of Westminster Abbey his imagination was kindled to new excitement by the very thought. His illustrations to *The Book of Job*, commissioned by Linnell and finally published in 1826, might barely have broken even financially, but at least the 'man of righteousness' had found some earthly reward.

The Ancients determined to follow Blake's artistic path, regardless of the fact that in so doing they were cutting themselves off from current artistic fashions and hence commercial success. As young men they were not worried by what the world thought of them; they had their brothers to reassure them, to understand and support them, and to defend them in the face of ridicule. They established a regular monthly meeting – a gathering of 'The Blessed in Council' – to be held in each other's homes, though most often at Calvert's, where his long-suffering wife would attend to their every want as the evenings lengthened and their visionary fervour gradually gave way to ridicu-lous jokes, moral intensity to merciless teasing, and prayerful solemnity to an irreverent sense of fun. Blake, when he was feeling well enough, would occasionally come along. He understood the importance of a shared sense of purpose for he liked to imagine the great Renaissance artists as being like the Holy Apostles: working together 'engaged without jealousy . . . in the carrying out of one great common object'. But it was Palmer, more than any of them, who cherished the idea of community. He devoted a great amount of energy to trying to corral his scattered friends. 'It is wonderful,' he said, 'what good things may be suggested where nothing offers at first by the laying together of two or three heads.'[24]

Shoreham

The beautiful was loved for itself
from *The Letters of Samuel Palmer*

As a boy, Palmer had lived only a short walk away from the tollgate
which crossed Kent Street Road (now the Old Kent Road) between
the Old Dun Cow and the Green Man, levying the traffic which
passed in and out of the city from the south. The smart post-chaises
dashing in from the provinces, the lumbering farm wagons piled high
with produce, the packhorses floundering under unbalancing burdens,
the slow plodding cattle and the flocks of panting sheep: all passed
along this crowded route. And, as a child, Samuel must sometimes
have stood there gazing, wondering about the world from whence all
these things arrived. Young George Richmond certainly did. One of
his earliest memories, he recalled, was of watching the great horse
carts coming in from the country with harnesses chinking and bright
flanges fluttering, while the little gypsy children, too exhausted to
walk any further, lay rocking in great nets slung underneath. To him,
he remembered, these vehicles had seemed like the harbingers of
some charming rural land.

As a young artist Palmer had dreamt of turning rambles and sketching trips into something more lasting. London was a vast, polluted
mire of men. The 'Great Wen' was how the pamphleteer and cham-
pion of rural England William Cobbett had described it in 1820. To
a bewildered Thomas Carlyle, arriving in 1824, it was like paying a
visit to Bedlam. 'Of this enormous Babel of a place I can give you no

account,' he wrote to his brother. 'The flood of human effort rolls out of it and into it with a violence that almost appalls one's very sense . . . and with the black vapour brooding over it, absolutely like fluid ink; and coaches and wains and sheep and oxen and wild people rushing on with bellowings and shriekings and thundering din,' it was, he said, 'as if the earth . . . were gone distracted'.[1] 'Nobody is healthy in London, nobody can be,'[2] declared Jane Austen's valetudinarian Mr Woodhouse. And little wonder: there was not a man or woman who lived there, announced a writer in the *Quarterly Review*, whose skin, clothes and nostrils were not loaded with a compound of powdered granite, soot, and still more nauseous substances. Even the city's spiders were said to be so befuddled by pollution that they could not spin their webs straight.

To Palmer, suffering so persistently from respiratory complaints, the idea of rural escape was especially enticing. Increasingly he began to look towards Shoreham for his dreams of 'that genuine village' where, as he was later to put it, he 'mused away' some of the best years of his life.[3]

The village of Shoreham lies less than thirty miles to the south-east of London in the county of Kent. Nowadays, crawling out from the capital through an all but unbroken suburbia, it only takes about an hour to get there by car. Alternatively there is a train from Victoria which, crossing the Thames, rattles out past the back yards of Clapham towards Bromley beyond which patches of woodland begin to line the track. Soon, the traveller is moving through opening landscapes, past paddocks of muddy ponies and steepening fields as the railway curves round to enter the Darent Valley, running the length of a line of green pastures that rise up towards hills with wooded horizons. But when Palmer first started visiting the village, the suburbs had only just begun their inexorable creep. There was no train to startle the hares from their nibbling or put up the herons from their patient watch. Even the toll road, that unspooling precursor of ribbon development, did not pass through the village, and Palmer and his fellow Ancients, if leaving on foot from London at dawn, would have arrived in the village by the light of the moon.

It was a difficult journey. The soil, 'being wholly chalk and very stony' rendered the road 'not very pleasant to travel at any time', recorded Edward Hasted in his 1797 *History of Kent*. Palmer and his friends must have felt a little like Chaucer's fellowship as they passed the Tabard Inn in Southwark from which the medieval pilgrims had five hundred years earlier set out and, leaving the city behind them, adjusted their stride to the long journey ahead. They could seldom afford the stagecoach, although there was one which, leaving at twenty past nine in the morning, would drop travellers three hours later at the top of Morant's Court Hill from which it was a gentle half-hour walk (or cart ride) down into the Darent Valley. At other times they would hitch a lift with a local carrier, riding on one of the fruit carts or hop wagons which plied a regular trade with the capital, or clamber on to the back of some lumbering wain.

On his first visit, Richmond liked to remember, he had been accosted by a gentleman farmer on horseback who, scanning him closely, had politely inquired if he knew any lad of his age in need of employment. Dressed in a nankeen jacket and white trousers, he had looked like a serving boy, the artist supposed. But dressing more in accordance with his social station could lead to other difficulties. One summer evening, weary from walking, he had flagged down a driver and, scrambling up gratefully into the roomy wagon, had soon found himself rocked off to sleep. It was only when the driver roused him at the parting of their ways that he had noticed the stains on his light flannel suit. 'What were you carting before you took me?' asked Richmond. 'Sile,' was the driver's laconic response. Clearly, the city-dwelling Ancients encountered a few problems on the path to their pastoral idyll; but once they arrived there they found the village of their dreams.

Shoreham, taking its name from the Saxon words *scor* for slope and *ham* for village, shelters in the seam of the fertile Darent Valley which has been pretty much continuously settled since prehistoric times. In ancient days the whole area would have been thickly forested. Woods of oak, beech and chestnut still cover inclines that are too steep to plough. But farmers had started their clearing long before the Ancients arrived there and, as the young Palmer first crested the lip of the valley, it would have been a richly agricultural view that he found himself gazing upon, with crops of wheat and barley turning gold in the sunshine, with orchards laden with apples and fields of twining hops. Sleek cattle would have browsed among lush water meadows and sheep grazed the rough heath lands of the High Weald beyond.

The River Darent loops its sparkling course through the valley, threading its way through ancient demesnes and verdant pastures, down narrow passageways that run between cottages, round pollard willows and under dappling oaks. 'The still Darent, in whose waters cleane/ Ten thousand fishes play and decke his pleasant streame,' wrote the Elizabethan Edmund Spenser,[4] a product of Palmer's old school Merchant Taylors' and a poet whose taste for archaic traditions he would share. Shoals of minnows still flicker, faint as pencil sketches in the pools of the river that, for Palmer, would have offered that lovely glint of water without which no landscape could to him look right.

Flowing over a shallow bed of speckled stones, the Darent was once a much broader, faster river than it is today: in Roman times it was navigable to boats which came upriver from the Thames. And before large-scale extractions diminished it so drastically that, in the 1970s, a weasel was spotted darting across its dry course, its current was strong enough to keep the wheels of several corn mills rumbling as well as powering a paper mill which, not closing until well into the twentieth century, provided a valuable source of employment in the region, especially for the women who shredded the rags. Palmer might have disliked the growing industrialisation of the countryside that such factories represented but he must have found it most useful to have a supply of thick, high-quality paper on hand; nor was he averse to hitching a ride with the rag carts that brought old clothes down to Shoreham from the East End.

A straggling village street flanked by cottages, many of them dating back to medieval times, crosses the river by a three-arched stone bridge which, though now much restored and remodelled, was designed in the thirteenth century to allow donkeys with a bale strapped to each side to pass. Palmer, who sketched it, was as charmed by its antiquity as he was by the picturesque houses which clustered around it: humble low-beamed dwellings with roofs of mossy thatch, their vegetable plots, fruit trees and flower gardens all carefully protected from winds and stray livestock by woven fences of willow. And yet, even in those days, Shoreham was changing. It had flourished in the century before Palmer arrived and, alongside the modest cottages, a handful of rather grander dwellings had grown up and now included Riverside House, an imposing edifice constructed in grand Georgian style by a successful eighteenth-century saddler, and Waterhouse, the spacious residence in which Palmer's father was to live.

———————

Palmer's introduction to Shoreham came most probably through his father. One of his cousins, Charles Wake, had been the vicar of the parish from 1775 to 1796. More importantly to the elder Palmer, it was known as a stronghold of Nonconformist belief, although some fifty years earlier when John Wesley had first visited he had provoked a riot, setting an outraged congregation of Anglicans storming and cursing and clanging at the church bells. Dissenting sects had subsequently put down roots in the region and flourished and Palmer's father was invited to become a lay preacher in the chapel at Otford, about a mile downstream from Shoreham village.

Sam, accompanying his father on trips to attend his new flock, had visited the area with some regularity after 1824. Several of the drawings in his surviving sketchbook – the views of clustered villages amid undulating landscapes, of distant spires and sloping meadows, of cloaked shepherds presiding over quietly grazing flocks – were probably done in the Darent Valley; a large bristle-backed pig, which he sketched as she watched warily over her litter, may well be the 'huge Kemsing Sow' that he mentions in an 1824 letter in which he uses Shoreham as his address for the first time.

Palmer was enchanted by the village. His works of 1825, including his glowing sepias, evoke the natural fecundity of its rural views. In the freshness of spring the following year he and his fellow Ancient, Arthur

Tatham, travelled down to Shoreham for a more protracted stay. Renting rooms in the ramshackle timber and weatherboard house of a local farmer, Arthur Tooth, (a house which is now known as Ivy Cottage and which, though much done up, still stands on the road that leads up out of Shoreham towards the church) they pooled their meagre resources and by dint of frugal management survived on a sum total of eight shillings a week – an allowance which was later cut to five shillings, two pence.

It was around this time, however, that the fiscal circumstances of the Palmer brothers suddenly improved. In 1825, William Giles died leaving both his grandsons a legacy which, when all the paperwork had eventually been completed, amounted to a far from insignificant £3,000 apiece. William decided on the strength of it that he wanted to become a sculptor. Samuel, no longer bound to London by the need to attract paying clients, was free to pursue his ambitions in remote rural peace. Towards the end of 1826 he bought a dilapidated cottage, small and dark and overrun by rodents. The Ancients nicknamed it Rat Abbey. But the determinedly parsimonious Palmer was unperturbed: 'I will not infringe a penny of the money God has sent me, beyond the interest, but live and study in patience and hope,'[5] he told Richmond. This cottage would remain his home for well over a year.

Meanwhile, Palmer's father had started muttering about taking a new wife, a prospect which did not please his prosperous brother Nathanial who, already irritated at having to support a sibling who persisted in dabbling so degradingly in trade, did not want to have to deal with any potentially embarrassing and financially cumbersome dalliances on top. He issued an ultimatum: either his brother would live the life of a gentleman of leisure, and live it as a widower to boot, or he would have to forfeit his annual allowance. The path ahead, for the time being at least, was plain. Palmer's father loved his books but his Baptist convictions were equally firm. He decided to accept his brother's terms, to relinquish his unremunerative business, leave his dingy London house and retire to Shoreham to pursue a leisured existence, with his own private library and Mary Ward as a housekeeper, and a local congregation to whom he could expound his ideas of salvation, hustling their souls heavenward, as his grandson was later to put it, 'with much sweating and thumping of cushions'[6] to expedite them on their way.

In March 1827, Palmer's father sold up his stock in a sale which, taking place over the course of three days, brought him £133.6s. Not long afterwards, packing up his books and domestic accoutrements, he carted his entire household to Shoreham. By the end of 1828 he was ensconced at Waterhouse, a pretty Queen Anne building which he rented at the bottom of the village, overlooking the pack bridge. It was not as ostentatious then as it looks now, for a Georgian façade has since been added giving it an air of contrived grandeur; but to the locals it would certainly have seemed a gentleman's residence with its six spacious rooms and its servants' attics, its little walled garden sloping down to the river and its expansive aspects of far-off tree-crowned slopes.

———

Shoreham felt like a secret haven to the Ancients: 'a valley so hidden', as Calvert was to put it, 'that it looked as if the devil had not yet found it out'.[7] Palmer would often paint it protected by a foreground of sheltering hills. It was his sanctum. Away from 'horrid smoky London with all its begrimed finery and sooty shows',[8] he could search for that simplicity of purpose which he so admired in Blake, a man who managed to live 'without a mask; his aim single, his path straightforwards, and his wants few' so that he could be 'free, noble, and happy'.[9]

Palmer had some time since abandoned his dandified pretensions. He had caught sight of his full-length reflection in a London shop window and, after a long pause for self-critical consideration, declared: 'No more finery for a gentleman as short as you!'[10] From then on his dress would be humble, if decidedly eccentric, as a caricature scribbled by Richmond in 1825 makes clear. The painter is depicted from the back, a dishevelled figure with voluminous overcoat, furled umbrella, clumpy boots and broad-brimmed hat. 'Learn thou the goodness of thy clothes to prize/ By their own use and not another's eyes,'[11] Palmer would chant aphoristically. He came increasingly to detest the affectations of fashion, preferring clothes made with a more rigorously practical regard for comfort, hard wear and, of course, pocket capacity.

In Shoreham he began to adopt the sort of biblical look which the Nazarenes had favoured and, in both a chalk sketch and a miniature done by Richmond in 1829, an idealised 'Ancient' emerges who, with his clipped beard and shoulder-brushing locks, serene downcast gaze and long antique robes, looks pronouncedly Christ-like – an association further affirmed by Richmond's first attempt at a portrait of Jesus. The robed and bearded figure who sits by the well in his 1828 painting of *Christ and the Woman of Samaria* bears a strong resemblance to Palmer who quite possibly posed.

To the locals, Palmer would have appeared outlandish. Beards were not much worn at that time, except by soldiers, and were considered positively suspect in Establishment circles. Even as late as 1840, when the radical Mr George Frederick Muntz appeared in Parliament with a flourishing growth of facial hair, there were many who felt that he was issuing his own peculiar hirsute insult to English parliamentary institutions. In more bohemian company, however, the beard was coming back and the once pink-cheeked Palmer was proud to be sporting his cutting-edge credentials. 'The artists have at last an opportunity of wearing the beard unmolested,' he informed Linnell that summer. 'I understand from the papers that it is become the height of fashion.'[12]

Palmer persuaded Mary Ward to stitch him a large and extraordinary cloak. In winter he would furl it warmly around him, pulling up its hood against the inclement weather; but in summer, when the heat in the valley was basting, he would wear a canvas jacket and a huge circular straw hat: a functional if flamboyant adornment which, cropping up in several of his paintings, became for this scion of a family who had made their money in millinery a long-cherished symbol of his Shoreham days. He must have made a peculiar sight, stumping about the hills, stool in one hand, umbrella in the other, pockets stuffed with sketching pads, long auburn locks straggling from under the brim of his great woven-straw cartwheel, while he peered at far distant views through spectacles so 'scratched and scribbled over' that their two misty spheres of light looked, he said, like 'the sun in a fog or a dirty dish in a dark pantry'.[13]

His fellow Ancients, however, did not follow his dress code. They couldn't afford to look so shambolic. It was all very well for Palmer, with his financial legacy, to enjoin his companions to trust in the Lord – 'our blessed Lord teaches us not to be anxious about the morrow' he told Richmond, 'spiritual difficulties should be the only serious trouble of a bright intellectual essence: other disturbances are for the most part terrific phantoms which vanish on approach'[14] – but the rest of the Ancients were encumbered by what must have felt like a far-from phantasmic need to earn a living. Even Calvert with his private income had to bear in mind his familial duties, not to mention his sense of social propriety. The only person who remained permanently in Shoreham with Palmer was his brother William, who by then was pursuing his own unpromising sculptural career.

Calvert liked to visit whenever he could and, in the autumn of 1825, he brought Blake and his wife along with him by stagecoach. The old visionary was very unwell by then and had spent most of that year confined to his bed, but though still plagued by shivering fits and his perennial stomach complaints, he enjoyed the trip, spending profitable hours tucked up by the fire discussing books with Palmer's father. It has been suggested that his *Jerusalem* was inspired by, if not actually written in, the village, that Shoreham's rainy skylines were his 'clouded hills'. The rest of the Ancients turned up periodically for visits, staying with Palmer at first in his rodent-infested hovel and later, and far more comfortably, with his father at Waterhouse. Sometimes they would lodge with locals as flurried exchanges of letters discussing rooms and their various merits and rental prices attest.

The ardent young men relished their time in the valley as much as any holiday. In 1827, in the month of May when the orchards and hedgerows were overspilling with blossom, the fields crowded with wild flowers and the pastures springing up lush, Walter, Sherman and Frederick Tatham all came to visit. A short while later, Richmond, having sold his first ever miniature for three guineas, rented a room from a labourer for two shillings a week – he was particularly delighted to discover that John Wesley had held a meeting in that very chamber – and joined his fellows in Kent determined to eke his money out for as long as he could. Richmond was always to remember those weeks. 'I believe no human being was ever happier than I was in that first independent taste of really beautiful countryside along with my dear friends,'[15] he would write.

Linnell had originally tried to dissuade Palmer from retiring to his rural retreat. He would be washed up in a cultural backwater, he had warned. But he also enjoyed periodic trips to the valley. 'I have been at many places,' he wrote after a stay in the summer of 1828, but 'I never was anywhere so much at liberty.'[16] He found 'benefit' and peacefulness in Shoreham's 'Sylvan Bower'[17] and he set about making his typically thorough arrangements to bring his entire family, his wife and their (by then five) children – the little Leonardos or little Ancients[18] as they were playfully nicknamed – down to enjoy the harvest home.

———

'If we wait for a pure community large or small while human nature lasts, we shall wait in vain,'[19] declared Palmer. He knew that the ideal society could never exist. And yet for all that the Ancients were rather fragmented, they had a powerful sense of shared purpose and prayerfulness, of friendship and happiness that enriched their lives. They sought out the simple pleasures of a world in which the spiritual was spied through the veil of nature and, as Palmer was later to put it, 'the beautiful was loved for itself'.[20]

They rose early at Shoreham, beginning their days – or at least *endeavouring* to, Palmer admitted – by dwelling on a passage from scripture. They gloried in the loveliness of the dawn, often rising in darkness and slipping out while the mists were still lingering low by the river and the oxen still drowsing unyoked in their stalls, to sit on their camp stools and watch for day's coming. And then, when the first creeping pinkness had flared and flamed outwards in a conflagration of dawn gold, they would gather up their things and walk home through its wonders together, singing praises to God for his radiant light.

Having breakfasted simply on bread and apples, they would bathe

in the river, even in winter when the swift icy currents must have
made them splash and yelp. Such vigorous daily ablutions were a new
departure for Palmer who had until then been content to wash only
once a week. 'I feel ever grateful to Mr Tatham for teaching me to
"sweeten my carcass",'[21] he would later write. For the rest of his life he
remained 'an inveterate body-washer'. The whole human race could
be divided spiritually into the converted and unconverted and bodily
into 'the washers and stinkers',[22] he concluded, and when many years
later a woman politely inquired of him what, in one word, he considered to be England's greatest national virtue, he pronounced without
a moment's hesitation: 'Cleanliness.' 'Yes! We may look down from
the organ gallery of St Paul's Knightsbridge in the London season and
say "Every one of you has taken a tub this morning!" In what other
country could *that* be said?'[23]

The Ancients would often spend the entire day out of doors, roaming
about in their valley of vision with their sketchbooks and brushes, their
pockets packed with apples and bladders of pigment and volumes of
poetry, their minds stuffed with visions of ideal delight. To read Palmer's
letters or look at his Shoreham pictures or even take a stroll through the
still largely unspoilt valley in which he lived, is to discover a sense of the
pleasures he enjoyed: the surging enthusiasms of spring when the
orchards are a frothing profusion of blossom and the pale pink of the
dog roses drape every hedge, when the woods are alive with the jays'
angry clatter and the young calves bleat shrilly from the little thatched
crofts; the sweltering delights of the summer when Palmer would stalk
through the cornfields, plodding slowly uphill towards the ridge-top
heights where crickets filled the air with their frying-pan sizzle and
speckled fritillaries skipped over the chalk. When the sun was too high,
he would often sit dreaming on the shady banks of the river watching
the flash of the kingfishers under the oaks, the damselflies flickering
and the trout lazily rising among the silver twist of the willows and the
glinting puzzles of gnats. In autumn, the valley was at its richest. He
would watch the stooping harvesters wading through the corn, feasting
on blackberries until his fingers were stained purple and crunching at
handfuls of hazelnuts. Palmer particularly loved nuts and would stuff

his enormous pockets full of them, cracking them loudly between his teeth as he shuffled through the leaves like some acorn-grubbing hog. And in winter, when the pace of life was much slower and the landscape more still, Palmer would often stay in by his fire to work, listening to the rhythm of the flails as they thumped the stone threshing floor, the rush of the river swollen up by rain, the tapping of branches against the panes of the windows and, occasionally, to the thick muffled silence of snow.

Sometimes the Ancients ventured further afield on their sketching trips, pausing in the hop gardens of the hamlet of Underriver, delighting in the architecture of the medieval Ightham Mote, visiting Edenbridge and Anne Boleyn's childhood home, Hever Castle, or walking to Chiddingstone about three miles beyond, the sort of picturesque village which Palmer would later revisit to find the mills, old forges and cottage doors which could lend character to his work. Occasionally they would follow the Darent upstream in the direction of Westerham from where, climbing up to the village of Brasted Chart, they could gaze out across 'the softly melting richness'[24] of a view which stretched on a clear day as far as the Isle of Wight; or they would make detours to other beauty spots, to the place they referred to as 'Pig and Whistle Valley' after the name of the flint cottage that stood at its head, or to the beacon at Rooks Hill overlooking Underriver. Palmer would later paint the view from its summit: a narrow slice of landscape leading towards far-off horizons of hazy blue. When Linnell came to visit, Palmer took him and his children on a tour of all his favourite sites. Linnell was 'delighted with the scenery', he reported excitedly to Richmond, 'and says he has seen higher hills but never finer scenes'[25] and the children were thrilled to be trundling along in an open cart.

It was landscape that the Ancients most loved, and particularly when they were wandering through it together, rolling along arm in arm, seeing God in everything from the little 'garden'd labyrinths' at the bottom of the valley to the great swelling masses of the 'thymy downs'.[26] These young men were not moving through the same world as the village dwellers, they were not wandering through fields that had to be ploughed, planted and cropped; seeing sheep which would stray if their watcher fell asleep or corn sheaves that would buckle the bones of their spines. Their suns did not rise on a day of hard labour or their dewy twilights bring a damp rheumatic ache. They were moving through the 'dells, and nooks, and corners of Paradise'.[27] The landscape of Shoreham had for them been transubstantiated by the poetry that they loved: they would often recite it as they drifted along, letting the rhythms of Virgil or Milton roll out along lanes and rumble down valley slopes. Palmer was always to be particular about the art of recitation. He would study how actors spoke. One did not make oneself heard over long distances by bawling, he would later instruct a young protégée, 'but by speaking very distinctly and giving . . . words their proper and proportioned emphasis'.[28] 'Do not grunt or snuffle the words through your nose or choak them in your throat or bite them with your teeth,' he would tell her, 'but throw them boldly out until they resound again.'[29]

Palmer was also a fine singer. His powerful tenor ringing out from the hilltops could be heard far down in the valley below. Sometimes, when the thunderclouds gathered in the summer's sultry heat, huge towers of cumulus massing along the horizons, building and boiling in vast staggering banks, the Ancients would wait out on the ridges until the tempest broke. Then, when the skies were shot through by great bolts of lightning and the rain was dashing down in sheets, they would make their way homewards through the storm together pitting their loud chorus against the rumbling thunderclaps.

The Ancients dined as simply as they breakfasted; probably, as was customary in those days, at about three o'clock. The mainstay of their diet was milk, eggs and bread, supplemented with the occasional piece of meat: perhaps a bit of mutton bought from some local farmer, a plump pheasant or partridge from the woods or on high days and holidays a fat goose. They would buy seasonal fruits and vegetables – radishes and gooseberries are mentioned – from neighbouring cottagers and throughout the autumn there would be an abundance of local apples, served up by Mary Ward in puddings and pies or roasted and stewed for the sake of the bowels with whose functions Palmer and his friends were consistently preoccupied. Sometimes they ate too much and Giles, taking a swim too soon after dinner one day, found himself greatly discomfited by the sensation that a large 'quartern loaf'[30] had got stuck in his digestive tract.

The apples would be pressed by the locals to make cider which, when the harvest had been good, could be bought 'undiluted and unadulterated',[31] for as little as a shilling a gallon: so cheap, Palmer told Linnell, who planned to take some back to London, that farmers were giving it to workers instead of the normal table beer. Palmer and his fellow Ancients never consumed anything stronger than this local brew, but they appeared to have drunk it in such profuse quantities that even heavily diluted it had an effect – not least if the bacchanalian antics depicted in Calvert's woodcut *The Cyder Feast* are anything to go by.

The Ancients particularly loved the 'perfumed and enchanted twilight'[32] of the warm summer evenings and long after the last heavy-uddered cows had swayed home from their pastures, after the weary labourer had returned to his supper and the slow grey heron flapped home to its roost, they would linger, swishing through the cornfields as the hills turned to dark silhouettes and the moon slowly opened her 'golden eye'. She shed a 'mild, a grateful, an unearthly lustre on the inmost spirits', Palmer said.[33] Sometimes, as darkness drew in, the young men would walk up through the village to a nearby chalk quarry and there, in a natural stone theatre carved out of the slopes, they would deliver a concert at the tops of their voices. They particularly loved Purcell's music to *The Tempest* (in those days it was thought to have been written by Matthew Locke), growing wilder and wilder as they sang it louder and louder, their faces glimmering eerily as they danced in the night. Often they set off on long rambles through the herb-scented darkness, their familiar landscapes made mysterious by the sprinkling moonlight. The locals nicknamed them the *Extollagers*, a mixture of extoller and astrologer, most probably, or as Palmer jokily defined it: one who 'went by the stars, a strange gentleman whose sketching stool, unseen before in those parts, was mistaken for a celestial instrument'.[34]

One of their favourite haunts, Finch recalled, was a tangled lane that led away from the village and was flanked by rows of old beeches with great writhing roots. Some years before, this lane had been the scene of a murder and the excitable Ancients thrilled at the very thought. The lane became their theatre, a site for re-enactments of fantastical scenes as the friends staged their own versions of the sort of spooky *tableaux vivants* that Fuseli's Gothic paintings had made so fashionable or made the dark corridor ring with their operatic renditions. One night they decided to walk to Bromley churchyard to meditate among the tombs, but were spotted by suspicious locals and reported to the watch who accosted them with raised bayonets accusing them of taking part in the then lucrative practice of tomb-robbing. The encounter came to nothing in the end. Everything was explicable. And the Ancients weren't deterred from undertaking further moonlit jaunts. Another night, the church clock had already struck ten by the time they decided on a whim to set out on an eight- or nine-mile walk along the ridges to Sevenoaks in search of a copy of the novel, *The Mysteries of Udolpho*: a ludicrously overwrought tale of supernatural terrors which, when first published some twenty years earlier, had whipped convoluted Gothic fantasies up into a fashion. Jane Austen had ridiculed it in *Northanger Abbey* in which her impressionable young heroine, riveted by such histrionic stories, starts to imagine her acquaintances to be characters in a lurid drama, but Palmer remained a fan of its author, Ann Radcliffe ('dear old aunt Radcliffe'). Some sixty years later he still had his 'ancient fragile'[35] copy of her *Udolpho* and wished that he could get hold of her other volumes in print of a size that his by then ageing eyes could read.

Local rumours would have done little to soothe the febrile imagination. Like most rural communities, the villagers harboured all sorts of superstitions, stories of spirits whose dread secrets had been passed down from generation to generation. They told tales of snakes 'of the bigness of a man's leg', of deadly lizards which 'basked sleepily on out-of-the-way banks where men never pass'.[36] One stout local yeoman professed that, jogging home from market through the valley at twilight, he had seen a flying reptile which by dint of whip and spur he had overtaken and killed, leaving its remains to be seen by all unbelievers the next day, lying on a wall at Otford, wings and tail, complete.

The arrival of Blake – a man who had played host to any number of otherworldly callers – only fanned their enthusiasms and one evening they all set off together to a 'haunted mansion in a shadowy paddock' where, as Palmer remembered it, 'sceptics had seen more than they could account for'.[37] Shuffling and whispering and hushing each other, glancing at Blake by the light of the veering lantern and giggling and nudging no doubt, they arrived and waited but any urge to laughter, however nervous, soon came to an abrupt stop when they heard a curious rattling. Drawing together they listened in a scared but expectant silence. It was Calvert, the most practical among them, who moved soft-footed towards the source of the sound while Palmer, more tentatively, followed with lantern raised. They listened again. Tap . . . tap . . . tap, came the sound. They peered more closely. And it was only then that they made their discovery: a snail was inching its way up the mullion, its shell tapping noisily against the glass pane. Not that this mundane revelation would dissuade them from their ardent belief in supernatural forces. Palmer was convinced that he had had a clairvoyant experience one night when, leaving Blake and his fellow Ancients in Shoreham, he set off on an errand to London. Not very long after he had left, Blake, sitting at the table, suddenly put his hand to his forehead and said: 'Palmer is come . . . he is walking up the road.'

'Oh, Mr Blake,' Calvert told him, 'he is gone to London, we saw him off in the coach.'

'No. He's coming through the wicket,' Blake clearly contradicted. A few seconds later the latch was indeed raised and Palmer stepped into the room. It turned out that the stagecoach had broken down just outside the village and so he had returned.

Palmer would relish such experiences all his life and would happily recount tales of mystic canary birds or haunted toy horses. He was delighted, some fifty years after leaving Shoreham, to find an article in the *Spectator* by someone who, while ridiculing rustic credulity, thought a terror of ghosts a far more reasonable response to tradition than mere dismissal of what one cannot at once explain. As Palmer himself rather pompously declared, having returned in 1870 to Margate where he had spent 'among the most interesting evenings of my life' in a haunted house, his impression was 'that, making all allowance for imposture and mistake, there was a residuum of evidence which no candid mind could resist'.[38]

The Ancients, however, only indulged in their eccentric nocturnal jaunts from time to time. In autumn, as the fragrant smoke of the homeward-plodding labourers' pipes drifted along the lanes, their own thoughts would also turn to the hearth. In the cold of the winter they preferred to remain by the fire. Frequently they would stay up into the small hours, working by candlelight as a little ink sketch of Richmond done by Palmer attests. Huddled up in his warm dressing gown, a long, tasselled night cap pulled over his head, he scratches away diligently at his engraving. It is his *Shepherd*, a note by Palmer informs us: an elegant but unfinished pastoral composition that had been inspired by the engravings of Blake.

Later, as an elderly hypochondriac nervously alert to potential causes of ill health, Palmer would repent these prolonged late-night stints. 'Sir Walter Scott got all his day's work done before breakfast,' he informed a pupil. 'I fell early into the opposite habits which I deeply regret.'[39] But at the time those long winter evenings, pulled like warm coats around them, felt delightfully homely, especially after Palmer moved from the incommodious Rat Abbey into the far more comfortable Waterhouse. He loved the 'never-cloying luxury' of long 'quiet intellectual evenings to those who are fagged out by the day'.[40] Gathered round the fire, the Ancients would listen to the music of the river as it rushed down to the millrace, to Palmer playing his fiddle or picking out tunes on the piano, while Finch sang along choosing the sort of 'sweet pathetick'[41] melodies that his friends most loved.

Long after the last amber glow of the neighbours' candlelit lattices had faded, the young men would be sitting there, indulging in their agreeable ceremonies of pipe-smoking and snuff-taking, puffing and tamping and pinching and blowing as they sipped at their bowls of 'dear precious green tea'.[42] Palmer and Richmond (whose mother sent him parcels of tea and sugar from London) had a particular passion for this drink and a letter passes between them in which Palmer minutely instructs his friend on how to discriminate Hyson (which should be 'of a full-sized grain, of a blooming appearance, very dry, and crisp') from its superior Gunpowder (which 'should have a beautiful bloom upon it, which will not bear the breath', be of 'greenish hue' and 'a fragrant pungent taste').[43] But green tea – or *terre verte* as they called it, after the artist's pigment – was their particular favourite and even years later a bowl of it would stir nostalgic memories for Palmer of quiet Shoreham evenings and 'nice long old-fashioned talks'[44] by the fire.

These conversations were made up of an 'entertaining medley'[45] of poetry and art, religion and politics, though they could easily descend into acrimonious theological bickerings, not least when Palmer's father was entertaining Primitive Baptists or Linnell had invested in the latest proselytising tract. Palmer relished a tough quarrel and revelled in long-running intellectual tussles. But more even than talking, the Ancients loved to read. 'Blessed books – any one of which is worth all the toggery we ever put on our backs,'[46] said Palmer. With '*opodeldoc* [a powerfully aromatic liniment, supposedly invented by Paracelsus, made of soap dissolved in alcohol, to which camphor and herbal essences, most notably wormwood, had been added] rubbed into the forehead to wake the brain up' and 'a Great Gorge of old poetry to get up the dreaming',[47] he was happy. When the wind howled bitterly round the chimney pots and the rain beat in gusts against panes, he and his fellow Ancients would place the steaming teapot by the fire and, reaching down the tall folios from the bookshelves, tuck themselves peacefully into their tomes. These precious interludes, passed 'recreating myself with good books',[48] were times which Palmer was always to look back on and treasure. 'I am really glad I had a dose and glut of reading at Shoreham,' he would write many years later, for some savour of it always remained, he said, 'like the relish of wine in an empty cask'.[49]

Eventually it would be time to retire. Palmer would go up to his bed, with its mattress of local sheep's wool ('a feather bed costs 14 guineas and is not my lot'[50]) with a hop sack coverlet thrown over it if he needed extra warmth, and lie there listening to the calls of the owls as they swept through the trees, the creaking of the floorboards and the bark of the foxes. And maybe, beyond that, so constant that he barely even caught it, the deep background hum of a profound sense of peace. 'We less enjoy life than listen to the sound of its machinery,'[51] Palmer later wrote. He would always look back to his time in Shoreham as a moment of blessed tranquillity; as a time of stillness which for the rest of his life he would seek.

———————

William Blake died within a year of Palmer moving to Shoreham. Richmond gave Palmer the news. 'He died on Sunday night at 6 o'clock in most glorious manner,' he told him. 'He said He was going to that country he had all His life wished to see & expressed Himself Happy, hoping for Salvation through Jesus Christ – Just before he died His Countenance became fair. His eyes Brighten'd and He burst out in Singing of the things he saw in Heaven.'[52] It was Richmond who finally closed Blake's eyelids and kissed him as he lay in his work room in Fountain Court. John Linnell, with characteristic efficiency, helped to arrange the burial and five days later the Ancients followed Blake's humble elm coffin to the dissenters' burial ground in Bunhill Fields in north London where both his parents had already been buried and where their brilliant son was now laid, at a cost of nineteen shillings, in a common grave. Palmer wasn't there. It was a loss he must have felt keenly, despite his conviction that they would meet again in heaven one day. For the rest of his life he kept among his most treasured mementos a message card designed for Cumberland, the last work Blake had completed, and his pair of big, round, steel-rimmed glasses, their lenses bleared by many years of use. The memory of Blake bound the circle of Ancients even more closely together. They were to become his most impassioned defenders. 'He was one of the few to be met with in our passage through life, who are not in some way or other, "double-minded" and inconsistent with themselves; one of the very few who cannot be depressed by neglect, and to whose name rank and station could add no lustre,'[53] Palmer would say.

It was Linnell, however, who was most immediately affected by his death. He had been much involved in his affairs during his last feeble months and had lent Blake's widow, Catherine, the money to pay for the ceremony, moving her afterwards into his Cirencester Place studio ostensibly as a housekeeper, but in fact to take care of her. He had lost a friend whom he had profoundly respected and his health began to break down shortly afterwards. One day, queuing at the bank, he found himself too weak to wait any longer and had to return home. Soon, all other restorative measures having failed, he was compulsively inhaling twelve bottles of oxygen a day.

In 1828, finding the constant back-and-forth journey too taxing, he moved his family back from Hampstead to a rented house in Bayswater. But he still kept up a punishing work schedule: rising early in the morning to work at his painting, continuing his teaching (he was by then much in demand as a tutor), educating his children, making bread (he would often leave his sitters for a few moments to knead the dough), brewing beer and, as if all this wasn't sufficient, hatching a scheme to build a new house. Having consulted with the architect Tatham, undergone all his usual pecuniary calculations and negotiated a complex web of barter arrangements by which he would trade paintings for building work, he embarked on the project. By the autumn of 1829, foundations had been laid in Porchester Terrace and, within the stipulated year, the new home was finished, by which time Linnell, having taken a hand in everything from the drawing up of the first plans to the digging of the cesspool, was installing a bread oven and a cast-iron kitchen range.

Beside all this determined industry, the un-timetabled hours that he passed in Shoreham must have felt even more beguiling and back in London, after a visit, he began dreaming of pastoral Kentish scenes. Palmer, manifestly delighted, did everything he could to encourage his return. A succession of letters passed back and forth between them, discussing potential accommodation, organising help from a farmer's daughter (down to the specific details of her responsibilities: her father would not like her to wash dishes or be under the cook doing scullery work), negotiating prices, giving the times of the coaches and making arrangements to meet them. Palmer would happily walk up to the toll road at the top of the hill at Shoreham on the off-chance that Linnell might be on a certain coach. He worried about whether his mentor could bear the uncushioned jolting of a cart without springs and on one occasion, when Linnell was feeling particularly weak, the Ancients procured a wheelbarrow in which to push him about.

The Palmers did everything they could to make their guests welcome at Waterhouse. There was always a bowl of apples left out on the table and a kettle of tea left brewing on the hob. When Calvert and his wife came to visit they were given the best room because they were married and, when one of their sons fell dangerously ill, the Palmers looked after him in Shoreham while he convalesced. 'In all probability it saved his life,'[54] the boy's grandmother thanked them. If there were not enough rooms, Palmer would move out to lodgings above the village bakery and, if walkers from London arrived in the middle of the night, his father would not only get up to greet them but give them his own bed so that they could enjoy a well-earned sleep.

Palmer made as few visits as possible to 'the great national dust-hole'.[55] 'I purpose never again to see London by daylight,' he declared in 1834. Between 1831 and 1835 he bought four more properties in Shoreham which he let out to locals, planning to live off the meagre rental income until his career gathered pace. He would own these cottages for the rest of his life. Meanwhile, his fellow Ancients ran his errands in the capital – visiting framers, looking out books, delivering messages or purchasing materials that ranged from the sheets of thick Bristol board, which he most liked to draw on, to a mussel shell of powdered gold for a miniature that he planned to paint. Palmer, in return, dispatched potatoes to Tatham at two shillings a bushel, sacks of hops to Linnell and to Richmond flagons of cider for his bowels.

Alone in Shoreham, however, Palmer greatly missed his friends – he laments not being present for a cricket match in Linnell's garden – and constantly chivvied his fellow Ancients to visit: the harvest is coming; the days are glorious; the hopping season has begun, the weather is fine, they must hurry before it breaks. 'Why do Walter and Mr Calvert fancy Shoreham a hundred miles off?' he complained in 1828. 'Let them get on the road by chance and walk a bit and ride a bit and they will soon look down on the valley.'[56] The winter months when the roads were not conducive to travelling, when the weather was 'fogg'd and cloudy' and the 'landscape a sickly white or grey',[57] often left him solitary and in the summer, when sudden rains turned the roads into mires, sending torrents rushing down the hillsides and leaving the fruit carts stranded up to their axles in three foot of water, he would feel the inconvenience of his isolation acutely.

The Ancients kept in touch by writing long letters to each other in which they discussed their activities, ideas and discoveries. 'Punctually devote half an hour every evening to setting down the prominent circumstances of your day; particularly anything pictorial or intellectual,'[58] Palmer instructed Richmond as he set off to Italy in 1828. 'Pray write me a more minute account than the last of what you get up to "from morn to dewy eve".'[59] He fretted about the parlous state of the postal service with its delays and misdirections. 'I want so much to be talking to you that you see I cannot wait to be coming to town,' he told Richmond in a letter which 'dribbled out' as he walked in the neighbouring Lullingstone Park, as he sat in the peace of a local farmer's garden or scribbled at a table after supper at home.[60] These periodically updated missives took the place of a conversation; a pen, the place of an arm tucked companionably into his own.

Palmer in many ways found writing a more natural form of expression than painting. 'It is very much easier to give vent to the romantic by speech than to get it all the way down from the brain to the fingers' ends, and then squeeze it out upon the canvas,'[61] he told Calvert in 1837. To consult the archives of the Victoria & Albert or the Fitzwilliam Museums, to read through page upon close-packed page of his sloping sepia-inked scripts, is to gain a vivid sense of his life and character. A barrister who had once met Blake over dinner, described him as having delivered an unmethodical rhapsody on art, poetry and religion throughout the meal. Palmer's letters have something of the same rambling flow. They encompass anything from the most solemn disquisition on artistic beliefs, to a boyish discussion of bowel movements; from a profound profession of faith, to a fussy itemisation of costs. They have a delightful freshness. The reader is introduced to a character unfurling in all its many aspects, from the heights of its idealism to the depths of its disappointments. A picture is offered of Palmer in his many moods: passionate, punctilious, pious, fun-poking, pompous, provocative, self-pitying, appeasing. One hears him haranguing or assuaging, whining or exulting; finds him madly excited or gloomily melancholy, ridiculously grandiloquent or just downright silly. Sometimes, Palmer pours out his thoughts in a stream of consciousness ('autobabblery'[62] as he describes it), sometimes he flits from idea to idea as when he moves in a trice from discussing the 'perpetual miracle of life'[63] to the price that he should pay a Mr Steggle for a picture frame. Sometimes, he writes with premeditated gravity in a neat legible script with barely a crossing out; sometimes his letters are ornamented with drawings in the margins, packed with afterthoughts and cross-scorings and strings of postscripted points.

Palmer tried to draw the brotherhood more tightly together through his letters, passing on news, offering words of encouragement or conveying frequent remembrances from one to the other. The Ancients would also use drawing in this way. Like the Nazarenes before them, they would sketch each other, studying the lineaments of each other's faces, becoming familiar with expressions and moods. Such likenesses could affirm a sense of shared purpose. When Richmond exhibited his 1829 miniature of Palmer under the title of *Portrait of an Artist*, it was an assertion of his faith in the future of his friend's profession.

More often, however, their sketches were less serious. The Ancients were little more than boys – and were even mistaken for schoolchildren as a tale, which Finch liked to tell, shows. One day, out for ramble, they had stripped to the waist to wash in a village well only to find themselves suddenly surrounded by locals who, thinking them truants, wanted to call the constable. It was only when a man ran a finger across one of their cheeks that, feeling the bristles, he realised: 'No, these ain't schoolboys. This is an old file!'[64]

The young men revelled in boyish teasing, in practical jokes and self-mockery. A caricature of Richmond catches him 'in the full swing of his glory', his tail coat flapping as he twirls upon a pair of horizontal bars. And in a little self-portrait, Richmond presents himself as a dunce, smoking a pipe and wearing a fool's cap. There are pictures of Palmer in big round glasses and ridiculous hat, or singing with his mouth wide-agape as a frog's, or shambling absent-mindedly, his umbrella clutched upside down. 'Sambo Palmer', Richmond inscribed this sketch. The Ancients liked nicknames. They called Blake 'the Interpreter', Michelangelo 'Mike', Linnell's children 'the little Leonardos', and Richmond's newborn baby 'the Chevalier', short for 'Chevalier-New-Come'.

Beyond the solemn purpose and the religious piety of the brotherhood, lay the simple enjoyment of a gang of young men who loved laughter and jokes and bawdiness, ridiculous puns ('I would rather have queer notions than queer *motions*'[65] Palmer declares as he returns yet again to the subject of costiveness) and ludicrous rhyming ditties. 'I am in one of my fits, again,' Richmond wrote. Palmer would often be reduced to rolling incapable on the floor: 'a kind of delightful hysterics', as he described it, when he would 'yell and roar' like a wild beast.[66] They all relished teasing except the solemn Calvert who as a result became the butt of their jokes. A high-spirited Palmer once affronted him by singing *The British Grenadiers* at the top of his voice when he had been told not to. Calvert's consequent anger lasted for more than thirty-six hours. They were the only three days that they ever hated each other, an affectionate Palmer was later to recall.

At Work in the Valley of Vision

Nature . . . transmitted into the pure gold of art
from *The Letters of Samuel Palmer*

To look at the pictures which Palmer painted in Shoreham is to see rural England through newly enraptured eyes. As he wandered the fields of the fertile Kentish valleys, along wooded ridges and down sloping pastures, among orchards and hop gardens, by hayricks and cattle sheds, he beheld a landscape transfigured as if by some miracle of divine grace. It was as if the whole world, 'passed thro' the intense purifying separating transmuting heat of the soul's infabulous alchymy',[1] had been transubstantiated. 'I really did not think there were those splendours in visible creation,'[2] he said.

Linnell, however, was keen that his protégé should return to academic basics and learn to master the figure and, for a while, Palmer knuckled down to anatomical studies. In 1824 he wrote dutifully to his mentor to assure him that had been working diligently on a drawing of a head. 'Have I not been a good boy?' he asked. 'I may safely boast that I have not entertain'd a single imaginative thought these six weeks.'[3] For many years he persisted, fitfully, in his attempts to represent properly the human form, even, every now and then, managing to make his newfound skills pay: in 1829, he complained of having 'a bothering little job of a likeness'[4] to finish. And yet, for all that he still dreamt of conjuring grand biblical tableaux, the only works that survive to bear witness to such high-flown ambitions owe far more to the landscapes of Shoreham than to studies in the life room. His *The Rest on the Flight to*

Egypt (*c.*1824) shows the Holy Family huddling among the valley's wooded hills.

Richmond encouraged him to follow his natural inclinations. 'Mr Linnell is an extraordinary man, but he is not a Mr Blake,'[5] he warned Palmer. But Sam, deeply reluctant to give any offence, found it increasingly awkward to extricate himself from Linnell's grasp. 'I beg to be understood as not so much positively asserting anything in this half-studied scribble on a very difficult subject, which is beyond me,' he wrote in an 1828 letter, his point soon getting lost in a thicket of circumlocutions: 'as, for the increase of my knowledge, putting forth a thesis by way of query, that where it is rotten it may be batter'd, thus avoiding to choak the throat of every sentence with "I humbly conceive I submit with deference" which had made those lines, if possible, more tedious than you will find them.'[6] Even when he did turn to landscapes, his tenacious teacher was there to instruct, repeatedly telling him to rein back his imagination, to stick more rigorously to the facts in front of him. Palmer, though underwhelmed at the prospect of studying the 'clover and beans and parsley and mushrooms and cow dung and other innumerable etceteras of a foreground',[7] once again knuckled under and obeyed. 'I have been drawing the Natural Fact till I am cold in my extremities,'[8] he informed his mentor in November 1828. 'I am desperately resolved to try what can be got by drawing from nature.'[9]

Linnell believed that naturalistic landscapes of Shoreham would be saleable, able to earn his pupil as much as £1,000 a year, but Palmer was not yet prepared to succumb to commercial tastes, to become one of the ubiquitous 'housepainters and sky sloppers and bush blotters'[10] who followed the precedents of Girtin or Cox. His talent, he believed, was a gift from God. It was not to be compromised for money or fame. 'Tho' I am making studies for Mr Linnell, I will, God help me, never be a naturalist by profession,'[11] he told Richmond in 1828. He still longed to set a visionary imagination free.

'I can look at a knot in a piece of wood till I am frightened at it,' Blake had said.[12] Palmer sought this same ferocity of focus. Placing his subject in the middle of the paper, he fixed upon it with an intensity that must have made his eyes water. Even a functional hop bin could become the subject of fascinated scrutiny. He drew one from several explanatory angles and made extensive notes on the leaves in the fields: 'The younger (& smaller) hop leaves are of a lighter & yellower green than the elder some of which are dark & cool and take very gray lights from the sky & sometimes a pole clothed entirely with the younger leaves is among the others quite a light yellow green & not only differs by colour from the rest but by being quite tender in its reliefs and shadows – from being thinner of leaves (more slender and regular in shape) without overhanging masses & deep shades under them.' His images began to take on an almost hallucinatory quality: details grew bigger; colours glowed brighter; forms became amplified.

In a series of studies of barn roofs and cow byres, done in around 1828, Palmer observed the patterns, tones and textures of the clustering moss: its deep greens and their olive-tinted contrasts; the pale primrose yellows and the richer tawny glows; the glowing ambers and ruddy browns; the roseate touches and rubescent blushes; the flaking crumbliness and the pillowing softness; the mottling dampness and the patches that had dried and peeled. His pigments built up a thick paste embossing the paper, mimicking the velvety growth that spreads over the thatch.

Palmer's paintings of trees were done with a particular sensitivity. He approached them as individuals to be understood as characters, appreciated for their histories and admired for their quirks. The mighty oaks of Lullingstone Park – noble descendants of the valley's ancient Celtic forests (the name of Shoreham's River Darent may derive from the Celtic word '*deruentio*' which means 'oak river') – were as much a part of his rural community as the aristocrats who had once gazed at them from their castle windows or the peasants who had taken shelter beneath their vast knobbly boughs. Anchored by their great, knotted roots to the very life of the Weald, he saw them as majestic giants. 'Milton, by one epithet, draws an oak of the largest girth I ever saw,' he wrote: 'Pine and *Monumental* Oak.' Palmer yearned to present them in the same way, but though he had spent all afternoon trying, 'the Poet's tree is huger than any in the park', he wrote.[13]

Palmer set out not simply to capture the tree's outward appearance, to describe its 'moss and rifts and barky furrows', but also to evoke a sense of its inner life: 'the grasp and grapple of the roots, the muscular belly and shoulders; the twisted sinews'.[14] To him 'the arms of an old rotten trunk' could appear 'more curious' than the brawny arms of the figure of Moses which Michelangelo sculpted for Pope Julius II's marble tomb. His trees come alive, possessed by their spirits as the woods in Blake's illustrations to Dante's *Inferno* were haunted by the suicides whose bodies were trapped writhing within their twisted trunks. And though Gilpin, the high priest of the picturesque, had dismissed the horse chestnut as 'a glaring object',[15] Palmer, perhaps enjoying the visual pun that its palmate foliage played upon his name, frequently made them a subject. He was the first to offer this familiar feature of his native landscape a place in the history of British art.

Like Turner who is said to have made as many as 10,000 studies of skies in his life, Palmer early got into the habit of making rapid pencil sketches of clouds. In later life he would often paint the vaporous ripples of formations that he called 'Margate-Mottle', so-named because it was in this seaside town that he would typically see their low fleecy reefs set on fire by the last rays of the sun. He greatly admired Linnell's aerial works: 'Those glorious round clouds which you paint,' he enthused in 1828, 'are alone an example of how the elements of nature may be transmitted into the pure gold of art.'[16] And yet for Linnell, as for Constable who would famously go out 'skying', such sketches were in large part a scientific pursuit. In March 1812, when a comet had become visible in the night skies, Linnell paid several visits to Cornelius Varley who was developing an instrument that he called the graphic telescope which, when pointed at a subject, projected its magnified image onto paper. Linnell had begun studying the solar system, mapping the planets in relation to the earth. That autumn he made the first of two records of the comet's position from the window of his house. Perhaps he interpreted its appearance as a heavenly sign for it was at this time, after much discussion with Varley, that he finally made his conversion to the Baptist faith.

And yet, where Linnell was fascinated by the facts of astronomy, Palmer was entranced simply by the sky's starry wonder. Though he did paint a double-tailed meteorite at Shoreham and later, towards the end of the 1850s, Donati's Comet (named after the Florentine astronomer credited with its first sighting) as it streamed over Dartmoor, he did not need such rare manifestations to inspire him. (The only other reference he made to a specific astronomical occasion was a mention, in 1856, of being summoned outdoors to witness a lunar eclipse.) The heavens in their everyday guise were quite magical enough. The celestial beauties to which his paintings bore testimony – 'the mottley clouding, the fine meshes, the aerial tissues that dapple the skies of spring . . . the rolling volumes and piled mountains of light . . . the purple sunset blazoned with gold . . . the translucent amber'[17] – seemed to him a manifestation of divine presence in the world. He sought out those moments – the flushed dawns and glowing twilights – in which he sensed its special benediction. He tried to capture the mysterious transformative effects of the night. The moon was, to him, the planet of poetry. Inside the covers of his pocket Milton he made a list of every lunar reference and, in the series of small Shoreham monochromes which he called his 'blacks' or 'moonshines', he picked out its silvery shining as it sprinkled the landscape with ethereal brightness, glimmering like fish-scales upon winding streams. In these little dark paintings, shadow becomes far more than a mere absence of light. It becomes a soft, breathing presence that transforms the world's mundane mass.

'I overspend that time in talking which should find me doing,'[18] Palmer wrote in 1828. 'Every day convinces me with wise and good Dr Johnson that this life is a state in which "much is to be done and little is to be known",' he told Richmond in a fit of industrious fervour. 'What is done at leisure is done wrong and whatever is done best, is done when there is hardly time given to do it in.'[19] Throughout his Kentish sojourn, Palmer applied himself to his work in sudden vigorous bouts. 'Talk of putting thistles under donkeys' tails to make them go!'[20] Determined to conquer the constitutional indolence of the daydreamer, he learnt always (as he would later tell anyone who would listen) to tackle any job that he felt disinclined to do first. He could be stubbornly persistent. In winter, huddled up in his cloak against the cold, he would work at a drawing until his finger bones ached. In summer, he would haul his artist's equipment uphill under a broiling sun. Often he would stay up drawing long into the night, sitting alone at his table, working up sketches by candlelight or later, when money ran short, eking out the single penny dip that he allowed himself daily for as long as he could.

He worked in a wide range of materials, using anything from the rough, thick papers produced in the local mill, to smooth, commercially prepared boards. Occasionally he would paint on a wooden panel and at one point he asked Richmond to bring him some slivers of polished ivory. It would seem that, following the lead of both Linnell and Richmond who briefly during the 1820s restored the art of the portrait miniature to a delicacy it had not enjoyed since the Elizabethan era, he was planning also to turn his hand to such dainty pieces but, if he did ever paint any miniatures, they have never been traced. For sketching, Palmer liked a strong grey-brown paper with a well-sized finish so that watercolour washes would not soak in too deeply, though for more detailed work he preferred a glazed pasteboard (called Bristol board) made of high-quality woven paper with a smooth surface.

Technically, Palmer was at his most experimental during his Shoreham period. Blake was his role model in this as in so much else. Preferring the precision of medieval painting to the blurry fluidity of the oils which had been prevalent since the high Renaissance, the old visionary had consulted Cennino Cennini's *Il libro dell'arte*, the famous 'how to' manual of the fifteenth-century craftsmen. He was looking to revive outmoded dry fresco techniques in which designs, mapped out on a rigid surface, were coloured with tempera – a fast-drying mix of pure pigment bound into a viscous emulsion with some water-soluble substance, usually egg yolk, but often glue or gum. This medium, drying in hard, translucent films, kept the crispness of outline and clarity of colour that Blake most admired. Linnell too was an inveterate meddler. As students, he and Cornelius Varley had indulged in a variety of experiments, eager to ascertain just how far a painter's materials could be pushed. Most commonly, an artist would thin heavy oil pigments with turpentine or linseed, but Cornelius tried adding gum copal to the mix, a natural resin which, though it would not evaporate as quickly as turpentine, added body to the colour and a heightened gloss. Linnell, who had witnessed the experiment, was later to put it to practical use. By the late 1840s, with characteristic self-sufficiency, he had all but stopped buying commercially produced colours and, building two iron furnaces at the bottom of his garden, was producing pigments and varnishes himself.

Palmer, too, persisted in testing new approaches and materials: abandoning precisely rendered details for a bolder handling, trying out richer colours and a more vigorous line, letting realism melt away into an atmospheric sense of mood. Sometimes he would build up thick areas of underpaint; often he would ink in dark outlines at the end; occasionally he would add pigments in big, bright, unmodulated blobs; more frequently he would mix them with other colours, keeping the density but playing down the glare. Sometimes paintings which had begun as water-based temperas ended up as oils. Palmer would stick the sheets of paper onto wood panels and continue to work, applying his pigment in thicker and thicker layers, adding more and more glue, mixing in dollops of ultra-glossy cherry gum and then adding sugar to try to bind it all together. Often his experiments led to unforeseen consequences. The Ancients particularly enjoyed telling the story of the time that he had manufactured an egg-yolk emulsion which, poured into a tightly stoppered bottle, he had deposited in one of his pockets in the hope that his constant movements would mix it up well. Not for the first or last time, however, something had got lost in the capacious compartments of his coat. The concoction was completely forgotten. The coat was worn daily until suddenly one afternoon as a detachment of Ancients was strolling through London, their senses were assaulted by an explosion so loud and a stench so unspeakably foul that all bar one of them were completely befuddled. Fortunately, this one (most likely Calvert, the most practical among them) had the presence of mind to pull out his knife and, ripping Palmer's pocket from its lining, hurl it complete with its sulphurous contents away into the gutter. The Ancients moved hastily off, but when they looked back they saw an old-clothes dealer darting to recover the discarded item who, no sooner had he grasped it, than he flung it away with such a dramatic gesture of disgust that they could never recall the event without laughing.

Other experiments, however, caused less amusing problems. The addition of too much gum would lead in time to cracking and Palmer, trying to achieve ever glossier effects to capture quite literally the glowing spirit of divinity, used a serious excess in his later tempera pictures. The thickly embossed surfaces of some of his finest paintings have deteriorated severely with time.

Palmer worked away 'with the patience of an ox'.[21] Year after year he submitted his annual quota of eight pictures to the Royal Academy. He was attentive to every detail of their making, from the first preparation of the surfaces down to the frames which Linnell's father would construct for him. Palmer may have chosen a life of eccentric seclusion, but he wanted professional recognition. And yet his early successes proved hard to follow. In 1825 he attracted the attention of the critics with two intensely bright landscapes. They possessed 'a clear and brilliant light and a vivid style of colouring which it would be vain for any other artist to hope to equal', declared the popular weekly periodical *John Bull*. It recommended visitors 'to seek out these gems'.[22] But to another journalist, the very same works seemed less eccentrically commendable than downright peculiar. 'There are two pictures by a Mr Palmer so amazing that we feel the most intense curiosity to see what manner of man it was who produced such performances,' the *European Magazine* mocked. 'We think if he would show himself with a label round his neck "The Painter of a View in Kent" he would make something of it at a shilling a head.'[23]

The next year an understated monochrome was not even noticed. In 1827 and 1828 all of Palmer's submissions were turned down. In 1829 two drawings were accepted, although even the artist found the committee's choice of his brawny Ruth striding home from the gleaning fields unaccountable. It was shown in the Antique Gallery where the hang was so bad that, in the opinion of one reviewer, the pictures might as well have been turned with their faces to the wall. In 1830 and 1831 Palmer again had no success and even though in 1832 seven of his eight submissions were selected they were consigned once again to the Antique Gallery, likened by the same reviewer to 'purgatory, if not a worse place'.[24]

The young painter returned the next year to submitting oil paintings, among them a rich autumnal depiction of gleaners at eventide and a picture of bustling harvesters amid profusions of glowing corn. The moon hangs low as a lantern in the surrounding elm trees; stars shine like spotlights from a transparent sky. Both panels were hung in the Great Room where the majority of visitors would have had a chance to view them, but, put into competition with Turner's first oil painting of Venice and his view of a storm-swept Seine, the little rural landscapes were all but overlooked. In 1834 a reviewer for the *Athenaeum* mourned the lack of 'that rare quality, imagination'[25] amid the general mass of domestic landscapes. But Palmer was growing disheartened by this time. He had chosen a tangled and long disused path and he was beginning to despair of it ever being opened again.

The viewer has to look back with modern eyes to understand the greatest painterly achievement of Palmer. The finest – and now most famous – of the works that he did while in Shoreham were paintings that he never in his lifetime showed. He kept them hidden away in the folder of his 'Curiosity Portfolio'.

'There is no excellent beauty without some strangeness in the proportion,' Francis Bacon had said. It was one of Palmer's favourite quotes. 'I believe in my very heart,' he told Richmond in 1834, 'that all the very finest original pictures . . . have a certain quaintness by which they partly affect us – not the quaintness of bungling – the queer doing of a common thought – but a curiousness in their beauty – a salt on their tails by which the imagination catches hold on them while the sublime eagles and the big birds of the French academy fly up far beyond the sphere of our affections.'[26] It is this strange beauty that may be discovered in his late Shoreham works. His *In a Shoreham Garden* and his *Magic Apple Tree* are works of mad splendour. Nature runs riot. Close observation combines with abstracted daring to capture and celebrate the exuberant fecundity of the world.

In his painting, *In a Shoreham Garden*, the blossoms of an apple tree break like a wave frothing over the picture. Blob upon huge blob, Palmer builds up the masses, an impasto exploding upon the surface of the board. He revels in the soft profusion of the pink-and-white petalled foam. *The Magic Apple Tree* glows like a great autumn bonfire. Palmer exults in the harvest's rich gifts. Colour becomes a pure sensual pleasure. These are paintings to glut the appetite. And yet their meanings remain elusive. Their subjects cannot be explained. Reality is transfigured as Palmer embodies his giddiest, his boldest, his most extravagant perceptions in paintings now hailed as the pinnacle of his Shoreham achievement. And yet, even as he captured the most exalted form of his vision, in the eyes of the world he was seen to have failed.

13

The Pastoral and the Political

I love our fine British peasantry
from *The Letters of Samuel Palmer*

The visitor to Tate Britain in London might easily wander past Palmer's *Coming from Evening Church* without so much as pausing. Barely the size of a piece of A4 paper, it seems hardly designed to draw the stranger up short. And yet, this is probably Palmer's most significant picture: it captures the essence of his Shoreham beliefs.

Palmer paints a procession of villagers winding their way homewards from the ivy-clad church that stands at the heart of their rural way of life. A line of domed hills forms the furthest horizon, encircling and protecting the pastor's congregation just as, on the far slopes, woven hurdles protect the shepherd's huddled flock. Framing tree trunks curve upwards, boughs interlacing to form a Gothic archway; cottage windows glow warmly from amid scrambling leaves and, as the church spire elevates its shining cross to the heavens, the light of a full moon falls like a benediction from above.

The natural and the spiritual merge in this landscape. Man lives in harmony with his community, with his rural surroundings and with his God. Palmer presents a vision of rural life as it may be shaped and protected by the traditions of the Anglican Church – and, in so doing, it turns out, he is making a direct political point. Clearly visible at the bottom of the painting is the inscription: 'Painted 1830 at Shoreham Kent S. Palmer'. Since this is one of very few works of this period to be signed and dated, it seems probable that Palmer chose to do so deliberately: a decision that makes sense in the light of upcoming events for, even as he was painting this beneficent fiction, a far harsher reality was beginning to take shape. The year 1830 saw the first rural unrest in Shoreham. It was the beginning of the upheavals that would lead to parliamentary reform.

Palmer's life spanned a period of great change. The traditional agrarian way of life was vanishing; the Enlightenment's rationalist certainties were fading and soon pretty much everything was being thrown into question: the nature of society, the basis of civil government, the doctrine of individual rights, the notion of political justice and the roles and the relationships of the sexes all found themselves coming under scrutiny as Britain moved towards the new values of a modern industrial world. However, even as swift currents were sweeping society onwards, tradition was dragging like a powerful undertow. To those who yearned for the safety of familiar shores, culture could create a protective haven. The visual arts – and most particularly landscape painting – had a patriotic role to play.

The mid-eighteenth century had seen the start of the widespread enclosure of Britain. As act after parliamentary act was passed (some 4,000 were to come into effect before the General Enclosure Act of 1845 enabled appointed commissioners to enclose land without applying to Parliament), the strip plots that dated back to a medieval feudal system were turned into larger fields which were then separated off from each other by hedges. The look of the British countryside was radically changing. At the same time, Romanticism was encouraging people to take pride in their native beauties. Why turn to the Roman *campagna* of Enlightenment tastes when Britain could boast noble views of its own? As piecemeal plots merged to create single holdings, the estate was presented as an alternative idyll: the cheerful peasants, nurtured and protected by landowners, working happily to produce the crops that would bring ease and prosperity to their nation. This was the contemporary version of the pastoral vision which Virgil had presented in his *Georgics*, a book that every educated schoolboy would have been expected to know. Its philosophies, adapted to Romantic sensibilities, had found full expression in Wordsworth's 1814 *The Excursion*, a poem which, exploring the political and economic pressures exerted upon the rural community, had suggested that the essence of English country life lay in a mystical connection between man, nature and God: a traditional order upheld by the local pastor and symbolised by the church spire which bonds earth and sky. This is the vision which Constable alludes to in his images of Salisbury Cathedral from the meadows. It is the picture which Samuel Palmer paints in his *Coming from Evening Church*.

The great estate, however, was not quite the private Elysium of the wishful imagination. With enclosure, the peasants were being evicted from their lands, driven into the cities of a burgeoning industrial revolution. England's supposedly idyllic rural communities were being drained. Traditions tend to feel most charming when they are finally vanishing. Palmer, in moving to Shoreham, was moving into a land of dreams that were crumbling just as he set out to capture them in paint.

The first census of Shoreham taken in 1841 (about five years after Palmer had left) records about a thousand people living in some two hundred households, the majority in the village itself, the rest scattered in outlying hamlets and farms. There were seven blacksmiths, nine carpenters and wheelwrights, a harness maker, a shoemaker and two keepers of shops; but for the most part the Shoreham folk would have worked on the land either as tenant farmers or their more humble labourers. Palmer painted them in his pictures: up at sunrise to yoke their burly brown oxen, shearing the sheep through the long afternoon, gleaning the fields by the last glow of the daylight or bringing in the sheaves under a shining moon. His work is full of rustic vignettes. He shows the felled tree trunk hauled slowly homewards, the farm wagon heaped high with newly mown hay, the reapers embracing their harvested corn bundles, the women balancing baskets of woven willow on their heads, the cattle quenching their thirst in the river's cool shallows, the crows as they circle the ploughman's fresh furrows, the sheepdog curled sleeping in its patch of warm sun.

Palmer knew several of his neighbouring landowners: Farmer Tooth with whose family he had first lodged and whose daughter Clarissa – or Clary, as Palmer knew her – was to be employed as a child minder by the visiting Linnell; Mr Groombridge the apple grower whose cottage the Palmers could see from their Waterhouse windows and in whose pleasant gardens Palmer often liked to sit; Mr Love, a hop grower whom he thought a fine farmer, and Mr Waring of Chelsfield who made the best cider. He enjoyed cordial relationships with several of the inhabitants of Shoreham's timber and thatch cottages, with Mr Brewer the tailor, Mr Gregory the baker and Mr Yates who lived on the terrace road. He would pass the time of day with Mr Barham, an old labourer with a bright and busy wife and two daughters, or wave to the Wilmot family of Goddington Mill or bid good morning to Mr Bailey, the carrier, who told him one day that he was as happy as a lamb with two mothers. When Bailey's young wife fell pregnant, Palmer described her as having a belly as large 'as if she had got the dome of St Paul's under her apron', and yet she still bustled about like a girl, he said; when the day comes, he told Richmond, 'she'll drop her kitten into the basket without any . . . parade and in a day or two be just as well as ever again'.[1]

These were all decent people running their modest households on cautiously metered budgets, as their numerous arrangements to let lodgings to Palmer's friends suggest. A Mrs Mills, for example, had a spare room but no bedstead to go in it and was not prepared to invest in one unless her prospective lodger would commit himself to staying for the whole of the summer. The Ancients enjoyed the lively gossip of locals. They laughed at the story of the local baker, a meek and grievously henpecked man whose wife, a jealous scold, would watchfully track him when he was out on his rounds. He had a pet jackdaw which had learnt to mimic this harridan. 'Ah, Thomas V . . . Thomas V . . . You hadn't a shirt to your back when I married you Thomas V . . .'[2] it would croak, until one day the baker, driven beyond the bounds of endurance, leapt up and wrung the bird's neck.

Richmond described in amused detail the clerk of a nearby chapel:

an aged war veteran who, having lost a leg, had had it replaced with a wooden one. The clerk would sit under the pulpit till the hymn before the sermon was given out, whereupon, there being no choir, he would assume the role of chief songster. As the first bars of the musical prelude were played, his grandson, a young ploughman, would march from the west end of the church to his grandfather's seat where, bending over as if about to play leapfrog, he would mount the old man upon his back. Out would ring the first words of the hymn: the clerk, from his new elevation, would deliver alone the first two lines. Then the youth with the old man on his back would march solemnly down the nave, the clerk singing lustily all the way from his strange vantage point. Up the spiral staircase the youth would steadily mount, the voice gradually diminishing before rising once more to an abrupt crescendo as an upper door opened, eventually to conclude with a stentorian finale as the youth deposited his cargo in the musician's gallery.

The Ancients would always stop to talk to the idling village simpleton who, in sunny weather, liked to bask away the hours upon the bridge. Richard Lipscombe, the jovial ostler from Otford whom Palmer knew as Dick, was another favourite with the young men. With his broad Kentish dialect, his simple piety and his talent for rhyme, he was like a character from *Pilgrim's Progress*, Richmond thought, or the 'inglorious Milton' of Gray's churchyard *Elegy*, and he would lend him edifying books on the pages of which he would pen his customary ditties: 'To turn down the leaves is a very bad plan/ So I always puts paper wherever I can.' Lipscombe was particularly fond of Palmer's father whom he knew as his preacher and described him in one of his impromptu poems:

> *Palmer is a man of God*
> *He is a sound divine,*
> *For when he doth expound the word,*
> *His face doth always shine.*

Years later, when the ostler had been laid in his grave, John Giles returned to put up a tombstone in his memory. It still stands in the shadow of the old yew in the Otford churchyard, a simple red sand-stone monument with a deep-cut cross.

Frederick Tatham visited a sick cottager, day after day for months on end, washing and dressing his sores, and Palmer put himself to considerable effort in his attempts to find a position for a local farrier who had lost his job. One of the principal purposes of Christian teaching, he wrote in a letter to Richmond, was to divert attention away from 'vile all-absorbing self' to the plight of the impoverished.[3] There is no doubt that there was a good relationship between the Ancients and the people whom they lived among. 'In time they . . . came to know us and we to love them,'[4] Richmond said. And yet, there was a fundamental difference between the simple Shoreham dwellers and the privileged urbanites who had decided to live among them. The stout barriers of class and convention had not really been overcome, as an episode involving a village woman, employed by Palmer's father, suggests. One day, while she was waiting at table it was pointed out to her that a plate was dirty. She picked it up, spat on it, wiped it with her apron and replaced it in front of the diner. 'Never let me see you do that filthy trick again,' her outraged employer had scolded, but the woman had just stared, astonished by this outburst; she had no idea of what she had done wrong.[5] The story of a cottager who had cooked up rat pudding was among the Ancients' repertoire of oft-recounted Shoreham tales; but it seems to have been told as a joke, none of the young men even pausing to consider quite how hungry a family must have been to have resorted to this unsavoury recipe.

'The jocose talk of hay-makers is best at a distance,' George Eliot wrote in *Adam Bede*, a novel which explores village life at precisely Palmer's period. 'Like those clumsy bells round the cows' necks, it has rather a coarse sound when it comes close, and may even grate on your ears painfully; but heard from far off, it mingles very prettily with the other joyous sounds of nature.'[6] Palmer, indulging his dreams of a pastoral idyll, did not see the realities of rural life. He did not consider the rheumatic damp that would have seeped into the watching shepherd's bones; the backbreaking ache of the bent reaper's pose; the terrible weariness of the labourer at the end of a day which, beginning even before the first scrawny cockerel had scrambled onto its dung heap, closed in an often fireless darkness with shivering families huddled on beds of flea-ridden straw. Palmer painted cottage windows glowing with a welcoming light. His more socially attuned contemporary, Eliot, spoke instead of 'little dingy windows telling, like thick filmed eyes, of nothing but the darkness within'.[7]

The inhabitants of Palmer's paintings are not real people. They are characters from a pastoral fantasy: denizens of flowered dells and fruitful landscapes fed by burgeoning nature with berries and nuts, dozing to the piping melodies of flutes while the mellow sun warms their plump cheeks. This is the world that he described in *The Shepherd's Home*, one of only a few of his poems to survive, in which he wrote of 'a little village, safe, and still,/ Where pain and vice, full seldom come'; where 'Clear, shallow, pebbled streams are found,/ Where many a fish doth skim and bound'; where 'trim cottage gardens' are 'intricate with fruit-bent boughs' and 'sweet young maidens . . . fairer than the milky lilies do appear'.[8] Palmer wanted to believe in a nurturing land which would provide for its people as the mother ewe in one of his images lets down her milk to a nuzzling lamb. He loved 'the jovial time of hop picking' when the whole village made 'sunshine holiday', when 'age and youth and childhood, merrily singing as they worked, garnered in the fragrant crop without the help of strangers'.[9] He relished the 'pretty picture' of harvest home when, the very last wagon loaded up, the children would ride home atop 'singing and shouting for joy' before retiring to the old farmhouse where, as Palmer looking back wistfully described it, 'all the poor people who have been reaping for so many days in the hot sun till they are as brown as hazel nuts – all these merry reapers have a good supper together with music and song and dances'. 'They worked hard for their master, and now he makes them happy,'[10] Palmer concluded, equating the feudal relationship of landowner and peasant with that of Christ and his Christian flock.

The reality was rather different from this rose-tinted idyll. The bucolic character, wrote the clear-sighted Eliot, was not always 'of that entirely genial, merry, broad-grinning sort, apparently observed in most districts visited by artists'.[11] An observer, 'under that softening influence of the fine arts which makes hardships picturesque', she wrote in *Middlemarch*, would find a village homestead delightful with its ivy-choked chimneys, its large porch 'blocked up with bundles of sticks and half the windows closed with grey worm-eaten shutters about which the jasmine boughs grew in wild luxuriance'. The mouldering garden wall with hollyhocks peeping over it, the mossy thatch of the cowshed, the broken barn doors: 'all these objects', when painted 'under the quiet light of a sky marbled with high clouds would have made a sort of picture which we have all paused over as a "charming bit"'.[12] As this fiercely moral and profoundly compassionate woman well knew, a grim reality blighted the pastoral whimsy and this was a particularly brutal period in the rural history of Britain.

Many of the poorest field workers were only able to survive because they could graze a cow, raise a flock of geese, collect firewood or grow a few vegetables on the common, a shared piece of land to which they had a traditional right by virtue of renting a cottage within a village. When this common land was enclosed they were deprived of their independence. Forced to sell the livestock which had helped to ward off penury, they had only their wages to rely on. Gradually, an underclass of agricultural labourers emerged. Many would not have been the sort of 'civil cleanly moral peaceable and industrious'[13] folk whom Palmer met in the farmsteads of Shoreham for, by the end of the 1820s, more than a third of the population of the Kentish weald was unemployed.

The Corn Laws, which had filled the coffers of Nathanial Palmer on whose annual allowance Palmer's father now lived, had spread hunger and distress through the very communities within which he preached. Many could no longer afford to pay for the grain from which they ground their bread. This state of affairs was exacerbated by the prolonged agricultural recession which followed the end of the Napoleonic wars. The poor rates – a tax on property levied by the parish to provide relief for those in need – should have helped but instead they further added to the problem as farmers, hoping that they could leave it up to the parish to make good any deficiencies, offered only the barest subsistence wage to their labourers; a sum which did not increase upon marriage or the birth of children. A family man could no longer take pride in being a hard-working provider; he was forced to depend on the handouts of charitable relief. And even when a farmer did pay a decent living wage, he still had to contribute to the poor rate and so ended up subsidising his less humanitarian neighbour.

After the war, when returning soldiers flooded the labour markets, the cost of parish relief soared. Farmers cut back even further on wages, often by laying off workers. This decision was made easier by the arrival of threshing machines, one of which it was reckoned in 1830 could replace ten labourers.[14] This deprived men of the threshing work that they had come to rely on to tide them over the bleak winter months. Life grew ever harder, as a wry Kentish rhyme records.

> *Pork and cabbage all the year;*
> *Mouldy bread and sourish beer,*
> *Rusty bacon, skim milk cheese;*
> *Beds of chaff and full of fleas,*
> *Who would like the living here?*

A few local parishes started subsidising emigration so that they could be rid of the excessive burden of maintaining the unemployed. In 1827, some seventy families from the Weald left England. Not far away, in Petworth, West Sussex, the Earl of Egremont offered to pay the passage to Canada for workers from his estate. He was praised for his magnanimity though, in truth, he had merely discovered a convenient way to dispatch a considerable problem along with any of the residual qualms of conscience that it had caused.

The outspoken radical William Cobbett – who had himself been a farm boy before a spell in the Army had expanded his horizons – toured the southern English countryside by foot and on horseback between 1821 and 1826 reporting on what he saw in his classic *Rural Rides*. He was clear as to the cause of the problem. It lay in the demise of the old English farmhouse in which the small farmer had provided board and lodging for workers whom he cared for as part of his family. They had tilled his few acres together and, at the end of the day, shared the fruits of their labour and the comforts of his home. There would have been a quart of beer, a good barley loaf and a bowl of potatoes, turnips and carrots from the garden and maybe some butter from the dairy wrapped up in a dock leaf and a hunk of smoked bacon cut from the storeroom's side of pig. But the days of 'the cask in the cellar and the flitch in the pantry were gone',[15] Cobbett wrote. Traditional steadings had been swallowed whole by 'bullfrog farmers', agricultural capitalists intent only on making a return on their money. An old farm table, spotted for sale at a country auction, summed up the situation for this writer: 'Squire Charington's father used, I dare say, to sit at the head of the oak table along with his men, say grace to them, and cut up the meat and the pudding,' he wrote. 'He might take a cup of strong beer to himself, when they had none; but that was pretty much all the difference in their manner of living. So that *all* lived well.' But as his son rose in his manner of living and expectations, Cobbett said, his need of luxuries, of wine decanters, of dinner sets and dessert knives, 'must of necessity have robbed the long oak table if it had remained fully tenanted . . . therefore, it became almost untenanted; the labourers retreated to hovels, called cottages; and instead of board and lodging, they got money'.[16]

By the end of the eighteenth century, the majority of farmers had become tenants of such wealthy landowners as the Marquis of Camden who, farming just a few miles from Shoreham, had, by Palmer's day, spread 'his length and breadth over more . . . than ten or twelve thousand acres'.[17] In 1830, out of all the agricultural land in England, *The Times* estimated that 90 per cent was farmed under lease.[18] Even worse, when the old beneficial leases expired they were replaced with vastly inflated rental values which reflected the sharp rise in farm prices during the war. 'The farmers have become labourers and tenants of little cottages for which they pay £5 or £6 an annum, though they cover a few rods only of that land which they had earlier sold for £2 an acre,' the newspaper reported.[19] Meanwhile, 'the farming servant is a miserable outcast . . . ill-paid, half-starved, heartless and exasperated'. He is reduced to 'little more than a labouring animal on the estate'.[20]

The Church did nothing to help. It still exacted its tithes. One priest, the Reverend Thomas Malthus, laying the problem at the door of a rising population, urged 'moral restraint'. He proposed that married labourers should abstain from sex while those still unwed should defer plans for matrimony until such time as they could be sure they could maintain a family without parish help. William Cobbett countered him vigorously, arguing that nobody had ever suggested controlling the birth rate of clergy or any other non-productive classes that drained public finances. Cobbett published a weekly newspaper, the *Political Register*, which, launched in 1802, soon established itself as a powerful radical voice. Landowners, he declared in his paper, were not any more valuable than their workers or more entitled to governmental protection. It would be immoral for them to continue to 'perpetuate their extravagant gains'.

Palmer and Cobbett both dreamt of a perfect rural community. But, in 1829, when the youthfully self-indulgent Palmer, mingling for the most part with gentlemanly farmers and so blind to the baser sufferings of the agricultural community, refused to see anything but his archaic ideal, Cobbett (who did not disapprove of the hierarchical society or wish for any class-based antagonism) was pleading with his countrymen to recreate a working alliance wherein landowners would recognise their duties towards their workers and represent their case to Parliament. He called for reductions in tithes, reform of the Corn Laws, a wider suffrage and an end to innovations in the Poor Law – not least those which allowed unemployed workers to be put up for auction, their labour sold to the highest bidder, or permitted paupers to be used quite literally as beasts of burden, set to dragging laden carts or shouldering towering stacks of wood. Time and again, even as late as the harvest of 1830, Cobbett was begging the farmers to share more of their wealth. Change your ways now 'or we shall be wide awake about the middle of next winter. The "grand rousing" will come from the fellows with hobnails in their shoes,' he warned.[21] These were the very hobnails that Palmer picked out in a sketch in which he posed a shepherd boy like a slumbering Endymion. This was the very year he was painting his *Coming from Evening Church,* a symbolic expression of an outmoded order, which, far from preserving a traditional idyll, was grinding the rural worker down into the dust.

By the end of the 1820s, a dangerous impasse had been reached. The inimical Cobbett again put his finger on the point: 'Your labourers hate you as they hate toads and adders,' he warned landowners. 'They regard you as their deadly enemies; as those who robbed them of their food and raiment, and who trample on them and insult them in their state of weakness; and they detest you accordingly . . . You know that you merit their deadly hatred; and then, proceeding upon a principle of the most abominable injustice, you hate them, and you destroy them, if possible, because you know that they hate you.'[22]

The peasants were trapped. A labourer could not make enough money to provide for his family and yet, at the same time, he was policed by a ruthless penal system in which stealing a watch could send him to the gallows and the snaring of a rabbit lead, under newly tightened game laws, to seven years' transportation. One of the amply laden apple trees which Palmer painted would have meant the difference between survival and starvation to a man for whom a ripe bough of russets provided food for his children and money for the rents that kept a roof above his head. 'Crime is the inevitable consequence of desperation,'[23] The Times warned in October 1830. In the autumn of the very year that Palmer painted his Coming from Evening Church, the greatest rural rebellion in English history broke out.

After harvest home, peasant workers would traditionally have found their next job in the flailing barns where, wielding a staff with a free-swinging stick at the end, they would have manually beaten the sheaves of the corn, separating the good grain from the husks and straw. But with the arrival of the threshing machine, this winter employment was coming to an end. As the nights closed in, tensions grew. Soon, desperate gangs of men, dressed in dark clothes and with blacked-out faces, set out hallooing across the garden of England. Armed with cudgels and hatchets, hammers, axes and saws – and sometimes even guns – they descended on farmsteads, smashing the detested threshing machines and setting fire to the ricks. Sometimes dozens of labourers would stand around watching as a farmer's annual profit went up in smoke. None would have dared to put out the flames and there was little the landowner could do in the face of such frightening insubordination: he could neither command his attackers nor guard his steading round the clock.

Towards the end of the year, menacing semi-literate notes began to drop on to doorsteps. These – perhaps inspired by the frightening missives that had been sent during the Luddite rebellion of 1811 – threatened death. Farmers risked being burnt alive unless they got rid of their threshing machines and improved the conditions of their labourers, the letters warned. They were signed 'Captain Swing', or sometimes just 'Swing'. No one was quite sure of the source of this sinister name. William Cobbett thought it came from that part of the thresher's flail which was known as the 'swing' or 'swingel', but a Kent journalist suggested that it originated in the signal call customarily given to haymakers who, having taken a break to sharpen their scythes, would be summoned back to their labours by their leader or 'captain' with a loud cry of 'swing'. It also had hair-prickling associations with the hangman. Whatever the name's origins, within days it had become synonymous with rural riots. Imaginations ran amok. Captain Swing was hailed by the country folk as an avenging hero. The authorities were desperate to catch him. But no one could identify him, most likely because there was no such person. Swing was a mystery, which made him an even more potent force in the minds of the illiterate farmhands who followed where he led.

For a few short weeks riots swept across the south of England, spreading westwards from Kent to Sussex and Hampshire. Poverty fought property; destitution battled possession. Every day new and ever more alarming reports flooded in. Armed gangs were tramping the highways; granaries, barns and hayricks, stacks of corn, clover and furze were going up in flames. The plumes of black smoke were like sinister beacons: they could be seen for miles.

In Kent and Sussex the protest became particularly fierce. A gang of several hundred labourers surrounded the mansion of the rector in Wrotham crying out 'Bread or blood!' and a baying mob was seen to attack the castle of Lord Abergavenny at Eridge Green, dispersing just before the soldiers arrived. Another gang dragged their overseer down the street and a parish officer was taken prisoner in a dung cart. Meanwhile, there were reports of arson attacks taking place in broad daylight, of fire-lighters tramping from parish to parish pressing even the most timid to join their mob, of suspicious outsiders hanging around farmers' markets, of plough boys compelled to leave their horses in the fields. All along the road to Canterbury the word 'Swing' was chalked.

Some feared that England was on the brink of civil war, or worse, revolution. The search for Captain Swing grew ever more urgent. Several landowners capitulated, promising wage increases. Others destroyed their machines voluntarily. Meanwhile, special constables were hurriedly sworn in and landed gentry were encouraged to volunteer as watchmen or to join night patrols. Police bodies were hastily dispatched to wherever it was believed that there would be a gathering. Rewards were posted up for the capture of the arsonists. Soon, men were apprehended just for being in the vicinity of an unlawful gathering. Brought before the courts they were hanged as a gruesome example to all. But by the time that Home Office ministers and local magistrates had finally developed an effective anti-riot strategy, the majority of threshing machines had either been destroyed or dismantled, not to appear again until steam-powered contraptions began to operate in significant numbers in the 1850s. The riots that for a few short weeks had held centre stage had, by the end of the year, died down. Only a few smouldering embers remained, glowing darkly in Kent where the movement had started, a latent spirit of underground resistance which would flare up periodically at times of particular hardship with the odd alarming fire or attack on an overseer's property.

Palmer was aware of the Swing rioters and would have seen the great conflagrations on the dark hills at night. One of his farmer friends, the hop grower Samuel Love, was among the first to suffer incendiary attacks. Palmer had described him as 'one of the best farmers hereabouts',[24] though evidently, as far as his labourers were concerned, he was among the worst. But Palmer did not understand the predicament of the peasants: he didn't share their lifestyles or ambitions or worries. He spoke a completely different language to their broad vernacular. He was even on the way to becoming a landlord himself – albeit on a modest level – for he had already invested a family legacy in the first of the five cottages in the village that he was eventually to own and let out. The Ancients might often have felt the pinch of straitened financial circumstances but, at a time when the local landowner Lord Gage was recorded as paying his hedgers and ditchers two shillings a week, Richmond, keeping meticulous account of his expenditure in Shoreham, was living on ten shillings – and he didn't have a family to feed. What to a young gentleman felt like extreme frugality, to the average field worker would have felt more like wealth. Where extreme privation to the former meant giving up green tea or snuff, to the latter it meant going to bed without supper after a hard day's work.

'Rural poetry is the pleasure ground of those who live in the cities,' Palmer later would write in an introduction to Virgil's *Eclogues*. His vision of Shoreham was an outsider's view. Describing its harvests as a wonderfully 'pretty picture'[25] he seemed rather more concerned that heavy rains would spoil perfect rustic views than worried that the labourers' crops would be ruined. Later he recommended the study of 'picturesque farm implements'.[26] Even where his works had some political resonance, he failed to ponder the more profound implications. As an eager young man, he had written to Linnell asking him to try to get hold of Blake's 'terrific poem'[27] on the French Revolution, but he was not a political radical like his visionary mentor. Blake, who had been imprisoned and stood trial for sedition, waged a lifelong war against state and Church, against an establishment which he saw as an instrument of repression and corruption. But Palmer, for all that he mourned 'the old manners', the days when, visiting a farmer in Edenbridge, he had seen the labourers 'clumping in their any-sounding hobnails, and dining cheerily at the side tables', did not seem to have been able to understand why suddenly these same peasants should have been meditating rick-burning while they eked out 'a quarter meal of baker's bread be-alumed and rancid bacon under a hedge'.[28]

The Captain Swing riots had all but fizzled out by the end of 1830 but they had not been fruitless. They provided a powerful impetus for political reform. This was badly needed. Aristocratic families dominated the political landscape. 'Rotten boroughs' – typically depopulated villages in which the electorate had dwindled to a tiny handful of constituents – had an undue influence on the make-up of Parliament because, however few its inhabitants, a borough had the right to elect two representatives to the House of Commons. Britain's parliamentary system no longer reflected the realities of a rapidly changing world. Six hundred and fifty-eight MPs had seats at Westminster, but neither Birmingham nor Manchester – both growing new industrial towns – were represented while the notorious Old Sarum, an abandoned relic of the medieval era, returned its two members despite being populated only by a few thorn bushes. There were also 'pocket boroughs' owned by major landowners who could choose their representatives and, since the ballot was not secret and voters were easily intimidated or bribed, they usually got the man whom they wanted in. Not everyone could vote anyway: in thirty-nine English boroughs the right was attached only to certain properties; in forty-three the electors were the town council; in sixty-two only freemen were balloted. In the counties, if you were a freeholder of property worth more than forty shillings you could cast your vote and naturally you tended to do so in deference to the wishes of the local landowner for fear that he might otherwise withdraw valued favours. Parliament was not for the people. It was more like an exclusive club: the aristocracy forming the House of Lords, their friends and relations along with a sprinkling of other gentry making up the Commons. A 'ruling few' dominated a 'subject many', as Jeremy Bentham famously said.

From around 1815 on, a deep sense of dissatisfaction had been swelling in Britain. By 1830, reform was firmly on the agenda. The violence of the Swing revolt, the naked contempt of the workers, the hopelessness of the gentry in the face of their fury, had finally convinced an aristocratic elite that their rule could not continue unless changes were brought into effect. Both the emerging industrial classes and the commercial middle classes had to be given a more significant voice. Under the Whig administration of Lord Grey, a bill for reform was presented in March 1831. It went through its many drafts and readings, passes and rejections, amid such dramatic scenes of contention that the very stability of society seemed often at stake, until eventually, in June 1832, the Great Reform Act received the royal assent and the political map of Britain was redrawn.

The act did not bring about universal suffrage. In its final form it increased the electorate from around 366,000 to 650,000. About 18 per cent of the total adult male population (very few belonging to the working classes) could vote. In towns the vote was given to all whose homes were valued for rates at £10 per annum. In the counties it was given to forty-shilling freeholders as well as long leaseholders and tenants who paid more than £50 per annum rent. This led to the redistribution of seats in Parliament: those seats with less than 2,000 voters – the Earl of Caledon's Old Sarum among them – lost their representation; others which had previously returned two members were reduced to one and all the seats thus gained were redistributed, twenty-two to towns such as Birmingham and Manchester which now had representation for the first time, and sixty-five others re-allocated to the counties, many of which were divided into two. Old corruption was not completely rooted out. Some seventy seats remained under aristocratic patronage. But this was the start: it was a landmark event in the history of English democracy.

———

Palmer felt as if the walls of his Eden had been breached. He was an old-fashioned high Tory who voted with what he believed to be the best motives. 'As I love our fine British peasantry,' he explained to Richmond in 1828, 'I think best of the old high Tories, because I find they give most liberty to the poor, and were not morose, sullen and bloodthirsty like the whigs, liberty jacks and dissenters whose cruelty when they reign'd, was as bad as that of the worst times of the worst papists; only more sly and smoothlier varnish'd over with a thin shew of reason.'[29]

Palmer was deeply distrustful of revolutionary principles. To him, the ancient institutions of England were sacred, and foremost among these was the Anglican Church. He had been unsettled by the emancipation of the Catholics; now he was deeply disturbed by discussion of the abolition of tithes, for this ecclesiastical tax – a time-honoured method of providing for the clergy which required members of a parish to hand over 10 per cent of their income – seemed to him symbol of the sacramental unity that existed between a pastor and his people. To abolish it, Palmer believed, would be to hurl a firebrand into the heart of the peaceful procession that winds its way homewards in *Coming from Evening Church*.

In 1832, with the passing of the Reform Bill, Palmer was finally dug out of his political corner. Believing that the only hope for his now defeated faction lay in winning seats in the upcoming general election, he laid down his brushes and took up a pamphleteer's quill, penning *An Address to the Electors of West Kent* in support of his local Tory candidate Sir William Geary. France, he warned, had 'obtained her freedom: and, alas! immediately lost it again, irretrievably: by confiding it, as the people of England are at this moment confiding their own – to revolutionary empirics . . . Shall we mistake her ravings for the voice of Delphic Sibyl' Palmer asked, 'and proceed to model, or rather unmodel, every institution of our country, and tumble them all together, into the semblance of that kingless, lawless, churchless, Godless, comfortless, and most chaotic Utopia of French philosophy? . . . Farmers of Kent – we are tempted with a share of the promised spoliation of the CHURCH! – There was a time when every Kentish yeoman would have spurned at the wretch who should have dared to tickle him with such a bait – to offer him such an insult! But piety and honour are in the sepulchre.'

'Is this the rant of a fanatic?' asked Palmer. The answer he offered was a resounding 'NO': 'It is the zealous but sober voice of one who dares to speak what millions think.' So, 'let us rally once more,' he concluded, 'round the noble standard of Old Kentish Loyalty; and defend it to the last . . . If we perish in the contest; let it not be, O spirit of Albion, as recreants and dastards: but with Thy standard clenched in our grasp, or folded about our hearts!'

Signing it 'an elector' – Palmer, as a property owner, was qualified to vote – he sent copies of the pamphlet to the local papers. The *Kentish Observer*, even though it supported the Tories, ignored it; the pro-reform *Kentish Gazette* dismissed it as the 'ravings of this maniac', and Linnell was far from happy, not simply because Palmer had taken an Establishment stance, but because he had parodied the language of the great republican Milton to do so: 'The same fountain does not send forth sweet water and bitter,' he declared.[30]

Palmer's candidate came last in the poll and the painter was never to resort to so direct a form of political involvement again.

The Sensual and the Spiritual

The visions of the soul being perfect are the only
true standard by which nature must be tried
from *The Life and Letters of Samuel Palmer*

It was not brutish indifference that left Palmer blind to the hardships of the labourer's life. 'Nothing more refreshes the spirits than a battle for the rights of the poor,'[1] he would later write. But as a young man in Shoreham, his head swirling with visions, he failed to see the reality that lay right in front of him because he was looking straight through it in search of some higher truth.

Palmer was inflexibly committed to a religious path. There was but one way to heaven, he informed Richmond in 1832, and that was a narrow one; there was but one Apostolic altar, one Holy of Holies, and that was the Anglican Church. To turn away from it, he believed, was to turn towards the devil of whose actual existence he remained all his life convinced. Satan's deepest artifice, he declared, was to infuse the mind with doubt as to whether there was any devil at all. Everyone, even the implacably anti-Establishment Linnell, would be regularly subjected to his rants, with only his 'poor dear old nurse' Mary let off the hook: 'though a misled Baptist,' Palmer wrote, he was sure that she would 'sing among the redeemed forever'.[2]

The Ancients in Shoreham all attended church regularly, said their prayers daily and set out to channel their talents along a religious course. Richmond's first Royal Academy exhibit was an 1825 painting of a recumbent Abel; the young Tatham completed a design showing the biblical Gideon and, Calvert's pictures before he finally let his pantheistic inclinations loose, making images of frolicking couples and pastoral nudes that had rather less to do with spiritual salvation than the sexual propagation of pagan fertility rites, were pervaded with Christian mysticism. 'These are God's fields, this is God's brook and these are God's sheep and lambs,' he once gushed as he showed off his latest landscape to Linnell. 'Then why don't you mark them with a big G?' his acerbic onlooker commented, alluding to the practice whereby a shepherd would mark his flock with an initial so that, if a sheep strayed, it could be identified.

Palmer never fulfilled his ambition to paint biblical subjects, but he discovered in landscape a parallel path towards God. 'What if earth/ Be but the shadow of Heaven?' Milton had asked in *Paradise Lost*. *Seculum est speculum* – the world below is a glass to discover the world above – the seventeenth-century clergyman John Flavel had said in his *Husbandry Spiritualised*, a volume which, finding religious significance in everyday rural practices, was to become a much favoured Shoreham tome. Palmer believed that, through art, the world could be elevated to a higher plane; that the painter, after a protracted struggle, could escape '"like a bird out of the snare of the fowler" from the NATURALISTIC . . . towards his "Jerusalem", the IDEAL'.[3]

Palmer's artistic impulses had found their beginnings in his love of church buildings. Now in Shoreham he turned the entire world into a cathedral for the worship of religion's higher mysteries. He did not see shabby shepherds, their skin grimed with grease; he saw an image of Christ caring for his earthly flock. He did not gaze upon groups of rough bucolics with grumbling stomachs and grimy clothes; he looked from afar and descried minor saints. In his transubstantiated realm, trees became the columns of soaring Gothic vaults; the full moon a rose window amid trellising boughs. Earth grew into a new Eden under his brush. How happy are those who 'find Him and adore Him everywhere, as they investigate His beautiful creation',[4] he declared. As he peered into chestnut flowers to paint the delicate pink stamens; as he watched a swallow's breast brushing the tips of ripe corn; as he noted every leaf shape, palmate, falcate and pinnate; or studied every texture, hatched, stippled and striped, he was trying to transcend the merely literal. The outward senses, he believed, could be turned against their own 'fleshliness'; they could be trained to 'drink in thro' their grosser pores wisdom and virtue to the soul'.[5]

It seems hardly surprising, then, to find that Palmer was a deeply sensual man. As someone takes care of the horse that carries him, he said, a person should take care of the body which carries his soul. He was obsessed with matters of health. Coughs, colds and sniffles were constantly debated. Damp, draughts and icy east winds were seen as a deadly peril; padding and defensive flannels a must. Gout, scarlet fever, jaundice and pneumonia were all ailments encountered in the course of his life, but in the absence of any more serious problem he would make a tremendous to-do over a scratch.

Short and rather stocky, with a tendency to corpulence, Palmer had a gluttonous streak. When he wrote of eating goose, 'that great king of birds', or its 'humbler but no less delicious relative, the duck',[6] it was with such orgiastic relish that a reader can almost see the grease running in glistening dribbles down his chin. The constitutionally lean Linnell mocked him for his greed. 'When Palmer a duck did buy/ he laid it not on the shelf/ but stuffed it full on the sly/ and with it he stuffed himself.' But Palmer grew used to such taunts and revelled in his luxuries. However busy he found himself, he would always try to find some time in the evening in which he could 'loll and roll about like a cat on the rug', he said. It was the best way to oil the wheels 'and make the old mud cart of existence roll on without creaking'.[7] He was a snuff taker and pipe smoker who found it hard to give up tobacco. Even cultural pleasures took on a sensual cast. The 'chastity of most of the Antique is too mild and pure for my gross appetite to relish', he wrote, and though he could imagine that some 'have a very refin'd pleasure in a boil'd chicken' he would take 'the *rich experience* of roasted goose' any day, which is to chicken what Michelangelo is to the Antique.[8]

Blake had seen sex as a form of spiritual freedom, a lack of restraint which could let the hidebound soul loose. All his life he had taken an obsessive, even pornographic, pleasure in the practice. The Ancients were a great deal less liberated. But still, a sense of their sexuality constantly simmers. Missing Richmond dreadfully after he has returned to London, Palmer resorted to a letter, 'that wing of lovers' thoughts', to fill the 'gasping hiatus'[9] that his friend's departure has left. 'Oh, if we loved one another's souls as we ought to love, methinks our eyes would so run down with rivers of water that we could scarce any more enjoy the shining of the sun,'[10] he exclaimed. He enjoyed a similar closeness to Calvert and, though few of his missives to this older man survive, even a fragment can convey their perhaps slightly suspect intimacy. 'Like a blind baby feeling for the breast knows the taste of milk,' but has 'a somewhat precocious appetite for cream', Palmer wrote, he could find the cream in one of Calvert's pictures.[11] All his life, he was to keep a handful of titillating woodcuts by his friend in a secret portfolio – 'mind toners'[12] he called them – and a few of the erotic prints once belonging to the Greek collector, Alexander Constantine Ionides (who, in the mid-1820s, had been a close friend of Calvert's) and now in the V&A, could quite possibly have been engraved by Palmer.

It has even been speculated that Palmer indulged homosexual tendencies. He was not an assertively masculine character, but there is no proof that the shared frolics and fervid intimacies of Shoreham ever amounted to anything more than an overspill of youth's frothing passions. Palmer's natural proclivities inclined towards women. He missed female company in Shoreham and, writing to London, asked Richmond to 'most adoringly, vehemently, and kissingly present my quaint but true knightly devotion to the young Ladies One and All'. His request that these ladies should honour him occasionally with their thoughts – even if it be 'only to set their pretty mouths a-giggle at the remembrance of my spectacles'[13] – offers a glimpse of the flirtations he enjoyed. At the end of this letter, in an impetuous postscript added apropos of nothing in particular, he declared: 'I am looking for a wife.'[14] A year almost to the day later he was still looking. '*I want a Wife sadly!*'[15] he confided to Linnell. He longed for 'a nice tight armful of a spirited young lady,' he told him a few weeks later; a 'young wife to kiss and be kiss'd by, on whose breast to lay a head aching with study into whose heart to pour our joys'. 'You *have* such a wife,' he wrote enviously: 'I only in feeble imagining.'[16]

Palmer's sexual frustrations may have found a focus in one of the Tatham sisters. Richmond, who had been employed as their drawing master, had already fallen in love with Julia, the elder of these girls. Palmer quite possibly harboured feelings for the other. But an impoverished drawing tutor and an eccentric recluse were far from desirable matches – and not least in a family which at that time was struggling financially. When an elderly peer made an offer for Julia's hand, her father decided to accept on her behalf. Richmond was heartbroken. His 1829 painting *On the Eve of Separation* shows a young couple clinging in desperate embrace. Julia clearly shared his feelings and, in 1830, she and Richmond eloped, travelling northwards in separate post chaises to the Scottish borders where they spent the night at the Crown and Mitre – the pillowcases were so dirty that Julia had to lay her silk petticoat over the linen – before being wed the next day over the anvil at Gretna Green. The Ancients had all been party to this plan. Palmer had lent £40 to pay for the venture and Walter had chipped in a further £12 loan. When the newly wedded couple returned south they found a welcome in Shoreham while Linnell played a persuasive role in convincing the irate father that this young drawing master was possessed of sufficient talent and ambition to ensure that he would eventually turn out well. He was to be proved right. By the end of the first year of his marriage, Richmond had finished no less than seventy-three portraits, earning £207 from which he could pay Palmer back – and with interest at 3.5 per cent.

Palmer, his closest companion now lost to him in marriage, found his thoughts turning more and more frequently to his own matrimonial prospects. It was fortunate that Linnell had the same faith in his talents as he had shown for Richmond's because Palmer looked no further than his own family.

Hannah (or 'Anny' as she was known), born in 1818 with Dr

Thornton attending, was the eldest of Linnell's nine children. Palmer had known her since she was five when she had been the first of the squabbling troupe who had tumbled out to greet him on his visits to Hampstead, when she had sat on Blake's knee singing his *Songs of Innocence* and received her first drawing lesson at the visionary's hand. Linnell had attended to the education of all his children himself, teaching them to read and write, introducing them to Shakespeare by acting out all the parts, his performances based on productions he had been to see with Blake. He had encouraged them to draw and set them at an early age to colouring his prints. Later, he would instruct them in painting and engraving, bringing them up in the proud belief that an artist's practice was a high vocational calling. All of his sons went on to follow careers as professional painters. The girls would have had to help out in the nursery and learn needlework, too, but there was little division between male and female when it came to household duties and Anny – who never grew taller than five foot – was often employed in the garden, digging for vegetables and lugging heavy watering cans. Such drudgery, she later believed, may have been detrimental to her health. If so, her mother's medical administrations would not have helped. Armed with her abridged copy of *Materia Medica* (a fat but obsolete volume on family doctoring) and an unfailing conviction in her powers of healing, Mrs Linnell would administer bizarre assortments of pills and home-brewed potions to her brood. In an era in which housewives commonly thought that the tail of a black tom cat would cure a sty and an onion stuffed in the ear ameliorate a painful toothache it was not unusual for medical treatments to do more damage than the original injuries.

Palmer approved of the Linnells' egalitarian methods and, for all that Hannah herself would voice conventionally effeminate fears, worrying that only a man could grapple with art and that she as a woman had too weak an intellect, he believed that much might be made of a woman if 'caught young' and especially if secluded 'from the cap-and-bonnet-society of her own sex'.[17] Hannah, he was delighted to discover, had been studiously trained up to be most industrious in her habits, not to hanker after the gewgaws and trumpery that befooled so many girls, and yet to be as kind, neat, clean, and orderly as any of them. In this curly-haired teenager he had found all the requisites of a perfect wife.

In July 1833, the twenty-eight-year-old Palmer made his feelings known to Linnell, and, though neither he nor Mary considered the young painter to be financially prepared to marry their daughter, he was soon to become an amorous caller at their Bayswater home. The girls, hearing his knock at the door, would run to greet him with bright eyes and hearty handshakes. Left alone in the drawing room, the courting couple would bend their auburn heads together as they turned the pages of books and talked. Sometimes, chaperoned by Anny's sister Elizabeth (with whom Palmer, for all that she was prone to fly into the exasperated rages which her father called 'fits', would forge a fond friendship), they would go out for summery evening walks or pay visits to galleries. They shared their love of art and Anny grew into an accomplished draughtswoman: snatching every moment that she could from her domestic duties, she would copy from old masters or work up her own designs. Palmer greatly admired such skill in a woman. Calvert's wife – his model for uxorious perfection – was also a talented painter who, when separated from her husband, would continue aesthetic discussions by correspondence and who, when her husband set up a printing press in his Brixton home, was prepared to rise from her bed in the middle of the night to prove a picture over which her spouse and some fellow Ancients had been brooding for the past several hours.

For a long time nothing was plainly spoken, but Palmer, right from the beginning, felt sure that his affections were returned. 'With respect to Anny's "sobriety",' he later wrote, 'I always looked upon it with a suspicious eye, knowing that the solemnity of young ladies under the process of courtship much resembles the demureness of a certain animal watching for a mouse.'[18] He was proved right. In the summer of 1835, he was handed a surreptitious note. 'I think it will please you to hear that my affection so far from decreasing in your absence increases daily,' Anny confided. 'I think of you more than ever and look forward to your coming back with stronger emotions of joy than I before felt.'[19] To Palmer the way ahead seemed clear. 'My energies are now at last unimpaired, because I have found vent for my strong and passionate love for women,'[20] he told Linnell in September 1835. His confidence was unshakeable, his affections unquenchable, his bond with Hannah grew every day more indissoluble, he said. And so the young couple became officially betrothed.

The End of the Dream

Pinched by a most unpoetical and unpastoral kind of poverty
from *The Letters of Samuel Palmer*

'If my aspirations are very high, my depressions are very deep,'[1] Palmer told Richmond in 1828. Though Shoreham was the place where he felt most ecstatic, it was also the setting of his most anguished despairs: 'Great hopes mount high above the shelter of the probable . . . know many a disastrous cross wind and cloud; and are sometimes dazzled and overwhelmed as they approach the sun; sometimes vext and baffled, they beat about under a swooping pall of confounding darkness; and sometimes struggle in the meshes, or grope under the doleful wings of temptation or despair'.[2] He learnt to accept, even welcome, these abrupt mood swings. 'My pinions never loved the middle air,'[3] he wrote. 'Better to cry and shriek and howl every morning and get a cosey oily hour out of the night, than to mix up joy and grief in the mortar of moderation till they neutralise and to smear the nasty mixture over the day.'[4] And yet, he would find himself increasingly suffering 'jaded halts of intellect', floundering through terrifying 'eclipses of thought': a 'living inhumement . . . equal to the dread throes of suffocation, turning this valley of vision into a fen of scorpions and stripes and agonies'.[5]

Such vividly felt despairs were not helped by his financial situation. By 1828 he was already overspending his budget and, by the early 1830s, struggling to live on the few shillings that his cottage rentals brought in, he cut back his expenditure to five shillings and two pence a week. An inability to pay for materials was beginning to curtail his ambitions. He feared he would have to hire frames for the Royal Academy exhibition. 'It is a very trying situation in which I am at present placed,'[6] he complained. If once he had dismissed financial worries as 'terrific phantoms',[7] he now reconsidered such glib pronouncements. 'Really a handsome income and personal influence do enable a man by his savings and his authority in society to do a very great deal for those two great interests . . . the Poor and the Church,' he informed Richmond. 'I do not think,' he continued, 'that Christianity is meant to damp the spirit of enterprise or the desire of success.'[8]

Palmer was only too aware of the professional gap that was widening between Richmond and himself, for his friend, while still enjoying the occasional Shoreham foray, was by then established as a society portraitist who could count William Wilberforce, Lord Sidmouth and the Bishop of Chester among his sitters. The young man who had once had to record every frugal expense, from the purchase of a gaiter strap to the repair of a shoe, would soon be earning £1,000 a year. 'As you are now become a great man I will address you on a sheet of my best writing paper not gilt edged and delicate like yours but rather too extravagant for me,'[9] Palmer began a letter to Richmond in October 1834. 'I am in solitude and poverty,' he lamented. If he could 'but get a twenty-guinea commission even if it were to take a view of Mr Stratton's conventicler or to draw the anatomy of a pair of stays,' he wrote, he should be 'as happy as the day is long'.[10] He ended up accepting a commission to clean a picture by the historical painter John Opie to make financial ends meet.

Prospects did not improve. 'Poetic vapours have subsided and the sad realities of life blot the field of vision,' he wrote in August 1835. 'O miserable poverty! How it wipes off the bloom from everything around me,'[11] he mourned as he touched Richmond for a loan of £3. His friend was quick to oblige. 'How sad to think that at 30 my dearest friend should be struggling to earn a few pounds a year unsuccessfully,' he scribbled on the margin of the letter he received. But if he pitied Palmer, it could hardly have been more than Palmer pitied himself. 'I am all in the dumps . . . and feel as if I alone of all mankind were fated to get no bread by the sweat of my brow . . . If you've a mangy cat to drown christen it "Palmer",'[12] he wailed. Financial matters had finally come to a head. The unworldly dreamer had to earn a living. He now determined to take any teaching job he could find and, until such time as he began to earn that wage, he would have to sell his pianoforte and a few of his beloved books. The prayer that had once seemed enough to support him felt no longer sufficient: 'Is daily bread promised to those who overspend their income?'[13] he asked.

Loneliness also began to weigh on Palmer's spirits. His once-treasured isolation had now come to feel more like abandonment. 'You shall see my body as soon as I come to town,' he wrote to Richmond in 1834, having given up hope of Richmond coming to him; 'but as to my poor mind I have been vegetating so long in solitude that I hardly know whether I've any left.'[14] Linnell seldom visited Shoreham by this stage. He had settled in his new house; his health had improved; he was travelling the country executing portrait commissions and selling engravings of his most successful works. The Ancients were drifting apart. Richmond was caught up with his burgeoning career and his family. Calvert and Finch remained mostly in London. Arthur Tatham was ordained and John Giles was kept busily employed as a stockbroker. Only Sherman and Walter, the least committed members of the group, were free to come and stay. Meanwhile, Palmer's father was preoccupied with his son, William, who, having decided that he did not like the life of a sculptor had taken up engraving instead, only to find that that did not much suit him either. Soon he was to cause the family even graver concerns.

Welby Sherman was a suspect character and, as early as 1828, Palmer was begging for help on his behalf. He had got into a 'most critical situation',[15] he wrote, which, though the nature of the problem was never specified, most likely had something to do with having borrowed money which he couldn't repay. Palmer tried repeatedly to put things right, allowing Sherman to make an engraving – a mezzotint, *Evening* – after one of his own pictures, trying to find him a market for his

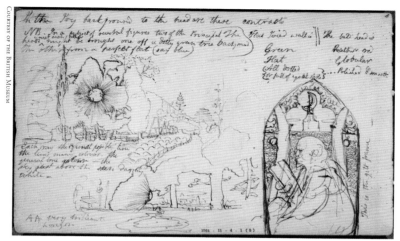

A page from Samuel Palmer's 1824 sketchbook. Palmer studies the way that light streams through shadowing foliage. He frames a single figure within a painted Gothic frame. Accompanying notes record precise visual details from the 'very brilliant horizon' to the textures and tones of the monk's bald head: 'rather red', 'globular', 'polished & smooth'.

Early Morning (1825). Palmer captures the quiet harmony of dawn in this delicate sepia. Doves call from the boughs of the crinkle-leaved oaks. A hare picks its solitary way up the shadow-streaked path.

William Blake and John Varley (1821) by John Linnell. The ebullient Varley is sketched in the middle of animated conversation; Blake is leaning back with an expression of benign detachment. Varley was probably trying to convince Blake of his astrological theories.

Portrait of an Artist (1829). When Richmond titled this miniature likeness of Samuel Palmer it was an act of affirmation, of faith in the future career of his friend who in Shoreham would sometimes don archaic robes like these.

Oak Trees in Lullingstone Park (1828). For Palmer, trees were far more than mere leafy adornments of a picturesque composition. They seemed like people: each with an individual personality and look. He saw in these oaks the noble descendents of the great Celtic giants which had once sheltered the valley of Shoreham, and he tried to evoke their monumental splendour as surely as Milton, in his poetry, does.

Coming from Evening Church (1830). This image distils the essence of Palmer's convictions. The natural and spiritual merge as villagers process home from their ivy-clad chapel beneath trees which soar upwards like the Gothic arches of a church. The light of the moon falls, a benediction from above.

In a Shoreham Garden (*c.* 1830). The extraordinary pictures which Palmer kept secret in his 'Curiosity Portfolio' are now considered among his finest paintings. They are works of splendour. Here nature runs riot in a profusion of pale apple blossom.

The Magic Apple Tree (*c.* 1830). Another of the works which were shown only to close friends, this painting glows as bright as an autumn bonfire. Palmer exults in the harvest's rich gifts. Colour becomes a pure sensual pleasure.

Yellow Twilight (*c.* 1830). 'In a half-lit room the drawing seems luminescent; both startling and tender,' wrote Palmer scholar Geoffrey Grigson, who counted it among the artist's very greatest works. 'In few things painted by an English artist is vision held so securely and with such simplicity and such delicate, grave concentration.'

The Harvest Moon (1833). Villagers harvest together through the star-spangled night, gathering in the natural bounty of the land. Palmer used oil for this painting and submitted it (along with *The Gleaning Field*) to the Royal Academy. It remained unsold.

Cypresses at the Villa d'Este (1838). Ruskin may well have been thinking of this study when he wrote that Palmer's 'studies of foreign foliage especially are beyond all praise for care and fullness'.

The Rising of the Skylark (c. 1843). A tiny oil panel is infused with an atmosphere of poetry. The spectator can almost hear the tumbling notes of the lark; sense the longings of the watcher who unlatches the gate.

King Arthur's Castle, Tintagel, Cornwall (1848–49). Palmer loved the wild moors and coastlines of the West Country. Here he tries to infuse a topographical study with Turner-esque energy, sketching the huge bluff of rock that Turner himself had once depicted, assaulted by powerful shipwrecking storms.

Opening the Fold etching (1880). The pent-up flock rushing outwards with the first rays of risen light reflects the longing of the artist who yearned for the dawning of a new world.

The Lonely Tower (reworked 1881 version). For the last fifteen years of his life, Palmer was occupied by his Milton project. This image – the last in the cycle but among the first to be finished – is the most evocative of his late works. A ruined tower stands on the edge of a cliff, a proud remnant of something that had once been great keeping solitary watch over the quiet of the night.

prints and begging Richmond to give him some encouragement. If Sherman could not find a way of making more than the piecemeal living he threatened to give up on art and go to sea, Palmer explained. In Richmond's opinion, this would have been the best thing for him: 'Mr Walter has gone to his nest,/ Mr Tatham is now in Edgeware,/ While Sherman in Hackney doth rest/ And Hackney'd he is I dare swear'. The loyal Palmer, however, was more sympathetic and continued to trust in Sherman's talent until finally this so-called friend let his true colours be seen. Having relieved William Palmer of a large sum of money, he fled with his ill-gotten gains to France. John Giles explained the whole sad story in a letter of 1836. A series of bets had been laid upon billiard games in which Sherman, winning again and again, had eventually managed to secure some £500, none of which could be recovered. Giles and Richmond, with typical solicitude, were the first to go and see what they could do to help William who, by then married and expecting a child, had been left all but destitute. The whole affair must have been a terrible shock to the ingenuous Palmer. How wryly he would have looked back on sentiments expressed just a few years before when, firmly believing that the Lord would provide, he had written: 'Mr Sherman will not suffer the devil to make him doubt and waver and falter any more about money for if there were no other right way of getting it we should find it dropp'd for us in the street.'[16]

By the 1830s, Palmer's rural dreams were fading fast. When in 1832 he was left another bequest he invested part of it in two cottages in Shoreham and with the rest purchased a house in London. Number 4, Grove Street, was a substantial ten-room building in what was then still viewed as a respectable spot, though its reputation was already on the decline. It was conveniently close to the homes of Palmer's friends: Frederick Tatham lived round the corner in Lisson Grove North and Calvert and Richmond were both to be found a brief walk away in Park Place, Paddington and Beaumont Street, New Road, St Marylebone respectively. The Ancients, even in urban exile, could meet once a month. And, just as importantly, Palmer was only a pleasant evening stroll from the home of Linnell and his family in Porchester Terrace.

Palmer had bought this new house as a teaching base. He found pupils without much trouble, for watercolour sketching was considered as much a part of a genteel education as reading or writing or playing the pianoforte, and by the early 1830s he had begun to travel back and forth frequently between the capital and Kent. But, even as he was encouraging his amateur clients, he was losing faith in himself. Analysing his work with a ruthless eye he discovered many faults and mercilessly listed them: 'Feebleness of first conception . . . consequent timidity of execution. No rich, flat body of local colours as a ground. No first-conceived foreground or figures,'[17] he recorded in a notebook. He was ready to clip the wings of his vision for the sake of public recognition. He wanted, he wrote in the autumn of 1834, 'as soon as possible to struggle up into repute'.[18] When, in 1835, Linnell set about touching up one of his paintings prior to its exhibition, Palmer acceded, allowing – not for the last time – his mentor to make such thorough adaptations that when many years later the work, for a period lost, came once more to light they accepted it to have been a joint effort whereupon Linnell began busily to meddle with it again.

Palmer's criticisms of his own pieces were unduly harsh, but as far as he was concerned such severity prepared the ground for the changes that he knew he had to make. By the mid-1830s he was in the mood to begin again. He engaged in endless elaborate experiments with materials and pigments. 'My cranium is stuffed with gallipots and varnishes,'[19] he wrote. It was around this time too that he began painting in oil out of doors. Inspired by a picture of Watermouth Bay which he had spotted in a shop window, he set off for Devon on the first of a series of sketching expeditions to the West Country and Wales. He intended to search out the sort of dramatic views – the craggy mountains and gushing waterfalls, the crumbling ruins and soaring cliffs – which Girtin and Turner had made so popular and which, at that time, could be sold for considerable sums.

Striding along Devon's windblown coastlines, Palmer must have felt an awfully long way from his fertile Kentish valleys, from the huddled farmsteads and fruitful orchards of his familiar Shoreham views.

Occasionally, to look at one of his West Country sketches, at some hulking promontory or deep plunging combe, is to sense the excitement of new discovery, to feel an infusion of energy as fresh as a lungful of blustery sea air. The following summer, 1835, he set off again, this time in the company of first Calvert and then Walter to Wales where they followed the course of the stream of fashionable watercolourists who would lug their easels along a well-worn route from the northern wilds of Snowdonia to the gentler Wye Valley in the south. Palmer was in search of 'Ossian sublimities',[20] but the trip was not the success he had hoped. The weather was *too* good. He saw too little 'of McPherson's mist and vapour';[21] Romantic topographers needed atmospheric vapours and thundery vistas, glimpses of distant peaks through chasms of rolling cloud. But the deeper problem for Palmer was that he would never truly share the topographer's commercial tastes. He would happily have swapped all Snowdon's precipitous dramas for the peaceful nook of Tintern Abbey. 'Such an Abbey!' he wrote: 'the lightest Gothic – trellised with ivy and rising from a wilderness of orchards – and set like a gem amongst the folding of woody hills.'[22]

Palmer returned home broke. He had to ask Richmond to send money to pay his fare home. Had he known in advance how much he would spend, his muse would have 'donkeyfied' upon thistles upon Hampstead Heath with a log round her leg, he complained, referring to the way in which grazing equines were hobbled to prevent them from straying. Worse, he discovered that his sketches were useless: despite careful annotations and passages of focused detail, they were too undeveloped and, back in the studio, could not be worked up into saleable views.

Undeterred, Palmer returned to Wales the next summer, this time with Calvert as his companion. It was, once again, a hard-working, low-budget trip. 'I am walked and scorched to death,' he informed the Richmonds; he lived on 'eggs and horny ham',[23] and did without shirts and socks, but his enthusiasm was undimmed. This was the trip, he hoped, which would lead to improved prospects, help him to make some useful connections and, even more importantly, lay the foundations of 'solid attainments'.[24] He did meet one potentially valuable acquaintance. He encountered the journalist Henry Crabb Robinson, who, taken by Palmer's 'eye of deep feeling and very capacious forehead'[25] invited him on a daytrip to some nearby falls. The outing, for both of them, must have been pleasurable. Perching on rocky outcrops that projected high above the torrent, they might have discussed Goethe, with whom Crabb Robinson was acquainted, or talked of the poetry of Wordsworth and Coleridge or gossiped about their mutual acquaintance, Blake. Later (though the whereabouts of the picture is no longer known) Robinson purchased the scene that Palmer had sketched as a souvenir of the day.

In a letter to Richmond, Palmer told the story of his meeting with a beautiful Welsh child in a dell. She had a beetle tethered on the end of a thread and offered to sell it to Palmer, assuming that he would then kill it. Collections of pinned insects were popular at that time. Palmer handed over his money but, to the seller's astonishment, he immediately let the iridescent creature go. It must have been an affectingly symbolic moment to Palmer who himself dreamt of such freedom. He was certainly working determinedly to attain it and spent his tour diligently visiting all the requisite beauty spots including the falls of Betws-y-Coed which, by the middle of the century, had become one of Britain's most frequented artists' roosts. Flocks of daubers would descend daily with their sketchbooks, huddling like birds on the surrounding rocks.

But what could Palmer add? He worked studiously, filling his sketchbooks with pictures, cramming their margins with notes: scribbled records of colours and shadows and textures, reminders of details that he did not have time to draw. He wanted to convey the atmosphere of the moment; to distil a mood as much as offer a description. Sometimes he would achieve his aim, capturing the wind as it bustled about among bushes or the flicker of light as it glanced over a pool. And yet Wales was already a cliché. All he could contribute was a minor footnote. If he continued simply multiplying pictures in the Welsh manner he would be miserable, he concluded. As for his connections, Robinson had turned out to have a journalist's fickle attention span and, just as he had eventually come to find Blake fairly tiresome, he also lost interest in the ardent little enthusiast with whom he had once passed such an entertaining day. Palmer's paintings at this time are only interesting in so far as they record his changing ambitions as, moving away from the Gothic, he nurtured a more conventional, classically inclined taste. The artist who had once described colour as a 'sugared spoon' to persuade the reluctant 'to swallow the ideal or severe',[26] now turned his talents to garish topographies inspired by the palette of Titian, whose voluptuous Ariadne he had recently taken a steamboat trip to Plymouth to see, investing a precious five shillings on the fare. 'Let everything be colour and not sullied by blackness,' was his new resolve.[27]

This feels like an abrupt volte-face, but it was not an arbitrary decision. Palmer was intellectually caught up in a Greek versus Gothic debate which, at that moment, was once more being evaluated. The publication of Augustus Pugin's *Contrasts* in 1836 was a landmark of the Gothic Revival. Classical architecture, Pugin posited, was quintessentially pagan and as such unsuited to speak of the values of a Christian society. Britain, he believed, should look back to the Gothic instead: to a style which had served a world of medieval faith. Palmer would have been in full-hearted concurrence had not Pugin, following his love of medieval religion through to its logical conclusion, converted to join the Roman Catholic faith. Soon Gothic architecture was widely associated with the inscrutable squabblings of the Oxford Movement and its convoluted arguments about ecclesiastical continuities. It put Palmer in a quandary. How could he, a staunch Anglican, now turn to its style as symbol of traditional values? The Gothic had turned into a piece of hotly contested ground. How could the Ancients still meet under its soaring arches? Palmer's Shoreham aesthetic, a bit like Tintern Abbey, had been left in ruins: it looked best when glimpsed nostalgically from afar.

The Ancients did not simply disband. 'The little knot of friends remains united,' Palmer assured Frederick Tatham in 1837, 'only if possible, more closely cemented than ever.'[28] And, although this is most likely a wishful overstatement, a group of them did continue to meet once a month. This regular gathering, an excuse for a party which would often extend late into the night, was remembered as an occasion of great excitement by the artists' families. Richmond's children would wait, noses pressed to the window of their Marylebone nursery, watching for their visitors to arrive: the artist carrying his carefully wrapped burden – a painting fresh from the easel or a sheaf of new sketches – while wife and offspring tagged excitedly along behind. For the first few hours the men would go into retirement in the study or studio where, amid a gathering fug of pipe smoke, they would remain closeted in solemn judgment on one another's progress.

But then the meeting of the 'blessed in council' would break up and it would be time for tea drinking and chatting and stories. The graceful Mrs Richmond, their 'fair Hebe', would deal out bowl after bowl of the 'oriental nectar' (green tea) while the children would crowd in excitedly to admire the Ancients' latest works. 'How solemn and how beautiful those freshly painted pictures appeared to us,' Calvert's son remembered, 'displayed in the light of candles . . . which were built up on books and pedestals in ecclesiastical fashion.'[29] They would gaze in reverence. But there was also much laughter amid the discussion. Sometimes the wet paint on one of the pictures, despite careful measures, would get smudged: it would lead to 'Turneresque subtleties', Palmer liked to joke. He was one of the merriest for, although Calvert's son commented on the amiability of Richmond, the modest reserve of Walter or Finch, the conscious twinkle in his father's eye, it was 'the oddity and humour of Palmer' that struck him most pleasantly. He 'interested and amused everybody' he said, especially at supper when he would find that the goose was too savoury or that the beer had too much froth.[30]

These gatherings would go on late into the night as the Ancients shared reminiscences about their Shoreham days, sipping drinks in between pinches from their snuff boxes. Finch would play the piano or Palmer his fiddle, while the rest would gather around to sing until at last, weaving a little, they would wend their way homewards, gazing up nostalgically at the stars and recalling the times they had wandered through the velvet Shoreham nights. 'We seem individually to be the odd volumes, and when together we form the complete set,'[31] Finch remarked.

And yet, for all that each of them dearly valued the company of his fellows, as artists their courses were diverging. Richmond was socialising doggedly to consolidate his portraitist's career. He was a charming addition to any polite gathering, not least when his attentive wife Julia was beside him, and although like Palmer he was a terrible hypochondriac – his diaries are peppered with records of indispositions and sniffles, cancelled appointments and suspended sittings – he still managed to complete several dozen portraits a year. He was never to be persuaded from his course again and though he was later to enjoy a friendship with John Ruskin who, for a brief while took quite an interest in the Ancients' lost dream, when Ruskin tried to lure him away from the comforts of commerce – 'Give my love to George Richmond,' he wrote in a letter from Italy, 'and ask him what the d he means by living in a fine house ... painting English red-nosed puppets with black shoes and blue sashes when he ought to be over here living on grapes and copying everything properly' – Richmond was not to be convinced.

Richmond does not belong in the first rank of portraitists, but what his pictures lack in psychological acuity, they make up for with careful observation. He had a sharp eye. Once, spotting some frescos in a blacksmith's shop, he popped in to buy them, only discovering later that they came from Ovid's family tomb; while a small crayon sketch that he did of Charlotte Brontë captured her so vividly that she burst into tears when she saw it for it reminded her so nearly of her recently deceased sister Anne. It is now seen as the definitive image of the author.

Richmond must often have missed his more carefree Shoreham days. In 1845 he took a holiday in Kent with his family, revisiting many of the Ancients' favourite haunts. But he remained contentedly living in London, a good but strict father to a growing family who, for all that he would deliver many sound thrashings, remembered him with as much affection as respect. Many years later his eldest son Willie would tell the story of how, as a child, he had sneaked off to the zoo without telling his parents. It had been a Sunday and so, to punish him, his father had given him the biblical text of the day to read. It was a passage in which St Peter compares the devil to a lion. Willie, summoned before his father to be tested, had started to repeat the story but when it came to the part about the leonine devil he had piped up: 'Papa, I have seen him today.' Richmond, unable to maintain his stern façade any longer, burst into laughter and his happy son was let off the hook. Richmond remained all his life a loyal supporter of Palmer. 'Among the many mercies of my now long life,' he later wrote, 'the friendship of Samuel Palmer was to my poor seeming . . . one of the greatest things that ever were given to me.'[32] Palmer valued him equally in return. 'You are fixed in my heart and it would want a very rough jerk to tumble you out,'[33] he declared.

Calvert, with his independent means, could have continued clearing the tangles from the Ancients' archaic track. The spirited woodcuts that he made during Shoreham days are still considered his liveliest and most inspirational works. But the boldness of Calvert's vision soon faded, along with its pervasive erotic energy, as increasingly he succumbed to the mores of Victorian society. He built a studio in his garden and retiring through a secret door behind a bookcase to this refuge would while away long hours, formulating complicated colour theories or rearranging his extensive library of classical texts, withdrawing further and further from the dreams of his fellows.

Finch pursued his painting career quietly for the rest of his life. He had a modest reserve which served him well in the society circles into which he ventured after being commissioned to paint views of Lord Northwick's mansion. He was a kind and sensitive companion. 'Whether grave or gay, he was always equal to the occasion endeavouring to understand and adapt himself to the feelings of those present,' it was later recorded; 'where dancing was the order of the evening, he seldom sought, as partners, the most attractive of the fair ones within his reach, but rather those whom others of his own sex might feel disposed to pass over.'[34] In 1837 he married Eliza, a fellow singer whom he had met through the Hatton Garden church choir, and from then on, undiscouraged by neglect or diverted by fashion, he continued to supply the annual exhibition of the Old Watercolour Society with a steady quota of poetic landscapes which, as one critic noted in 1835, never varied from year to year. Yet why should they when they were perfect of their kind, this critic asked? Finch supplemented his income by teaching and became a lecturer in later years. 'Art, like a mountain, must rise from a broad base of general knowledge and acute observation, but it rises heavenward and should ever culminate in the "beauty of holiness",'[35] he informed his students. He believed that he could disprove atheism by logic. Blake, who detested such rationality, would no doubt have found matter for argument but by then Finch had lost faith with the ideals of this mentor. 'He was not mad,' he would tell Blake's biographer, 'but perverse and wilful; he reasoned correctly from arbitrary and often false premises.'[36] The lives of the Finches and the Palmers diverged, yet Palmer was always to remember this calm, kindly creature with affection and respect.

Henry Walter had never really subscribed to the ideals of the Ancients, though his watercolour caricatures provide lively mementos of the group. Relatively little is recorded of his life after Shoreham except that he got married and moved to Torquay. Returning to the village one day with his wife, he didn't pause to chat as formerly with the simpleton who liked to loiter on the bridge. 'He had a *woman* with him,' the mournful fellow sobbed.

The Tathams, too, went their own ways. As a movement the Ancients had manifestly failed. They had attracted no followers, found no patrons, received no critical acclaim or provoked much new thought. In fact, about the only published response to their project had been an expression of mild bemusement. They may not have been remembered by posterity at all had it not been for the rise of the Pre-Raphaelites later in the century. This band of brothers, with the help of Ruskin as a patron, would revive British interest in a medieval aesthetic and rediscover the until-then-forgotten figure of Blake. It was Dante Gabriel Rossetti, the poet and painter at the heart of this group, who encouraged Alexander Gilchrist to embark on a biography of the great visionary, thus providing the Ancients with an opportunity to recount their own part in his tale. But by the time this biography was published the erstwhile Ancients had all but abandoned their Shoreham beliefs. 'We all wanted thumping when we thought in a dream of idealism that we were learning art,'[37] declared Richmond. Palmer was more nostalgic. As a young man he had annotated his copy of Payne Knight's *Analytical Inquiry into the Principles of Taste* with high-minded comments. Years later he added a far sadder note: 'I knew the positive and eccentric young man who wrote the notes in these pages,' he penned. 'He believed in art (however foolishly); he believed in men (as he read them in books). He spent years in hard study and reading and wished to do good with his knowledge . . . He has now lived to find out his mistake.'[38]

———

By the end of 1836, Palmer's father was also growing restless. Finding his gentlemanly existence increasingly unsatisfactory, he wanted to open an educational establishment in which he would be able to employ the now penurious William and, in January 1837, he signed a document agreeing for the annual sum of £30 to take premises in Speldhurst Street. For a further £18, he purchased the goodwill, the desks, forms and academy boards of a school. Palmer, concurring with an irate uncle Nathanial, thought it a 'ruinous step'.[39] To add to their worries Palmer's father once more professed a desire to remarry. 'O! for a wife – the joy of my life,' he would sing, taunting his domineering brother who immediately threatened to withdraw all financial support. A spat ensued which Palmer, with effusive professions of gratitude to his uncle, tried desperately to soothe. Like most of his father's 'sudden fancies', this one too, if left alone, would 'die a natural death', he suggested.[40] He was proved right. Before a year had passed the school had been abandoned, the second marriage had not materialised, and Palmer's father and Nathanial had been reconciled. But if once the father had been the provider of a home for the son, from now on it was the child who was going to have to take care of his parent.

Then, on 18 January 1837 – the nineteenth anniversary of Palmer's mother's death – Mary Ward died. For more than thirty years she had been a constant presence in Sam's life, accompanying the family wherever they moved, cooking and keeping house, mending clothes and admiring pictures. Palmer had used to play the piano to her in the evenings while she listened attentively through her battered ear-trumpet. Now, she was gone. Kissing her on her cold shrunken cheek, Palmer cut a lock of her hair and wrapped it in a slip of paper. He would keep it along with the treasured edition of Milton that she bequeathed him on her deathbed and a few other mementoes, including a pair of spectacles. Her loss was a final break with his youth.

Honeymoon in Italy

You are going to tread a holy ground, where
St Peter and St Paul have walked
from *The Letters of Samuel Palmer*

On Saturday 30 September 1837, after a courtship that had lasted for more than four years, Palmer finally married Hannah Linnell. She was nineteen and he was thirty-two when they signed their names in the register. And though Palmer would have liked to have professed his vows in church, in taking the hand of Hannah he was also taking her father ever more nearly into his life and Linnell, who, when he had married twenty years earlier had been prepared to travel as far as Scotland to avoid the priest, had insisted on a civil ceremony. The young couple, under a law which had only two months earlier come into effect, were conjoined in a ceremony solemnised by a registrar. 'S. P. was married at the Courthouse, Marylebone', noted Palmer several years later in his commonplace book: and 'he, a churchman!'[1]

For their honeymoon, the young couple planned to join the throngs of British travellers who, with the end of the Napoleonic wars, had returned to traipsing the Grand Tour trail. They would visit Italy. For Palmer it would be the fulfilment of a long-held desire. 'You are going to tread a holy ground, where St Peter and St Paul have walked before you,'[2] he had written to Richmond almost a decade earlier when his friend had first visited this land of artistic wonders. He had long dreamt of the luminous vistas of Claudean pastorals, of Donatello's divinities and Michelangelo's giants; he had imagined the heavenly music that would be played in churches, the medieval reverence of the peasants who prayed. Now he and Hannah were to join Richmond, his heavily pregnant wife Julia and their four-year-old son Thomas Knyvett (the sole survivor of the four children to whom she had so far given birth) on a voyage for which they all held great expectations, but none higher than Palmer's. Reputations could be made overseas. 'I hope to produce much saleable matter – and to make the "pot boil" with fuel "kindled at the muses' flame",'³ he declared. Richmond, quick to reciprocate the favour that Palmer had done him upon his own marriage, lent his friend £139 for the journey. A contract was drawn up, setting the interest at 3.5 per cent, though specifically stating that the money should never be demanded back at a time when its borrower would be inconvenienced.

Money, however, was not the couple's main problem. Hannah's mother presented a far less easily surmountable obstacle to their plans. A woman who could discover multifarious dangers in even the most ordinary course of London life, regarded the Italian venture as a dice with death in a land of perilous fevers and volcanic catastrophes, ferocious bandits and predatory priests and, perhaps worst of all, indigestible foodstuffs. For a while it had seemed as if Palmer would be travelling alone. It took all the persuasive tact of a conciliating Julia and all the logical pressure of a reasonable Linnell, to coax the neurotic matriarch into changing her mind. To prevent any last-minute backpedalling she was made to put her name to a written declaration of assent. Meanwhile Linnell, although initially he too had had his reservations, commissioned his daughter to paint a series of small-scale copies of the Raphael frescoes in the Vatican, as well as to colour a set of prints he had made after Michelangelo's Sistine ceiling. These tasks would provide her, he thought, with a project to occupy her as well as a source of much-needed income for he had given his daughter no dowry and she would be embarking for Italy with barely £10 in her purse.

In the weeks before leaving, Palmer set busily about his preparations: painting materials were gathered, packing attended to with militaristic rigour, a pistol complete with ammunition purchased (it was confiscated by the French authorities even before they got to Paris) and some 'curious modifications'[4] introduced to his bachelor wardrobe. Though these were not specifically described, they would no doubt have involved increased pocket capacity for, several months into his journey, remembering that he had not returned a borrowed book, Palmer wrote and asked his father to do so only to discover the said volume several weeks later bumping around at the bottom of his coat.

Palmer intended to make money by letting out his Grove Street house and, until such time as a tenant could be found, he left his brother to live there and take care of it with the help of his wife. It had seemed a convenient arrangement at the time. The feckless William had at last secured a job and was working as an assistant keeper at the British Museum.

Four days after the wedding, the Linnells and their children – Lizzy, Johnny, Jemmy, Willy, Mary, Sarah, Polly and Sally – gathered in their front garden to wave Palmer and their eldest sister Anny off.

Having enjoyed a smooth crossing by paddle steamer from Dover, the travellers arrived in Calais, the foreign cries of the French sailors echoing all about them as they dragged the boat shorewards, earrings winking in the light. It was here that Palmer paid his first visit to a Roman Catholic church (though, unsurprisingly, he did not tell Linnell); its richly furnished chapels and 'picturesque poor people . . . kneeling about the doors',[5] delighted his visitor's eye quite as much as the old-fashioned markets with their gay rustic costumes and profusions of bright fruit. From Calais, the Richmonds and Palmers shared a bumpy diligence to Paris, only getting out twice on the way for a quick stretch of the legs. Despite a few passages of 'pretty tolerable' scenery, the villages were mostly 'desolate and deserted . . . with not a gleam of cottage comfort . . . and instead of ruddy ploughmen, ragged, sallow, blue-coated monsieurs', the firmly anti-Republican Palmer recorded. The whole country, he observed, looked as if it had been 'purged, not purified' by its violent history.[6]

In the past, Palmer had referred to Paris as 'that metropolis of Apes'.[7] But now, passing a few days there, he spent every hour he could spare from wrangling with French officials over problems with their papers, admiring the antique statuary in the Louvre where, though three-quarters of the paintings he dismissed as 'of little interest',[8] Veronese's massive canvas *The Wedding at Cana* seized his eye. It would be worth travelling to Paris to see this one extraordinary picture alone, he concluded, though it was but the first of many pictures which he would complain could hardly be seen because they were hung in such gloom.

Leaving Paris, the two couples headed south-eastwards for the Swiss frontier; rattling along from five in the morning until six at night with only a brief stop for lunch they made their way upwards into the mountains, through steepening valleys and past plunging waterfalls, by cream-coloured oxen and tumbrels of purple grapes, before winding down into Lausanne and on round its lake. They were delighted by the precipitous drama of the Alpine landscape, which, as Hannah informed her parents with somewhat unwise relish, was scattered with crosses to mark the places where previous travellers had been killed. They crossed into Italy by darkness over the perilous Simplon Pass. From the balcony of a flower-trellised inn above Lake Maggiore, the honeymooners watched their first dawn breaking over Italy. Beyond them stretched the landscapes of the Romantic imagination. They were setting out together into their new life.

While the horses were rested for three days in Milan, the travellers went sightseeing. They were entranced by the cathedral's poetic gloom: 'a wonder of holy, Gothic', declared Palmer: 'its dim religious light gilds the very recesses of the soul'.[9] He admired a few drawings in the city library but was appalled by Leonardo's *Last Supper* which, hanging in 'the most dismal hall I ever saw', looked like 'a complete wreck'.[10] Then, leaving Milan, they headed south on an ever-more-glorious route which took them via Bologna, where they wandered through moonlit arcades, across Apennine landscapes and on down to Florence. 'Quaint, antique, stately, and gorgeous, and full of the gems of those divine and divinely inspired arts,'[11] this city with its dusky semi-barbarous cathedral, its sumptuous baptistery, its turreted palace and colossal statues seemed to Palmer like some old-fashioned yet richly wrought cabinet, containing in its caskets and curious recesses specimens of all that is sublime. But Rome, that 'wilderness of wonders',[12] was their ultimate destination. It was mid-November 1837 when the companion couples arrived and started sorting out lodgings for the duration of the winter.

Palmer at first was entranced. 'What shall I say of Rome?' he cried. 'Rome is a thing by itself which, once seen, leaves the memory no more – a city of Art which one . . . can scarce believe one has seen with these ocular jellies – to which London seems a warehouse and Paris a trinket shop.'[13] They watched the sun as it sank beyond the dome of St Peter's, visited the Colosseum by flickering candlelight, witnessed Pope Gregory blessing prostrate multitudes and joined their fellow English tourists for opera trips. For Palmer, the magic of unfamiliarity infused everything at the beginning, although the Richmonds, in their neighbouring lodgings, found the atmosphere rather less charming and three months later moved on.

It was not until May 1838 that the Palmers, disentangling themselves from the happy society of the many artists they had met, got going again, travelling to Naples to escape the rising summer heat. Their carriage, hopping with the fleas that had disembarked from an accompanying greyhound, was protected by a guard with two pistols for there had been several robberies on the marshes which they had to cross. Naples they found 'filthy and uninteresting';[14] their rooms were pestiferous dens with the foul stink of drains, and for all that Vesuvius bubbled fitfully away – they described dreadful rumblings and drifting ash and a sun that glowed red as if shining through a fog – they did not hang around waiting for the promised eruption, for the volcano, locals told them, could go on grumbling for weeks.

By early June, the Palmers were in Pompeii where they found lodgings in a rustic cottage at the edge of the ancient ruins. 'You can go into their kitchens and cellars and see their jugs and utensils,'[15] Hannah told her parents. She was spooked by the eerie silence that hung over the site and the skeletons of trapped prisoners still fastened by their chains. Palmer was astounded by the quality of the paintings: 'If these are the works of antique house decorators what must Apelles have been!!'[16] he exclaimed.

The sun was baking: by nine o'clock each morning the young couple were forced to stop working because of the heat. They spent August and September sketching in the cooler climates of the mountainous Torre Annunziata, Salerno and Corpo di Cava, before returning to Rome at the end of October in preparation for a second winter, throughout which Hannah worked on her father's commission.

Arriving back in the capital, they felt like old hands. They were welcomed as friends by their earlier acquaintances and met up with the Richmonds whose baby, born at the beginning of that year, had already cut six teeth. By the time Julia left the immortal city she was pregnant again.

From Rome, the Palmers took a diversion to nearby Tivoli – 'the most charming place we have seen in Italy'[17] declared Hannah with the effusive delight that marked arrival at any new spot – where they settled down for a month or so in rural lodgings. Palmer, taking advantage of the balmy late autumn weather, produced some of his best paintings before retiring to the hearthside to spend hours reading Shakespeare while his wife worked at resuscitating her tattered wardrobe. By New Year 1839 they were again in Rome where they remained before heading northwards for the summer, reaching Subiaco on donkey-back by June. The heat here was intense and, tortured by fleas, they moved a month later to the fresher climate of Civitella until the temperature there also mounted and an outbreak of plague sent them fleeing, travelling by mule under the light of a moon which picked out the speckled green corpses of abandoned plague victims, to Papignia, a picturesque little village in the Umbrian hills. From there they travelled via Terni back to Florence, where, passing the entirety of September and October 'wholly absorbed in art', Palmer became 'so imbued with love for the landscape of Titian and Giorgione' that he vowed never to 'paint in my old style again'.[18]

————

The letters written by Palmer and Hannah from Italy are irregular. They reached the Linnells haphazardly, sometimes in the wrong order, sometimes two at once; long and (as far as Hannah's parents were concerned) nerve-wracking interludes often fell between them, provoking terrible anxieties and leading to angry recriminations. Read all together, however, they give a vivacious account of foreign adventures. Palmer, who would pull out his pen as soon as the tea was drawing, had rather less time than his wife for writing; but their missives – his often poured onto the page without revisions or erasures, hers full of apologies for not writing sooner, for having bad handwriting, broken pens or for being too brief – bring their experiences to vivid life. 'An account of all the novelties which I have seen, if hung from the top of the Monument, would trail upon London Bridge,'[19] Palmer said.

He and his new wife observed everything wide-eyed, from the extravagant masquerades of the Rome carnival to a papal procession in which a white satin pontiff was borne aloft like 'something the English boys carry about on the fifth of November'.[20] They remarked on the 'dear precious shining heavenly faces' of the 'poor barefooted pilgrims'[21] arriving at churches to pray. They witnessed a monk securing his dinner by offering fish-market traders a coloured print of the Virgin to kiss in exchange for a small gift from each of their stalls: 'I think in Billingsgate he would find himself as much out of his element as the fish themselves,'[22] Palmer observed dryly. They met a curly-headed urchin who had been christened after Christ's prophetic cousin: 'I saw John the Baptist this morning eat a very large raw Cucumber for breakfast,'[23] Hannah said. And they watched a funeral in which boys dressed as angels carried the bier, their large pasteboard wings knocking against everything, and making, Hannah noted, the most uncelestial noise. They listened to nightingales, saw the oxen of Theocritus and the frescos of the Florentines, ate pomegranates and oranges and sketched cypress trees planted in the days of Ariosto. They crammed their letters full of detailed observations of everything: from the way that bedsheets, shaken out of windows, scattered passers-by with bugs, through how swaddled babies were hung up on hooks to keep them out of the way, to the heat of the door handles which could not even be touched. Nothing was too small to mention – from a screaming match with a curricle driver to the loss of a parasol.

The weather proved a matter of constant discussion. One moment Palmer was shivering in Rome 'wearing always two shirts and two waistcoats lined with flannel – and sometimes an India rubber cloak',[24] a few months later he was sweltering through the high summer of Pompeii. 'It is a labour here to lift my hand for a dip of ink,' he moaned, though at least he was being baked in a 'pleasantly ventilated oven'.[25] In Florence a stifling heatwave reduced him to the consistency 'of the jelly fish which we find on the sands'.[26] Food provided a source of at least as much fuss. They started off, Hannah assured her mother, by eating only the sort of things that they could be sure of: fowls, beefsteak, fish and veal, and, since all was 'cooked in the French way, covered with sauce and curiosities',[27] they left anything they didn't recognise. At first Palmer considered Italian cookery 'most hateful' – 'nothing portly, nothing round, majestic or profound in it'[28] – but in Rome he mastered a modestly priced bill of fare and, from the 580 dishes on offer, found six he could manage, though macaroni, he warned Richmond, was 'vile rubbish . . . most constipating . . . and hard of digestion', its effects only rectified by 'blessed bowel opening' oranges, grapes and figs.[29] But they soon grew accustomed to foreign eating habits and came to relish raw ham and fresh fruit for breakfast or the ample 'fat of the land' fare of mountain dwellers. Every dinner seemed to be 'better studied than the last',[30] the increasingly portly Palmer declared. In the course of his Italian sojourn he grew so fat that a visiting friend reported back to his family that he stood 'like a fixed easel'. 'Well you are likely to come home a man of substance in some sense,'[31] the sardonic Linnell remarked.

The Palmers described all their encounters with the natives, from the cries of 'Piccola Inglese', pursuing Hannah down the streets, to the body odour of the locals which Palmer found more problematic than their beliefs – though it was not just the human population that could be troublesome. The local fauna proved equally threatening, from the pack of fierce dogs which Palmer charged with his iron-tipped walking stick, through the wolves that supposedly prowled the wild mountain tracks (and which Palmer, hearing strange rustlings, one day bravely confronted, only to find that 'lo! up came a goat!'[32]), to the snakes and the scorpions that lurked under beds. And though, in the long run, none of these creatures caused them any difficulties (a scorpion was even popped into a box as a present for Hannah's little brother), the mosquitoes turned out to be a constant torment. Palmer and Hannah spent many a sleepless night rubbing themselves alternately with soap and vinegar, pacing their rooms and scratching, before eventually one day deciding to travel ten miles by donkey (Anny falling off on the way when the girth suddenly broke) specifically to buy nets. Even these didn't entirely solve the problem since the nights were so hot that even a layer of gauze could become unbearable. The fleas – F sharps, they called them, F for their initial letter and because their bites were so sharp (whereas the bed bugs were known as B flats, B for their initial and because the insects were flat) – proved to be a particular trial. Palmer suffered 'perpetual minute venesection', he said. 'I suppose daily body washes are peculiarly tempting to vermin,'[33] he groaned, unwilling to give up the personal hygiene that ever since Shoreham had remained a point of pride.

Despite such tribulations, however, the Palmers soon began to feel at ease in Italy. In Rome, they met up round a trestle table every evening for dinner and animated discussion with a colony of English artists. They discovered a Protestant church, and they quickly learnt to make friends with fellow travellers, a cast of characters that included a Mr Macdonald, a Scotsman who angrily stormed out of the room when one day a rude comment about the bagpipes was passed (Palmer was not the offender but tried to make peace, he assured Linnell) and the artist Edward Lear whom they met in Civitella and who played the flute for an impromptu ball. A year into her trip, Hannah was not remotely worried to find herself travelling in the company of complete strangers. 'I made myself at home with them in minutes,' she wrote, 'though at first they gave me the usual fashionable glare which I am now so used to that it does not in the least discompose me.'[34]

Soon the Palmers were taking siestas and speaking passable Italian. Hannah befriended the locals with particular ease and an Italian lady in Papignia was so grieved at the prospect of their eventual parting that, amid profuse tears, they exchanged locks of hair. In her second winter in Rome, Hannah started Italian lessons with a man whose brother was a captain in the Swiss Guard. The Palmers became seasoned travellers.

They found out how to face down the wily *veturino* drivers, to bargain with shop keepers and boil up coffee in a tin in their room. They learnt to carry their own soap because there was never any on the washstand, to sleep between blankets when the sheets were damp, to hire a boy to fend off the people who would crowd them while they were sketching and, when communicating with locals, to exchange decorous English manners for boldly flashing eyes and a loudly raised voice. Unfortunately, it was only many years after leaving that Palmer learnt that burning camphor could keep mosquitoes away.

As soon as she arrived in a new lodging, Hannah would pull out her knitting and make herself at home. 'Travelling is nothing when one is used to it,' she airily informed her sister. 'A clean coarse mattress in a little hot room without a single decoration'[35] came to feel like a blessing. The Italians, she enthused, were 'truly delightful people'; she praised their warm-hearted affection, the way they would jump up and hug. 'We are such a cold set of people,' she remarked.[36] She was particularly charmed by the way that the villagers would kiss her hand in the street and say '*Buon-giorno Eccelenza*'.[37] They were 'wonderful people in spite of their fleas',[38] Palmer declared. 'I have learned more of mankind since I left England than I did all my life before . . . [I] fancy I know how to get through the world pretty well.'[39]

———

Though the Linnells had had qualms before the wedding of their daughter, Hannah's honeymoon letters were designed to reassure them. 'The propriety of our marriage is a thing I never doubt for a moment,' she told her mother a few months after leaving. 'If Mr Palmer had come abroad without me you would have lost me altogether as I am quite sure I should not have lived.' 'I am fatter and better than I have ever been in my life.' 'Mr Palmer is kinder to me than even I could have expected.'[40] 'We live in increasing mutual delight in each other's society'. 'We have not had one quarrel yet, and I do not think there is any fear with so kind a creature.'[41] Palmer, in his turn, was equally enthusiastic. 'Anny is exactly the wife I wanted,' he told Linnell. 'My anticipations of happiness' in her society 'have been most fully realised and every day I think brings an increase of affection without exception or alloy.'[42] He especially liked her high-spirited moods. 'I had no notion she had so much sparkle and buoyancy,' he declared one evening when, fearing that she might have been unsettled by the bustle of the Roman carnival, he had approached her 'thinking to comfort her very tenderly' only to find to his amazement that she had leapt up and, bursting into laughter, had started to dance and sing. 'I thought myself a tolerably merry animal,' wrote Palmer, 'but I am quite a Simon Pure compared with Anny who is all dance and frisk and frolic.'[43]

The young couple's missives offer glimpses of close mutual happiness: of Anny giggling as she mischievously erases a bit of a letter that Palmer is writing, or laughing open-mouthed as her husband, kneeling on the carpet before her, attempts to stuff three large onions into a duck. When Julia Richmond brings news that Anny has permission to draw a privately owned Titian portrait, Palmer is so pleased that he falls upon the floor and, kicking like a lady in hysterics, seizes a tambourine before leaping up to perform a Bacchic dance. Linnell would no doubt have considered the response a trifle undignified, though the Richmonds would more probably have understood, for it was in a letter to them that Hannah told of how she had had to tick her husband off for his 'most beastly' trick of trying to cram as many grapes as possible into his mouth at once 'till the juice ran out of each side, like the lions of the Roman fountains!'[44]

Palmer and Hannah – often mistaken by shopkeepers for brother and sister – were much at ease with each other and it is perhaps surprising that, in the course of their honeymoon, she never became pregnant. Perhaps the couple deliberately avoided conception because they feared that it would interfere with their future work. Having travelled with the expectant Julia, they would have been only too aware of the awkwardness; Hannah had often been snappy with the Richmonds' four-year-old son and perhaps did not want to shoulder the burdens of motherhood quite yet.

The creation of paintings – not progeny – lay at the heart of the Palmers' plans. Sam intended to return to England with a portfolio of drawings to sell as well as sheaves of preparatory sketches for more significant commissions; Hannah too had ambitions which he took as seriously as his own. He believed her capable of great things. 'I should like to fight up into fame and get her a Greek and Latin master from Oxford – Novello for music lessons – I see her quite a Lady Calcott,' he wrote, referring to the wife of a naval officer who, when her husband was at sea, became a writer of children's and travel books: 'tho' I hope she will be more – namely a fine and original artist'.[45]

Hannah often found drawing frustrating and sometimes, losing her temper, she would hurl down her papers and stamp on them in pique. If it were not for Palmer, she told her parents, she would have given up for good. But he was a patient master and soon she was producing what she believed might be saleable sketches while he coaxed her on, always ready to hail each new effort as her finest so far. In Rome she would set off for the Sistine Chapel with her basket of painting materials and stay there from nine until four in the afternoon, working on her copies of the Michelangelo frescos for her father's commission, while her husband would find some other spot to sketch. They would take it in turns to grind colours for each other's boxes, sometimes share a hired model or draw side by side in a scenic landscape. A comic pen sketch by a fellow artist, Penry Williams, captures them at work: the bespectacled Palmer and his bonneted wife perch on a rock like a pair of puffins while half a dozen other artists roost all around. Anny was particularly taken by the picturesque local costumes and, taking a brigand's wife as her first sitter, made the first of a series of records of the exotic Italian dress. She planned to turn these drawings into a book. She also dreamt of selling a set of five etchings done after her husband's pieces to a London publisher. Palmer could thereby become 'as much known in a week, as he would become by a year's private circulation of the etchings',[46] she wrote.

They were both optimistic. It was in Italy, after all, that artists from the idealising Richard Wilson to the atmospheric J. M. W. Turner had made their names. But talent alone, they discovered, was not quite enough. Where Richmond had arrived in the capital armed with a bundle of introductory letters, Palmer had brought no recommendations and without them, he soon realised, Rome's social circles remained resolutely sealed. He grew increasingly self-conscious about his lack of social graces. While Anny, he told her parents, 'will do very well for society . . . "I – the dogs bark at me as I halt by them",'[47] he wrote (quoting from Shakespeare's *Richard III*). His eccentric dress sense can hardly have helped, not least as his journey progressed and he hatched idiosyncratic plans to avoid the darning of stockings which involved cutting patches from one bit of footwear and tacking them on to the other's sole. Where Hannah was present-able – she even invested in a new evening dress for Roman parties at which artists' wives, she noted, dressed more like queens – her husband, however passable he tried to make himself, always looked in comparison with any regular dandy much like a coal barge beside a royal yacht.

Richmond did his utmost to help, introducing the couple to Joseph Severn, a pivotal figure in Roman society, and securing for Palmer a commission from John Baring to paint a panorama of Rome. But even the Richmonds' young son could spot Palmer's social failings. 'Tommy sends his love . . . and says that you must not eat the backs of the sticks that we have for dinner,' wrote Julia: 'meaning that you began to eat the asparagus at the wrong end.'[48] Palmer became increasingly troubled. 'All who know us by sight, know us as nobody, and as creatures whom nobody knows,' he lamented.[49] How galling it must have been for him to meet a young artist who (in his opinion) could not draw and, even more unforgivably, had been heard dismissing Michelangelo's *Last Judgement* as 'a mass of rubbish'[50] get two fifty-guinea commissions from the Russian ambassador and an introduction to the Duke of Sutherland. 'There seems to be a great chasm between me and gentility,' he mourned: 'that gentility which I despise, but of which I should like to suck the sweetness.'[51]

Linnell was not worried. 'I think it of far more consequence that you bring home plenty of fine studies rather than fine connections,'[52] he reassured his son-in-law. But success remained elusive. Though Baring was interested in a pendant piece for his Roman panorama and Palmer spent weeks grappling with possible compositions, the banker employed another artist in the end. Nor did Hannah's commission from her father go well. The colouring in of his Sistine engravings may have been anticipated as a pleasant enough pastime, but it turned out to be a strenuous, time-consuming, neck-cricking feat.

————

As Palmer's time in Italy progressed his relationship with Linnell grew increasingly strained. Hannah's parents missed their daughter. They worried about her health, especially when the country was struck by an outbreak of cholera, and although at first the young couple sent back constant reassurances – bowels are reported on, diets assiduously monitored and an account of sudden hair loss by Anny meticulously proffered along with the benefits of Veritable Moelle de Boeuf oil, the application of which brings back her curly auburn mop – no profusion of reassurances could ever be quite enough. Palmer entreated his mother-in-law with ever-growing exasperation to dismiss her excessive anxiety. She must get over her 'dread of boats and drownings and moving accidents by flood or field', he admonished; he felt provoked to intemperance by what he described as an 'unjustifiable and distrustful anxiety' which 'embitters and falsifies'.[53] 'Your daughter is well and unhurt,' he insisted towards the end of his trip 'and has spent nearly two years acquiring intellectual and moral power, and experience which will . . . lead her safely through the mazes of life.'[54]

Linnell, though more sanguine than his spouse, was not much easier to deal with. His very first letter to his daughter reproached her for not writing sooner and suggested a strict routine whereby missives – which he would pay for – would be dispatched once a month. When this did not happen as planned he grew more insistent and blamed his son-in-law. 'Why did not that Bartholomew Pig write?' he demanded. 'Was he so tired going halfway up the hill that he has not yet got over it?'[55] he asked, alluding to the portly Palmer's failure to climb a steep slope to the hill-top statue of Santo Carlo Borromeo.

The balance of an already unequal relationship had finally tipped. Palmer's letters were increasingly stuffed with professions of gratitude, persistently proffered compliments and ingratiating requests for advice

– should he draw entire scenes or only details; should he concentrate on foregrounds or backgrounds; should he draw figures on the spot or in the studio? – while his father-in-law ever more firmly took the upper hand. By the time the young couple had been away a year, Linnell was instructing them as to when they should don their warm stockings and flannel drawers. Where once he had had faith in Palmer's artistic future – admiring his lack of compromise much as he had admired Blake's, describing his own practice, in comparison, as an inferior 'pettifogging'[56] path in which success had been sacrificed for the sake of a family – over the course of the honeymoon he progressively lost confidence in the son-in-law for whom he had once fostered such hopes.

Religion, predictably, became a point of contention. Though Hannah went to some lengths to explain how much Roman Catholicism disgusted her – not least a ceremony in which two lambs were blessed and their skins used to make monks' cowls – Linnell's festering suspicions that Palmer harboured Romish tendencies eventually found expression. There was no disguising his tone of voice when Palmer anticipated the pleasure of paying family visits when they got back home. 'It is all very nice what you say about home at Grove Street and your visits to Bayswater with only the wooden bridge to get over etc. – but it appears to me there is another Bridge which you have assisted in building and keeping in repair for some years and which is rather a barricade than a means of communication. I mean that Asses Bridge of Superstition built with nothing but the rubbish of human tradition – obscene, false and fraudulent.'[57]

Money turned into another source of friction. Palmer's financial affairs were not running smoothly. Grove Street remained untenanted, in large part because the next-door house had been rented by a pair of prostitutes who advertised their services by throwing up the sashes and shouting out of the window. Palmer's father had by then left, moving to Aylesbury to become the pastor of a congregation of only nine people, and leaving Palmer's home to the improvident William to take care of. But William, having adopted a foundling from the workhouse, was using the Grove Street front parlour as a bedroom, which was hardly conducive to paying lodgers.

Palmer badly needed the money that the letting of Grove Street would bring. He politely but firmly pressed his brother for rent, but though William had plans to follow his father into the country and set up a school, for the time being he could not pay. He even hatched a shady plan to sell Palmer's Shoreham cottages – a scheme to which Linnell, efficiently, put paid. Meanwhile a strange and never-quite-explained affair occurred whereby charges were brought against William for the barbarous treatment of his adopted daughter. The child was removed. The rumours were eventually proved unsubstantiated but by the time that William was asked to take the child back, his wife was expecting a baby of her own.

Without any rental income, any sales of his work in Rome exhibitions or any private commissions coming in, Palmer found himself falling into dire financial straits. 'Pray tell me what you mean Samuel, by the gloomy picture you draw of your funds, tell me how much money you have spent?'[58] Linnell asked him in June 1838. The news which Palmer sent back was not good; though Linnell laughed off his wife's worries that their daughter was starving – Palmer would eat the geese from the Capitol before he starved, Linnell joked – matters grew more pressing. Palmer, for all his penny-pinching, bargaining and making-do, was barely able to manage and, reduced to delineating his expenditure in humiliating detail, he handed over all financial responsibility to his father-in-law who, in return for providing regular funds, took the fiscal control that he would keep for the rest of his life.

Linnell's commission was also becoming a source of friction. A project that had initially been greeted as a 'joyful business'[59] was beset with problems, not least among them Hannah's frail constitution. At first, walking across the city every morning to set herself up in the Sistine on a folding camp stool, she had enjoyed the feeling of being a professional artist, but after a while the long hours spent amid chill damp stone, craning up into the lofty gloom, scanning the ceiling with the help of small mirrors or squinting against the glare of the light, had started to take a toll on her eyesight and health. A job which – after Palmer's long and timidly circumloquacious negotiations – would bring in only six shillings and nine pence per drawing was not worth so much effort. And yet Linnell was implacable. It had to be done, he insisted, and in the end Palmer (helped by Albin Martin, a pupil of Linnell's who had been dispatched to join them as much as a parental spy as travelling companion) had to waste precious time that should have been devoted to his own portfolio, revising and correcting every one of his wife's works. By the time the Palmers finally left Rome after a second winter, he had spent more than a third of his stay completing what, in the long run, amounted to little more than a colouring book.

———————

For much of his time in Italy, Palmer had found himself working feverishly against the clock. The honeymoon would have been far more fulfilling had he had the leisure to venture off the beaten track, to discover landscapes other than the tourist's hackneyed spots. But there was no question of prolonging a sojourn which had already lasted so much longer than the year that had originally been planned. The Linnells were outraged when the idea was even mooted. And so, as the summer of 1839 progressed, the Palmers' thoughts turned more and more to home. Hannah grew effusively excited at the prospect of seeing her family and though the thought of London's 'filthy smoke and black chimney pots'[60] sickened Palmer, he was at the same time eager to begin proper work. 'When I left England my mind was like a house full of furniture and utensils some good and some bad. I think the bad are now thrown out of the window and the good put into tolerable order so that I know pretty well what I want,'[61] he wrote a few months before returning. 'I long to leave study making,' he added a while later. 'I have had a glut of roaming.'[62]

By August 1839 the Palmers were on their long homeward trek. They would have taken a boat from Marseilles, but they dared not trust their precious cargo of pictures to a long sea voyage and so, by the end of October, they were trundling steadily northwards at the rate of thirty or forty miles a day. Hannah could not resist telling her mother one more bloodcurdling story, recounting in detail the crossing of rapids on the flooded River Po. Palmer was more concerned to make completely sure that his brother would not be in the house when he finally got back, but added a little pencil note to the end of a letter from Hannah. It is scribbled from the very top of Mount Cenis: 'We have crossed the Alp and left Italy!! "Farewell happy fields where joy forever dwelleth. Hail railroads! hail!'[63]

News of Hannah's return had sent her siblings capering like savages around the frosty London garden. They were thrilled when the Palmers at long last arrived back; when they saw the sister who had left them two years earlier now turned into a well-travelled woman who could speak Italian and had learnt to fire a pistol in an olive grove. But for Palmer the homecoming was tinged with sadness. He would never forget the contrast between the brilliant skies and the marble buildings of Italy and the filthy Thames warehouses that greeted him on his return. He was often to dream of one day returning. But he never did. Only sometimes, when the sunburnt Italian organ-grinders stopped outside his London house, Palmer would speak to them in their native language and, where most people considered them to be public menaces, he would pay them a shilling to go on playing for a while.

Back in England

Real life began

from *The Letters of Samuel Palmer*

'Real life began', noted Palmer many years later, as he looked back at that moment in the autumn of 1839 when he and his wife had returned from their two-year honeymoon. They had been eager to embark on the next phase of their life, but Hannah's parents had had other plans. They wanted their daughter to live with them at their home. She 'must be *ours* again for a time',[1] Linnell insisted in a letter. He went into a sulk when his son-in-law took a rare stand. 'I do not like the word "*must*",' Palmer replied; Hannah's 'filial affection and veneration' would always remain with her father, but 'her *obedience* is transferred to me'.[2] In the end, Hannah spent only a few days in Bayswater while her husband busied himself with other tasks: retrieving his portfolios from the snares of customs officials, addressing various financial muddles and making the Grove Street house feel more habitable.

Lisson Grove had first started developing in about 1720 when, with the sudden expansion of London, the village of Lisson Green had provided labour and service to the capital. But the construction of New Road (later called Marylebone Road) in 1756 had made it much more accessible. Its leafy byways had attracted several well-to-do residents including the historical painter Benjamin Haydon and the sculptor Charles Felix Rossi who carved the classical caryatids that can still be found ranked along the front of the nearby St Pancras Church. But Palmer was a latecomer and although the locality was still just about presentable, it had already entered a period of decline. The itinerant Irish labourers who had first arrived there in the 1830s to build the canal which cuts through dank alleyways and tunnels under roads, had made it their home and, as their shoddy dwellings multiplied, it would soon be little better than a slum.

The street in which Palmer lived no longer remains but a few surviving Georgian houses – two-bay red-brick buildings – still give an idea of what it must have been like. It was modest, and though the Palmers in the long-term hoped to find somewhere less cramped, for the time being they were happy. Their house, with its ten little rooms and its field out at the back, felt palatial, Hannah said, when compared to Italian lodgings and so, with the outside repainted, with old furniture and kitchen utensils borrowed from Palmer's father and a brand new mattress purchased for their bed, the couple set about constructing a shared domestic life. Neither of them was particularly suited to the task. Palmer had always had Mary Ward to rely on and had not fared well when, after her death, he had been forced to live under the hired administration of a Mrs Hurst who had left his damp clothes draped along the passageways and heaps of dirty saucepans piled up in the sink. With Hannah as his wife, domestic arrangements were hardly set to improve. She knew little about housekeeping. She certainly couldn't cook. A maid called Peacock was employed: a slovenly dogsbody whose methods were slipshod. The Palmers were, for the time being, unconcerned. They were set on a loftier artistic course. Their work would be their haven. 'Whatever I do,' Palmer wrote, 'I wish our painting room to be the cleanest in the house – that however I be kicked about in the world I may be able to retreat thither with Anny as to a little pleasant mountain in the desert – and there try once and for all to do something which may rescue me from neglect and contempt.'[3]

———

Palmer had set off to Italy full of optimism for his professional future. He had put in long hours on his honeymoon trip, watching for his subjects like a tiger watching for its prey: seizing upon landscapes and monuments and old master paintings, figures and foregrounds and poetic effects. Buildings and costumes, cascades and mountains, distances and outlines, tonal juxtapositions and atmospheric skies had all been assiduously added to his artistic stock. Little could distract him from his task: not even the swarm of wasps which, attracted by the honey with which he kept his colours moist, had besieged him in Subiaco, crawling about his face and spectacles and 'eating little clean, round holes into the oil paint'. 'But never having, on any consideration, left off a sketch from external annoyances,' he later told a friend, 'I persevered to the end; only moving my arm and hand very gently, as I knew they were insects full (as the novelists say) "of just pride and proper spirit"; and by respecting their heroic instincts, I came off unstung.'[4] Sometimes his fingers had grown stiff and painful from clenching his pencil; sometimes, hauling his heavy sketching apparatus uphill, he had rubbed his hip bones raw. For a while he had complained that he had hardly been able to squeeze his brushes, though this, it had turned out, had been caused not by hard work but by an attack of gout.

Palmer had tried to learn whatever Italy and its old masters could teach him: he had noted how tenderly Michelangelo depicted the strongest muscles or the way in which Titian would deepen his celestial blues so that subjects could glow more brightly when set against them. His Baring commission, a *View of Modern Rome*, had been of a size and complexity he had never before ventured but it had had a striking clarity, learnt at least in part from the Veronese which, painted in the 'highest key of light' and with the 'purest brilliancy of colour',[5] he had seen and admired in the Louvre. Later, struggling to compose a classical counterpart to his modern panorama, he had faced such frustrations that after a while he had turned quite yellow and grown so thin that he could pull out his waistcoat three inches from his stomach; but determined to do it or die, he had done it in the end.

'I now see my way and think I am no longer a mere maker of sketches, but an artist,'[6] Palmer had written a year into his trip. He had felt a sense of 'enlargement'[7] he said – and not just as a result of too many good dinners. He had discovered the dangers of yellows, found out how far to venture 'a good deep green' or which passage of a picture needed particular attention and which might be skimmed over with a rapid touch of the pen. Though only one known work survives from this particular period (a coloured study of the hermitage at Vocatella), it demonstrates how much he had learnt since discovering back in the studio that his *plein air* Welsh sketches were unworkable, for this delicate architectural piece is a finished drawing of the sort that he had long aimed for, 'with effect, foreground and figures quite settled'.[8] It was this type of drawing, he believed, that would be most useful to him on his return. The 'good deep greens'[9] also played a part, most notably in his studies of an ancient cypress avenue in the gardens of the Villa d'Este. As Palmer had wandered the grounds of this extravagant villa with their nymphs and their fountains, their grottoes and lakes, he had bitterly regretted not having known of them earlier. 'I have seen nothing like or second to it,'[10] he had said. In his sketches he had endowed the cypresses, towering sentinels of bygone Baroque splendours, with a grandeur quite lacking in more conventional treatments; not least that done by Linnell's acquaintance William Collins who, having met the Palmers in Rome (and passed on troublemaking gossip to the Linnells) had probably recommended the villa as a picturesque site.

Palmer had regretted the long hours wasted on helping his wife with her father's commission. 'I try only to choose in each place what seem to be the very essence and what I think it probable we may never see again in our travels,'[11] he had written as he had all but dashed along, desperately concerned to make the most of each moment. Towards the end of his trip he had been convinced that he had found a new way forward. His habits had undergone 'a complete renovation',[12] he said. And though he would still long in his heart to make one last 'humble effort after deep *sentiment* and deep *tone*',[13] he had vowed to 'make a steady effort to turn all to account'.[14] And so, at the beginning of 1840, banishing poetic dreams to a single private hour every morning, he began dedicating the rest of his working day to whatever drudgery was required to adapt old visionary tastes to the demands of the new Victorian era which had dawned with the 1838 coronation during his time away.

The Palmers had returned home with over-stuffed portfolios. 'They are twins,' Palmer had joked; 'Mrs Palmer's drawings and my own. Dear little creatures! They will I hope, support *us* instead of our having to keep *them*.'[15] Now he and Hannah, putting up a smart little brass nameplate on their door, mounted a selection of the best of these pictures before setting about grinding palettes of fresh pigments and embarking on new work.

Palmer decided to establish his reputation with a series of large, elaborately detailed, brightly coloured watercolours, which he hoped would lead on to oil commissions. Thoughtfully composed and competently executed, they are appealing enough, but they lack the atmosphere of his Shoreham pieces. Palmer was trying too hard to emulate the sort of 'light and pleasing construction' which he thought people would 'like to have on their walls'.[16] Trying too hard to please had always been one of his problems. The small yet poetic works that he had dreamt of producing in Italy, seeing how grand Titian and Domenichino could make the tiniest landscapes, never materialised. Instead his images became increasingly conventional, garishly tinted and lacking in life, as can clearly be seen in an 1845 watercolour of the Villa d'Este cypresses. The replica loses the spirit of the vivid sketch. The public was unimpressed. Nobody came to call at the Lisson Grove house. Nobody was interested in the paintings of the bright-eyed young couple who sat forgotten in their pokey studio, the pictures from their wedding trip stacked unwanted against the walls.

One of Palmer's watercolours was shown at the Royal Academy in 1840 but after that pretty much everything he sent in was rejected. The fashion for Italian views had passed: 'Italy has been painted out and out and we are weary of its splendid scenes and contemptible people,'[17] the *Athenaeum* had declared in 1833. Artists such as David Wilkie, John Frederick Lewis and David Roberts were tempting the public with more exotic scenes. The wonders of the Orient – its biblical landscapes and archaeological monuments, its Islamic domes and its vast sandy deserts, its camels and date palms and peacocks and gazelles – were now preferred. These were the marvels for which Venice had seemed only a preparation – and Palmer had not even got as far as that.

At first, the couple earned something from the sale of Linnell's engravings after their Sistine Chapel images: work by Hannah's father always fetched a good price. But Hannah's plans to make a series of ten etchings after her husband's views of Rome came to nothing and though she occasionally sold one of her copies from old master paintings, her drawings from Raphael, hung in pride of place in the Linnell family drawing room, were not so appreciated by more dispassionate observers. Sir Augustus Calcott declared them a 'very inferior and exaggerated version'[18] of their fine originals – though he probably would not have been so dismissive if he had known how much youthful energy they had cost.

Palmer's hopes fluttered briefly when his work caught the eye of Ruskin whose *Modern Painters*, first published in 1843, had made him the most famous cultural theorist of his day. He had probably been pointed in Palmer's direction by Richmond who had painted his portrait in 1842. Ruskin, who criticised the old masters for inventing their landscapes rather than studying from life, appreciated the sensitivity of Palmer's perceptions and he was probably referring to his sketches of the Villa d'Este cypresses when in an 1846 edition of *Modern Painters* he described him as 'deserving of the very highest place among the faithful followers of nature', praising in particular the fullness of his studies of 'foreign foliage'. 'His feeling is as pure and grand as his fidelity is exemplary,'[19] Ruskin wrote. But this moment of appreciation never flourished into widespread acclaim for, in 1848, the Pre-Raphaelite brotherhood was founded, a gathering of fervent young painters and poets who set out to reform art by rejecting the academic formulas of such practitioners as Sir Joshua Reynolds (whom they called Sir Sloshua) who, as they saw it, simply parodied Renaissance models. The Pre-Raphaelites advocated a return to the sort of direct observation that Palmer too admired. Their heartfelt appreciation for the early Italian and Flemish masters was not far from that which the Ancients had expressed. But the brightly coloured canvases of Dante Gabriel Rossetti,

John Everett Millais or William Holman Hunt, in which every minute detail – every petal of a meadow flower or hair of an animal, every wrinkle on the skin or embroidered stitch on a costume – is attentively picked out, far more nearly accorded with Ruskin's liking of scrupulous observation than Palmer's conceptions of poetic landscape. Palmer did not feature in Ruskin's disquisitions again.

Nothing concrete came of Palmer's time in Italy except when in March 1846, well over six years after he had returned, Charles Dickens, needing illustrations for his forthcoming travelogue *Pictures from Italy*, approached him, a planned liaison with another artist having failed. For a while the excitable Palmer must have thought that his prospects were improving. He was offered the commission. He was to receive twenty guineas – a sum agreed upon only after a flustered consultation with Linnell – to do four wood engravings similar to those used as vignette illustrations for a comparable volume: Samuel Rogers's by-then enormously popular blank verse poem *Italy* which had been illustrated by Turner and Stothard. And though an initial hitch at the publishers sent his spirits into a tailspin – 'I am weak as a rat and a spectacle to the little boys in the street as I totter along'[20] – the transaction eventually was carried through. Dickens was detached but affable. 'I beg to assure you that I would on no account dream of allowing the book to go to Press, without the insertion of your name in the title page. I placed it there, myself, two days ago,' he told Palmer who was worried that he would be sidelined. 'I have not seen the designs, but I have no doubt whatever (remembering your sketches) that they are very good.'[21]

Dickens might have been confident, but Palmer was not. Unaccustomed to working to a deadline, he soon found himself in difficulties. He couldn't make it clear to the block-cutters exactly what he wanted. His proofs were an impenetrable mess of scribbled suggestions and appeals. An awful lot of trouble was taken for the sake of four small illustrations – they show the Villa d'Este at Tivoli, the Colosseum in Rome, Pompeii's street of tombs and a vineyard scene in which the plants clamber up tree trunks like twining hop stems – and when the travelogue was republished some fifteen years later another artist was commissioned to add further images. Palmer's collaboration with

Dickens came to nothing. It was one of the great non-encounters of the nineteenth century.

————

Outside his work, however, Palmer found times of contentment, especially in those moments spent with old friends. With relations patched up with the Linnells, there was much shuttling back and forth between the two households, many pleasant evenings passed around the fire and, in the summer of 1840, Palmer and Hannah took off for Shoreham with all the Linnell children in tow. Taking rooms in a rambling old mansion, they reacquainted themselves with the pleasures of village life, enjoying long walks and feasting on mulberries, stuffing themselves with poultry and filberts and figs. 'John nearly turn'd over a rock which would have done credit to Ajax. Willy's mouth is elongated into a perpetual smile – and Lizzy is getting as fat as a butcher's wife,'[22] Palmer wrote to Linnell who, striking a characteristically thrifty bargain with the driver of a two-horse fly (whom they forced to take a detour to avoid paying the toll), soon travelled down to join them with his wife. On the return journey Linnell tried to make similarly economical arrangements, negotiating with the owner of a furniture wagon that was returning empty to London, but his wife, perhaps thinking of the gossip that such a mode of transport might arouse amid neighbours, put her foot down and firmly refused.

Palmer was delighted to be back amid his circle of fellow Ancients. Richmond by this time was living in Beaufort Street, an artistically fashionable area of the Thames embankment at Chelsea. He was never to mention or make application for the honeymoon loan and seemed surprised when, in 1844 and with Linnell's help, Palmer finally paid him back – though without the interest that had been mentioned in the initial agreement. 'He asked me if I had sold all my drawings,'[23] Palmer said. But financial disparities could not alter the warmth of the relationship between the two old friends and when Palmer sent him a note one day inviting him to come over and join him and Giles for a dinner of goose but asking him to excuse 'the roughness of things',[24] Richmond promptly replied: 'I will excuse all things *but your* asking me to excuse anything. Do you remember who lent me £40 to get married, who gave me and mine a hearty welcome and a house at Shoreham, when such a welcome and a house were most needed, and think you my dear Palmer that the kind friend who has done all this and much more is the one to ask me to excuse "the roughness of things".'[25] Over the next few years, Richmond and Palmer could be found sharing feelings on pretty much anything from the development of their painting through thoughts on new publications or passages from scripture to the progress of children. They would keep each other constantly up to date, inquiring attentively after health, congratulating each other on any successes, sympathising with losses, and consulting on everything from the purchase of a pianoforte to the colour of wallpaper.

Palmer's relationship with Richmond's wife, Julia, was particularly tender – she inviting him and Hannah to holiday with her in the country or to celebrate a wedding anniversary or share in their happiness at a daughter's betrothal. Palmer, in return, wrote attentive letters, recommending books, indulging in the sort of detailed medical discussions which would have delighted a caring mother or recounting his latest joke: 'Why is an oyster the most anomalous of animals? – Because he has a beard without a chin, and is obliged to be taken out of his bed to be tucked in.'[26] There was something almost feminine about Palmer's gentle character and Julia was the first of several women with whom he was to go on to foster warm relationships.

Palmer and his cousin Giles returned enthusiastically to their 'theological bickerings'[27] and annual Christmas reunions. Calvert, too, despite a slight frostiness caused by the fact that he had never once bothered to write to Palmer in Italy (and when confronted with this had claimed that the letter had been lost), was back in the fold. When Palmer later made a trip to the Devon haunts of Calvert's youth he was reminded of his friend every turn of the way. 'How great and important an addition to the happiness of my little life [has] been your united friendship,' he wrote to Calvert and his wife.[28] The core of the little circle of Ancients had been re-established and, though in circumstances very different from old Shoreham days – they had wives and children, 'dear young friends shooting up and spreading now like poplars and cedars'[29] – a fundamental affection remained, a source of deep happiness to the still struggling Palmer as well as more practical help whenever Richmond passed a client along.

The greatest joy of the Palmers at this period was the arrival of their first child – Thomas More Walter George – who, born in 1842 on the same date as Palmer (27 January), was named after that English Reformation martyr and 'model of Christian laymen'[30] whose image his father had once hung on his Shoreham study wall. Thomas More had been a staunch Roman Catholic but Palmer had admired him nonetheless, believing that he and his fellow saint, the blessed John Fisher, whose portrait he had also nailed up, would 'frown vice and levity'[31] out of his home. George Richmond, whose name was also encompassed in the infant's moniker, was his godfather.

Palmer, as a young man in Shoreham, had talked of the carrier's wife dropping her baby like 'a kitten into the basket', but there could be nothing so casual about Hannah's pregnancy, especially not with the neurotic Mrs Linnell about. Retiring to Thatcham in Berkshire in the summer before she gave birth, Hannah had nursed her swelling stomach in healthy rural surroundings. The peace had been as beneficial to her husband as to his still unborn son and Palmer, perhaps finding a new confidence in his coming fatherhood, had painted what at the time were considered among his better works, two of the watercolours being selected for exhibition and another, presented to Linnell in lieu of an earlier £5 loan, becoming the only one of his pictures which his father-in-law would ever deem worthy of keeping – though it may have been desired more as a memento of the period that had given him his first grandson than of the talent of the man who had painted it.

Thomas More, a tiny lace-swaddled creature, would become the repository of a hundred ardent hopes. And yet, for all the happiness that he brought, he added to his parents' already significant financial concerns. 'It is more difficult at present to get than to save,'[32] Palmer had noted in his first year back from Italy and, hoping to tide things over until trade picked up, he had sedulously set about making personal savings, giving up snuff and sugar in his tea, rationing butter and soap

and limiting himself – and the 'great reads' of which he had spoken so
longingly in Italy – to two candles a night. But still, the money would
not stretch. The Palmers were pushed into making embarrassing economies when, after Palmer's father had taken back the furniture which he
had lent them, they were forced to trawl through the then famously
shoddy Wardour Street stores. Hannah wrote to her father afterwards
asking him not to mention this little spree to one of their cousins who
knew the Richmonds. 'To Mr Richmond it is not well to confess yourself obliged to be economical,' she explained.[33]

Meanwhile, Richmond consulted Palmer about whether or not he
should move his practice to grander London premises. His friend
offered his customarily frank advice. 'A large house in the central part
of the West End would leave you not a moment to yourself,' he discouraged; 'it would become the resort of a host of acquaintance – and you
– however unwittingly – would go the round of fashionable visiting
and late hours.'[34] Palmer did not crave the society artist's life – which
was just as well for it was not within his reach. His domestic circumstances only worsened when his father decided that he wanted to move
back in with them. The Palmers, in Italy, had envisioned this happening and had considered it a bonus in so far as it would have meant that
they could share the cost of a servant. What they had not foreseen was
that, by the time the old man eventually decided to come, he would
have been stripped of his annual stipend. The long-suffering Nathanial
had at last had enough and Palmer's father had been reduced to selling
his piano and books to pay his bills. For a while, Palmer tried to
persuade his parent to lodge with a sister in Margate, but accused by
this sister of neglecting his filial duties, he had been forced to capitu-
late. His father moved into Grove Street which meant that the couple
not only had to start paying for extra domestic help but give up their
long-planned painting studio to provide him with a room.

Palmer, as usual, turned to Linnell asking him for help in securing
his father a situation first in the newly founded London Library and
afterwards in the British Museum where, he felt sure, there would be
posts to suit. His reprobate brother William might at this point have
helped. He had worked there himself. But he was not around, having

indeed, as Palmer had requested, cleared out by the time that the honeymooners had returned – though not before pawning all the paintings that Palmer had entrusted to his care. Palmer had got back to Grove Street to find that all of the works which he had asked to be so carefully stored were in hock, owing, a pathetic letter from his brother informed him, to 'illness and other unlooked for exigencies' that had placed him in 'circumstances of perplexity and distress'.[35] It may have been at this time that William also purloined one of Blake's notebooks from his brother. He was to sell it to Rossetti in 1847 for the sum of half a guinea telling the buyer that it had been a gift from Blake although, given his devious inclinations, it seems more likely that he had stolen it from Palmer. And though William had promised ardently to redeem his brother's pawned works (he had hoped to do so before Palmer's return, he said) it had been left to Palmer to pay the nine pounds one shilling and eight pence while William, who by then had been contemplating an emigration to New Zealand, had kept his profile low.

Just when Palmer's family situation was beginning to look impossible, he received a letter from his father informing him that he had wed. The bride was a Mrs Mary Cutter, a forty-eight-year-old silk weaver who owned her own business and was, according to one report, good-looking, refined and intelligent to boot. She had a clergyman brother who, as a prolific author, would have shared the literary interests of old Palmer and, even more importantly, she had her own home: a large top floor which she shared with a great, bulky loom. 'The access to it is uninviting and the whole is mean, but she is a prize,'[36] records a scribbled memorandum found among Palmer's papers. The stubborn and unpredictable old man might, once again, have abased the family reputation by associating with trade, but the news came as a relief to his son. 'I can only declare that I ever have desired and do most heartily desire your welfare and happiness,'[37] he wrote in a dumbfounded letter, having just been appraised of this development.

Watercolour pigment has been used as a medium for sketching for hundreds of years but it was only during the last decades of the

eighteenth century that artists started to explore its possibilities more
fully. They discovered that by using washes of colour rather than line
alone, by creating texture and depth through scraping and sponging
and rubbing with breadcrumbs, they could turn a tinted drawing into
the sort of complex work considered worthy of appreciation in its own
right. It would be a long time, however, before such pictures gained
proper recognition. As far as the Royal Academy was concerned, oil was
the only medium to work in and when some luminous little watercolour landscape slipped into the summer show, it would more often than
not be occluded by a flashy oil drama or hung to least advantage in
some dingy anteroom.

In 1804 the Society of Painters in Watercolours had been founded to
give watercolourists a higher professional standing and, in 1805, it had
staged its first public show. By 1807, it had become known as the Old
Watercolour Society after a rival organisation – the Associated Artists
in Watercolour – had been set up. Both did much to establish a new
respect for the medium and even though Turner, its most accomplished
exponent, could not join for he, as an Academician, was precluded
from becoming a member of other institutions, the balance of opinion
was beginning to swing.

Palmer, as an ambitious young man, had dreamt of success as a
painter in oils. In the early 1840s he began work on a glowing panel
The Rising of the Skylark which, based on a sepia sketch of a much
earlier date (and followed some time afterwards by an etching bearing
the same title) was painted '*con amore* in the superlative degree'.[38] He
infused the oil-painted image with his undiminished sense of nature's
poetry. It is not hard to believe, as Palmer himself later did, that with a
little help at this critical moment he might have been put on the path
to being recognised. But neither this little panel nor his (now lost) *Job's
Sacrifice*, also done at this time, met with any encouragement. It must
have been galling – especially when his father-in-law was attracting
high praise for his own biblical works.

Discouraged, Palmer turned more and more often to watercolour
and, in 1843, his career as an artist in this medium was finally determined when he was made an associate of the Old Watercolour Society.

Once he had envisaged such a membership as a mere fall-back position, but by the time that he was finally elected, he was overjoyed. He wrote to the secretary of his 'deep sense of honour'.[39] At last, he had received some professional recognition. He would be joining the society of such admired forebears as David Cox and Peter DeWint, as well as that of his fellow Ancient, Finch.

The joy – and relief – of his election was further enhanced by a sale of a watercolour for £30 to the Art Union, an organisation which, founded in 1837 to foster an interest in the fine arts, required members to pay a guinea a year as a subscription fee in return for which they would receive an engraving. The funds which the Art Union accrued were spent on the purchase of art considered of merit. Palmer relished this mark of appreciation as much as the cash. But Linnell, revealing the cruel streak in his character that would glint ever more fiercely as time went on, dispatched a taunting message to his son-in-law. 'S.P.U.R.I.C. to B P.S.P.W.C . . . U but and ME it is all fiddle DD; I.O.U. no N.V.' This is to be interpreted: 'SP you are I see to be President of the Society of Painters in Watercolour. But between you and me it is all fiddle-de-dee. I owe you no envy.'[40]

Unfortunately, Linnell was before long proved right. Palmer's election caused no more than a passing ripple in the proceedings of the society. The work of the members was too disparate. The intricate little birds' nests of William Henry Hunt, the prettified peasants of Miles Birket Foster, the exotic foreign landscapes of John Frederick Lewis, were all too different one from the other to launch any concerted assault on critical tastes. A reviewer in the *Spectator* suspended his verdict the first time he saw Palmer's work in the society's annual exhibition. The fiery sunsets were so crude, he said, that it would be better to wait until the following year to pass judgement. Palmer sold only three of his quota of eight paintings, and those to a neighbour of Linnell's. The next year when the critic returned he decided that though Palmer was ambitious and had an eye for colour, the sky with its radiant sunsets was the only good part of the picture. The artist, he concluded, was too unskilled to achieve the poetic effects at which he aimed. And although in succeeding years the works which Palmer exhibited were described as 'dazzling' or 'too clever and original-looking to be overlooked', over-looked is exactly what they were in the end. Palmer's initial burst of optimism slowly fizzled out, leaving only the dull ashes of a dogged determination that would carry him onwards through the decade that he would then have to wait before being elected a full member, rather than a mere associate, of the Society.

The prices fetched by watercolours seldom reflected the hours that went into their making. Palmer needed to supplement his income. In 1843 he returned to teaching. Linnell encouraged him. It was better than pot-boiling, he said: churning out 'cheap pennyworths of Art'[41] that would only degrade his talent. Richmond, employing Palmer to instruct his own daughters, was quick to recommend him and Linnell, likewise, introduced him to moneyed patrons. Palmer's election to the Old Watercolour Society would also have helped: indeed, the very day that he was informed of it, Lady Stephen (the wife of a successful banker and prolific author who had helped Linnell to sort out the deceased Blake's affairs and later sat to him for a portrait) inquired whether he was a member before asking him to come round and give lessons twice a week. It was the start of an acquaintanceship involving repeated and pressing invitations to come and stay with the family in Dorset – invitations which Hannah persistently, and at the risk of real rudeness, refused. She was reluc-tant to leave her precious baby in some far-off nursery while she sat trapped politely in the drawing room.

For most of Palmer's pupils, painting was merely part of a reper-toire of desirable accomplishments. They had no real feeling for their subjects, he said, and in nine cases out of ten simply wanted some fine touched-up drawings for public show. 'A good bold quack with plenty of tact, a comely presence, and well-cut Hoby boots, would beat any real artist out of the field as a teacher,'[42] he declared, telling the story of how Turner, when he had tried his hand at instruction, had been discharged for incompetence. And yet Palmer was popular. He was a patient, attentive and – when he came across a student who was prepared to 'take pains', to produce proper studies instead of 'a parcel of half-studied fragments'[43] – a passionate teacher who believed that, if his pupils did not master the basic grammar of drawing, they would 'come out as like each other mentally, as a batch of rolls out of the oven'.[44]

He would prepare a drawing while his young protégées looked on, explaining his methods and encouraging them to take notes so that in their next lesson they could imitate his model. Sometimes they would draw from portrait busts or plaster models and, in spring, when the weeds in his ill-kempt Grove Street garden shot up lush and green, he would fling open his windows and teach drawing from nature. Over time he fostered some lasting acquaintanceships with his pupils, most notably with a Miss Louisa Twining, a member of the tea-growing family, and with a neighbour, Miss Wilkinson, who lent him her copy of *The Times* every day. His relationship with these women was to continue for years and he was also to grow very close to Laura and Julia, the two Richmond girls.

Palmer was an assiduous taskmaster. 'All who draw from Nature must be exact,' he said. 'I would rather see young people play at marbles [than pursue an inexact education] – for there they do manage to be exact as they can – and so far it is a true educational exercise.' To turn the pages of a small, bound sketchbook in the Ashmolean, is to sit quietly in on one of Palmer's lessons. Here is page after page of anno- tated sketches, of neatly pencilled notes on light and shade, outline and form. Here are lists of recommended colours and recipes for combining them to make tints; suggestions as to how to layer these tints on paper and advice on capturing distances, sunsets and the 'EXPRESSION' of nature. Palmer's correspondence with Louisa Twining constitutes among the most detailed and lively expositions of an artist's technique. 'Take hot-pressed *thickest* imperial [paper],' he tells her. 'Put bistre into a *swan pinion* . . . and outline firmly . . . Keep on refreshing your ink outline as you go on . . . When you use heightening lights, on a tree already painted for instance, do the lights first, delicately and sharply with white; when dry add the colour . . . No scrubbing and fumbling with colour dried hard,' he admonishes. 'Until a vituperative dictionary is published, I can't tell where to find any epithet vile enough to hit this kind of work.'[45] He would treat each pupil as an individual. 'You are the only lady to whom I should recommend *dashing*, but I advise you to *dash* at these,' he instructs Miss Twining. 'Turn your swan pen into an anchor and then be bold . . . sometimes painting with your brush, then with your fingers. With his finger, they say, Titian put his last finish; it is a wonderful instrument.'[46] Palmer himself would certainly use his own: as he fought to capture waves smashing against Cornish rocks, his prints appeared amid the boiling spray.

In her memoirs, Miss Twining recalled his lessons with the greatest pleasure, remembering how his 'original and striking conversation' would be mixed with 'the profoundest rules and directions concerning art'.[47] She went on to become a prominent philanthropist and campaigning reformer who published books and pamphlets, several of which she would send to Palmer. The conversations he enjoyed both with her and with Miss Wilkinson ventured far beyond painting to encompass anything from the methods of poorhouse schooling through artistic discoveries ('Beware of the notion that shadows cannot be cast *upon* water . . . I lately saw the shadow of a pier cast upon the sea, and its colour thereby totally altered by losing the warm sunlight'[48]) to the prevention of sunstroke. They continued to exchange letters and pay occasional visits late into his life. His relationship with young Julia Richmond was even more established. As he watched her grow up and get married and have children of her own, an open and affectionate correspondence continued which ranged from music and poetry to personal anecdotes, from fun-poking disquisitions on the frivolities of women to fussing imprecations not to sit in wet shoes.

Over the years, Palmer's teaching practice expanded and he may even for a while have teamed up with a figure-drawing instructor, Miss Meakin, who seems to have lodged for a time with the Palmers or, at least, given their home as her accommodation address. All his former pupils – except for members of a certain Campbell family whom, after they left off coming to him, he avoided with exaggerated tact for fear that they might think he was touting for business – returned to him again and again. His system of payments was eccentrically complicated, his charges varying from one guinea for two-and-a-half hours to ten shillings and sixpence an hour if less time was required, unless the teaching took place in his home when he asked for only seven shillings. He worried about what he should charge such wealthy clients as the Duke of Buccleugh, who expected him to travel to their country estates, and, with habitual indecision, he had to consult Linnell.

For many years, teaching would provide Palmer with his main source of income. Though he sometimes longed to abandon it – 'if I could but stand the loss of the first disentanglement . . . I think it would be a hundred times overpaid'[49] he declared – he could not make that first break for, however meagre the end-of-season sums may have been, they were all that lay between him and the humiliating handouts of his father-in-law.

———

Teaching duties kept Palmer in London long into the summer, when the capital sweltered in a miasma of filth. 'What use I could have made in the country of these three weeks of fine weather!'[50] he cried in an 1847 letter to his wife. As he threw up his window sashes, gazing out hopelessly at a patch of withering grass, he must have longed to be tramping the wild landscapes of England. He would take a brief sketching tour almost every year, sometimes in the height of the summer and sometimes in early autumn. He always went south, far preferring 'dear old spongey Devon',[51] that 'loveliest of lands'[52] to the dramatic austerities of the windswept north. He preferred 'the ancient granges and manor houses which are to me the gems of England . . . the grand large cottages (for grand they are) . . . buttressed with stone and ribbed with heart of oak' to a good many Loch Lomonds with their 'lumpish mountains and leaden lakes'.[53] Palmer visited Wales in October 1843, Guildford the following year and Princes Risborough in Buckinghamshire the year after that. August 1846 was passed in Margate; in the summers of 1848 and 1849 he travelled again to the West Country and, throughout the late 1850s, he would repeatedly return.

Palmer was thorough in his explorations. He scrambled about with a guidebook always to hand for fear that without it he might miss a fine sight – he recommended John Murray's because 'it is written by an artist and has a real savour of Devonshire Perception'.[54] All the best things, he believed, lay hidden in chinks and combes; to find them, he said, it was essential to walk, to get as close as possible to the edges of cliffs and brows of hills. Those who lease out the carriages, he warned, tended to get set down on the wrong side of the chasm, to be left 'gaping at the opposite cliff – while the real spectacle is what they are standing upon' and usually strewn, he added, with 'Pic Nic bottles and broken plates'.[55]

His sketching trips were a vital source of refreshment. 'I can *begin* my subjects . . . in London,' he told Hannah, 'but when *Italian* weather sets in I should like to get out of town directly, if it were only for a week . . . The weather from which I get my subjects and my suggestions for the remainder of the year is that dazzling weather when all the air seems trembling with little motes. A week of that is, to me, worth three months of ordinary fine weather. It is then I see real sunsets and twilights.'[56]

Where other artists travelled in luxury with well-stocked portmanteaus and elaborate painting boxes, Palmer took only what he could carry by hand. He liked to tell his pupils the story of Turner who, to the list of implements he needed, would add 'myself', wisely knowing, Palmer said, 'that it was better to forget some of his colours than not take the whole man to the work'.[57] Donning his plainest clothes, a broad-brimmed hat to protect him from rain or sun and heavy hobnailed boots for the steep mountain tracks, he would slip a tin box of spare pigments, an old campstool and his lunch or dinner into a wicker hand basket. A capacious sketching portfolio (big enough to carry a good supply of paper, together with two large but very light wooden palettes) would be slung round his shoulders by a large strap. Everything else went into one of the accumulation of pockets in which were stowed away the 'all-important snuff-box', knives, chalks, charcoal, coloured crayons, sketchbooks, water bottle, poetry book, diminishing mirror and a pair of 'large, round, neutral-tint spectacles made for near sight'.[58] Little wonder that, waddling about with all these encumbrances, he got mistaken for a pedlar by a pair of fellow artists, Richard Redgrave and Charles West Cope, future friends who first came across him one evening at an inn in Wales.

To look at his 1847 *Gypsy Dell by Moonlight*, its ragged travellers huddling about their bright fire while the darkness gathers around them and a barn owl glides from the rocks, is to suspect that Palmer is not merely appealing to a then popular taste for pictures of travelling folk which the painter Francis Topham had turned into a fashionable speciality, but remembering his own happy days as a roamer, whether wandering free over the hills of Shoreham or clambering the shaggy moors of the West. 'In exploring wild country I have been for a fortnight together uncertain each day whether I shall get a bed under cover at night; and about midsummer I have repeatedly been walking all night to watch the mystic phenomena of the silent hours,'[59] Palmer wrote. He revelled in his precious weeks of freedom, sheltering out on the hills in a rough shepherd's hut; disembarking at a lonely little cove near Clovelly, his shoes filling with water as he leapt from the boat; getting trapped by the tide in a cavern at Kynance as (rather like Turner who had lain down at Land's End so that he could look up at the rock face) he scrambled under a cliff to find the right sketching point; or lying unclothed in bed while his rain-drenched garments dried over the kitchen fire of an inn. Little wonder that so often he caught dreadful colds.

This socially inept little man felt far more at ease scrambling about in the mountains than negotiating the pinnacles of London society. He felt quite at home as, guided only by the sound of the torrent, he clambered down a Welsh rock face at dusk or joined the evening gossipers in the chimney corner of a hostelry. He would sit as the villagers smoked peacefully over their tankards, or join them eating their pilchard pies 'clouted' with clotted cream. He would chat to a landlady in the kitchen one evening as she milked the goat; or scratch the pigs that snubbed about in the yard. Such scratching seemed to the animals, he observed, 'a pleasure equivalent to honours among mankind'.[60] And when one week in Wales the weather was particularly wild, he walled up by a fire, reading his way straight through a seven-volume edition of Samuel Richardson's *The History of Sir Charles Grandison* for the second time.

Palmer would return to London laden with work: with the sort of broad landscape sketches that he had learnt to do in Italy, with crayon studies of dawns and sunsets and twilights; views of wheat fields and coastlines and mountains and farmyards; studies of foliage and wild-flowers, rustic cottages and ancient machinery. These would be worked up into the elaborately composed landscapes that, throughout the 1840s, he continued to produce. But they, like the Italian compositions that he worked on simultaneously, had little success. His admiration for nature was undiminished, but he had lost his idiosyncratic panache. The rich glow that used to illuminate his images was replaced by a superficial garishness. His handling had grown increasingly conven-tional. He had sacrificed personal vision for a fashionable style that he hoped would please.

With growing desperation, Palmer tried to identify the causes of his failure. His energies were dissipated in endless theorising, diffused in the slew of notes that he accumulated in a portfolio labelled 'Written Memoranda' in which, like some mad secretary taking minutes at a meeting between an artist and his subject, he tried to record on paper every difficulty of composition and design. The world's natural phenom-ena were boiled down into columns and bullet points and lists and laws. But it did no good. In the decade that followed the birth of his son in 1842, Palmer, according to his accounts, sold some forty-five pictures for an average price of around £16 each. This was simply not enough to support a family and, in one letter to Linnell, he confessed that he had 'only one sovereign in the house – most of which will be paid away today'.[61] Hannah could not help. As her work was again and again rejected, her hopes declined apace. The once-spirited little redhead turned picture after picture face to the wall.

———

In 1844, Hannah gave birth to her second child, a grey-eyed girl who was christened Mary Elizabeth. Family life offered the Palmers some consolation for the loss of their once cherished vision – of husband and wife working away busily in a peaceably shared studio, he stretching the canvases, she grinding colours, while some bright little maid made their beds and boiled the dinner potatoes. Palmer would read aloud to his wife in the evenings and in 1848, away on a sketching trip, he wrote to tell her how greatly she was missed. 'Your charms my dear Annie are no weak inducement to lure me back,' he pined. 'To me you are fairer than at 17 and though by this time I have got pretty well used to your scolding your love is always fresh and always precious. I hope to prove myself worthy of it by renewed exertions in Art.'[62]

In Italy, Palmer had felt himself a manly figure, protecting his pretty young wife from the improper advances of impudent Neapolitans, beating off a wild cow in the Roman *campagna* with his sketchbook and confronting a furious knife-wielding landlord with aplomb. Now, he found himself unable to provide properly for his family. And, as Anny finally abandoned her artistic aspirations, and with them the engagement with painterly problems which would have led to a sympathy with her husband's plight, she began to turn more and more to her parents. Linnell became an increasingly overbearing presence in his son-in-law's life. On top of this, Palmer's health was not good. 'The filthy coal pit of London'[63] aggravated his asthma, leaving him debilitated, wheezing and weak. The man who had used to stride lonely hills by moonlight would no longer go out and deliver a letter of an evening in London because he was fearful of catching a cold.

Financial anxieties strained Palmer further. Turning his problems over and over in his head, he was all but incapable of making decisions. He continued to consult Linnell on everything, from how much he should charge for his services as a teacher to which doctor he should hire to attend on his children. At one point, Linnell took it upon himself to go behind Palmer's back to John Giles and ask him directly how Palmer's finances stood: Giles was persuaded to impart some information, though later wrote refusing to disclose anything further and expressing regret that he had already told so much. This stand against his authority must have taken Linnell aback for, more usually, when god-like he dispensed money or advice, it was received with tail-wagging gratitude by his son-in-law. Meanwhile his adoring daughter seemed almost to have equated him with a divinity. Writing to thank him for funding a recuperative trip to Margate for her and her son, who had both been ill, she declared the improvement in their healths 'a great blessing for which I feel a great thankfulness to God and to you for so kindly helping us to procure it'.[64]

A new low point in Palmer's career came in 1846 when an art dealer called round to Grove Street full of extraordinary professions of indifference as to buying. He could only be persuaded to stretch his humiliatingly low offers for Palmer's paintings when he learnt that Linnell had had a hand in retouching a few. Instead of feeling mortified, Palmer wrote gratefully to his father-in-law. With an 'hour or two of your skill on the Ponte Rotto', he told him, that painting too might also sell.[65]

───────

As Palmer watched his ambitions grow increasingly improbable, he laid more and more store in the future of his son and set about trying to turn him into a paradigm of religious piety, of diligence, learning and devotion, of filial obedience and moral rectitude. His dreams were to become a heavy burden on the delicate young boy.

Palmer was a devoted father. He would carry Thomas More around the city on his shoulders, hoisting him even higher when he wanted to see above a crowd; take him on day trips to Primrose Hill to drink tea; invite him into his study and show him how to draw, teach him his alphabet from a big box of letters or how to play the piano by putting his fingers on the keys. Often he would read to him from his own favourite volumes so that the cadences of Blake's *Songs of Innocence* were interwoven with More's earliest memories and by the age of five he had learnt *The Lord is my Shepherd* by heart.

More was not yet three years old when he received the first of the many letters that his father was to write to him. Palmer sent it from Guildford. 'I went so fast in the steam coach!' he wrote. 'How you would like it! Here are high hills and the birds sing in the trees.' 'Who loves Thomas More?' he asked at the end of the letter. 'PAPA!' came the answer in capital letters.[66] Palmer was attuned to a child's imagination. He knew how to select the stories that would most delight his son and often added illustrations to the margins of his letters. He sketched a fair that he had seen in Surrey, telling his son of its 'little men not so high as the table . . . and men without arms that could hold a pen between their toes . . . and a learned pig that knew his letters'.[67] He dispatched missives from purple moors where, had his son been there, he said, he would have lain down to roll in the heather; or from sandy beaches in which he would have loved to dig. He wrote from a pier from which a little girl had just taken a six-foot tumble without breaking anything (though More, who was delicate, had just broken his leg by tripping in the hall); and from landscapes which had once been trodden by a race of giants. Their bones could still be dug up from the soil, Palmer said. His descriptions could be wonderfully vivid. 'I wish you were here,' he wrote from a rocky promontory, 'although you would really be frightened to look down from these savage rocks at the foam of the sea far beneath dashing against them. For some moments perhaps the waters are sucked into a black cavern, and then forced out again in a cloud of white foam with a deep growl like thunder.'[68]

Palmer greatly missed his son when they were apart. He tried to keep up their lessons. Transcribing two bars of music, he instructed More to: 'place your thumb upon C' and 'play slowly'.[69] He told him to shut his eyes when his face was being washed so that the soap wouldn't sting. He explained how italics work – 'read the slanting words a little more loudly than the rest'[70] – and, having sent a postscript requesting him to send a kiss to his little sister, he remembered to tell him: 'P.S. means "Post Scriptum – or after written".'[71] As the boy grew older he began to respond, sending his father drawings – 'I think the man sitting upon the coach box is the best you have done'[72] Palmer praised – and then, at the age of six, his first letter. And yet, for all his manifest tenderness, Palmer never passed over an opportunity for moral instruction. It began in his very first letter when More was instructed to: 'Ask GOD to make you a good boy,'[73] and it never stopped from that point on. A lively description of a travelling fair with its mermaid woman and fiery lynx was spoiled by what, even in an era of Victorian values, must have sounded a death knell to joy. People come from as far as fifteen miles to enjoy the fair, Palmer wrote, 'but I think that is silly because it takes up

so much of their time. I think we should spend our time in doing
things that are useful – in learning to *make* things – being careful not
to break them – and we should try to be very good and wise.'[74] The
moral hectoring seldom let up. 'The way to become Good is to pray to
the Good and Blessed God to make you good,'[75] he informed two-year-
old More. 'Talk to your Mamma about the Holy Child Jesus,' he
instructed him when he was three. 'You should try most of all to be
good at those times when you feel inclined to be naughty,'[76] he told
him. 'My dear boy pray daily to the blessed Jesus to make you something like what He was when He was the same age as you.'[77]

Anything could provide the excuse for a sermon: a walk to a cliff
edge was fodder for a grim meditation upon the end of the world and
the loss of a tooth, in exchange for which More had been given a book,
the starting point of a lecture on loss and gain. The letters stacked up
into a weighty burden of advice. It was not unusual for the period.
Nursery stories of that era were heavily freighted and often frightening
to boot. Anna Laetitia Barbauld's *Lessons for Children* was among More's
bedtime books. He knew the tale of the little lamb that, not liking to
be penned up at night, had ignored its mother's warnings and stayed
out after dark to play. The wolf had come along, carrying the errant
creature away to 'a dismal dark den all covered with blood and bones'[78]
to feed it to her cubs.

Palmer's attitude to his son's education was similarly unsparing. 'As
you read every day with your Mother I shall expect to find you improved
when I return – therefore *take pains* or I shall be sadly disappointed,'[79]
he wrote in 1845. Even as More was learning to read – and he was told
to read very clearly attending to punctuation – it was suggested that he
should also try to write; as soon as he could write well enough to send
his father a letter he was being pushed to embark on a journal – a
journal that, moreover, he ought to keep up every day. As soon he had
mastered his own lessons, More was enjoined to start instructing his
little sister, passing on to her everything that he had himself been
taught. First he was simply asked to show her the alphabet – 'play at
PEEP BO with the letters',[80] Palmer suggested – but soon he was
expected to teach her also the errors of naughtiness. Next Palmer

instructed More that he must look after his mother as well, to be kind and take care of her when she was ill. 'What a high ladder is that of Christian perfection!' Palmer had declared;[81] his poor son was placed on the first rung and set struggling to get to its top.

A similarly narrow path was being prepared for little Mary. She was barely three when Palmer wrote to her brother who was holidaying at the seaside: 'Tell Mary that I love her dearly and that when you dig a grave, a deep wide grave in the sands, she must help you to bury the giant Naughtiness.'[82]

The family had gone to Margate for the sake of More who was a sickly child, but it was the strong little Mary who, a short while after their return, fell desperately ill. 'What would you do if you were in my case?' Palmer wrote frantically to Linnell. He was in a state of 'horrible perplexity' about the incompetence and high fees of the pair of doctors attending. They offered conflicting opinions. One told Palmer that if his daughter managed to live through the next twenty-four hours, she might get through her illness. But 'I am cut to the heart to see how they have begun,' Palmer wrote, for the little girl had spent a sleepless night, coughing incessantly. The other doctor assured him that the girl would recover: 'But how comes it then that the old cough has returned with redoubled violence?' the stricken father asked. 'Every cough is a dagger to me,'[83] he wrote. Palmer had tried to turn his Lisson Grove study into an artistic haven, decorating it with paintings and etchings and classical busts, but none of these could mean anything now. Cancelling a work trip, even though the doctor had told him that it would be fine to go, he sat in a torment of anxiety. 'I EARNESTLY trust Mrs Linnell will be able to see us today – I have sent for both doctors – I remain in an agony of distress,'[84] he wrote.

'*Could* Mrs Linnell do us the great kindness of coming *immediately?*' a panicking Palmer implored. 'Dr Mackenzie gave 6 drops of laudanum last night which Anny thinks has caused the sad state of Dear Mary this morning – We have both with one consent – dismissed Dr Mackenzie and depend up Dr Mackintyre – but alas I fear too late.'[85]

The last words of the letter are almost illegible. Palmer was distraught. And though his earnestly awaited mother-in-law did eventually arrive, she was too late to help. 'My dear daughter Mary Elizabeth *died* at 25 minutes to 6 p.m.,' he recorded on 15 December 1847. 'She was three years and nine months old.'

Eleven days later, Palmer recounted the details. 'Her mother was sitting at the end of the bed when Mrs Linnell said "I think she is gone." Anny put her face close to Mary's, but could hear no sound of breathing. Her eyes were open and fixed, but her face turned deadly pale . . . SHE WAS DEAD. Mrs Linnell closed her eyes. The last I saw of her dear grey eyes was in the afternoon, when I watched them. The lids closing a little over them made it seem like a mournful and clouded sunset. She had appeared for the most part unconscious for two or three days, but on the morning of the day she died Anny was going to bed, when she held up one trembling arm and then the other. Anny put her head down between them, when she held her tightly round the neck for about a minute, and seemed to be thus taking a last leave of her mother. She had done so to me about two days before.'[86]

Palmer and his cousin Giles were there when Mary was buried in All Saints' Cemetery, a peaceful private burial ground in Nunhead in the then still undeveloped outreaches of Camberwell, where mourners could wander among neoclassical monuments, along meandering paths overlooking leafy views. 'It was not until some time after dear Mary's death that we had any notion as to the cause of her illness,' Hannah would much later write. 'The doctors could not understand the seizure, and asked several times if we knew of her having swallowed anything. At the time the questions were *asked* we did *not* know – but afterwards dear More remembered having seen his dear Sister suck (when playing in the field adjoining the house) a poisonous weed which when the stalk is broke yields a fluid which looks exactly like milk.'[87] It is possible that Mary had found a Euphorbia, the milky latex of which is an extreme irritant, blistering skin and burning the throat if even its fumes are inhaled. When ingested, it can lead to death, especially in a young child. Post-mortem examinations of victims have revealed severe inflammation, and sometimes even perforation, of the stomach wall.

Palmer felt completely defeated. As he bent over his paintings or sat through his teaching engagements, his eyes would blear over and his voice start to choke as memories of his golden-haired daughter drifted through his head.

The Years of Disillusion

O! this grinding world
from *The Letters of Samuel Palmer*

'Life,' said the erstwhile mariner, Edward Calvert, 'is like the deck of a battle ship in action – there is no knowing who will go next.'[1] After the death of Mary, Palmer's old friend came round to Grove Street every evening to keep him company in his grief. 'Bitterest anguish would have been less bearable but for your . . . sympathy and vividly remembered kindness,'[2] Palmer would later write. He mourned the loss of his 'dear sweet'[3] girl. 'Words of comfort sound very hollow,' he wrote three years later to Richmond when he also lost a baby daughter. 'The blow has fallen; the affections are lacerated,' the 'wisest words' can only be 'miserable comforters'.[4]

But if Palmer was left desolate, it was even worse for his wife. She desperately gathered every last relic of her lost child, stitching a cushion cover from her baby clothes, caressing the casts that had been made of her tiny hands and feet. Sorting through every fragment that would bear testimony to her daughter's brief life, she turned up a letter from her husband. 'If Mary is going to be naughty,' he had instructed More, 'call out "Mary take care of the wolf!"'[5] 'I cannot remember one single instance in which dear Mary shewed any disposition to be "naughty". She was most loving and kind to everyone,'[6] Hannah scribbled in the margin. Private recriminations may have followed this loss.

———

For the sorrowing parents, every room of Grove Street was haunted by memories. They no longer wished to live there and, within a few months, decided to make a new start. It would be as good for the family's health as it would be for his profession, thought Palmer, for Lisson Grove with its damp clay soil and disreputable neighbours was becoming an increasingly insalubrious place and soon he was consulting Linnell on a cottage in Kensington that he and Hannah were hoping to rent.

Kensington in those days was still separate from the capital. An outlying town that had grown up in the seventeenth century around the palace to which William III had decamped because of his asthma, it had long been considered a desirable spot, and though by the time the Palmers moved there it was already far from rural, it still remained pleasantly peaceful in parts – its quiet lanes lined by little wooden fences, its cottages pretty and its gardens lush. In March 1848, the Palmers moved into Number 1A, Victoria Road, a picturesque if rather rickety dwelling with a thatched roof, uneven floors that threatened to collapse into the cellar and a garden which boasted its own apple tree. A few minutes' walk away were Kensington Gardens which, with their gently lilting pastures, their calm ponds and spreading trees, offered a far better apology for the country than what Palmer had described as the 'dank' and 'consumptive'[7] Regent's Park. These would provide not only a good sketching spot but a pleasant place for Hannah to wander and a fine playground for the six-year-old More.

'I look out of the window – several birds are singing – the sun shines so brightly upon the slates – and the white houses look as virtuous as Vesta,'[8] an uplifted Palmer told Julia Richmond a few months after moving. 'I sit and think of you every morning under the cedars in Kensington Gardens,' Hannah wrote fondly to her father. 'The sheep [are] so tame that they come all round us and the birds sing gloriously overhead. I take my work and my camp stool and we are out 3 hours every morning.'[9] But just as the Palmers on honeymoon in Italy had greeted every new staging post with panegyrics of delight before finding only too quickly that its novelties had palled, within a few months of moving neither of them was feeling so cheerful and Palmer was subsiding into one of his periodic glooms.

A cholera epidemic which had swept across Europe finally broke out in this leafy London borough. Inhabitants were warned not to wander along the Serpentine. 'Noxious effluvia' were 'reeking from its lovely ripples',[10] Palmer said. Hannah and More, fortunately, were away holidaying in Balcombe but the fearful Palmer hastily equipped himself with a medicine to be administered at the first hint of a symptom. Consisting of opium, fennel and black pepper compressed into a tablet to be crumbled or chewed with a tablespoon of brandy or water, it sounds an improbable prophylactic, not least when accompanied by tight ligatures of tape tied just above the knees and elbows to prevent the blood from rushing to the extremities; but the father of his friend Charles West Cope (one of the artists whom Palmer had first met in Wales) had apparently been saved in this way.

Palmer's anxieties mounted. 'How the gratings smell tonight,' he informed the perennially sympathetic Julia Richmond as he sat down to reply to an invitation she had sent him that evening. 'The drains in London are of themselves enough to breed a plague.' And, if the prospect of a deadly epidemic was not bad enough, he whipped up more worries, fretting over the health of a society in which crime had 'reached its ackme': 'women in Essex [were] murdering their husbands by wholesale' and an eight-year-old boy had dispatched his little sister, neatly tidying away his instruments before his mother came home.[11] Palmer had clearly been brooding over lurid newspaper reports. But the next day, as he finished his letter to Julia, the morning had dawned bright and clear and he laughed at his morbidity of the previous night.

His other problems, however, were less easily solved. He felt, he said, 'MISERABLY HAMPERED' by his duties.[12] Whenever he tried to get away to the country, 'some horrid teaching engagement' would 'snare him by the leg'.[13] How could the omnibus office at Paddington be compared with Devon's Mount Edgecombe, or the Kilburn Road with the 'thunder fraught' Hamoaze (the estuary of the Tamar)? he wondered.[14] The warm weather that delighted those holidaying in the country seemed to him, stuck in the capital, more like a glaring and uncomfortable heat.

'I must, D.V. [*Deus Vult* or *Deo Volente* meaning 'God willing' is a medieval acronym that peppers Palmer's letters and notes] strike out at once into a NEW STYLE. SIMPLE SUBJECT; BOLD EFFECT; BROAD RAPID EXECUTION,'[15] he resolved after a sketching trip in 1847. From the late 1840s a new energy infused his work. He visited King Arthur's Castle at Tintagel: a huge bluff of 'tumbled about'[16] rock that Turner in 1815 had painted, assaulted by powerful shipwrecking storms. Discovering a little hut in which he could shelter, he sketched the rocky masses heaving upwards like waves against his horizon; a sudden rainy squall blowing across the slopes, tossing glittering seagulls and fragments of light.

Palmer also embarked around this time on a series of literary scenes. He painted the departure of Ulysses from the sea-nymph Calypso's rocky home: their sad farewell set against the sinking sun's gold. He depicted Christian's descent into the Valley of Humiliation: a lowering drama that discovers a lone hero on the brink of his greatest battle. Accounting meticulously for every literary detail – the red cloak that falls from Christian's shoulder reveals that his back is unprotected by armour which is why he will later stand and fight the foul fiend Apollyon rather than flee – Palmer worked for hours on each of these pieces. Yet, exhibited at the Old Watercolour Society in 1848, his image from *Pilgrim's Progress* was returned unsold. The picturesque formulas of such fellow members as Thomas Miles Richardson and William Collingswood Smith (both elected associates in the same year as Palmer) were far more widely preferred. A disappointed Palmer vowed to 'foreswear HOLLOW compositions' such as Calypso; to stop painting 'great spaces of sky' and 'TAKE SHELTER in TREES'. 'Directly poetical subjects are less saleable,'[17] he decided. But his tastes were too deeply engrained to abandon. He was stranded on rocky islands of romance. In 1850, he chose a subject from *Robinson Crusoe*, a novel which must have appealed particularly to a painter who had been all but marooned.

Like the famous literary outcast, he made the best of what he had: which was watercolour. Working on large pieces of board, he continued

to test the capacities of this medium, tackling his ambitious subjects
with panache, infusing his elaborate compositions with light. He still
harboured yearnings to become an oil painter and, though for a while
these were encouraged by his close friend, the enthusiastic amateur
artist and deaf mute John Reed, for all his persistent efforts, for all the
notes that he kept so punctiliously in a portfolio devoted to the mysteries of this material, his hopes were consistently frustrated. Palmer ran
down an analytical dead end. The stacks of stretched canvases, primed
panels and never completed pictures that were discovered after his
death in his lumber room bore a sad testimony to his failed dreams.

Palmer, however, was learning to work a little more quickly, for,
though he compared his paintings to 'apples which will not ripen till
they have been kept a long while in the cupboard', he no longer 'pored
and bored'[18] over them as he used to, he said, but instead worked on
four or five at once. In 1852 he sold everything at the Old Watercolour
Society exhibition and afterwards received a commission from a Mr
White – albeit a small one to be sold at a third of the exhibition price
– who subsequently asked him to do a further seven pieces. Then at
last, in 1854, after an eleven-year wait in which the continuing appearance of his name in the lower list – the list of associate rather than full
members – had come to feel like an annual stigma, he was elected a full
member of the Old Watercolour Society. He was as relieved as he was
delighted. 'Almost every member said I ought to have been in before,'
he wrote.[19]

———

The family can hardly have looked forward to Christmas 1848 as they
approached the first anniversary of little Mary's death, but it was to
turn out to be even unhappier than they had anticipated. On 17
December, Palmer's father died. The generous if chaotic old man who
had been so much a part of Sam's carefree childhood, of the dreams and
delights of his rural Shoreham days, had rather faded from his married
existence, his paternal role supplanted by the more competent Linnell.
His sudden death stirred up deep sediments of memory, unsettling
emotions of gratitude and regret. 'The first gush of tears came with the

thought, "How he loved my childhood's soul and MIND – how he laboured to improve them, sitting in the house and walking in the fields!"' Palmer wrote.[20] He had lost his gentlest and most faithful ally. That spring he was to lose another when, in April 1849, Henry Walter, his boyhood friend and fellow Ancient, also passed away. Palmer, recovering from a protracted bout of illness, felt 'worn through with the dejection of the sudden news and the prostration of utter fatigue',[21] he told Richmond. He could not even get down to Torquay to pay his last respects for he had cried off from so many teaching obligations that he could do so no more.

Thomas More must have wished that Palmer had taken a leaf from his own father's book for, where the young Sam had been set free to discover his own course, More found himself forced upon an ever more narrowly prescriptive path. Intense religiosity was part of every Victorian upbringing. Achievement was highly valued in a progressive age. Contemporary attitudes to education were caricatured by Charles Dickens in his Dombey and Son, in which the unfortunate scion of the eponymous Dombey is put into the hands of a teacher whose system is 'not to encourage a child's mind to develop and expand itself like a young flower; but to open it by force like an oyster'.[22]

'Education,' said Palmer, 'including at its foundation the fear and love of God, is all in all.'[23] He regarded the process as a personal hobby, if not a holy calling. Schoolwork he believed to be 'nothing short of divine'.[24] There was nothing on earth more delightful, he declared, than the training of one's child. His son, even more precious now that Mary was gone, was his guinea pig. He set about giving More a thorough education with nothing 'loose or slippery' and no 'show or parade'. Palmer, who admired Milton for knowing Homer by heart before he was sixteen, saw difficulty as a challenge and diligence as the vehicle by which one could rise to meet it. It is 'very difficult to do anything well from the blacking of shoes upwards',[25] he said, but by taking pains one could achieve things both wisely and well. He believed firmly in the advantages of parental influence. He would not, he insisted, hand over his first born to some hired pedagogue, to some crinoline-clad nurse bawling angrily at her charges. 'While ladies say they can't trust their servants with their keys,' he wrote to Miss Twining (who, having written a pamphlet on workhouse schooling, was always prepared to discuss such matters), 'we see that they *can* trust them with their children: trust them at a most impressible age to take their shape and bent of mind and soul from hirelings! What then is the momentous business that can drag the mother from those dearest hours of her life, *her mornings with her children?* No business at all. You have answered the question. It is the hatred of conscientious painstaking in which and through which alone comes the delight of duty.'[26] 'Home influence is maternal influence and *that* we *know* has formed the best and greatest men,'[27] he concluded.

Palmer, however, believed with Locke that children's constitutions could be 'either spoil'd or at least harm'd by Cockering and Tenderness'.[28] He vigorously espoused the virtues of beating. 'Flog on!' as his great aunt had said when an uncle, who had run away from home to enjoy the 1780 riots, had been found asleep among the cavalry horses in the Royal Exchange. Palmer would sometimes tell the story of one of his cousins who, though he had known perfectly well how to spell a word in his school book, had stubbornly refused to prove it to his parents. 'They gave him a cold bath, whipped out the demon for a time,' Palmer remembered. But it always came back. Once, Palmer had managed to coax the boy into spelling the word privately. He had done so correctly, and his cousin had reported as much; 'But soon after he was up the next morning he was playing hare to the hounds round the garden, till they caught him at last and brought him in for a birching.' That 'birching was blest' Palmer had concluded, for 'I saw him the other day, a worthy, cheerful old gentleman'.[29]

The 'most calamitous of our birthdays', Palmer once declared, was that on which we 'become too old for whipping',[30] while 'the disuse of those few moderate twigs of birch in our nurseries', he told a friend many years later, 'is a patent infatuation'.[31] And yet, for all his strenuous advocation of the virtues of corporal punishment – 'Will boys learn at home without the distant probability of the strap?'[32] Palmer wondered – the rod remained in his house for the most part a mere threat. He rarely punished and, when he did, the penalties imposed were slight.

Indeed, looking back many years later on his efforts to educate his son, he declared paradoxically that 'the peculiar excellence of home teaching' lay 'in the earliest lessons being made pleasant', that a child should be beguiled and not beaten and that – bar an occasional correction for idleness – for every cuff given by an ill-tempered parent, the parent deserved to receive a dozen back – 'and pretty hard ones too'.[33]

The foundations of More's future were dauntingly solid. 'I do think a boy should *know by heart* and *understand* some short Latin Grammar – the Eton say – and should go through the first book of Euclid with a private tutor before going to school,' Palmer said.[34] Latin was fundamental – 'for without it I do not think the best English has ever been written or spoken: and as speech pre-eminently distinguishes us from the brutes . . . we ought surely to speak well'[35] – so, though prosody could be deferred for a while, irregular verbs and syntax needed to be 'thoroughly mastered so that they can never be forgotten – and syntax wants the pains of home teaching that it may be *understood* as well as got by rote'.[36]

More was encouraged to draw. He was taught to read aloud, enunciating properly so that he could entertain his mother while she was sketching or amuse the family as they gathered round the fire. He shared his father's love of music and played the piano; one day, when their piano tuner failed to turn up, Palmer worried terribly that the jarring notes might do his son's ear lasting damage. More particularly liked the organ. As a fourteen-year-old, on holiday in Margate, he would rise at half past six to spend his mornings playing Handel and Corelli on the instrument at the town baths. A year later, officiating temporarily as an organist at a church in Earl's Court, he proved highly proficient, playing the congregation out with a rousing *Hallelujah Chorus*. He and his father filled happy hours discussing 'fugues, stop-diapasons, open-diapasons, double-diapasons, the swell, swell-couplers, principals, fifteenths, sequialteras, bourdon, and double sets of 32-feet pipes!'[37] Palmer recalled. And, in 1858, he took his son to Crystal Palace where they drifted happily about amid the displays of pictures 'while from the distant, great organ, sweet streams of melody spread like perfume through the halls'.[38]

Lessons were not always plodding for More. His father knew how to
kindle the imagination. As he lectured his son on the evils of cruelty, he
reminded him of the biblical story of Jezebel. 'I wonder what Jezebel
was like when she was a little girl,' he wrote. 'You may try to draw her';
and there followed the sort of imaginative contemplation that must
have informed his own narrative works. 'I should make her with proud-
looking eyes – turning up her nose at everybody and in very fine clothes.
She was fond of dress to the last – but while she was painting her cheeks
and making herself so fine that morning – she little thought of the
hungry dogs that would tangle their fangs among her laces and
gimcracks.'[39]

Palmer was prepared to sacrifice everything for the sake of his son's
education. A landscapist could make a better living in the country, but
he remained in the capital because it was the best place for schools. His
efforts paid off. Having finished his preparatory education under the
auspices of a Kensington clergyman, in 1858, at the age of sixteen,
More went on to gain a place at Kensington Grammar School where he
not only won several prizes but became a great favourite of the headmaster. He got into the highest class, Palmer told Miss Wilkinson
proudly. It would still be some time before he looked back on this
moment with the bitterest of regrets.

———————

While Palmer had limped impecuniously on through the late 1840s
and into the 1850s, Linnell had continued to take great strides as a
painter. His 1848 *Noah: The Eve of the Deluge* works like a powerful
vortex, sweeping the eye inwards with its glowing force. Ruskin noticed
it at the Royal Academy exhibition of that year and though he misread
its subject, referring to it as *The Retreating Storm*, he nonetheless
mentioned it in an updated edition of *Modern Painters* as 'characterised
by an observance of nature scrupulously and minutely patient . . . only
to be understood by reference to the drawings of Michelangelo'.[40] By
the early 1850s, Linnell was being hailed as one of Britain's most collect-
able landscapists. Dealers were buying up any work that they could. A
picture of quoit players which Linnell had first sold to Sir Thomas

Baring (the father of John Baring who had commissioned Palmer in Rome) in 1811 for seventy-five guineas was sold by Christie's in 1848 for a thousand. Problems with forgeries would soon arise and, before long, Linnell would find himself being asked to verify a work so often that he began to charge a £5 fee.

Soon, no longer tied to the capital by the financial necessities of portrait commissions, he was planning to leave Bayswater. In May 1849, on their way to Edenbridge to inspect a possible site for a new home, Linnell and his son James found themselves waiting at Redhill, in Surrey, to change trains. Energetic as ever, Linnell filled the time with a brisk walk up the nearby Redstone Hill where he was so taken by the views that stretched outwards in all directions that he decided on the spot that this was where he would live. Eleven acres had been put up for sale by a London stockbroker. Linnell bought them at once.

Picking a vantage point on the brow of a well-timbered hill sloping down towards the west, he set about designing and building a substantial Reigate-stone house, adding sixty-three more acres to his original eleven, personally supervising every stage of the construction himself. By the time he had finished, Redstone was an impressive mansion with terraced grounds and magnificent views. It was near enough to London for him to take the train in easily, and also to Brighton for his wife to make trips to the shops or the beach. In July 1851, the Linnell family finally moved.

Redstone was organised around work. Two huge painting studios of the sort that Palmer could only have dreamt of took up the entire first floor; one was Linnell's, the other for the use of his sons, both by then also practising as professional artists. A lobby lined with plaster casts separated them. Downstairs there was a large sixty-foot drawing room with two entrances, so that it could be divided if necessary with a partition, while the windows of a spacious library offered an ample view over flowerbeds and lawns towards the wilder vistas of Linnell's own woods. In the evenings Linnell would gaze through these windows out over the sunsets which, famously glorious because of the red earth in the area, he would paint. How Palmer, who had studied a sunset 'over the *same* piece of rock and sea'[41] for three weeks in Cornwall, would have loved such a view! Instead, back in London, he had to climb up to the attic and, standing on tiptoe, strain his neck out of the nursery maid's window to get even the tiniest glimpse of the sky.

Linnell was lord of all he surveyed at Redstone. No one could arrive at the front door without him throwing up the sash and issuing his challenge. He might not have been quite as ferocious as his hound, Niger – it had to be shot after biting a girl who was delivering eggs – but still regular tradesmen preferred to dodge round under cover of the trees to the entrance at the back of the house. The local hunt was also upset. Used for decades to drawing cover in the mature oak woods, they resented the territorial fences that Linnell put up. A long battle ensued which Linnell won in the end. His house remained a stronghold, an empire over which he presided. There, unimpeded, he could pursue his painting, pore over his books of Hebrew and Greek, grind his corn, bake his bread, brew his ale and thunder forth his opinions to a well-disciplined family which increasingly seldom dared venture dissent.

––––––––

In 1851 the Palmers also moved house, taking up residence in 6, Douro Place. It was only a short walk from their previous cottage, but it was considered an upward move. Douro Place was a pretty cul-de-sac. The then fashionable sculptor, John Bell – his dramatic *Eagle Slayer* was to stand at the heart of the Great Exhibition that year – had a house on the corner. But, if a succession of social luminaries arrived at that end of the street, the other, where the Palmers lived, was blocked by a high brick wall.

Number 6 – now singled out by an English Heritage plaque as the home of Samuel Palmer – is, by current standards, a substantial residence: a four-storey Georgian building set in quiet seclusion, it would be far out of the financial reach of an unsuccessful artist today, but in Palmer's era it was considered a modest establishment. The visitor, arriving through a green wicket gate, would follow the path through a shady patch of garden which was cheered up in summer by abundant marigolds, to a flight of steps with a tangle of white roses growing around its railings, leading up to the front door. It was dark inside, the daughter of their neighbour, Charles West Cope, remembered, with a long low room on the left as you entered, the floor of which sloped steadily down towards the windows. There was no studio. Palmer used a corner of the drawing room. It had a southerly aspect, which he liked, even though it looked onto the houses opposite. Palmer tried to make the best of this far-from-perfect set-up, settling down amid his clutter of artist's materials, mended picture frames and homemade portfolios and, in memory of Shoreham, planting a root of hops among the garden's lilac bushes.

Many happy hours were spent in that home. Cope's daughter would much later describe them, recalling how Hannah would caution the guests about the sloping flagstones, remembering her 'pretty gentle way and voice' and how Palmer would sing as he played the tall silk-fronted piano or tell the children blood-curdling stories about wolves in which the creatures' far-off howling seemed to draw nearer and nearer and nearer as the children clustered about him, half-frightened, half-thrilled. She particularly remembered the magnificence of his voice 'rolling out *By the waters of Babylon*'.[42] This psalm of exile must have meant a lot to him. He was a suburban outcast of his rural dreams. And it would only get worse. The green spaces of South Kensington were being rapidly buried under stucco. 'They have so built us up with great houses,' Palmer mourned, 'as to destroy the elasticity of the air.'[43] Sometimes he would burn blotting paper that had been soaked in salt-petre in his bedroom so that he could breathe better. The acrid vapours helped to clear his lungs.

His health was declining. Throughout the 1850s he was regularly ailing. Appointments were frequently cancelled or postponed. He blamed his impaired constitution on the transition from Italy's dry summer climates to London's damp clay. Coughs, colds and wheezes seemed constantly to plague him and, by 1856, he was referring to himself – albeit mockingly – as 'a wretched invalid'.[44] The enthusiastic young visionary who had used to ramble all night across the Kentish Weald was now entering his fifties. Winter, with its 'bitter weather and untoward rains',[45] herded him towards his hearth; but in summer it wasn't much better. 'I DREAD the DUST of town, which withers me whenever I go out,'[46] Palmer moaned. Hannah would apply mustard plasters to his chest. But she was not well herself. She had suffered several miscarriages before finally, in September 1853, giving birth to a third and last child, a son who was christened Alfred Herbert: Alfred after the king and Herbert in honour of the poet. For some time his father called him the former and his mother the latter; but in the long run it was Hannah who won out. The boy was known as Herbert, or Hub for short. Cope and Reed were his godfathers.

From the beginning the infant was sick, succumbing to fevers, convulsions and fits. Dr Macintyre once more became a frequent – sometimes a daily – visitor, and Mrs Linnell, with whom Palmer shared few other interests, became a medical confidante, privy to the details of every symptom and remedy. The baby was prone to squinting, Palmer told her in 1854. 'We . . . have noticed it all along at intervals.' '[Dr McIntyre says] it might proceed merely from wind or from a very serious cause, congestion of the brain.'[47] Within such wide parameters, there was plenty of room for anxieties to run amok and the unfortunate infant was subjected to an assortment of unpleasant treatments that ranged from the administration of grey powders to the lancing of its gums.

Later that year, Hannah, the baby and his nurse, went to stay at Redstone while Palmer, freed for a few days from teaching commitments set off – with the help of £5 from Linnell – for a holiday with More. Herbert grew temporarily stronger but by 1855 he was seriously ill again and, had it not been for the advice of Dr McIntyre, would have been 'laid by the side of his still dear little sister',[48] Palmer wrote. By the time the baby had recovered the whole family was exhausted: Hannah had sat up with him every night but one for six weeks, while the nurse had never got to bed before two in the morning. Preparations were once more made for a recuperative trip to Redstone. 'We have indeed much reason for thankfulness,' a relieved Palmer wrote, 'when after fever and insensibility we see our poor Herbert amusing himself with his old playthings and playing his old tricks.'[49]

It was around this time that Palmer developed a fascination for homeopathy. This system of medicine, based on treating a patient with highly diluted substances which trigger the body's natural system of healing, had been introduced into Britain in the 1830s by an Edinburgh trained medic, Dr Quin, who while travelling in Europe had met Samuel Hahnemann, the founder of this holistic discipline. By 1850 he had founded a homeopathic hospital in London and by 1858 had negotiated an amendment to the Medical Act as a result of which homeopathy became not only tolerated but in many cases preferred to traditional treatments – perhaps hardly surprising in an era when mainstream practitioners regularly advocated such measures as bloodletting, purging and the administration of Venice Treacle: a mixture made up of sixty-four substances among them opium, myrrh and viper's flesh.

Palmer invested in a homeopathic box containing sixteen different medicines: – 'all that are wanted for domestic practice',[50] he announced with satisfaction – and from this time on would self-medicate enthusiastically. Pulsatilla taken alternatively with Aconite, he informed Julia Richmond, had done wonders for his eyes. Vision which had grown bleared from hours of close work had been suddenly and almost miraculously restored. He sent her *Chamomilla* for the colds of her children: he had twice cured a three-year-old by administering six globules dissolved in water, he assured her, and he himself, recently caught out in the driving rain without an overcoat, would surely have succumbed to one of his frequent flus had he not happened to have had his box of medicines in his pocket. '2 globules of Dulcamava made me as safe as if I had been sitting by the fire!'[51] Palmer believed in homeopathy, much as he believed in haunting, he said: 'because, if you sift both questions till you sift your arms off, there is still a residuum of evidence that cannot be got rid of'.[52] Besides, he insisted, the practice saved him money. By curing a miserable cold in the head in just a few hours he was enabled to start work again immediately and so save himself not just ten stupefying days of miserable snuffling but a considerable amount of money too.

Money continued to be a trouble to the Palmers. Doctors – and towards the end of the 1850s there were sometimes two in attendance – had to be paid for, quite apart from Herbert's illnesses, Thomas More was never strong. The rent at Douro Place was higher than that at their previous cottage. The income from Palmer's Shoreham houses was small and though, in 1851, Linnell, who was party to all his son-in-law's pecuniary arrangements, had helped him to increase the rents, this did not always have quite the desired effect. A Mr Foreman, who until then had paid regularly, fell as a consequence into arrears.

Economies had to be practised at Douro Place. They came fairly easily to Palmer who, though occasionally tempted by some fine old book or print, was a man of simple habits. But Hannah found them far harder to bear. Having lost all confidence in her own talents as an artist, she was not far from losing faith with those of her husband too. Her father had already done so and when, in 1850, Hannah's younger sister Polly had got engaged to Calvert's son, Linnell, anxious that the same mistake should not be repeated, persuaded her to break the betrothal off.

_____

'Women, well governed, are dear charming creatures,' Palmer confided to Richmond in 1851. 'Though (between ourselves),' he added, they are 'wonderfully feline' and most to be doted upon 'when their claws are in'.[53] But Anny's claws were now more often unsheathed. The woman whom he had once affectionately called 'Bantam' now took the nickname 'My Lady Superior'[54] or 'Head of the House' to his 'tail'. 'My timidity has left me in a minority of one,'[55] Palmer wrote. Hannah, comparing her humble circumstances with the comforts of Redstone, felt increasingly dissatisfied. She yearned for a fashionable lifestyle of the sort that a successful Academician would provide. She wanted a smart house with elegant furnishings and so set about creating it, investing in the sort of accoutrements that could ill be afforded. 'I could have bought all the books it is good for anyone to read for the money this table and these chairs have cost – have furnished an immortal mind for what will not half-furnish a room,' Palmer wailed to his father-in-law after one of her sprees. 'Groaning under mahogany',[56] the letter is signed off.

Instead of the single, part-time maid that Hannah had once thought would be sufficient, she now employed two servants who, as often as not, only added to their problems. The cook acquired so much money while working for this penurious family that she bought herself a watch, while an Irish girl, upset by an argument over the baby's milk, stormed out at an hour's notice and demanded a full month's wages, thereby shoring up all Palmer's prejudices against Roman Catholics.

These maids became Hannah's cohorts in her unremitting battle to keep up appearances. Periodically, even the reluctant Palmer would be winkled out of his study as they set about a vigorous cleaning in which closets were emptied, books dusted and sometimes disposed of and plaster casts all too often carelessly smashed. 'I am getting used to it, and have ceased to feel much annoyed at the reckless destruction,' Palmer wrote to his wife who had gone away (to Redstone presumably) leaving her husband to cope with the domestic onslaught. But even he found it hard to maintain an air of peaceful resignation when, visiting a friend, he spotted a bas-relief identical to one that his maids had recently broken placed on prominent display above the parlour door. 'What egregious blockheads we must become if we ever more attempt to vie with people who have fifty times our income!'[57] he mourned.

Palmer enjoyed going to parties, especially those involving gatherings of artists, for artists he believed had a great deal of humour. His wife, however, wanted him to attend the sort of 'midnight dissipations' which he hated – smart social gatherings in which cards and music were considered more important than conversation and in which, when people did talk, they engaged in the sort of gossip which Palmer most deplored. Gossips, he remarked, were like flies, settling 'with satisfaction on every little heap of filth and refuse',[58] whereas we should be more like bees, collecting honey as we roam.

Far too often for his liking, Palmer would find himself lurking on the sidelines of some social gathering, a small, bespectacled figure pulling a capacious snuff box, rubbed to the warm glow of an aged Titian painting, from the pocket of a dishevelled coat and blinking myopically at the melee before him. He got far more pleasure, he said, from the few tranquil moments that he and his wife would spend afterwards at home, she reading aloud to him from a life of George Herbert before bed. 'What poor, fun-loving babies we are – here upon the verge of eternity,' he wrote bemusedly to Reed. 'All is puzzle and a heterogeneous heap of inconsistencies so wild and strange that, but for their daily experiences they would be incredible. Thousands lavishing, thousands starving; intrigues, wars, flatteries, envyings, hypocrisies, lying vanities, hollow amusements, exhaustion, dissipation, death – and giddiness and laughter, from the first scene to the last.'[59]

———

Hannah hero-worshipped her father. 'You live on a *hill* in more senses than one,' she told him in 1858: 'standing on the vantage ground of truth higher up it seems to me than anybody else in the world . . . I long to toil up after you though to reach your height would be impossible even with your helping hand.'[60] She began to spend more and more time at Redstone. Linnell, always ready to encourage her visits, might have been suspected of wilfully undermining her marriage had he not also been the provider of the funds that kept her household afloat.

Where once Hannah had defended her husband against the accusations of her family ('I find Mr Palmer so different, from the misrepresented accounts of his opinions and practices in London,'[61] she had written from Italy), she was now more likely to concur with their criticisms. One evening, having tucked up his trousers to keep them clean as he walked to the Richmonds', Palmer had forgotten to untuck them again and had spent all evening wandering about with his socks on show. It was obviously a faux pas. 'Had I maintained three wives at once, had I sent my children to boarding school at Sierra Leone, I verily believe I should have committed no crime so capital in the eyes of my beloved countrymen as that which I perpetrated last night at your house,'[62] he wrote in self-mocking apology. But where Julia, his hostess, was quick to laugh off such solecisms, his wife Hannah was mortified.

Other more serious problems arose. At one point a religious spat broke out between Palmer and Linnell: injuries were aired, resentments nurtured, tales carried, taunts delivered and theological minutiae picked over in petulant detail. Hannah even risked injuring Palmer's relationship with Giles on the grounds that so many members of his family (though not Giles himself) were Roman Catholic and, if there was one thing on which Palmer and Linnell could agree, it was that Catholics were suspect and not to be tolerated. Another time an argument blew up over a minor indiscretion in which Hannah had gossiped to her father about the private affairs of the Old Watercolour Society. Towards the end of the 1850s, Thomas More became the cause of a huge family row.

More, by then in his late teens, was often refractory. He could be conceited and wilful and he also had a penchant for practical jokes which – though no specific examples were mentioned (except his buying a peashooter, unbeknownst to his mother, with which he ended up hurting his mouth) – were clearly the sort of pranks which would not have gone down well in Redstone's regimented world. 'I have known for long that More is too much indulged, but my being at home makes very little difference in that respect,' Hannah wrote to her father, who considered her son spoilt. One day More invited his friend Charles Cope over for an impromptu lunch at his grandfather's, a meal at which Linnell, who planned his time precisely, liked to meet dealers and do business. He got very unsettled – and would even fly into a rage – if his routine was disturbed. Another time Linnell, who was inordinately proud of having taught himself Latin and Greek, had laid a classical trap for More from which the boy had extricated himself with self-confident arrogance. Linnell had been greatly irritated, not least because he suspected that all the effort that went into More's education would only prepare another Anglican clergyman. 'You have saddled your hobby of scholastic learning with a worldly object like Balaam,' Linnell wrote to More. 'You do not see the messenger of God blocking up your path but keep spurring on the exhausted flesh . . . Seek a living apart from all ecclesiastical dignity which is no dignity but a degradation.'[63]

The initial cause of the controversy that in 1859 arose over More remains unclear, but the animosity that resulted was only too manifest. The boy had been sick but the Linnells refused to have him to stay at Redstone. The Palmers, it was hinted, did not show proper gratitude. A favour had been followed, it would seem, by reproachful taunts. Letters passed back and forth. 'I wish I knew in what way More has offended you; for every grandfather's house is open to his grandchildren: no mother is left to beseech it as a favour especially for a convalescent child,'[64] wrote a placatory Palmer. Linnell remained unconvinced. Hannah's brother James entered into the fray and eventually the whole affair was superficially settled, though lingering resentments continued to simmer. When Linnell sent a soothing letter, inviting Palmer and his son to stay, the offer was stiffly turned down. A few months later, More was ill again and was sent to recuperate with friends in the country. Linnell dispatched a present of home-brewed beer and was whole-heartedly thanked by the boy who bore no lasting grudge. But the relationship between Palmer and his father-in-law had been irreparably damaged. Where Palmer used to sign off his letters to him with affec-tionate subscriptions, now they tended to end coolly with a standard: 'yours truly'.

Hannah, however, whose 'filial reverence', said Palmer, amounted 'almost to worship',[65] stayed more and more frequently at Redstone, leaving her husband alone to the companionship of his cats. Palmer was more or less contented. He loved listening to the 'furry orchestra'[66] that these creatures would strike up at night in the streets and for a truly peaceful evening, he told his friend Reed, 'there *must* be a cat upon the rug – a sedate well conducted tabby – contemplative of temperament – shutting her eyes or blinking as she muses upon her last mouse'.[67] But he missed the warmth of the family circle, with its singing tea kettle (he always preferred the vociferous kettle to the silent urn) and its piano playing, its poetic recitations and its fireside chat and he often felt sidelined and defeated, as if he merely plodded on for the sake of his children. 'I am prepared to lead a life hopeless of any earthly good, and to persevere to the utmost of my power in patient well-doing, unappreciated and ridiculed,'[68] he wrote miserably to Hannah in 1856. When his former pupil Louisa Twining returned some sketches he had lent her, he was pathetically grateful that they had been of use. 'I shall value them the more for having afforded you some quiet recrea-tion,'[69] he told her. He must have wished that his wife was more like this highly motivated woman. When men tend upwards, he wrote to

Miss Twining, they move towards 'hallowed intelligence', while women aspire to 'seraphic love'. But 'when they tend downwards the man falls towards brutality, the woman towards *trumpery*'.[70] Occasionally his resentments towards Hannah found a direct voice. I have been 'ill-used and unjustly neglected as an artist, as well as in many other ways',[71] he told her in 1856. But he didn't elaborate.

Palmer must greatly have missed the company of Blake, a man who, like Socrates, he said, had declined the common objects of ambition. His old mentor was much in his mind at this time because, in 1855, Palmer was approached by Alexander Gilchrist, a young writer and art critic who, embarking upon a biography of Blake, was looking for people who had known him personally. Palmer responded enthusiastically and he and Hannah spent many evenings reminiscing while Gilchrist took notes. On one occasion they became so absorbed in looking at portfolios of drawings that they lost track of time. Dawn had broken by the time that the party disbanded. The Palmers' servants had got into a terrible state, fearing that their employers had both been murdered and their bodies disposed of in a roadside ditch. Palmer, however, must have treasured this opportunity to talk. It gave him, albeit temporarily, a renewed sense of relevance, especially when Linnell, who had expected also to contribute, had had his offer turned down. He had wanted to take control of the project but Gilchrist had not been prepared to hand over his editorial independence.

———

Work had always provided a refuge for Palmer in times of trouble and in the 1850s he discovered a new outlet for his talents. He turned to etching for the first time. It is surprising, perhaps, that he had never tried it before. Small-scale monochromes were suited to his way of working; but, until he first took up the etcher's needle as a middle-aged man, he had not suspected quite how perfectly this scrupulous discipline would suit the proclivities of his mind, body and soul. It rekindled not just his enthusiasm but the visionary spirit of his art.

In February 1850, Palmer became a member of the Old Etching Club, a small association of professional artists (many of them

Academicians) that had been founded twelve years previously with the aim of promoting a practice that, until then, had been seen principally as a means of reproduction rather than as a way to do original work. Members met regularly to share expertise, exchange criticisms and opinions, and occasionally to quarrel – not least about the division of the money that accrued when, having pooled their resources as they did periodically to publish a small collection of etchings, they found themselves in possession of a modest profit.

Palmer's probationary plate was a picture of a willow bending over a river. He had already painted a watercolour of the same tree, bringing to it the vivid sensibilities of someone who has lain down and dreamt under those very leafy branches, followed the sweep and the twist of their pliable limbs, listened to the wind as it twisted through the silvery foliage, the water as it slipped beneath a shadowing trunk. This is the mood that he captured in his etching plate. On the strength of it, Palmer was unanimously elected to the Society.

In the etcher's studio, inhaling the smell of nut oil and varnish, beeswax and lamp black; surrounded by iron pots for boiling, flat pans for warming and tallow candles for blackening; by racks of needles and burins and scrapers and burnishers; by stacks of translucent paper and copper etching plates; by old rags for wiping, pumice for polishing, silk for spreading, feathers for smoothing and muslin for drawing up the ink, he found a milieu in which he felt at home.

Etching is a laboriously complicated and painstaking process that demands precision and patience. An extract from William Faithorne's *1702 The Art of Graving* gives an idea of quite how arduous it can be. 'Use water and a grinding stone for polishing your plate, then go over it with a pumice stone, then again with a fine smooth stone and some water. Then go over it with charcoal, and remove any small strokes or scratching with a steel burnisher. Then clean it with stale bread or chalk. Smooth the varnish over the plate. Take a great tallow candle with a short snuff, then apply the flame to the varnish with the snuff of the candle,' instructs Faithorne; and all that before the art of designing has even begun. His advice continues: 'Dry the plates on a fire, place your needle in firm wood of six inches or less; whet the needle with an oilstone and prepare for the graving. You must place the knob or ball of the handle of your graver in the hollow of your hand and, having extended your forefinger towards the point of your graver, laying it opposite to the edge that should cut the copper, place your other fingers on the side of your handle, and your thumb on the other side of the graver flat and parallel with the plate.'[72] Palmer, pursuing the all but interminable stages of this discipline, was set on an often perplexing, frequently frustrating and occasionally heart-breaking path. But learning by a process of trial and error that error and accident themselves could be turned to account, he gradually progressed in his art.

His early attempts he described as 'a scramble of uncertainties from beginning to end'.[73] Working on his second etching, an 1850 copy of his *Skylark*, he passed 'a whole day in nearly burnishing out a sky that was overbitten' for 'the perverse acid *would* bite skies and nothing else' and 'the delicate upward flush of early dawn over thin vaporous cloud' was achieved only at a painstaking second attempt in which he went 'half through the copper'.[74] His *Christmas* or *Folding the Last Sheep*, done in the same year, in which a homecoming shepherd fastens the hurdle that encloses his huddled flock, makes skilled play with the contrasts between the softness of the moonlight and the window's welcoming glow. It is a fine piece of work. But many years were still to pass before Palmer had truly mastered the practice. Even a decade later he was still tackling obstreperous technical difficulties, recording how he had just spent several tedious days working 'in a ghastly frame of mind' trying to prove a plate that he had etched on some detestable old second-hand Club copper from which a previous image had already been scraped. 'I gave myself up for lost on Saturday at 5.30,' he noted, 'but, by a desperate perseverance, had singed the last neck of the hydra by 6.15.'[75] Palmer was prepared to labour on and, with the example of Blake a guiding beacon, with the shadowy mazes of Rembrandt and Dürer to inspire him and the advice and encouragement of his fellow Club members, his great skills as a print-maker slowly became manifest.

Palmer had the right temperament for an etcher: success in the medium, he wrote, 'depends on delight in solitude and locked doors, a contemplative mood and intense concentration'.[76] Alone in his studio, images dropping gently into his imagination, sinking down gradually through layer upon layer of thought until they came finally to rest in the sediments of his mind, he would work slowly and patiently for hour upon hour. Years could be passed developing a single copperplate. His *Weary Ploughman*, begun in 1858, was worked on until 1865, by which time it had gone through eight states. At that point the copper was finally abandoned (though only destroyed ten years later when his son discovered a publisher on the verge of reissuing it without his father's consent and destroyed it as Palmer had requested). Occasionally the changes he made would alter an image fundamentally: an etching begun in 1861 as a picture of Hercules chasing the cattle-rustler Cacus was transformed over time into an image of a kneeling peasant girl and a boy washing sheep. More often, however, Palmer's alterations involved the minute tuning of tones, the tiniest adjustments of balances of dark and light as, penning endless minutely complicated annotations for printers, he tried to coax out the subtlest poetic effects.

Palmer had fallen under the spell of the 'teasing, temper-trying, yet fascinating copper'.[77] Its difficulties, he wrote, 'are not such as excite the mind to "restless ecstasy", but are an elegant mixture of the manual, chemical and calculative, so that its very mishaps and blunders . . . are a constant amusement', and although 'the tickling', sometimes amounted to torture, on the whole the practice kept 'a speculative curiosity'[78] alive: very like gambling, he said, except without the guilt or the ruin. Etching spared Palmer the 'death grapple with colour which makes every earnest artist's liver a pathological curiosity',[79] he told Philip Gilbert Hamerton, the author of *Etching and Etchers,* a popularising book on the subject which would eventually help lead to a renaissance of this much neglected form.

Palmer – to whom a whole chapter of this seminal volume was devoted – became one of the keenest proponents of this so-called 'etching revival'. If he could have made the practice remunerative, he said, he would have been happy to do nothing else. But he couldn't. He had to restrict the practice to intense periods squeezed in between the demands of his watercolour painting, his teaching and his family life. He was only ever to finish thirteen plates in his life.

In 1856, Palmer showed two large watercolours, both inspired by Milton's *Comus*, at the Old Watercolour Society. 'Works of high imagination and extraordinary power,' declared a critic in the *Guardian*.[80] 'Compositions of this imaginative kind are rare among our watercolour artists, and make an agreeable contrast to the general realism which prevails,' declared a writer in the *Critic*.[81] Such praise inflamed Palmer's hopes. He pored excitedly over the copy of the newspaper that Julia Richmond had sent him via one of his pupils. But the pictures never found a buyer.

Such moments of optimism were inevitably followed by disappointments and glooms. 'One day he finishes a castle in the air – the next he mourns over its ruins,'[82] his son Herbert said. 'My whole life . . . has been little more than one *continued* punishment – flogging upon flogging – each before the last "raw" was healed,'[83] Palmer groaned. He was only half in jest. Sometimes he felt as if his work was 'a yoke and a burden': 'I feel as if I were repeating myself and have very little impulse or enjoyment in it,'[84] he told Hannah. And although, periodically, he would make a concerted attempt to pull himself together, getting up thirty minutes earlier so that he could have breakfast over and done with by half past seven and, vowing to continue this reform, bringing his whole schedule forward by yet another half hour, none of his efforts would better his plight.

As a painter he was passed over – and most pointedly by his father-in-law who in 1852 sought out the Pre-Raphaelites one varnishing day at the Royal Academy and invited them over to Redstone for lunch. William Holman Hunt and John Everett Millais both accepted and many years later the former was to describe the visit to Linnell's first biographer. 'The house was new; the fare was simple but most liberal, and the host was reigning in patriarchal state. After the midday dinner taken in a large hall with the door open to the breezy hills, some choice wine was brought up from the cellar, and over this he assured us of his admiration of particular works which we had done.'⁸⁵ Palmer, in contrast, was not encouraged either to come often or stay long at Redstone. Indeed, Linnell seems seldom to have passed over an opportunity to ridicule or humiliate his son-in-law. When Palmer told him excitedly of how, by chance, he had just met Calvert in the street – 'It was so delightful to roll along arm in arm at the old pace. How truly learned he is on Art!'⁸⁶ reported Palmer – the acerbic Linnell copied out the passage and illustrated it with a sketch showing two stout figures, one leaning upon the other, staggering from a doorway upon which he had printed in large letters the sign 'Pure Gin'. A pawnbroker's shop is depicted nearby. And when a drip of snuff dropped from Palmer's nose, staining his letter paper, Linnell burnt it fastidiously before penning a mocking note of complaint. Palmer received the criticism good-naturedly, countermanding accusations in farcical legalese, but Linnell's reply, scorning the vicious habit of stuffing noses with the nasty weed, transformed a trivial matter into a spiteful attack.

Herbert thought his father would have been better if he had remained unmarried. 'Imagine the results if, unhampered [by] a Kensington villa, two servants and an idol,' he wrote – the idol being Thomas More – 'he had been able to depart each spring, carefree and happy, and practically rich to new beauty and old associations.'⁸⁷ Palmer would probably have concurred, albeit for very different reasons. Parental anxiety, which began, he wrote, 'when a child begins to walk, for beginning to walk is beginning to tumble',⁸⁸ turned a screw on the heart. When, at the end of 1859, the family was struck down by scarlet fever, he grew almost demented with worry. The 'pain suffered for sick children, of anxiety terror and sometimes inconsolable grief – are a very very abundant offset to the desolateness of celibacy,' he told Richmond. 'We should by no means persuade those to marry who are content to be single.'⁸⁹

'O! this grinding world there is no Leisure for anything,'⁹⁰ Palmer, in 1843, had cried out to his wife. Now, fifteen years later, he felt completely crushed. He began commending mournfully sentimental poems about death to Hannah. 'I could go quietly,' he told her, 'like a poor sheep under the first hedge and lie down and die.'⁹¹ To Richmond, he described himself as 'a squashed worm'.[92] 'I seem doomed never to see again that first flush of summer splendour which entranced me at Shoreham,'[93] he lamented. He was in his mid-fifties. His dreams were all past. He had become nothing but 'a living flour mill which has to grind corn for others',[94] he wrote.

A Bitter Blow

The Catastrophe of My Life
from *The Letters of Samuel Palmer*

Even as Palmer's dreams were being ground down to dust, his hopes for his son mounted higher and higher. Hardly a letter passed between them which was not burdened with educational, moral or religious advice – and usually all three at once. Little wonder that More often yearned to escape. For a while, he dreamt of going to sea. The life of a mariner must have felt far more enticing than the career of a clergyman which his father had in store but, discouraged from the other side by a disapproving mother, nothing ever came of his nautical plans.

More did make one spirited bid for freedom. At the age of fourteen, he and Richmond's son, Willie, ran away from the homes where they were 'nurtured like cucumbers',[1] and, with four pence between them, set off to seek their fortunes alone. Many years afterwards, Willie (by then Sir William Richmond Blake) described what happened in the adventure that became known to both families as 'The Escapade'.

He and More were great friends and, since early childhood, had spent many happy hours in each other's company, sharing a piano teacher and reading books together, making suits of armour out of paper and glue and playing chess secretly late into the night. But, Willie said, they felt restricted by the artificiality of town life and so decided one day to escape to Windsor. It was March when they set off in a pair of greatcoats purloined from their parents, getting as far as Hammersmith before, remembering that they had no money to pay for their supper, they decided to call in on some nearby Palmer relations to borrow half a crown. They then trotted determinedly on and, though questioned by police on Barnes Common, were not detained. As they crossed Bushey Park, they imagined that they were living the free life of their fathers at Shoreham.

At Teddington they spent the night at an inn and, waking the next morning, More ordered shaving water, even though there was not a hair on his smooth pink cheeks. Meanwhile Willie, turning up his Eton collars, cut off their corners to make them look like the fashionable stand-ups of the day. The pair then set off again, practising a sermon which they intended later to deliver for money and, eventually reaching a small village, they walked about advertising their upcoming perform-ance before retiring to a pub. Willie sketched a portrait of the landlady in return for their lunch and it was while he was doing so that the pair were finally apprehended and returned by the police to their panic-stricken parents.

Their punishments were stern. Cope was called in to deliver a two-hour lecture to More, while Willie was made to learn by heart the letters sent by friends condemning his selfish flight. The incident, though it did nothing to affect the friendship between the two families, was accorded a disproportionate gravity. The two boys were forbidden from meeting and a short while later, when by chance they passed in the street, More turned his head and looked the other way.

He was set firmly back on his unrelenting path. By the age of sixteen he had won a place at a first-rate grammar school in Kensington. He is 'a diligent student . . . never idle for a moment . . . a very pleasant and intellectual companion',[2] his father recorded; William Haig Brown, the headmaster − known as Old Bill to the boys − concurred. He and Palmer join pedagogical forces. As they saw it, they were arming their pupil for life. But More must more often have felt that he had a hydra-headed monster to battle. No sooner was one task completed than the next cropped up. No sooner had one discipline been mastered than another awaited. Even on holiday, he was pressed to rise early and dedi-cate two hours to Homer before breakfast had been prepared.

Palmer set intellectual achievement over everything. 'Skill in music and cricket will not in the least avail you in a college examination,' he warned.[3] He discouraged most sport. More did not like it much anyway: boxing, in those days a regular part of a schoolboy's curriculum, made his head feel fuzzy. He preferred more gentle amusements. Inspired most probably by the publication of Philip Henry Gosse's *Evenings at the Microscope* in 1859, he wondered about getting such an instrument of his own. But Palmer was not to be persuaded. He was distrustful of science. Even if More were to find a flea as big as a mastiff, he said, he doubted that it could hop so far into the invisible world as if he watched his morals instead. He was far happier when he found his own enthusiasms reflected in his son. The boy 'foams with the book mania',[4] he proudly informed a friend – though he and his son never communicated more nearly than when they found themselves sitting in the drawing room at Douro Place, playing the upright piano with its red, pleated silk front. More's piano teacher, Mr Woolman, became an admired family friend and, as so often with people who were struggling to make ends meet, Palmer went out of his way to help him to find work.

One of More's favourite pastimes was grangerism, a hobby involving the taking apart of a book so as to reconstruct it with lots of additional illustrations collected from other volumes that had been cut up. More had been introduced to this activity – named after the Reverend James Granger because his 1769 *Biographical History of England* proved a much-favoured volume for illustration in this manner – by his friend Mrs George, a woman who had once been admired for her beauty and her ability to drive a four-in-hand, but was now ancient and massive with black gleaming hair and brilliant white teeth. She lived a reclusive life amid a profusion of eighteenth-century treasures, with only 'Old Tub' her maid and her youthful memories for company. But More would spend hours in her Mayfair home, snipping and sticking as he chatted away.

Mrs George was an eccentric choice of friend for a teenage boy, but at school More had been bullied. Had he been stronger and fitter he might have stood up to his classmates. He was funny and lively, clever and daring, but his health was failing and, at the beginning of 1859, he fell dangerously ill. Palmer, though concerned, did not cease to push his son and before long More was confined to his bed with a writing desk balanced on his knees and his schoolmaster visiting, inviting him to borrow any books that he required. More penned poems to his class-mates, which apparently brought tears to their eyes when they read them. He clearly had his father's taste for sentimental verse.

That summer, on holiday in Hastings, More was constantly badg-ered by letters from his father. Though he was not idle, Palmer told him, his danger was '*aliud agere*'[5] – a propensity to let the mind drift away from the matter immediately in hand. More kicked against the traces. A man with no '*aliud agere*' was likely to be a mere animal, he replied. His father was determined to keep him firmly in harness. Concentration, accuracy and 'painstaking' were indispensable, he insisted and the ensuing holiday which More took in Berkshire was punctuated by reminders that he was about to enter his decisive year; that his chances of going to college – and he needed to win an open scholarship – would depend entirely on the next few months. He must not just do the requisite work, but do it as if he *liked it*. He must measure himself only against the very best.

More entered his final school year, but that December, first he, then his brother, contracted scarlet fever. Hannah spent hours in the sick room with sponges and compresses, potions and broths. This time it was Herbert who caused the greater concern. But by the next term More was off school again, recuperating in Surrey from a bout of rheumatic fever. Fretful letters arrived from his father: 'If you go in to the garden without a cap your complement of life will be ended,'[6] he admonished. And yet, even as he warned him neurot-ically against damp shoes and long walks, he goaded him to keep up with his work. More went on to come second only to the head boy in his end of term exams.

If More had won a place at Oxford, his father would have been prepared to follow him, to make a new start himself; but during the ensuing term the boy's energy began seriously to flag. Several times, overcome by sudden drowsiness after his three o'clock dinner, More fell asleep at his desk. He was mortified to find that these lapses offended his master, a teacher with whom he would often stroll, arm in arm. He penned his apology in verse:

> *St Paul was preaching, Entychus*
> *Unhappy fell asleep*
> *Unable though attentive all*
> *His wakeful sense to keep.*
> *He fell from the window – and if I*
> *From prized favour fall,*
> *Would choose to sleep as he had slept*
> *Unless awaked by Paul.*

But, though the master quickly forgave him, the dreadful tiredness did not pass.

In the summer of 1860, More took a walking holiday with a school friend, Arthur Symonds. They toured Surrey and Kent, and, even if the trip was somewhat less impulsive that the infamous 'Escapade', the pair enjoyed some fairly lively boyish adventures all the same. One day they had a narrow escape when, dashing for shelter from a sudden downpour, they found themselves struggling to get through a gate. At that moment a great fork of lightning struck the road just ahead of them. Had it not been for the obstacle, they would have been standing at the exact point which it hit, More told his mother, who had already been quite enough alarmed by the fact that he had not carried an umbrella, without a frazzling lightning fork being added to her fears. More revelled in the freedom of his tour and wrote a poem which he illustrated with little sketches afterwards. But his father, who believed that two hours of work in the morning were worth four in the evening, was anxious that his Greek was being left until too late in the day. He was as much relieved as delighted when his beloved boy was safely back and, ensconced at the home of a Mrs Hodges in Kent, had resumed a more sedentary life. 'I trust your legs sowed their wild oats and that you will see the folly of fatiguing yourself,'[7] Palmer wrote testily, as though a few days spent wandering about the home counties without galoshes had been some perilous adventure.

In March 1861, More's health again broke down. Cadaverously thin, he left school to stay with friends in Slough while his father set off, trawling the country with sketchbooks and carpet bag, to find some suitable spot for the boy to recover. After much tramping, he alighted on High Ashes, a small farmhouse perched on the brow of a steep heathland slope a few miles from Abinger in Surrey. Palmer's artist friend, Redgrave, had a country cottage nearby. Linnell, although he never visited, considered it too bleak a spot for a convalescent, but to More's eight-year-old brother it seemed an earthly paradise. Herbert ran amok, playing with the local boys and riding the shaggy-hooved farm horses, until eventually his mother had to rein him back in.

Soon the invalided More was also out of bed and, though too weak to do much more than just vegetate – he was living discreetly '*à la cabbage*',[8] he joked – he passed the time gazing out of the window towards pearly horizons of a hue that would have been familiar from his father's work. He pressed spring flowers and started learning the violin. His father, who had lent him his fiddle, teased that he would frighten the pigs with his tuneless scrapings.

As More grew stronger, he started to ramble about in the knee-deep heather, to follow the threads of silvery brooks or shoot rabbits in the furze. His father was predictably alarmed, fearing that he would either blow off his hand or fall foul of game laws. He recounted the story of a man who had shot dead his sister by mistake. Palmer had no time for country sports. 'How few are out of their teens at sixty!' he once wrote to Reed. 'How few people have put away their toys. They have only changed them – grown out of their pellet and popgun into partridge shooting.'[9] Meanwhile a chest full of Latin and Greek books, rail-freighted down from London at considerable expense, awaited More's attention.

Palmer, throughout More's rural sojourn, was kept by his work in London where the discovery of the bodies of two dead cats in his garden further added to the city's more general miasma. He had caught a spring cold and felt fit for nothing but lying on the sofa and dozing. Every now and then he would dispatch fretful missives to his family, ticking More off for addressing a letter incorrectly, pontificating on the benefits of fresh milk, recommending shin-of-beef soup simmered down into a delicious jelly, reminding Herbert, who on first arriving in the country had been temporarily struck blind by a bad case of sunstroke, to remember always to carry his parasol.

In May the weather took an abrupt turn for the worse. As a damp eastern wind set in and a dirty yellow fog descended over the capital, Palmer began to grow fearful that his son was in too exposed a spot. Anxious letters fluttered back and forth between Kensington and High Ashes as Palmer discussed the possibility of joining his family, worrying that there would be no space for him in the cramped accommodation, vexed by the cost of renting an extra room and dispatching More to the neighbouring farm to inquire about empty lofts.

While he was in the country, More received a congratulatory letter from a school friend to tell him that, on top of other awards, he had won the Latin prize, even though he had written only fifty of the hundred lines set. It was better news than his father could send. At the Old Watercolour Society exhibition his works had been dismally hung. The committee excused itself by saying that his pictures were so powerful that nothing could stand against them; but the outcome was that only three of the seven works submitted had been sold. The painter was in low spirits. 'If this should be the last time I write to you – let me *beseech* you to "remember your Creator in the days of your youth",'[10] he wrote morbidly to his son. He could not have known that this would indeed be the last letter he would ever send his son. Instead of growing stronger, More suffered a relapse.

Many years later Hannah still recalled the morning of her husband's arrival at High Ashes farm. More, sitting at the table, had looked suddenly up and said: 'I fear I shall not be able to stand up to receive my father when he comes.'[11] He had rallied a little however in the ensuing days and found that, with the help of a stick, he could walk. A little donkey chaise was procured and, twice a day, propped up with pillows and with his mother walking beside him, he was jogged along through the shade of the pines. Meanwhile, Palmer's spirits also began to pick up. He strolled through the woods to watch the sheep being washed in a mill pond and sketched the shearing and branding that was taking place at the farm. He wandered the high slopes and looked out across vaporous views. He was beginning to feel happy in this rural spot.

Embarking on a series of watercolours, he started dreaming of extending his stay – he could get twice as much work done when away from Kensington, he said. He made inquiries as to renting a cottage for the winter and, writing to the Gilchrists who lived in Guildford and to James Clarke Hook, a nautical painter and Etching Club member who lived in Hindhead, he asked if either of them had heard of anywhere. Typically, the brief became progressively more fastidious: it was not just a cottage he needed, but one which was high, with a dry soil, a westerly aspect and a railway close by. But soon he had other concerns to distract him. More took a sudden turn for the worse again. 'Pray excuse the . . . incoherent scrawl,' Palmer ended a letter to Gilchrist: 'Poor More's illness quite upsets my brain.'[12]

By the time Palmer had consulted an eminent surgeon and fellow Etching Club member, Sir Francis Seymour Haden, it was far too late. As he marshalled his thoughts with a few hasty memoranda, it was plain quite how grave More's condition had become. In 'frequent and distressing pain', Palmer scribbled: 'unable to walk but by effort. Dreadfully depressed irritable and nervous . . . frightened . . . talks of his grave and his shroud – asks us to let him alone that he may die . . . Complains of tender breezes on a hot day as chilly.'[13] For more than a year he had shown an extreme sensitivity to noise, Palmer reported, and for even longer than that his hands had been trembling. When out in the donkey chaise, he had begged to come home after three-quarters of an hour. Even the slightest toss of the animal's head had seemed to startle him. He complained of a dull pain. Hannah saw in his eyes the distressed look of an epileptic she knew.

Sir Francis Haden's answer is lost. It is possible that More was suffering from severe heart disease following his attacks of rheumatic and scarlet fever, or that he had a cerebral tumour or a leak of blood in the brain. It is doubtful whether a diagnosis from Haden would have helped: and even if it could have, arriving on 11 July, it arrived too late.

In the evening of Wednesday 10 July, Thomas More fell into a dreadful and protracted fit. His parents were distraught. A farm lad was dispatched to fetch the Redgraves and, though the artist was away, his wife Rose roused a garden boy to carry the lantern and made her way quickly through the dark pine woods. Doctors were sent for; but High Ashes was isolated. Nothing could be done in the interim. Rose stayed up with the family all night. But shortly before dawn, More slipped into a coma and by quarter to six on the morning of 11 July 1861, without ever waking, he had died.

Palmer was not beside him at the moment that he finally passed away. On hearing that his first-born was dead he uttered an awful ringing cry and rushed from the house in a bewildered agony, never to re-enter again. The doctor, arriving too late to do anything for the original patient, was by now more concerned about his parents. Palmer, forced into a carriage, was driven to the house of his brother-in-law James Linnell, and Herbert too was taken there. But the grief-stricken Hannah remained. Even after her father arrived, trying to persuade her to come back to Redstone, she stayed by More's side. 'Leave the dead to bury their dead,' Linnell told her. But Rose Redgrave stood firm against his bullying: 'I will not allow you to carry off your daughter till her son is buried,' she said.

———

Palmer could not bear to attend his son's funeral. It took place a few days later in the nearby village of Abinger. 'The lark has risen, and birds are singing in the oak wood, but this . . . is the last day on which anything of the dear one whom I have cherished will appear above earth,' he wrote as he sat at his window, watching the dawn breaking, his heart aching with loss. 'Our birthday was the same . . . Jany. 27. O! that today I could be laid beside him,'[14] he cried.

The loyal George Richmond was there at the graveside; his son Willie was beside him. The boy had come down a little earlier to try to comfort Hannah and, bidding a final farewell to his childhood companion, had sketched a last portrait as a memento for his parents. It was a gift for which Palmer would always be grateful. 'I would not lose it for the world,'[15] he said. But it would be a long time before he could even bring himself to look at it and he was later to ask Willie if he would make another drawing, only this time showing More as if he were still living – 'if it were only a pencil line that might keep before me his *living look*', he implored.[16] Calvert and Gilchrist were also there in the church-yard and, though it wasn't the custom for women to attend funerals, Hannah crept down in the twilight that evening to stand by the side of the newly filled grave.

The gravestone was chosen after much discussion with Gilchrist. The mourning Palmer, welcoming the distraction offered by this small employment, managed to rouse a faint spark of his former spirit and began searching for masons, discussing the prices and haulage costs of pieces of Portland stone and weighing the tasteful simplicity of a London designer with the cheaper local productions of a Guildford stone yard. But it was Hannah who did most of the travel-ling to Surrey to make arrangements for this monument, and it was Gilchrist who planted the flowers around it. Palmer would not visit the grave or even go near it, he said, until it was opened to place him forever at his boy's side.

———

Palmer's heart had been torn up by the roots. From the depths of his despair he cried out to his friends, writing on black-edged paper first to Calvert – for it had been he who had been 'first in kindness when dear little Mary was called away'[17] – then to Richmond and Finch. Their love came to feel doubly precious to him in his time of grief. But though there were many – from the tactful and attentive Gilchrist to the bereft Mrs George – to offer their condolences, each fresh reminder only rubbed his wounds raw. 'Here is the consummation of all our twilight walks and poetic dreams,'[18] he wrote bitterly to Richmond. He had been smitten by a blow from which he could never fully recover and, but for his last son, dear Herbert, he said, he and Hannah could only hope that their own lives should soon end.

Every morning he would rise to an appalling sense of absence. He would struggle through his days searching only for distraction. And even in sleep he could find little rest: he was tormented by dreams in which he saw his son alive again, felt his arms round his neck or heard his voice singing. The whole terrible scenario had been only a nightmare, the boy would say, and for a second, after waking, a sense of surging joy would remain before reality seeped back in and the knell of despair rang once again in his head: 'More *is* dead More *is* dead'.[19]

Palmer had never assumed that his life would be easy, but he had believed that honest industry would lead him to a tranquil old age; he had dreamt of the 'attachment and veneration of children'[20] and yearned to leave behind him at least one who might 'grow up to atone by a wise and useful life for all the bread and beef I have eaten'.[21] Now all this had been snatched away from him: 'swallowed up in "a darkness that may be felt"'.[22] 'What *can we* do who are left behind?'[23] he pleaded. Turning to Richmond, helpless as a child in his 'low grovelling agony', he bared his grief. 'We are . . . like wrecked sailors on a spar drifting we know not whither,'[24] he wrote. 'The great deep of the heart and the understanding is broken up . . . and strange dark shapes move about like those said to have been seen in that first eruption of Vesuvius.'[25] Palmer was tempted to 'moral suicide', to a doubting of divine goodness. Who could tell how much more suffering he could bear, he wondered? His eyelids had become stiff with weeping. Who could plumb the empty depths of human misery, he cried?

For month after month, he stumbled helplessly on. His health began seriously to flag. By September the doctors had become gravely concerned. Palmer was ordered to drink strong beef tea every four hours day and night. But life to him had become an insupportable burden. He felt crushed by its weight and, though occasional echoes of his former self survived – 'Affectionately yours, A Vapour'[26] he subscribed a letter to Richmond, just one of several almost playfully self-deprecating monikers ('the eel', the 'crushed worm', 'sand of the desert') that he at this time adopted – his letters, crossed with erasures, scattered with staccato exclamations, were outpourings of pure grief. 'O! that the dead could speak to us,'[27] he mourned. But they couldn't: and the silence was almost too much for him to bear.

He was the 'most wounded crushed and insignificant of human beings',[28] he said: 'a blighted palsied parboiled creature'; 'a poor crazy carcass'[29] 'worthless other than as a curiosity'.[30] 'I have said unto the worm thou art my sister,' Palmer wrote.[31] He could not settle to his painting and yet every hour unoccupied drove him further towards madness. When he caught flu, he was pleased to be at least stupefied; when he recovered, his health felt like a curse for it only left him more sensible to the pain of his grief. On hearing that 'dearest dearest Finch'[32] had suffered a stroke (his second) he wished that he could die instead of his old friend. It was only after many weeks had passed that he could even say: 'Yesterday was the *only* day a part of which I have not passed in bitter weeping.'[33]

The father's anguish would only have been heightened by the appalling suspicion that he, at least in part, might have been at fault. The doctors decided that More had died of a sudden effusion of blood on the brain. 'Over-work!' Palmer blurted out to Richmond in his first dreadful rush of despair. Yet if he feared that his relentless study programme had been too much for his son, it was a secret remorse, never openly acknowledged but left to fester and nag. 'I really *did* treat the dear boy liberally and handsomely,'[34] he later told Julia Richmond. 'I always discouraged head work for a long while after dinner – and at one time played a game or two at backgammon every afternoon with him to *keep* him from study,'[35] he informed Gilchrist. The death of his son was the fault of the climate, he later insisted. 'Had we and the grammar school been in a dry bracing air I think my dear one would have been with us now,'[36] he wrote. But it was not his correspondents who needed such assurances; it was Palmer himself.

Palmer and Hannah returned only briefly to London. Neither could bear the idea of remaining at Douro Place. They could never have gathered again in that cosy parlour without the ghost of their dead son drifting among them; they could never have played the silk-fronted piano without seeing his pale hands moving over the keys. Besides, as Palmer told Richmond, they did have *one* child left and – even if they seemed almost to have given up on him already – they still wanted to do the best for him, which would entail finding 'a tolerably bracing spot'[37] out of town where Palmer could get on with the work which would provide for what remained of his family.

Where to go, was the problem. The grieving Palmer was too sad to care about scenery: a beautiful view gave him 'no more pleasure than the contemplation of the kitchen sink'.[38] But while his wife wanted only to linger in the place where she had last seen her son, to have remained at High Ashes would have been more than Palmer could bear and so, two weeks after the death, the Palmer family were to be found in a cramped, rented cottage on Redhill Common, close by to the Linnells, where they planned to stay while they looked for somewhere else. The banalities of house-hunting at least offered Palmer a sense of pragmatic purpose. He was not unaware of the bathos of the situation: 'The drooping head over which angels watch must be lifted up amidst this unfeeling hard world of ours and – degraded in men's eyes by the sorrow which should make it sacred – peer about and "look sharp" and go on the tramp after hideous boxes with stuccoed sides and slated roofs – called Houses! And we must frequent the sweet society of house agent and pore over their mystic books.'[39]

He wanted a healthy rural place, within easy train distance from London, near to Hannah's family and with a grammar school for Herbert, who, he said, must be educated and not left to run with the village boys. Redhill seemed to offer a solution, except neither of them liked the place: even the sight of the railway line, down which their dear boy had gone to die, was harrowing, wrote Palmer, and the view it offered towards the slopes of Leith Hill where their son lay buried was dreadful to his sight. And so, despite all the help and advice of the many friends to whom the Palmers had recourse, the search for a home for the time being proved fruitless. By the end of the summer they had moved into another set of rented lodgings in Reigate.

Palmer crept into that cottage, Herbert remembered, 'like a sorely wounded animal no longer able to meet his kind'.[40] 'All that is left untouched by the finger of woe is the black cat who was found this morning purring in the copper with two kittens,'[41] Palmer told Julia Richmond. Soon this contented feline would be his only companion, for the cottage was not only incommodious, but damp and, at the doctor's recommendation, the rheumatic Hannah and delicate Herbert retired to Redstone. It was a return which would surely have been encouraged by Linnell, not least since his own wife had fallen ill that summer. He also extended the hand of friendship to Palmer, sending him (as he had once done to Blake) a ton of coal so that he would not be cold. The gesture, however, though thoughtful, was not sufficient to re-warm the relationship between them and the occasional letters Palmer wrote to Linnell during this period are brief, businesslike dispatches. The last token strands of the friendship between them were being allowed to snap.

With nobody but Herbert's old nursemaid to care for him, Palmer was abandoned to his solitary grief. The six months that followed were probably the most melancholy of his life; but he struggled against depression, resolving at the very least to do his duty, to get on with the work that he could not afford to neglect, especially since More's illness had incurred heavy medical costs. When not painting, he tried to 'ward off the ghastly thoughts' among his 'dear kind books'.[42] It proved a fairly effective policy. Not only did five drawings by him appear in the 1862 summer show but, in the 'sweet society' of the authors he loved, he found himself 'as little miserable as one can be who, in the world, must never more be happy'.[43] He found in the Bible – particularly in the morose narratives of Job and the laments of Exodus – emotional fellowship. And though, when the gospels of two Sundays in succession could proffer nothing more comforting than first the parable of the barren fig tree and then the story of the buried talent, his mind was driven to ever more painful meditations, his faith in the long run stood firm. We may sail in an egg shell, with a straw for a mast and a cobweb for a rope, he wrote, quoting from Ben Jonson; but '*then* comes the voice from Heaven, bidding us open our eyes and see, and stretch out our hands and *grasp* the ANCHOR OF THE SOUL . . .'[44]

The people he most loved provided another source of consolation. 'Having nothing left which I do not expect to lose, my entire earthly solace must henceforth be in the wellbeing of my friends,' he told young Julia Richmond, and he implored her 'whenever another little budget of events accrues' to write. 'Do not "wonder" in future whether

"I shall care to hear from you" for though you are a very young lady you are a very old friend.'[45] It must have tugged at his heart strings to hear that her brother Willie was winning prizes at the Royal Academy, but he still sent the boy a message to say how much he would like him to visit – though, since it was December and he knew how valuable daylight becomes in winter to artists preparing work for Academy exhibition, he would understand if he did not have the time. He fussed over the news that his old friend Richmond had a cold, putting it down to the dampness of the clay he was sculpting, recommending that he light a fire in his studio two hours before he enters so that he may go into warm vapour rather than the chill dank.

Palmer missed his family. When he felt lonely at tea time, he would set out a chair for his little cat Trot. 'Up jumps poor puss and between us we make a segment of the circle,' he told Mrs George. 'Even the dumb creatures have gratitude and love in their measure, and the time will come when we shall know that the sagacity which finds a new planet is less essential to the perfection of our nature than gratitude and love.'[46] He was sympathetic when his brother William yet again presented a problem. After more than twenty years working at the British Museum, William had lost his job in the Department of Antiquities, having been absent through illness (he was suffering a disease of the cranial bones and rheumatism, the minutes of a museum sub-committee record) for almost a year. He was facing imminent beggary, said Palmer, who, having apparently forgiven his deceitful sibling for pawning all his pictures, set about trying to contact trustees who might be persuaded to secure more than the basic superannuation allowance for a man who had four mouths to feed. 'The future of my poor brother's children *rankles* within me,' for they are 'clothed with all the desolateness and none of the poetry of sorrow',[47] he told Richmond who in his turn, as so often, tried to help out. For a while, it was hoped that William's son might be employed in his place as a museum attendant, but although by January of the following year the father was receiving his £46 pension, there is no record of his boy having been given the job.

Palmer had always been generous but the deep sense of charity that characterised his later years was engendered by sorrow. 'Perhaps without sorrow there is little sympathy for others,' Palmer suggested; 'for by sympathy I do not mean any amount of good nature, but fellowship in suffering.'[48] Affliction, he wrote, 'acts like a vigorous stonebreaker upon the flint of our hard hearts'.[49] And yet, beyond all the brave efforts to rebuild his life, his sadness always lay waiting; often he could do nothing to fight but gave way to his grief. 'Today the first snow has fallen upon *our* dear boy's grave!' he wrote that winter to Mrs George as he sat alone by his fireside, the wind moaning round the house. 'It is a foolish fancy; but I have always felt it very sad that, while *we* are warm by our winter fireside, those precious limbs, mouldering though they be, of our lost dear ones, should be far away from us, unhoused and in the damp, cold earth, under the wind, and rain, and frost.'[50]

———

The single greatest help to Palmer's recovery came in the form of another death. At the end of November, Alexander Gilchrist passed away. Palmer had grown close to him over the five or so years that he had spent working on his *Life of William Blake* and had enjoyed many hours at his family home in Cheyne Walk. He had helped to nurse him through the bout of scarlet fever that had eventually killed him. By shifting his focus from his own loss to a fellow sufferer's predicament, Palmer may have been saved from a more prolonged personal collapse. He proved a staunch friend to Gilchrist's wife, Anne, doing whatever he could to console her, to sustain her spirits and offer her new hope. The letters he sent her were his longest and most philosophical meditations on the process of mourning and Hannah joined him in sending messages of support. 'Women who have suffered your bereavement,' she told the new widow, 'are said to be under the *peculiar* protection of the Almighty – subject to his *peculiar* care tenderness and love.'[51]

Anne Gilchrist, left so suddenly to fend for herself and her several children, was grateful for their kindness, but she had little time to meditate upon her loss. Among the first tasks that faced her was the need to move house and, barely a month after the demise of the family breadwinner, she had left London and was renting a cottage near

Haslemere, while she, like the Palmers, looked for a more permanent home. Though Palmer bombarded her with advice, when it came to practicalities he was completely ineffectual. When Anne was suddenly required at short notice to move he was too busy to help. Within two weeks, she had found a house on her own and by April 1862 she was ensconced in nearby Hindhead.

Palmer persuaded her that she should, with his help, complete the Blake biography left unfinished by her husband. The task would become a source of great solace in their shared grief. Roused from his lethargy, Palmer attended to it punctiliously, correcting anything from basic facts through philosophical meanings to punctuation marks. He was particularly keen to make sure that no indecent or coarse words or irreverent references would be included as Blake, he explained, had often been provoked to write by intense irritation with the result that some of his sentiments could appear blasphemous, and blasphemy, Palmer believed, would have blighted the chances of the book. As a result, the work of a hero whose fierce spiritual purity he had never really understood was subjected to a prudish censorship. His attempts at bowdlerisation, however, were not always successful. There was a story often told by Blake's patron, Thomas Butts, who said that, calling round on the poet one day, he had found Blake and his wife sitting quietly in their summerhouse freed of 'those troublesome disguises' which have prevailed since the Fall. 'Come in!' Blake had cried: 'it is only Adam and Eve, you know!' Husband and wife had, apparently, gone into character to recite passages from Paradise Lost in their little backyard Eden. Palmer had dismissed this tale. It was unlike Blake, he said. It would be better excised. It remained, however, though other passages did not.

Palmer's beloved Milton would have been outraged: in his *Areopagitica* he had launched a fierce attack on censorship. But Palmer was delighted by the results of all his efforts, shame-sparing asterisks included. He could hardly contain his effusions when, in November 1863, the finished volumes finally arrived. Cutting the pages, he read wildly all over the place, relishing every aspect of the work. 'Surely never book has been put forth more lovingly,'[52] he cried. He predicted many print runs and dreamt of debates carried on in periodicals. And even though these were not immediately to come about, Palmer, in collaborating so impassionedly with the Gilchrists on this biography, undoubtedly played a major part in setting off the process of reassessment which, over the ensuing years, was to turn a forgotten engraver into an exalted figure in British art.

After publication, however, his correspondence with Anne Gilchrist rapidly fell away. Perhaps she was too occupied with caring for her family, or maybe she had grown tired of his sententious outpourings on anything from child-rearing practices to the problems of country bakers. But the friendship had served its most important function, setting Palmer back on course to continue the next phase of his life. It was not that the Palmers would ever forget their eldest son: Hannah kept all his possessions – from a bookcase full of the bargain volumes that he had used to rummage for in the Farringdon Road market, to his old schoolboy essays. Palmer, in a drawer in his study, kept a handful of other treasured relics. He seldom dared look at them, but he liked to keep them near him. More remained an obsession. The nineteen-year-old whom a headmaster had praised in the prize-giving two weeks after his death as a boy of unusual promise, became elevated in his father's memory into a very paragon.

20

Redhill

Midnight has struck – and the hours – however slowly,
creep towards dawn

from *The Letters of Samuel Palmer*

Palmer had dreamt all his life of a rural existence but in May 1862, as he packed up his paintings into a few small boxes to leave for his last ever home, it was not to some pastoral idyll that he found himself moving but to the suburban realities of Victorian life. The house was Hannah's choice. Palmer had spent seven months hunting fruitlessly, tramping – even in a weakened state when two miles a day was the most he could manage – fourteen miles of coach road from south to west Surrey; but nothing he found met his fastidious criteria. Hannah, wanting to be near her family, finally settled on a modest, detached house in Mead Vale, a suburb of Redhill, in the borough of Reigate.

Redhill, named after the local common that was itself named after the red fuller's earth – a clay used until the end of the nineteenth century for absorbing grease from natural wool in a process known as 'fulling' – which was mined in the region, was a new town that, since 1818, had been gradually creeping across the waterlogged wastelands flanking the increasingly busy London to Brighton Road. With the opening of the railway in 1841 it had flourished and, by the time that the Palmers moved there, its population had risen to around 10,000. It was about 'as ugly a town as you could find', declared Herbert, 'with no history beyond the history of the railway, and no old association'.[1] The same might be said of Redhill today: a soulless aggregation of Edwardian leftovers and harsh modern blocks with a pedestrianised shopping precinct instead of a heart. But nowadays, Palmer's leafy suburb of Mead Vale is more readily associated with the town of Reigate: the more appealing Georgian neighbour with which Redhill merges as it leaks down the A25.

It is still possible to follow – give or take a few traffic junctions – Palmer's instructions for how to get from Reigate Town station to his home. A road leads steadily uphill between lines of new houses and a sprinkling of prettier cottages that he would have known. Keeping the old stone wall of Reigate church to the right, as Palmer suggested, the walker follows the road round and then upwards into a world of big gardens and gravel driveways, double garages and magnolia trees. The solitary gas lamp which once marked the Palmers' lane has gone, but the house – at the top of a road that is now called Cronks Hill – is still there, tucked away at the end of the little right-hand turning. A big solid building on the corner was Palmer's landmark.

Palmer's home is now called the Chantry, but then it was called Furze Hill House and was marketed by the letting agents as a Gothic villa. It could hardly have felt further from the aesthetic that Palmer so loved. What today's buyer might covet as quirky seemed ridiculously preten-tious to his tastes – not that he, in a state of depression, could rouse himself much to care. It met his requirements. It was built on high ground, standing about 400 feet above sea level, and yet was not lofty enough to be bleak. The soil was dry. 'We see the evening reek stopping just below us,' he wrote, and if it often 'strikes cold' just at the bottom of the hill, 'all is dry and pleasant above'.[2] It was cheerfully near to a town and, with two stations nearby, it would take only half an hour for Palmer to get into Charing Cross, while Brighton, where Hannah could go shopping, was also conveniently reached by rail. When the wind was in the right direction you could even smell the sea breezes, Palmer observed – or at least those who didn't take snuff professed that they could.

To stand there today – if the clutter of houses that have subsequently clambered up what used to be furze-covered slopes is disregarded – is still to appreciate the potential of this spot. Over the tops of the trees,

panoramic views stretch across a wide valley to the distant South Downs
in one direction, or along the gently undulating horizons of the sandy
Kentish Hills.

———

Furze Hill, built in 1858 by a man called James Fisher whose initials
along with the date still adorn a quatrefoil on one of the three bays that
form the house front, is constructed of local Reigate stone. It is a
curious not to say somewhat fantastical place. Its steep pointed gables
and central arched door echo the architecture of the chapel which
reputedly once stood on the site. A little bell tower and gargoyles add
to the ecclesiastical effect though the further adornments of decorative
ridge tiles, of carved wooden finials and fancy bargeboards, make it
look as much like a gingerbread house. The visitor, entering through
a neo-Gothic arch, finds himself standing in a dolls-house version of a
medieval hall, its high roof open to the rafters, a big open grate inviting
a fire. The three main reception rooms lead off from this hall, for the
house was first built for an immobile old lady who wouldn't have been
able to negotiate the stairs which lead down to the basement where the
kitchen, scullery and servants' quarters would formerly have been
found. These basement rooms, though small and low-ceilinged, do not
feel too dingy or cramped as the house is built into a hillside and they
open out airily onto sloping lawns at the back.

Hannah was delighted with this quaint if somewhat inconveniently
organised home and even Palmer, for all that he would mock its gentility, endowing each of the rooms with a pretentious nickname (he called
the drawing room 'the saloon'; one bedroom 'the boudoir'; another,
which was damp, 'bronchitis bower'; and a little downstairs closet
where some of his old books had to be stored away 'the butler's pantry'),
could be persuaded to acknowledge its merits. 'I sometimes think what
a pretty little box it might be,'[3] he admitted. Hannah set busily about
making it so: arranging various ornaments on a heavy oak sideboard;
placing a statue of Hercules on the marble mantelpiece; hanging the
prized copy of the Titian that she had painted on her honeymoon;
putting her husband's drawings in the dining room; piling Blake's

engravings from Job and Dante on a grand piano, finding another spot for his Virgilian woodcuts and choosing only the gilded and leather-bound books for the stack on the table to create an elegant but learned effect. Palmer's less presentable treasures – the skull of a man said to have been killed in the Battle of Hastings, his shabbier volumes, or the parcel which, wrapped in grubby brown paper and found (after Palmer's death) to have contained the manuscript of an unpublished poem by Blake – were stuffed out of sight into closets and cupboards.

Palmer for the most part left his wife to arrange things as she liked. He had only ever known of three domestic establishments in his life in which Sarah obeyed Abraham, he said. She was the 'Head of House' and 'Tail wags placably', he declared.[4] And so a man who considered a fine cat to be the only 'really beautiful ornament of a living room'[5] bent to his wife's bourgeois will. Life in what Palmer called 'Filigree Folly' dictated that a nosegay should be placed right in the middle of the table and the books arranged in 'solemn parallelism'[6] to its sides; that geegaws should be arrayed on empty mantels and druggets laid down to indicate routes between doors. And though when Hannah was away Palmer would replace the gilded 'fal-lals' on the dining table with a 'mighty mass of Virgils'[7] – 'then indeed,' he told Herbert, 'I felt that things looked "respectable" in the true sense of the word, and not in the sense of "keeping a gig"'[8] – for most of the time he let his wife hold sway. His only caveat was that he should be allocated his own inviolate retreat, a place to which he could withdraw to work, read and sleep. A little fifteen foot square bedroom just off the main hall is the one that he chose. This room, shut away from the remainder of the house by a wood and ironwork door, became his den. It fell far short of the perfect painting room which he had long imagined he might one day work in – one which would have 'glass at top and windows all round – closeable by shutters'[9] – but at least he could make his own, even if sometimes it felt more like a trap. There being only one entrance, when visitors called round whom he did not want to meet, he would have to hole up there until they had finally left.

Palmer made the place snug – which to him meant happily disorganised. He crammed it with the hoarded treasures that he had only just managed to rescue, his wife having instructed the removal men to leave most of them behind. The furniture, from the rough-hewn shelves through the primitive palette racks to the decrepit armchair, was decidedly shabby and the house-proud Hannah, poking her head round the door from time to time but only rarely daring to make a domestic raid, deplored their very presence in her home. But Palmer stood stubbornly against her social pretensions. It was not that he could not afford better – his paintings were beginning to fetch higher prices and commissions were arriving in a more predictable flow – but he wanted his study to stand as a last protest against 'cursed gentility'.[10] Almost everything in that room was makeshift, his son remembered, and there was little that did not bear evidence of his father's clumsy tinkering.

Lodged in the depths of his dilapidated armchair, Palmer would preside over his hoarded clutter. Behind him, along one length of wall, were row upon row of curtained shelves laden with plaster portrait busts, wax sculptures, boxes of pigments, brushes and books (with at least four dictionaries among them) as well as his private gallery of little antique casts which he kept safe in a series of specially adapted cedarwood boxes. Here too, lying about gathering nostalgia and dust, were his precious relics of happier times: an old-fashioned smock of the sort that would once have been worn by farm labourers; the battered tin ear-trumpet that had belonged to his nurse; the violin, now unstrung, which would once have struck up its tunes on the banks of the Darent and on which his son had first tried to learn. Palmer himself would never play it again for the music only reminded him of how much he had lost. Running down another side of the room were wider shelves bulging with homemade millboard and canvas folders and box portfolios into which artworks of all sizes and subjects, differing media and degrees of finish were sorted. Nearby stood a chest of drawers, holding anything from the cherished mementoes of his dead children to a little box labelled 'brights' in which, carefully wrapped in white paper, he kept his most luminous cakes of colour. And on top of the chest balanced an old packing case which Palmer had turned into a cupboard and in which he stored his etching materials and kept a small collection of miniature classical busts, each carefully wrapped in a protective calico bag. This was his favourite corner of the room. It may well have been here that he hung the tiny glowing rectangle of Blake's *The Spiritual Form of Pitt Guiding Behemoth*; this little gold-tinted tempera – now in Tate Britain – was owned by Palmer until his death.

There was not much room for manoeuvre. The painting table – a rickety wooden washstand – creaked under a hoard of piled china palettes; brushes of all sizes from the broadest fresco painter's hog bristle to the miniaturist's hair-point sable; mugs of water, saucers of pigments and mixers' gallipots, most of them stained with the rich colours in which Palmer delighted and whose succulent recipes he was constantly reinventing. A further table was laden with heavy folios and quartos and a bed was pushed up against another wall leaving only one place where the easel – a student's simple construction of plain deal wood – could be set. Palmer barely had room to back away from it to assess what he had done.

Palmer fitted Venetian blinds on the windows which had to be lowered at noon, but still the sun would come slicing through the slats, sending reflections from the garden shimmering round the room. Eventually he painted the glass with whitewash.

———

For the first months at Furze Hill, Palmer continued to live the life of a recluse, his painting the only refuge from despairing thoughts. 'I am *obliged* to work, for I dare not leave leisure,' he wrote. 'There is a time for prayer and a time for sleep; but every other *moment* I am obliged to snatch from the monopoly of grief.'[11] Even a couple of vacant minutes could be the 'leak through which the black waters gush'.[12] He would often have to struggle to see his work through his tears. Frequently, unable to sleep, he would sit up late into the night, writing letters, or rise in the lonely darkness that preceded the dawn. He felt listless and dull, as if his skull was full of sawdust, he said. He could find no inspiration. Each new day felt like a burden to which he had painfully to stoop. By the end of that first summer at Furze Hill, he had lost his appetite. He took comfort only in contemplating the fewness of the years he had yet to live.

His relationship with Hannah remained distant, and though in the evenings they would still sit together perusing volumes of sermons or reading aloud passages from their respective books, their intellectual ways had wandered along different paths. Palmer must have felt a wince of envy when he heard from a former pupil that she was learning to engrave so that she could illustrate her husband's forthcoming book on human bones. Once, he and Hannah had had shared ambitions too.

With Redstone less than two miles away, Hannah saw her family more than ever. It must often have been awkward for Palmer who, in moving there for her benefit, had lost his teaching income and so, for all that he was doing a little better as an artist, still depended heavily for financial help on his father-in-law. But Linnell, delighted to have his daughter back, made their situation easier when, two years after the Palmers had taken the tenancy of Furze Hill, he bought the house from the local builder who let it and gave it as a present to one of his sons, John. Palmer was no longer directly beholden to Linnell and John proved a kindly and considerate landlord who, leasing the property at a much-reduced rent to the Palmers, eventually bequeathed it to their son Herbert in his will.

Linnell and Palmer never re-established the close friendship they had lost. The former's beliefs grew even fiercer with age and in 1864 he published a tract, *Burnt Offering not in the Hebrew Bible*, a discussion of his views on the mistranslation of the Bible. Visitors to Redstone were invariably handed a copy. Palmer, in his turn, could still be tactless and awkward and though Linnell would still occasionally come to visit his daughter, these calls became less and less frequent, all but ceasing after 1862 when his wife fell ill. In September 1865, Mary Linnell died and was buried the next week in the Reigate churchyard. Linnell was glad to have a Nonconformist minister to read the service. Thirty years earlier, when he had buried his father, he had had to perform the ceremony himself.

The next year, 1866, Linnell started regularly seeing an old friend of his wife's. Mary Ann Budden – or Marion as she was called – had known Mary Linnell for more than twenty years, but now the widower discovered that he had much in common with her, most importantly fervent Nonconformism and a fascination for Greek. In July that year, at the age of seventy-four, Linnell proposed, and Marion accepted; but although he wanted to be wed as soon as possible, she persuaded him to wait until after the first anniversary of his wife's death. That September they were married in the local registry office. Linnell had been told that it was not customary for the bride to come to the groom but he had disregarded the convention. 'There is full authority for it,' he declared. 'Rebecca came to Isaac. Why should not Mary Ann Budden come to John Linnell. The only difference I see is that Rebecca brought all her wordly goods on a camel, whereas my bride's belongings came by Pickford's van.'[13]

As the months passed into years, Palmer slowly grew reconciled to his grief. In society he appeared so cheerful, so animated in conversation and so ready to join in a hearty laugh, that a guest remarked that he seemed a *bon vivant*. His immediate neighbours might not have agreed. Palmer would hide himself away when Hannah's acquaintances called. He hated the pretensions of the local 'villarians' as he dubbed them, far preferring 'good stay-at-home sensible Christian people' to these 'pleasure-taking ninnies and jackadandies with their "aesthetics" and exhibitions and Soirees and concerts and quizzing glasses'.[14] Herbert always remembered how one of them, convinced that an etching had been done with pen and ink, set out to elucidate the matter by scratching at one of his father's finest proofs with a knife.

Palmer, however, was unsuited to solitude. He had barely been at Furze Hill for a month before he began recommending its merits to his former London neighbour Charles West Cope, trying to persuade him to buy a nearby plot. It was a pleasant enough place, he encouraged: far enough from 'the dismal sentiment' of Redhill not to be tainted and with 'pastoral crofts' and 'overhanging orchards' and a two-mile run along the hill tops for his children to enjoy. He held out the added temptation of blooming sunburnt country girls as models to work from. 'How is it that the very artists who live to embody ideal beauty can confine themselves to London skins?'[15] A couple of months later he

tried to tempt Richmond and then Giles with other plots and a short
while after that wrote to Richmond's daughter wondering if any of her
friends would like to rent a nearby house. Palmer may have felt that any
happiness could only be momentary, 'like tinsel and spangles on a black
ground', but still he missed company. 'Seeing the face of a friend does
us much good; and we seem for the moment cheerful and merry,'[16] he
wrote. If a man has lost his last earthly hope, he said, one last crumb of
comfort can be found in his speaking of his misery to a kind friend.

He was cut to the quick when, in the summer of 1862, after suffering a succession of strokes that had left him largely paralysed, the
companion of his childhood and fellow Ancient, 'that *good* man Mr
Finch',[17] died. He was buried in Highgate Cemetery. Palmer penned a
little 'In Memoriam' that would appear in a first edition of Gilchrist's
biography of Blake. He encouraged Finch's widow to gather her own
thoughts, which she did, publishing her *Memorials of the Late Francis
Oliver Finch* in 1865, a book which included among other testimonials
Palmer's own recollections of his erstwhile companion. 'In Finch we
lost the last representative of the Old school of watercolour landscape
painting,' he wrote. 'If among Blake's deceased friends we were suddenly
asked to point to one without passion or prejudice, with the calmest
judgement, with the most equable balance of faculties and those of a
very refined order, Finch would probably have been the man . . . among
Blake's friends he was one of the MOST REMARKABLE – remarkable
for such moral symmetry and beauty, such active kindliness and
benevolence.'[18]

Meanwhile, the genial Richmond continued to move from success
to success. In 1860 he had been elected a member of The Club, an
exclusive gathering founded by, among others, Joshua Reynolds,
Samuel Johnson and Edmund Burke. In 1866 he was made a Royal
Academician. The letters that passed back and forth between him and
Palmer, though less frequent than formerly, were just as impassioned.
'Almost tomorrow morning', Palmer dated an 1869 missive in which
he decided to disburden himself of intemperate attitudes to atheism.
Rationalism, he raged: 'it is only infidelity with a fraudulent label'. His
excitable arguments flew vigorously on before, pausing for breath, he

drew his rant to an end 'with many apologies for my garrulity'.[19] Richmond would occasionally come down to spend a few days at Furze Hill, or Palmer would see him in London when, staying in the home of Giles, they would all three meet up.

Giles continued to spend Christmas with his cousin. From the time of his arrival, Herbert remembered, he and Palmer would retreat to the study where, secure of all interruption, they would converse of old days, 'deploring modern innovations, and extolling antiquity'. The 'plethoric "Shoreham Portfolio" was invariably in requisition', recalled Herbert,[20] its dusty colony of pictures carefully leafed through, placed image by image on the easel for eager discussion. There was not one of these works that was without its story, or that failed to call up a host of associations, which, even at second hand, had a charm of their own. 'To hear those two old men talking together over that portfolio was to live through the seven years of secluded happiness over again,' said Herbert: 'to abandon oneself to the same enthusiasms, to see the same "visions", and to creep with awe or shake with laughter at the stories and adventures'.[21] Year after year, Giles's admiration for these pictures augmented and, one by one, he would buy them until he was the owner of several of the very best. And each purchase, Herbert remembered, would lead to some refreshing paint touches for which it was necessary to re-open the ancient oil-colour box. Its smell of copal and spike-lavender would stir more memories up.

An occasional letter to Calvert also survives, although Calvert by now had become something of a recluse. He had lost his visionary spirit and, befriending the fashionable artist William Etty, had sacrificed his integrity so far as to become little more than a mimic of this then applauded painter's style. His work was so derivative that when, in 1850, at a sale of Etty's work, Calvert had seen a painting of his own being sold he had shouted out to the auctioneer: 'That is not Etty's,' to which the auctioneer had replied: 'A gentleman present has declared that the study is not genuine, but buyers would do well to bear in mind that the same gentleman was bidding for it.' Calvert dissipated his talent on pointless projects, among them the development of an impenetrable musical theory of colour: it climbed from the 'golden earth' of the chryseic, he suggested, ascending through the rubiate to the celestial saphirrine. Even Palmer thought he was wasting his time. Deputed by friends to express his misgivings, he wrote Calvert a letter which, thankfully, his old friend decided to take in good heart. 'You have been friendly enough, under the delicacy of suggestion, to caution me in regard to my protracted study of colour,' he wrote in 1868. 'You will be glad to hear that the past summer saw the chase . . . at an end, though not abandoned.'[22]

Palmer maintained several of his more recent London friendships, including those with the artists Hook, Cope and Redgrave. Sometimes they would go to stay with each other, and when they were apart they would enjoy lively epistolary interchanges on anything from the profundities of Milton to the manifold advantage of larger engravings (Palmer argued this last point by using handwriting that grew first larger and larger and then shrank again to a size that could hardly be read). He was delighted to hear from his former pupils and, though Palmer was no longer being paid to teach them, the Misses Twining and Wilkinson continued to receive pages of the most punctilious painting instructions, painstaking descriptions of his own slow-learned and long-practised techniques.

Palmer also engaged with eccentric affability with several of his neighbours: a preacher whom he had met in the lane and regaled with horror stories of extravagant living and the distortion of the human skeleton through the use of stays ('which surprised him', Palmer observed[23]) and a Miss Thomas who usually called round as he was about to have dinner. He would eat in front of her 'like the Kings of France', he wrote. 'I told her I was not up to the politeness of the French Court in the reign of Louis XIV. When the king would show a particular mark of favour, he took a morsel of something, a sweetmeat perhaps, and having bitten of a piece for himself, sent the rest down the table to the favourite guest.'[24] Palmer must himself have been the subject of much amused local gossip.

Other new friendships were struck up. In the summer of 1864, Palmer advised Edwin Wilkins Fields, a law reformer and amateur artist, on a forthcoming trip to Cornwall in a letter which, coming

complete with a little illustrative sketch, was packed with helpful information on anything from viewpoints to guidebooks to how to keep his
feet dry. Fields, an old friend of Henry Crabb Robinson, was a great
admirer of Finch and proposed that Palmer should do a series of illustrations to accompany a memoir. He was disappointed when Palmer
refused, not just because he didn't have the time, but to translate Finch's
pictures into 'dashing woodcuts would be as difficult', he explained, as
'to write a nightingale symphony for a brass band'.[25] Palmer and Fields
maintained a lively correspondence punctuated with occasional visits
to each other's homes. 'Will you name an hour for a "hot joint" or leave
yourself free and have it cold?'[26] Palmer wanted to know in advance of
one of his calls.

Frederick George Stephens, a former artist turned critic and collector, was another new acquaintance of Furze Hill years. He had been a
founding member of the Pre-Raphaelite brotherhood, posing as
Ferdinand being lured by an impish green Ariel for Millais and as Jesus
washing the feet of Peter for Ford Madox Brown. Stephens, however,
had lost faith in his own talents and, putting down his brushes, become
a public mouthpiece for the group instead. By the time he met Palmer
he had written a number of books, among them a monograph on
William Mulready. He may well have been contemplating his next
subject when he first came to Furze Hill. If so, the plan never matured,
but he appreciated and collected Palmer's work and, as the Keeper of
Prints and Drawings at the British Museum, relished the opportunity
of discussing the treasures of the museum's collection with a fellow
connoisseur.

Palmer had a particular fondness for the company of young people.
His friendships with men and women whom he had first known as
children flourished into a fond maturity. Julia Richmond remained a
particular favourite. When she told him of her engagement to a Mr
Robinson whom she had met in Iona, he was almost as thrilled as a
parent might have been; later he took so much pleasure in the news
of the birth of a lively daughter (christened Iona) that he said he felt
like an honorary grandfather to the child. The other Richmond children were also important to Palmer and though, especially in the

months immediately after More's death, he found it painful to imagine their close family life – their 'dear parents sitting down in the evening surrounded by their treasures'[27] – he remained in many ways a part of their precious circle. 'A letter would refresh me, but I like a long one full of matter,'[28] he told Laura. Walter and John were treated to a somewhat gruesome meditation upon how suffering leads to sympathy ('I dread coming near anyone who has never been in trouble,' Palmer told them; 'he might tear me in pieces for his amusement; as the old feudal lords . . . When, after a hard day's hunting, they came home very tired, it is said that they found warm human blood refreshing to steep their feet in'[29]). He warmly congratulated Inglis on his academic success and earnestly warned him against drinking cold water when he was very hot and the illness not long after their wedding of Willie Richmond's wife led to endless fussings about 'defensive flannels',[30] recommendations of milk and cream with a dessert spoon of brandy and optimistic tales of neighbours who had survived with only one lung. Unfortunately Inglis's wife had tuberculosis and died little more than a year later.

Frances, Redgrave's eldest daughter, had also become a friend. Herbert particularly relished her visits. When she stayed at Furze Hill, he remembered, 'it seemed changed, glorified serene and full of new interests'.[31] Palmer greatly enjoyed the company of her younger sister too. He nicknamed her 'Preceptress' after she had teased him about his grotesque attempts at pronouncing French – shove-do-over for *chef d'oeuvre* – and this intelligent young woman, brought up by her father (of whom she was later to publish a memoir) in the company of Academicians, fostered a deep and lasting affection for him in return, as well as a firm belief in the integrity of his work.

Palmer took a warm interest in the wellbeing of Cope's son Harry whom he had first got to know in 1863 when, escaping an epidemic that had broken out in Kensington, he had come to stay for a few weeks at Furze Hill. He continued to follow the boy's progress from then on, imagining him busy over his books in his 'snug quaintly-angled room'[32] when he went up to Oxford. And Hook's son Bryan – another friend of Herbert's – was also a favourite. 'You and I are such old friends that I

quite missed you,'[33] Palmer told him after one visit and Bryan became
the beneficiary of Palmer's favourite pieces of advice: he was instructed
to always tackle the most unpleasant task that faced him first and to
give his whole mind to one thing at a time. You will call me 'a fusty,
rusty, musty, old "fogy" for my pains', Palmer wrote before teasingly
arguing that, though fogy was slang, one of its definitions (Palmer
would frequently have recourse to his several dictionaries) was 'a stick-
ler for old things', which was not, he insisted, a term of reproach.[34]

The most important friendship which Palmer forged in his Furze
Hill years was that with a neighbouring family, the Wrights. Mrs
Wright was the daughter of his own father's bookish companion Dr
Williams (in whose Nonconformist library the records of Palmer's
birth had been lodged) and she, having married a wealthy parson,
Thomas Preston Wright, now lived in Reigate in a grand house with
extensive grounds, a model farm and stables. She had two sons: John
Preston and Thomas Howard. They were still schoolboys when the
Palmers moved to Redhill and he would entertain them with tales of
his Shoreham antics which years later they would parody in a humorous story set in the fictional headquarters of Cobweb Castle. As they
grew up – John going to Cambridge and taking holy orders to end up
eventually as Prebendary of Hereford Cathedral, Thomas studying at
Oxford and becoming a barrister – they offered an increasingly treasured companionship. He took to them almost as if they had been his
own, Herbert recorded, welcoming their visits 'till in time these
became a settled ordinance interrupted only by school and university
duties. Poems, essays, magazine articles, red-hot schemes for various
sweeping reforms – all were brought and laid before him; but not
always with the anticipated success in securing a straightforward
opinion.'[35]

Shut away in the studio, seated either side of the table – John Wright
with a meerschaum, Palmer with an old-fashioned churchwarden's pipe
– long, animated, opinionated, sometimes mocking and occasionally
intemperate discussions would take place, their favourite point of
dispute being the relevance of antiquity as Palmer defended ancient
authors and their philosophies from the ingenious and often feigned

attacks of these ardent exponents of contemporary thought. When the boys were away at university they kept up their varied and vehement conversations via letters, sometimes infrequent, sometimes arriving in flurries, dense with allusions, quotations and references and burdened, as so often, with endless advice. Here in these missives was Palmer's mind in full flight: they are not the 'negligently elegant . . . natty native grace-Gainsborough kind of letters'[36] which fashion found tasteful; they poured from his mind like a pent-up torrent. Here Palmer would pick up ideas and run with them, or return over and over to some favourite *bête noire*; using one tiny incident as an excuse for a sermon, railing and preaching, recommending and advising, ranting and confiding, fussing and fuming and dragging entire casts of peripheral characters into the debate. In one letter, Alcides, Cerberus, Lord Bacon, Bishop Horsley and Pythagoras all crop up in the space of a few paragraphs. The boys would write back and Palmer would carry their letters about in his ample waistcoat pockets for days, perusing them frequently, picking over their points one by one.

Sometimes the Wright brothers must have thought him an insufferable fusspot. Once he managed to turn Howard red with rage. But for the most part they enormously appreciated Palmer and, many years later, after his death, they wrote to Herbert recalling their memories of his father. 'Though he doubted human nature and belittled and abused mankind, at times with freedom and acerbity, he never distrusted a human being,' they reflected. 'I never heard him utter a hard word of any person in the world and I do not believe that he cherished a hard thought of anyone he had ever spoken with. His attacks were not against men and women but against qualities, vices, wickednesses . . . if he had striven with every fibre to make himself an ordinary being he would have failed . . . his was the life that knew nothing of the common and sordid incentive to action,' they said.[37]

———

The Palmers settled into a routine at Furze Hill. Breakfast would be early and was invariably followed by family prayers at which Palmer would read from the Bible, selecting passages he thought apposite or revisiting such grisly old favourites as the story of Judith or Ahab and Jezebel. Then, if the weather was good, he would spend half an hour in the garden before giving Herbert his lesson and himself retiring to his studio to work.

At home he always wore shabby, paint-stained clothes, rescued from a marauding wife who would have preferred to see them burnt. He would find strange and elaborate techniques of repairing them, recalled Herbert, who became his co-conspirator. Together they would stealthily patch up his battered old shoes by a laborious but 'entirely original process'[38] of their own.

Palmer's working time would be undisturbed – except at such moments of high drama as when some tinkers came round and turned out their donkeys to graze on his lawn, whereupon Palmer summoned help by loudly tolling the bell, the rope of which dangled down from its tower into his studio room. They would have dinner around midday after which Palmer would relax for a while, puffing away at his pipe and reading a novel and more often than not nodding off for a nap. He would then work again until tea time at five o'clock. In winter, after tea, he and Herbert would occasionally play backgammon before Palmer, pulling out a novel by Scott or Dickens or a volume by some favourite poet, would read to Hannah and Herbert until it was the boy's time for bed. Palmer read very slowly and clearly and without affectation. 'He abhorred few things more than quick reading,' Herbert said, and detested 'the modern custom of abbreviating the preterites' as a 'barbarous innovation'[39] that destroyed the sonorous rhythms of English. But some passages – particularly the biblical story of Lazarus who had risen from the dead – would move him so deeply that he would be forced to lay down the book. Palmer hated any disturbance when reading. Interruptions always seemed to him to come at some important moment and he would ostentatiously stop short if there was even so much as a whispered instruction to a servant, a tinkling of tea things or a rattle in making up the fire.

In the summer, when the evenings were long, Herbert and Palmer would go for a stroll, wandering along the ridges, down through the furze slopes and by fields of young corn. 'Few sunsets have seemed comparable in beauty to those he showed me,' Herbert later remembered, 'and when he could go no longer the twilights seemed to lose half their poetry.'[40] Afterwards, when Herbert had gone to bed, Palmer would light his little paraffin lamp – Nancy he called it (he often gave names to familiar or particularly loved objects) – and return to the 'congenial solitude'[41] of his room, preparing designs, compiling portfolios or just sitting and pondering one of his 'unsettlers': the paradoxes which he collected and liked to subject to his patient processes of thought. These came in such forms as: 'How is an artist to be a Christian if, as Michelangelo said, "Art is jealous and demands the whole man?"'[42] Usually, with his paraffin lamp glowing and a pot of green tea on a tray piled with books, he would read late into the night, anything from favourite old classics through volumes of sermons to the periodicals to which friends and family gave him subscriptions as a gift. For many years his little black cat would sit on his knee, patting the leaves with her paw now and then. When she finally died, he mourned for her loss. 'I dearly love solitude, but miss poor Tabby,' he wrote to his son.[43]

Sundays were rigorously observed. Palmer would don his best clothes: a vast broadcloth coat fitted with enormous pockets and a cravat of an obsolete fashion, which he would tuck into his buttoned-up double-breasted waistcoat. Attired like this, he looked so clerical, Herbert remembered, that a rural clergyman had once asked him to assist with the service. Old-fashioned silver spectacles with very broad rims were used for distant objects; but sometimes these were exchanged for a more ordinary pair which, once lost, he would stumble about groping for, with much accompanying grumbling, often treading upon them in the process of looking. The family would set off early to morning service, walking along the ridge that led from their house to the church. They always got there in good time so that Palmer could study the readings before the rest of the congregation arrived. He particularly loved the collects and psalms. 'The poor world-withered heart begins to open like shrivelled leaves in a gentle summer shower'[44] when it hears them, he said, and when he found their cadences massacred, their ancient phrases scrambled by some young High Church reader, his face would darken with anger. When the service was over, however, religious observances were done with for the day. Palmer was not a fanatic and though he refused to sign any petitions calling for the opening of art galleries on Sundays, he disliked the idea that this day should be made miserable by forcing children to put their playthings away. 'A little child brought up in this way asked its mother what Heaven was like,' he once told a friend. '"My love," said mama, "Heaven is a perpetual Sabbath"; upon which the poor little thing expressed a wish that, when she died, she might go *elsewhere*!'[45] 'Unaffected piety was as marked a feature in his character as a craving for knowledge,' said his son, 'but he never attempted to cram either intellectual or moral food down unwilling throats. The young mind was allured but never driven to its fairest pastures.'[46] Readers of his unrelenting letters to More may be surprised by this opinion. Perhaps Palmer had learnt a lesson. Certainly, for the devoted Herbert, a Sunday spent with his father was counted the happiest day of the week.

'Herbert is a most dear amiable charming child,' Palmer had written shortly after his eldest son had died. 'He has lived with me eight years without once displeasing me – but they say he is too weak to be educated – and education including as its foundation the fear and love of God is all in all – besides experience leads me to suppose that I shall lose him like the rest and I love him violently.'[47] Palmer seemed almost frightened to open his heart again and Herbert, still only seven when his elder brother fell sick, must often have felt himself to be inadequate. He longed for his father's approval; but instead, after More's death, came a long separation. He was taken by his mother to live with his grandparents. To a boy who had just spent the summer running free with the farm lads, riding shaggy horses and roaming wild hills, the routine at Redstone must have felt oppressive. It was not a relaxed place. Frances Redgrave remembered visiting as a child. Though she had liked chatting with Mrs Linnell by her bedroom fire, she had always been wary of the presiding patriarch. Where Palmer's conversation had always been 'so delightful and so amusing and so enlightening', Mr Linnell's remarks on the whole were admonishing, she recalled.[48]

Palmer described Herbert at the age of ten as looking 'old and unchildlike'.[49] He had had a difficult boyhood. Growing up in a house of mourning, he remembered often being miserable during his years at Furze Hill. Trips with his mother into town did little to alleviate loneliness since, what might otherwise have provided a pleasant opportunity to get out and meet neighbouring children, became an ordeal because of his clothes. Dressed in homemade petticoats with a frill for a collar and a ridiculous coat, he was openly mocked by the local boys as he passed. When no one was visiting – which was often – he was much neglected. His mother would retire to her study to write letters and his father to his studio to paint, leaving Herbert alone amid the polished mahogany, the neatly ranked ornaments and regimented books. A visit to the Wright family was a revelation. 'For the first time I saw toys and games (of which there were a multitude in the "Play-room"),' he remembered, 'and for the first time I tried to take a share in a round game. And it was there on Xmas Day 1862 at the great glittering table I saw for the first time what English hospitality and unstinted wealth could accomplish with unostentatious pride. There also I saw with astonishment the great pile of presents round the Xmas tree for everybody in that great company down to the cowman and the page. It was then that I received my first gift a little pencil case.'[50] The younger son, Howard, was to become Herbert's close friend.

For years, however, Herbert's main companion was Palmer, though he was only too pitifully aware that he was not the first choice. 'You may please God be a balm to my heart – but I fear the odds are against it,'[51] his father had once told him. And yet, as Herbert pragmatically put it, he was 'one of those who love the society of their children and, as we were now thrown together more than before, I soon learned to look upon him not only as a most indulgent teacher, but as a favourite companion'.[52] To the isolated Hub, to be with his parent was to step into a charmed sphere. He hardly missed playthings, he said, for there were artistic projects to take the place of toys and Palmer knew how to make these amusing. One of Herbert's earliest memories was of sitting in a baby chair helping to mount drawings: 'an opportunity for mischief and mess which he turned into an elementary lesson in painstaking',[53] he recalled. Palmer bore patiently with childhood bunglings and he and his son became brothers-in-arms against Hannah's domestic onslaughts. They would retreat into the studio together to work on assorted makeshifts, to mend slippers with boiling cobbler's wax or prepare materials for art. Sometimes they made expeditions to other parts of the house for various purposes kept secret from Hannah, once firing a gun up the flue of the hall chimney in a catastrophic attempt to clean out the soot.

Herbert would have liked to have gone to school but his parents were terrified for his health. 'Dear Herbert is so delicate, though without any specific disease, that we hardly think he will live to grow up,'[54] Palmer told the boy's godfather, Reed. Besides there was no educational establishment in the area that seemed quite to suit because, although there was a local grammar school with a clergyman for a headmaster, Hannah, having heard that the blacksmith's son went there, wouldn't let her own son attend. Palmer mocked her snobbery and yet accepted it: Herbert was kept at home where his father started teaching him, giving him lessons in Latin, arithmetic, drawing and English. These were administered in infinitesimal doses, Herbert remembered. He would have liked to work more, but Palmer, while acknowledging that he was quite as quick as his brother, would not let him, even when he was twelve, spend more than half an hour with his lesson books.

When Harry Cope was sent down by his parents to avoid a London epidemic, or when the Redgraves and their daughters came to visit, Herbert was thrilled. He loved his stays at the Hooks' or the Wrights' and was delighted when he was sent a little white dog called Phil to look after. He fed it sugar lumps and rolled around with it playfully on the lawn. Unfortunately the dog was less happy, growing more and more homesick, expressing its grief in a continuous falsetto howl until eventually, making a dash for the gate, it escaped. When it returned a week later it looked emaciated and the pads of its feet were quite worn.

A friend encouraged Herbert to start collecting beetles, a hobby that soon developed into an entomological mania as he spent hour after hour in pursuit of butterflies and moths. He wanted to be a naturalist when he grew up. His father was not completely discouraging. 'He allowed me to gloat over my captures,' Herbert remembered, 'thinking that good might come in the shape of nicety of handling, and habits of observation.'[55] But when he tried further to enlist his father's attention and showed him his boxes and setting boards he was firmly rebuffed. 'The proper study of mankind is man,' his father admonished with a quotation from Pope. He far preferred 'the other B – Biography' to beetles. 'It's biography that makes moral muscle,' he said. 'All the great men have set venerated models before them, and tried to work up to them.'[56]

For all the many years that he had lived in rural Shoreham, for all the long hours he had spent admiring natural beauty, his father could not have answered even the most elementary questions on the sciences, Herbert said. Palmer could not have recognised any but the most common of plants, insects or birds. Herbert did not give up his hobby, however, and his uncle, John Linnell, who had become the curator of the entomological collection at Reigate Museum, would occasionally invite him to visit. Herbert learned to handle the tiny brittle specimens without breaking them and it was to this precision of touch that he was later to attribute the aptitude for etching which his father would one day appreciate.

Herbert's other childhood pastime was, somewhat improbably, military drill. It was Mrs Redgrave who had recommended it, she alone realising that the boy, walled up with his grieving parents and lacking proper exercise, ran a very real risk of going into decline. There followed, Herbert said, 'a long and delightful period of instruction by an ex-sergeant major of the Grenadier Guards; whose course in my case went further than usual and included Broad-sword exercise with single-sticks'.[57] It was to lead to a lifelong fascination with firearms. When Herbert was seventeen, the eccentric Mrs George presented him with a gun: a splendid fowling piece that he showed his drill master. 'The sergeant thought the stock quite a master-piece,' Palmer recorded, 'and kept fondling it after the manner of a doll.'[58]

Herbert came to enjoy an increasingly vivid relationship with his father who little by little, amid constant fears of overtaxing his mind and perpetual anxieties over his health, began cautiously to expand his education. Realising that his son would never acquire enough classical learning to follow a leading profession, he would have liked him to have become a farmer instead but there was no prospect of ever being able to purchase enough land, so Palmer, without paying the slightest heed to Herbert's zoological bent, decided that he should become an artist. This, Herbert said, revived a love of teaching which thereupon began 'every day and more or less, all day'.[59] 'For more than fifteen years I was gradually taught S.P.'s views on the principles of Art,' he said: 'on composition; on clouds and skies; the imperative importance of linear and aerial perspective; and a host of other matters which went to form his great tests of good and bad in Art – to form his intensely earnest creed.'[60]

At the age of fourteen Herbert was enrolled at the Royal Academy Schools. He was beginning to learn a profession – 'a great Christian duty'[61] Palmer told him, but an arduous task. Letters from father to son were increasingly crammed with instructions. Palmer wanted to give Herbert the sort of academic grounding that he himself had lacked. Geometry and perspective had to be properly tackled, he told him; and though the former could feel like that 'sudden check presented' during a field walk in Cornwall by a high stone wall, there was 'nothing for it but to get over'.[62] Further to that, the figure had to be mastered. 'Don't think it's enough to let a lesson merely lie upon memory,' Palmer said; 'make sure that it enters you as a power.' It is 'of very little use to know how many degrees the scapular bone will stretch to, unless you fix the information by making small sketches of your own.'[63] Withdraw to the quiet of the library, Palmer recommended and, after issuing page after page of advice, he instructed his son to read it all twice. Everything could become a lesson, Herbert remembered. 'All that we did in the garden – all that we saw through the trees of the wide view over Surrey and Sussex, he used to explain in order to demonstrate his views and his principles in regard to composition, and chiaroscuro, and colour, and Poetic Art. The Past for Poets; the Present for Pigs.'[64]

Herbert was steeped in his father's vision: quirky and stubborn, outmoded and strange; but always infused with an animating passion.

'How could a child, even a stunted, prematurely old, and ignorant child, avoid the fascination of such a teaching?'[65] he asked.

The garden was one of the greatest shared pleasures of Palmer and Herbert. It was a steep stretch of land divided by a holly and laurel hedge from the precipitous furze field beyond, with sloping lawns and two cedars around which rabbits chased and a copse of larch and beech that was rustling with squirrels and birds. This was their little kingdom – or at least the small patch that lay outside the studio window was for, though a gardener (taking his orders from Hannah) kept the lawns and the flowerbeds in strict suburban order, one little area was exempt from his jurisdiction. There in that corner, Palmer told Julia Richmond, 'nothing that is beautiful comes amiss'.[66] All his favourite flowers grew in untidy profusion: foxgloves and harebells, honeysuckles and primroses; wood anemones and narcissi, his 'dear convolvuli'[67] and 'loveliest of all'[68] the woodbine. Pottering about in his patched old shoes, wielding an enormous worm-eaten whalebone-ribbed umbrella wrapped clumsily with string, Palmer tended them all. Each was a friend. His 'pet narcissus' was 'the eye of the garden';[69] the blue gentian which flowered so delightfully in January was procured because Mr Ruskin had described it as growing so profusely and brightly in the Alps that walking amongst it had felt almost like walking through heaven; and, if the gardener surreptitiously flung one of his plants over the hedge, he would bring it back tenderly and replant it again.

The garden was far from the lush Eden that he would have hoped, for the soil was dry and sandy, and water, a precious commodity pumped up by hand from a tank, was so limited in summer that it had to be bought for a ha'penny a bucket, and even though Herbert and Palmer, inspired by a passage from the *Georgics*, together devised a system of artificial irrigation, many of the plants would still wilt away. Palmer would save all his washing water for his pets. And when a new maid, set to weeding, accidentally uprooted the harebells that for three years he had been encouraging, Palmer gave way to one of his rare angry fits. Another was provoked when Hannah dispatched a housemaid to tell him that his trousers were embarrassingly shabby. Palmer took his walking stick, his son remembered, and started violently lambasting the ornamental yew.

Palmer and Herbert would sit in the garden listening to the white-throats and nightingales that sang in the hedges (though Palmer would complain that the latter kept him awake). They would watch the thunderstorms as they came rolling in. His pleasure in these storms, said Herbert, 'was quite as keen as in the days when the peals, rolling from combe to combe among the hills had called forth the Ancients from their cottages' and 'as a tempest crept towards us in twilight . . . the flashes, to his delight, sometimes revealing stupendous chains of cloud mountains – we simply revelled in the sight, till the great drops upon the dust and the crash of near thunder drove us in doors'.[70]

Sometimes Palmer, with Herbert beside him, would range further, cutting low winding paths through the surrounding shrubs. These led to hidden arbours from which they could peep out secretly at surrounding views. Once they made a little bench together. Palmer was not a proficient carpenter but he had a reverence for all handicrafts and lamented the 'moral debasement' of a society in which 'court dress was looked upon with more respect than a carpenter's tool basket'. 'The things in harmony with religion and art,' he said, 'are not fashionable follies but tool baskets, spades and ploughs, house brooms, dusters, gridirons and pudding bags.'[71] On another occasion, Herbert recalled, 'by means of prodigious expense of time and toil, we raised a small hillock ("The Spectacular Mount" as we called it) whence, over a very unclassical paling, we could get a downward glimpse of the steepest slope . . . and imagine if we liked, that it was haunted by a faun or two, or perhaps a beautiful Dryad.'[72] With the help of their fantasies (and the large heap of kitchen breakages which had gone into the construction of their 'Mount'), a prim suburban patch was transformed into a charming wilderness in which every twig had its work to do: it helped to shut out the sight of the hideous slate-roofed villas which, as the months went by, were steadily multiplying below.

By the time he was sixty, Palmer had lost all his former pleasure in walking. 'How much has been written upon exercise, how little upon keeping still,' he complained; and yet 'we owe the discoveries of Newton not to his legs but to his chair.' He would recount the story of how the great thinker, when lodging out of town, had been seen lounging about by his landlady who had declared that he was but 'a poor creature and would never be anything better than a philosopher'. The people in the next house had also seen him sitting by the hour in the garden blowing bubbles of soap and had concluded that he was an idiot. 'How proud I should be to be thought an idiot by most people I know,'[73] Palmer wrote. He preferred the universe of hill and dale that could be found in the Belvedere torso, he said, to the undulating landscapes of Reigate, but instructed to take more exercise he would embark obediently every morning on what he described as 'my monotonous walk'.[74] There were only two practicable routes and both had been spoiled by development. Flinging on an old garden hat and a veteran Inverness cape, seizing a pocket edition of *The Bucolics*, he would stride to a certain five-barred gate, touch it and then stomp back in disgust, much as a member of a chain gang goes back after exercise to prison, Herbert wrote.

Once Palmer had thought that he would go mad if he couldn't escape on his sketching trips, but after moving to Redhill he never returned to the wilds of the West Country again. Memories of journeys made with More crowded too painfully upon his mind; besides, as he aged, bad weather and the illnesses which accompanied it began to take an ever heavier toll. Instead, he made do with sketching what he could see from his windows. Matter abounded, he insisted, even though the sunset couldn't be properly seen and, apart from a sewage works, there was not 'that sparkle of water which no landscape can be without' for the 'sullen Mole' that wound through the valley, when it could not run underground, seemed to him to make a point of running out of sight. Herbert vividly remembered his father's joy when, one year, after heavy rains, this sullen Mole revealed itself as a veritable river winding in and out among the spreading meadows.[75]

Palmer continued, however, to make the occasional trip to Margate, even though in his last years these trips would be made alone since the resort was no longer considered sufficiently fashionable for Hannah. The train had made holiday excursions cheaply available to the masses and, as Palmer explained to Redgrave, 'people won't go there; for if they do they see poorish folks enjoying themselves, which of course is quite shocking!'[76] Hannah now preferred Brighton. 'One *must* be genteel writing to *Brighton*,'[77] Palmer told his son, the words in italics being scripted with an elaborate flourish. He did not accompany his wife in 1865 when, complete rest having been ordered after illness, she took a long autumn holiday with her sisters for which her father paid and again, in 1866, his family travelled without him to 'that respectable mud-side resort, *The Marina St Leonards*'. 'I *can't* make the letters slant enough,' Palmer mocked.[78]

In the summers Palmer regularly paid a visit to James Clarke Hook. His relationship with this artist is a little unexpected. The athletic Hook was almost fifteen years younger than him and when he had first walked into an Etching Club meeting Palmer certainly hadn't foreseen that he and his wife Rosalie – 'so discreet, so genial, and so good'[79] – would become such close friends. Beyond art they did not share many interests: Hook loved sailing and fly fishing and shooting; but Palmer would look forward for weeks to a stay in his Surrey home for, Herbert said, 'loving dearly the breath of cows, the sweet smell of the new furrow, and all the wonders of the gardener's art', Silverbeck seemed (as his sketchbooks and letters testify) an Elysium compared to 'the prim, densely peopled neighbourhood of Red Hill'.[80] Herbert loved the company of Hook's sons, a pair of amphibious boys, never happier than when in water and always keen to tempt visitors, Palmer among them, onto the pond for a voyage in one of their homemade craft. The attendant catastrophes were proverbial, Herbert recalled.

During the annual cleaning onslaught Palmer would still be turned out 'neck and crop for a couple of days',[81] while his books (no volume too venerable for its covers to be banged), his papers, portfolios and plaster casts were deposited on the lawn to be vigorously dusted, while carpets were beaten, floors re-varnished and armies of earwigs routed from his painting rags. He would find refuge with friends, usually

Hook or Richmond, while Herbert remained a loyal ally on the home front, receiving letters of detailed instruction on such tasks as the oiling of shelves. 'What a hideous vortex is all this domestic perturbation!' exclaimed Palmer. 'Orpheus looked back on purpose: he dreaded a second bout of housekeeping.'[82]

The occasional trip made by Palmer to London was always preceded by a tremendous kerfuffle as Herbert, who loved to accompany him, remembered only too well. 'For days, perhaps weeks, beforehand,' he said, 'a list of things to be seen, done and got, was carefully compiled . . . and the route was systematically planned out so as to economise time to the utmost.' Then 'on the eventful morning, the broadcloth coat with the long, flowing skirt was brought forth, and the white cravat was adjusted with unusual care. One or more sets of underclothing were donned, according to the time of year, and sometimes indeed a second pair of trousers in severe weather. The silver spectacles were reluctantly laid aside for those of thin steel, and a mighty silk hat was disinterred from a box where it dwelt secure for months together . . . I verily believe that that hat,' Herbert added, 'was the biggest that could be bought. The label on the bandbox had been directed by the hatter to "The Rev S. Palmer" and there was certainly a sort of very venerable curl about the brim.'[83]

Arriving at the station at least half an hour too early, father and son would walk back and forth, Herbert squirming with embarrassment at the attention which his father's outfit attracted while the pacing Palmer remained perfectly oblivious. Even if its oddness were pointed out to him, he would not, Herbert wrote, have been in the least put out. It was not that he wilfully sought eccentricity but few things, he believed, were more pernicious than the dread of being peculiar. Once in London he devoted himself to showing his son everything of interest that lay in their route, stopping dead in the middle of the pavement, regardless how crowded, to point out some church spire or memorable spot. On one occasion, Herbert recalled, when his father had been walking with a young friend, Palmer had suddenly drawn up short before a milliner's shop and begun with some vehemence to declaim loudly against the 'Jezebel Tops' within. This was his name for the silk-ribboned bonnets on display for the biblical Jezebel with her love of finery had become for Palmer the very paradigm of a woman of high fashion. A few passers-by, scenting his eccentricity, had stopped and his father, turning, had found that his erstwhile companion had fled in mortification and that he was standing alone at the centre of a gathering crowd. And yet for all the embarrassment that his father would cause him, what Herbert remembered most particularly about Palmer was his unfailing courtesy to everyone he encountered, regardless of class or wealth.

Palmer always had an aim in mind on these trips: some mission that, in his pencilled list of things-to-be-done, had been printed in large letters. He made the most of his opportunity to visit the London galleries and could remain in front of one painting for an hour or more, sometimes returning with amusing anecdotes of things he had overheard while he stood. Once, while 'drinking in'[84] a work by Fuseli at Somerset House, a man and a woman had come by. 'What's that?' the woman had asked. '"Oh, that's *imagination*," said he, with a most contemptuous emphasis upon the word. "Come along!" giving her a vigorous pull to the next picture.'[85] Once, on a cold winter's day, 'swathed like a mummy and at risk of [his] worthless life',[86] Palmer went to London expressly to look at a canvas by Poussin; on another occasion the object of his journey was to study 'a bit one inch square, in a single picture'.[87]

Usually he would meet up with old acquaintances, joining Richmond in the portrait gallery or dining at Giles's house. He was tremendously touched to find himself welcomed. 'I am everywhere claimed by friends,' he told Herbert, 'and all but pulled in pieces with kindness. The finest Burgundy is broached.'[88] Occasionally he would make a much-treasured purchase: an old book or print, a photograph of some favourite picture or a miniature antique bust. 'These were the things that found their way into his bag or pockets during the day,' Herbert reflected, 'and they gave him that keen pleasure known only to cultured men of small means who grievously pine for an object for months before they venture to buy it.'[89]

For the most part, as the 1860s progressed, Palmer preferred to remain at home. His letters are peppered with excuses and apologies for cancelled plans. His 'old acquaintance asthma'[90] remained a problem and he was constantly afflicted with colds because his house – for all that it had been chosen for its bracing dry atmosphere – turned out to be horribly exposed to the winds. 'The Draughts', he called it at the head of one letter. 'Bronchitis window', he addressed another. The East wind could discover him even in his bed. And so, more and more often, he remained housebound, sitting in his studio bundled up against chills, watching the evenings drawing in earlier and earlier, the leafless tree branches being battered by rain. It must have come as quite a shock to the valetudinarian fusser when his younger brother, William, died first. Five years younger than Palmer, he was only in his mid-fifties when he passed away in 1866.

Palmer's study was his kingdom, a walled citadel in which everything mattered and meant something to its eccentric ruler. Words would be chalked up on his easel, clues to some truth or maxim which he wished to keep in mind. 'Parsley' was one that Herbert particularly recalled. It referred to an anecdote he had recently read which had been related thus: 'I happened one day to converse with an excellent French cook about the delicate art which he professed. Among the dishes for which my friend had a deserved reputation was a certain *gâteau de foie* which had a very exquisite flavour. The principal ingredient, not in quantity but in power, was the liver of the fowl, but there were several other ingredients also and among these was a leaf or two of parsley. He told me the influence of the parsley was a good illustration of his theory about art. If the parsley were omitted, the flavour he aimed at was not produced at all; but on the other hand, if the parsley was the least excessive, then the *gâteau*, instead of being a delicacy for gourmets, became an uneatable mess.'[91]

Palmer would talk to himself as he shuffled about, chatting away audibly with imaginary companions who were familiarly known as Mr Jackson, Mr Jinks, and Mr Jick, and who played an everyday part in the family circle, though a new housemaid, whose previous master had also talked to himself and had ended his days in a mental asylum, would be heard after a couple of days in her new post bewailing her bad luck to have entered the service of yet another gentleman who was 'queer in the head'.[92] It was the same girl, Palmer was to recall, who had expressed her astonishment that her employer should have two frames of tailors' patterns hanging up in the drawing room: the 'patterns', it turned out, being Blake's *Pastorals*. But Palmer was untroubled by what people thought of him. He continued, unperturbed, in the quiet tenor of a life so peaceably uneventful that small occurrences of a sort that would more normally be forgotten became, much to the amusement of friends, progressively magnified by his imagination until they were remembered as great adventures.

The Milton Series

I am never in a 'lull' about Milton . . . he never tires
from *The Letters of Samuel Palmer*

With the loss of his son, Palmer had lost also his faith in painting. 'It seems to me better,' he wrote, seven years after More's death, 'that a man should be a good active citizen and a good Christian, than able to tickle and amuse the public by any dexterity in the arts.'[1] And yet he kept on working. His pictures, watercolours of sheep shearers bending to their labours, of oxen ploughing at sunset and maids milking in fields, are amalgams of his pastoral memories. He wandered back through his dreams like some homecoming ghost. But the world through which he drifted had been irrevocably lost.

Palmer, peeping with xenophobic eyes at the French Revolution, may once have worried about revolution in England by a rising underclass, but it was not a peasant rabble that was now threatening his country: it was people like him. In the decades following the 1850s, the once small and sharply defined middle class began expanding enormously. Profits engendered by the industrial revolution led to the growth of banks and accountancy firms, insurance and advertising companies, trading and retail outlets. Office life flourished. In London, huge armies of functionaries set up home at the fringes of the city and, from the late 1860s onwards, in new dormitory towns. File after file of terraced or semi-detached buildings marched outwards across the fields, a brick and mortar testimony to the power of a new propertied class.

These functionaries came, broadly speaking, to be seen as the lower-middle class while those working in the professions, the doctors, lawyers and clergy, the more respectable shop owners and businessmen with gentlemanly origins and university backgrounds, slowly hived off into an upper-middle class. Leaving the filthy industrial ghettoes of the cities and the identikit terraces of their expanding outskirts, they moved into airier, more socially exclusive suburbs. There they built the sort of houses that they felt could reflect their superior status. They indulged in their fantasies, adapting the architect's pattern book designs with towers and bay windows, balconies and porches, steep slate roofs and fancy shingles. These were the homes that Palmer watched multiplying out of his window. 'Little villas with big names ... and genteel mansions, each with a smaller garden and a more imposing façade than its predecessor, engulfed field after field,'[2] wrote Herbert. For Palmer, it felt like the last straw when the only old farm that was left in the region was bought up and converted into a hideous 'park' with trim roads, iron hurdles and manicured grounds.

Palmer was only too aware that he himself occupied the sort of Gothic Revival fantasy which he most detested, or that he too benefited from the 'metallic pea-shooter',[3] the train which made living there possible and which could transport him to the capital within a few hours. And yet he shared few of the interests of his neighbours. He mocked the gentility to which the upper-middle classes – bound to the gentry by virtue of being property owners – aspired in order to maintain their distance from the workers below. He deplored the ridiculous etiquette of these 'carriage and poodle people':[4] men in sparrow tails sipping coffee and dandies in fashionable horse-drawn gigs. He mocked the ludicrous elaborations of Reigate speech. 'The white convolvuli are commencing their tortuosities,' he laughed. He despised the 'genteel-life-servant-keeping-system'. If he were alone again, he said (and often he must have wished that he was), he would live in a hut near a wholesome cookshop and be his own housemaid and char.

'We are such geese of routine, such fools of fashion,' he wrote, 'that if rat pie ... I beg pardon, tart is the genteel word, became a favourite at Balmoral, in a short time they would be seen on every dinner table in London, with tails elegantly coiled and arranged outside the crust.'[5]

'If we merely ask ourselves what people will say of us then we are rotten to the core,'[6] he declared. 'Sometimes,' Herbert remembered, 'when a friend was dining with us, my father would appear at the table with a ring upon his little finger, an unwonted ornament which he would ostentatiously display. The guest was sure, sooner or later, to notice not only the ring (it was a plain, substantial-looking hoop) but a markedly genteel bearing and gesture. But, towards the end of the meal, a dangling screw would appear where the stone is usually set, thus showing that the jewel was nothing more than a new and highly lacquered picture-frame ring. This, the wearer would continue to show off with mincing attitudes and "Reigate-genteel conversation".'[7]

Female fashion in all its perverse manifestations became Palmer's particular bugbear: the low-cut evening dresses worn in all weathers, the 'shameless bold-faced-jig Jezebel tops' that are 'miscalled bonnets',[8] the enormous cage crinolines, 'meshes and lime twigs of Parisian Strumpets',[9] the predilection for little feet 'not perceiving that largeness and littleness are equally deformed and that the beauty of any part lies in its just proportion to the whole';[10] and perhaps most abominable of all: the fashion for tight stays. On this last subject, Palmer was at one with the author Charles Kingsley, a vociferous member (along with the artist G. F. Watts and the architect Edward William Godwin) of an anti-tight-lacing league. Again and again Palmer railed against the 'curse' of these 'Babylonish gyves'. 'It is the business of the Devil to deface the works of God, and of God's loveliest work,' he would thunder: 'these hateful corsets cramp and impede the vitals, utterly destroy the shapeliness and grace which we in our hopeless barbarism fancy they improve, and even twist and distort the bony structure. They impair the action of the lungs and heart, corrupt the breath, prevent ease and gracefulness of movement and sometimes any sudden movement at all but at the cost of sudden death.'[11]

The decline of religion was another thorn in his side. In the fast-growing towns, neither Anglican minister nor Nonconformist pastor could maintain proper contact with his congregation – not even with the indirect allurements of charitable handouts or free education in Sunday schools. The latest scientific discoveries did not help. The faith espoused by Paley's *Natural Theology*, a foundation stone of Palmer's religious belief, had been steadily eroded by strong new currents of evolutionary thought. The discovery of fossils in Tierra del Fuego had posed possibilities which the biblical creation story could not account for. Charles Darwin's 1859 *On the Origin of Species* shook the moral and metaphysical framework of Western civilisation: it questioned the belief that man was set above the beasts, a unique species sharing in and aspiring to divine love. This greatly disturbed Palmer who kept up to date with developments by reading periodicals. Deplorable as he found 'the encroachments of tasteless dissipation upon all that is most precious in English domestic life, there is yet a viler and more alarming defection,' he declared, which is 'that air of independence of God'[12] that rises from 'athletic young atheists who have outgrown their souls'.[13] The whole mental and moral atmosphere reeked with infidelity,[14] he ranted. Educated Christians were becoming less religious than the average pagan of antiquity. The nation, quite literally, was going to the devil. He would not part with Chapter 58 of Isaiah for all the dismal millions of ages or cavernous bone-grubbing of the geologists, he insisted. His faith was that of Augustine and Anselm, Bacon and Milton, Dante and Pascal. 'Would these men have thrown away their Bibles because coral reefs took a long time forming, or somebody fancied himself the grandson of an ape?'[15] As far as Palmer was concerned, progress was never so rapid as when it was running down hill.

———

Palmer withdrew into the peaceful world of his study as he had once withdrawn to the seclusion of a rural valley and it was there, amid loved books and artistic treasures, amid prayers and meditations and rambling memories, that he rediscovered a lost vision. It might not have been as fervid as it had been in Shoreham, but during the Furze Hill exile of the final part of his life he worked on the finest pictures he had created since his youth.

'If we had ventured into his study on a certain autumn day in 1864,' Herbert wrote, 'we should have found him, glue-brush in hand, joining together two millboards with a broad strip of rough canvas. When this was dry, behold a primitive portfolio! We should have seen him fix upon it a great label bearing the giant letters "MIL", and then begin a long and thoughtful search through the other portfolios, which, crammed to bursting, lined the room. One by one he reflectively picked out from the classical divisions of each, sketches from nature, small and large; highly finished or mere pencil indications with written memoranda, and tiny effect "blots" on scraps of paper.'[16] This was the start of one of the two projects that were to dominate his last two decades.

The inception of this project has, slightly fancifully, been compared by a previous biographer, Raymond Lister, to that of the commissioning of Mozart's *Requiem*. The great musician was approached shortly before his death by a mysterious stranger whom he, perhaps already suffering fits of the hallucinatory fever that would eventually kill him, thought to be an emissary of the supernatural world. The music of the *Requiem* obsessed Mozart until the end of his life. Palmer's commission was less dramatic but equally strange; and a grave and portentous stranger also called the tune. His name was Leonard Rowe Valpy, a Lincoln's Inn solicitor who included John Ruskin among his clients and pursued an ardent and often strongly opinionated sideline as a connoisseur and collector of art.

Palmer, for all that Ruskin had never followed up his first passing interest in his work, had continued to admire this critic and, in 1870, would gratefully receive a copy of his *Queen of the Air* inscribed 'Samuel Palmer with John Ruskin's love'. He shared his appreciation for the Pre-Raphaelites and he and Millais had found much to agree upon when they had one day happened to find themselves standing side by side admiring a painting by Turner. 'What an admirable man Rossetti must be!'[17] Palmer had exclaimed on first encountering his poetry. Rossetti in his turn had found much to praise in Palmer's work. He predicted a successful future for his poetic landscapes and he was right. In the wake of the Pre-Raphaelites' espousal of the Ancients' belief in the spiritual integrity of the medieval art, there was a noticeable shift in critical opinions of Palmer. To a cultural world that had been introduced to the myriad-hued canvases of Holman Hunt, Palmer's blazing sunsets and flaring dawns no longer looked startling. 'Mr Palmer may

rush into chromatic regions where other artists fear even to breathe,'
wrote an *Art Journal* critic in 1866, 'but still in the midst of madness
there is a method which reconciles the spectator to the result.'[18] Palmer
came to be seen as an exponent of what one writer labelled a 'polychro-
matic school'. 'Mr Ruskin in past years pronounced this artist the
coming man,' the *Art Journal* declared in 1866. 'Accordingly Mr Palmer
now realises his prediction.'

In 1863, Valpy had bought one of Palmer's paintings from the winter
exhibition of the Old Watercolour Society. It was a small (now lost)
landscape showing a chapel by a bridge. Valpy had contacted the painter
and – in a first sign of the opinionated bullying that would lead to later
collisions – had asked whether he would take the work back and tone
the light down a little. Palmer, bending as was too often his wont to the
demands of an overbearing character, had obliged and so had begun a
friendship which, developing through copious correspondence, was to
play a stimulating if sometimes upsetting role in his declining years,
rousing Palmer from his isolation, stirring his mind to fresh argument
and his imagination to renewed vigour even as his physical capacities
began to fail.

Herbert, ten at the time of first meeting Valpy, was not inclined to
like him. His face was keen, stern and dark, he recalled, with a low
retreating forehead and black hair in places turning grey. He had a
'reluctant smile, and a deep, deliberate diction [that] seemed to forbid
the associating him with any of the luxuries of life, or (save in religious
matters) with its emotions'. When it came to 'the lighter vein of table
talk', he was even less responsive that Linnell.[19] He also 'had a fine
repertory of what he imagined to be studio gestures', Herbert noted
acerbically, exclamations and attitudes of a sort from which Palmer was
completely free.[20] He believed himself to be a man of distinguished
sensibilities who 'sought refreshment in nature's deepest and highest
utterances'; who could 'revel in the tints of a dying bramble-leaf, and
who could fling his law, and his caution, and his seriousness behind
him, before a beautiful landscape or a resplendent sunset'.[21] These
poetic inclinations impressed Herbert's open-hearted father. When in
the summer of 1864, Valpy contacted him, wondering if he had

'anything in hand which specially affected his "inner sympathies",[22] Palmer wrote excitedly back: 'You read my thoughts! . . . Only three days have passed since I did begin the meditation of a subject which, for twenty years, has affected my sympathies with sevenfold inwardness; though now, for the first time, I seem to feel in some sort the power of realising it.'[23] This long-dreamt-of project was a set of small works inspired by Milton's meditations on mirth and melancholy: *L'Allegro* and *Il Penseroso*. Palmer had frequently painted other Miltonic subjects, but these two pastoral odes – for which Blake had once completed designs – appealed to his deepest affections.

They would hardly have appealed to the tastes of his times. The mid-Victorian preference was for big, polished pictures that told colourful stories; that conveyed moral messages or captured the densely packed drama of contemporary life. William Powell Frith's panorama *The Derby Day*, with its crowds of top-hatted race-goers, its fashionable carriages and barefooted gypsies, its picnickers, yokels and acrobats, had stolen the show at the Royal Academy in 1858. A rail had had to be erected to hold back the gawping crush. Hubert Von Herkomer had found enormous popularity with his conscience-stirring depictions of the lives of the poor and Ford Madox Brown had been admired for such sentimental scenarios as *The Last of England* in which a pair of anxious emigrants are shown huddled on the deck of an Antipodean-bound ship, or his richly symbolic *Work* which, taking him twelve years to complete, set out to show labour as it affects all strata of society. Landseer, too, had become a great favourite with his anthropomorphised portraits of pets and his proud cervine monarchs, which, presiding over their wild Scottish glens, had done much to popularise the Highland dream which the Queen and her consort had first made fashionable by decamping for Balmoral. Royal holidays in Deeside set a new trend for country life. But sporting pleasures amid heather-clad rocks could hardly have been further from Palmer's pastoral ideal.

Palmer was only too aware that in accepting Valpy's commission much would have to be sacrificed, but he was prepared to make the commitment and finally, in April 1865, after months of contemplation and planning, it had been settled that there would be eight, small watercolours, four from *L'Allegro* and four from *Il Penseroso*. He initially intended them to be twinned, demonstrating oppositions of mood and varieties of effects to their best advantage and though in the end he did not achieve this, doing three from the first poem and five from the next, echoes of the planned pairing can still be spotted. The optimistic promise of a rising sun, for instance, may be compared to the quiet solemnity of a gathering dusk.

Palmer embarked on his Milton project with a spring in his step. 'Without aiming at anything beyond or outside my tether,' he ventured, 'I hope, if it be not presumption, to produce a few things that may justly be called a work of art.'[24] These works of art – though the final one was never quite finished to his satisfaction – were to become his obsession for the last seventeen years of his life.

Palmer ransacked his portfolios, perusing his sketches, bringing together the best of them, combining 'mappy Buckinghamshire treat-ment'[25] with 'southern Dartmoor sentiment',[26] to evoke that imaginative realm in which he had wandered since boyhood. It must have been a delight – most of all when he drifted back through memories of Shoreham: 'It is a breaking out of village fever long after contact,' he said.[27] The commission was never far from his thoughts and, although beset by other duties, he managed to work away '*heart* and *soul*'[28] in whatever time he could spare, sometimes first thing in the morning, sometimes last thing at night. 'Milton's nuts are worth the trouble of cracking,' he told Valpy, 'for each has a kernel in it. Monkeys and illus-trators are apt to make faces when they crack and find nothing.'[29] Confined to his chair by an asthma attack, Palmer made the most of his indisposition, leafing through his portfolios and, one evening, while chatting to John Preston Wright, he paused suddenly in mid-flow, asking his friend to remain in position because he wanted to sketch the way his coat was falling for one of the works.

The Milton series spent a great deal of time packed safely away in a special bone box. But Palmer had always been a slow worker. 'When our work is on the easel, I wish we were obliged to sit a quarter of an hour with our hands tied, to have time for forethought,'[30] he had once told a pupil. He did not want to add one touch without proper consideration, he said. Often he would pause, just at that moment when he was about to apply the paint and, quite unconsciously, lay his palette and brushes aside to sit there instead, gazing for hours at a time. He had to wait for the right moment for, as he told Valpy, there are 'gossamer films and tendernesses . . . which are not always done at the proper time, but come strangely when one cannot account for it'.[31] His inching progress was the result of a minutely calibrated balance between technical knowledge and poetic inspiration, between judgement and impulse, thinking and feeling, fear and joy.

Valpy was initially very much involved in the process. Palmer informed him of every development, from the breaking up of a crimson tone which he thought would depress a saffron to the improvements that might be effected by a few faint touches of grey. Though Valpy was rather too literal-minded for an artist who sought out the spirit not the letter of a text, Palmer hoped to persuade him along a more imaginative path. As he exulted in the 'unutterable going-in-itiveness'[32] of his project, he failed to heed warning signs. Palmer had been put into artistic harness, Herbert observed, with the interfering Valpy holding the reins. Before long, he feared, Valpy would be riding roughshod over his father's sensibilities. The Wrights felt a similar distrust, Howard at one point becoming so incensed by the lawyer's pomposity and the dull drone of his talk that he withdrew to Herbert's bedroom to unburden himself of his contempt. The judgement of the youths was, unfortunately, to prove only too right.

Valpy grew increasingly impatient at the long delay. Soon a taut courtesy took the place of enthusiastic optimism; the correspondence thinned until, in 1875, Palmer, whose letters had once poured out in an excitable gabble, found himself struggling to put his emotions into words. No amount of explanation could stand in for feeling, he said, citing the story of Lord Stafford's housemaid who had stood leaning on her broom before a wondrous Claude not because it excited her curiosity, he explained, but because 'she thought she was in Heaven'.[33] Claude and Poussin, he said, 'did not attempt to satisfy that curiosity of the eye which an intelligent tourist ever feeds and never sates'. They were not attempting merely to reproduce a scene: 'They knew that every hedge-row contains more matter than could be crowded into a picture gallery; and that supposing they could deceive the eye, the real impression could not be completed but by touch and hearing – the gushing of air and the singing of birds. They addressed not the perception chiefly, but the IMAGINATION, and there is the hinge and essence of the whole matter.'[34]

It was pretty much the whole matter as far as Palmer and Valpy were concerned. An acquaintanceship which would probably have contin-ued on a remote but equable level came to an abrupt end when Valpy, in 1879, almost fifteen years after he had first commissioned Palmer, decided that the artist should reduce his fee. Palmer was deeply wounded. 'I loved the subjects, and was willing to be a loser in all but the higher matters of Art and Friendship,' he wrote. 'I do not in the least complain that I have lost a thousand pounds by them . . . but I considered your taste and feeling so much above the ordinary standards that, in order fully to satisfy them, I have *lavished time without limit or measure*, even after I myself considered the works complete.'[35] But, having given up so much time – 'such a *ridiculous* amount some would say'[36] – he decided to continue as he started and keep on doing his very utmost to the last.

———

Palmer had begun work on his Milton series at a time when it was becoming fashionable for artists to show their sketches: a rapid – and hence highly profitable – form of expression that could summon from its viewers an immediate response. But Palmer thought this practice superficial, a symptom of urban society's more general malaise. He sought instead a more profound form of perception, a spiritual revela-tion that would come only through long contemplation and meditative prayer. The eight Milton pictures ripened slowly to fruition, *A Towered City*, *The Lonely Tower* and *The Dripping Eaves* being completed in 1868, *The Curfew* in 1870, *The Waters Murmuring* in 1877 and then *The Prospect* and *The Open Gate* eleven years later in 1888, while the last

image, *The Bellman*, he never considered to be fully completed. Together
they represent the summation of his watercolour career: Palmer, sinking
slowly down through the sediments of his memory, brought his imagination to rest on a bedrock of undisturbed myth. As his mind wandered
amid the lands of his literary visions, amid Arcadian dreams and
Virgilian stories, medieval fantasies and Spenserian pastorals, he drew
together the images that had informed and shaped his own life: the
sleeping shepherd that he had first admired as a student; the 'monumental oak' which Milton had inspired him to draw, the pastoral
beauties of the Ancients' Kentish valleys, the tall craggy skylines of his
Welsh sketching trips; the luminous seascapes of tramps around Devon;
the thick-moted sunlight of an Italian honeymoon. He remembered
the classical aesthetic of Poussin; the tranquil poetry of Claude Lorrain,
the crepuscular mystery of a Gothic aesthetic, the vaporous atmospheres of Dutch landscape.

Palmer was by then an old man. His eyes were dimming, but his
memories glowed all the brighter for that. He was becoming like the
bellman of his final painting, a lone figure walking through huddled
village streets, tolling the passing of a day at its close. As the horned
cattle clustered in the lee of the hedgerows, as the labourers sat to their
suppers by shining lamplight, as the church tower reflected the last
glories of sunset and the chimney smoke rose into a gathering dark, he
marked the passing of an era of pastoral peace.

The Lonely Tower

A mysterious wisdom won by toil
William Butler Yeats, *The Phases of the Moon*

The Lonely Tower is the most evocative of Palmer's late works. It shows a ruined turret standing on the edge of a cliff, a proud remnant of something once greater keeping solitary watch over the quiet of the night. Far below, a crescent moon drifts from a cloud-streaked horizon; above, the sky's violet spaces are twinkling with stars. A late traveller guides his ox-cart along a track that winds through one corner. Two shepherds gaze upwards from the grassy foreground. They are contemplating the lantern which glows from the tower's upper window: a bright ember burning on the edge of the world. A barn owl skims pale as a ghost along a shadowy stream bed. It feels almost as if it could fly free of the picture: the spirit of this twilit vision released.

When the first version of this watercolour was exhibited at the Old Watercolour Society in 1868 it was accompanied by the quotation from *Il Penseroso* that had inspired it:

> *Or let my lamp at midnight hour,*
> *Be seen in some high lonely tower,*
> *Where I may oft outwatch the Bear,*
> *With thrice great Hermes.*

As he sat up late at night, alone in his studio, Palmer must have empathised with Milton's solitary thinker. Through his studio windows he could see as far as Leith Hill. It was probably the fortified folly that still stands upon its summit that he painted. To Palmer this monument would have been freighted with significance: it stood near High Ashes farm where More had suffered his last illness and beyond it lay his son's never-to-be-visited burial place. Palmer painted a picture laden with coded references to his lost boy. The position of the stars – he painted Ursa Major (the Great Bear) in accordance with Milton's poem – is that which would have been observed on the day of More's death. In the bewildered agony of that grief-stricken moment, the bright patterns of this constellation had been branded onto his memory.

The other major project that obsessed Palmer throughout the last years of his life also developed out of his relationship with his son. Palmer had always loved Virgil's *Eclogues* and for decades had dreamt of making his own English translation. After More's death this project became to him a precious 'resource in the deepest distress of mind',[1] he told Calvert whom he frequently consulted on the more puzzling Latin phrases. Palmer explored everything from the history of the poems' scholarly exegesis, to their possible relevance to the modern political world. His texts were never far from his side and, in 1863, required to have his photographic portrait taken for the Old Watercolour Society, he posed with a copy of the *Eclogues* in his hand. 'You can cut out [the Virgil] and throw the old man who holds it in the fire,'[2] he wrote as he sent Calvert one of the prints.

If a visitor to Furze Hill had examined the pile of books that lay on Palmer's table they would have found among them one in manuscript form: 'a manuscript so interlined, erased, and cut about for the inser-tion of new slips of matter, that but little of the original volume remained',[3] Herbert said. But no one ever caught him perusing this because a knock at the door was a sign for it to be hastily slipped away. Herbert alone was party to this project and he was highly scep-tical. 'I think the idea of having his name associated within the covers of a real, published book, with the work of an immortal poet, betrayed him into unwonted castle building,'[4] he wrote. Certainly, to the modern reader who stumbles across the volume that was only finally published after Palmer's death, the heavy-handed rhymes, ornate language and coy bowdlerisation feel more ludicrous than evocative: Palmer turned the second eclogue, a hymn to pederastic love, into a decorous heterosexual poem.

When, in 1872, he had all but completed his translation, he took Hamerton into his confidence who managed with some difficulty to persuade him that the *Eclogues* should not be published without accompanying illustrations. And so, in May of that year, fleeing the annual spring-cleaning, Palmer took refuge in Margate where he embarked on the second phase of his Virgil project. By the time he came home he had decided upon the ten subjects he would draw and one or two of the designs were already in a fairly advanced state. He imagined, Herbert recalled, that there existed some wonderful new photomechanical process which would make perfect facsimiles of his work; but there was not and so eventually, after long and unfruitful discussion, Hamerton suggested that he might start etching instead. He can't have known what this would mean, said Herbert, to a man who was 'incapable by nature and training of doing anything whatever by halves', who had 'throughout the whole of his life been mountaineering among the mental Alps that were always overtopped by some still more inaccessible peak'.[5]

A vision of an exquisite little headpiece at the start of each eclogue began to develop in Palmer's head. He would aim for 'poetic compression' rather than 'landscape diffuseness'[6] and so the works would be small. But this was not an undertaking that could be measured in terms of size. Laying in a dozen tremendously solid copperplates and a stock of the fiercest nitrous acid, Palmer was embarking on a project which, though calculated to occupy only 240 square inches, would take up the rest of his life.

'Once more . . . the doors of the little Etching cupboard stood open, the acid fumed and needles were diligently sharpened . . . the conversation ran on half a hundred delightful technicalities,' Herbert wrote, his own interest flaring as the etching began. 'The "Vs" became a by-word between us,' he recalled; 'a portfolio full of the most carefully selected material was promoted to a chair of its own; an old cigar box was made into a rack for ten plates' as a 'sole remaining hobby' took the bit between its teeth.[7]

Progress was predictably protracted. 'It is *my* misfortune to work slowly,' Palmer had once told his friend Hamerton, 'not from any wish to niggle, but because I cannot otherwise get certain shimmerings of light and mysteries of shadow.'[8] This was an artist who 'would sooner die that put a pinch of incense on the great golden altar of Mediocrity,' his son said, and his 'ten poor little Vs',[9] of which not a line could be put down without premeditation, were more deeply thought out than anything else he had ever done. His father crept painstakingly into the 'mystic maze'[10] of his work. 'Copper bites into time as greedily as acid into copper,'[11] he lamented. But with one of his 'dear teazing, tickling'[12] plates before him and a beloved needle, sharpened three-quarter-wise like a bayonet, in his hand, he did not miss the bright tinctures of his watercolour palette at all. Outline, he had always believed, was the one 'great difficulty; the only first step and great accomplishment of art'. Once that had been attained, the 'prey' was caught and the rest was merely 'cooking and garnishing it'.[13] Having lost sight of this purity for so long amid the colourful palettes of Victorian fashion, he returned to his ideal: the 'aerial gloom'[14] of the etcher. He would become so utterly absorbed, he once told Howard Wright, that time and place would vanish. He would step into the world of the picture he was making: into 'that land never to be reached but always to be striven for'.[15] 'Those who have seen him sitting, sable in hand, hour after hour behind the tissue paper, pencilling in varnish silver cloudlets round a moon; or have seen him revelling in the ferocity of the seething mordant with which he sometimes loved to excavate an emphatic passage will not wonder that he achieved only thirteen etchings in his life,' his son said.[16]

———

How different his life had become from that of his old mentor. Linnell was by then a fêted Victorian figure. Sitting in his grand library at Redstone, bringing fine brandies and clarets up from his extensive cellar (when the doctors advised him to give up drinking he abandoned the former but stubbornly continued to drink wine into extreme old age), he would entertain the many dealers who came to call. Offered both his ale and theology at table, they preferred the former, he observed, his penetrating stare magnified by the two pairs of spectacles which he wore, one on top of the other, for close work. He was under no illusions. He called these middlemen the 'DDs', which stood for 'Dodgy Dealers', and always insisted on taking a deposit even when negotiating with the most reputable of firms. Linnell seldom worked for more than two hours consecutively on any one picture before changing it for another canvas or alternative pastime. He had always considered himself to be above all else a craftsman and he churned out his landscapes like he churned out his batches of bread. At their best they were as muscular as ever: loudly proclaiming the majesty of nature, they appealed to the bold tastes of the era's self-made men.

Palmer, in contrast, lived a secluded life. Much of his time was passed in peaceful musing as the greater proportion of any picture that he did was achieved, his son said, not by manual work but mental concentration. To the industrious Linnell it would have looked like idleness; but Palmer's contemplation was often so profound that even his wife would not venture to disturb it. Furze Hill House would remain silent long into the night while only a mile or two away, at Redstone, Linnell would be presiding over a drawing-room gathering, 'loudly laying down the law on politics and wrangling over the daily newspapers'.[17] The work on his easel upstairs would be forgotten until the next day.

In 1875, Linnell was given his first one-man show; but his eyes were fading. He found it increasingly difficult to authenticate the paintings which dealers brought him and occasionally he made a mistake. Once, he had condemned a picture outright, only on further inspection to discover that it was one of the several Palmers which, thirty years earlier, he had retouched. Problems were beginning to arise with his home-made varnishes and some of his earlier canvases were flaking and cracked. Linnell's health was also deteriorating. Sometimes he complained of giddiness. His memory was failing him and often he found himself confused. He had rheumatism in one hip, wore a hernia truss and had to cup his hand to his ear when anyone spoke. But he still remained stolid in faith, firm in conviction and stalwart in character. When one of his sons, Thomas, a twin who had a limp and a stammer, announced that he was going to marry the serving girl to whom he had proposed while she was cleaning the grate, all the family was affronted except this stubborn patriarch who, never forgetting his own humble origins, was prepared to accept a housemaid as his daughter-in-law.

Holman Hunt, calling at Redstone with his wife, offered among the last descriptions of Linnell. He was greeted at the door, Hunt remembered, by the master of the house with his Bible raised aloft, demanding in stentorian tones to know whether he had mastered his New Testament teachings. 'He would not allow me to evade the question,' Hunt said. It was as if he had recognised that he was coming towards the end of his life and that there would never again be an opportunity for him 'to deliver his sacredest message of all to me, and he would not fail, although when he regarded my reply as failing in thoroughness, he had to reproach me, which he did unsparingly'.[18]

Linnell, Hunt said, was a man who 'all his life had striven after truth in way and in word'.[19] Herbert was less tolerant: he detested his grandfather's 'raging rancorous homemade religion'[20] and, acutely aware of familial strains, regarded the old man as a bullying martinet. He disliked staying at Redstone. Hannah, after the death of her mother, began to spend less time there too. She grew gentler and more loving towards Palmer as she entered old age and gradually, united once more in spirit and affection to the man whom she had married when she was little more than a child, became once more his indefatigable companion, always to be found close beside him, solicitous for his happiness and watchful for his comfort and health.

Forty years earlier, as a young artist in Shoreham, Palmer had dreamt of a wife who would read to him when his eyes were tired; now Hannah spent her evenings doing exactly that, or just peaceably sewing while he sat and wrote letters – often, for the sake of economy, on torn-off half sheets of paper that his correspondents had not used. One day, they were to be found sharing the sort of playful in-joke that, as newlyweds in Italy, they had enjoyed. Mary, their maid, had mentioned something called an 'anversand'; the pair of them, pricking up their ears 'with the most conjugal unanimity', set off on a humorous quest to find out how others of their household pronounced the word. Jane, from Redhill, it turned out, had 'always had a name for "&": she calls it an ampsisand', while their man-of-all-work informed them that he always heard it called 'asverasand'.[21]

Steadfast in their affection for their 'dear old church of England',[22] Palmer and Hannah continued to attend services together on Sundays, two small bundled figures among the poorer members of the congregation, preferring always the humbler place to the prominent pew, though, when a High Church service was introduced, Hannah, more wary than her husband of extravagant ritual, decided to move to an evangelical congregation while Palmer continued to worship at the local church.

Sometimes, in the afternoons, they would go out for country drives. Hiring a cart, they would trundle away until the odious villas had been left far behind them and they were creaking along through the open countryside. Both Palmer and Hannah were apprehensive about horses and Palmer was almost as nervous of the contraptions that they pulled: 'In all vehicles but a wheelbarrow or a bicycle,' he warned an old friend, 'it is useful to remember that there are but two or four lynch pins between us and death.'[23] But, with the sleepiest and most venerable of ponies in harness and the most soothing of drivers atop the box, they would jog along the lanes or creep up the steep hills enjoying the fine views that unfolded around them and condemning any modern innovations which they came across. Their favourite route lay through Gatton where a line of ancient yews marked out the old pilgrims' way. It was here Herbert said that, from the vantage point of the fly, his father had made his last drawings from nature. They are just a few lines, but they show that he had not lost his affection for trees.

Among the most vivid images of the Palmers in old age is that offered by Hamerton's wife who, preparing a memoir of her late husband,[24] recalled a visit that they had once made to Furze Hill. It was only in the late 1870s that the Hamertons, after long correspondence, finally paid a much-anticipated visit. They were disappointed when, arriving at the house, they were told that Palmer was confined to his bed, far too ill to get up and play host to anyone.

The Hamertons were shown into the dining room to be offered refreshment before taking their leave. 'The room was warmed by a good fire, but darkened by the blinds being down and the curtains drawn,' Mrs Hamerton remembered. 'The rays of a golden sunset diffused through the apertures a strange and mysterious glow.' This, she wrote, 'suddenly seemed to surround and envelop an apparition, standing half visible on the threshold of the noiselessly opened door. A remarkably expressive head emerged from the bundle of shawls, which moved forward with feeble and tottering steps – it was Mr Palmer. His wife could not trust her eyes, but as soon as she became convinced of the reality of his presence, she hastened to make him comfortable in an armchair by the fire, and to arrange the shawls over his head, and knees with the most touching solicitude.' Clearly Palmer would still go to some lengths to find the intellectual companionship that he had all his life sought. '"I could not resist it," he pleaded; "I have looked forward to this meeting with so much longing."'

'His eyes sparkled, his countenance became animated, and regardless of his wraps, he accompanied his fluent talk with eloquent gestures – to the despair of his wife, who had enough to do in replacing caps and rugs,' Mrs Hamerton said. 'He put all his soul and energy (and now there was no lack of it) into his speech.' His conversation kindled the enthusiasm of his listeners who were charmed by his liveliness and riveted by his anecdotes of Turner and Blake. But he was attentive too, Mrs Hamerton remembered, and would listen 'with so vivid an interest and sympathy that his mere looks were an encouragement. My husband was afraid of detaining him, but he declared he felt quite well and strong – "the visiting angels had put to flight the lurking enemy".'

Palmer felt so revived in the course of the visit that he even felt hungry and so, 'nothing loth,' his guests recorded, 'we sat down to an excellent tea with delicious butter and new-laid eggs, with the impression of sharing the life of elves, and of being entertained by a genie at the head of the table and served by a kind fairy. This feeling originated no doubt in the small stature of Mr and Mrs Palmer; in the strange effect of light under which our host first appeared to us, and lastly in the noiseless promptitude with which the repast was spread on the table, whilst the darkness of the room gave way to brightness, just as happens in fairy tales.'25

Palmer described himself as a hermit in his last years. Less and less often would he pay evening visits to old friends in Reigate. Away from familiar surroundings he would grow horribly flustered and he could seldom find the strength to go to London any more. Even climbing the steps to the station platform would take his breath quite away; if he did use the train he would travel 'swathed like a mummy'26 in shawls. By the end of the 1870s he no longer even troubled to send his apologies to the Watercolour Society or Etching Club when he missed their meetings. The president of the former greatly missed him as much for his role in discussions as for their exchanges of snuff but, having lost 'that locomotive power which distinguishes the animal from the vegetable kingdom', said Palmer, they could not 'expect monthly excuses from a cabbage'.27

Confined to the house and, when the weather was cold, to just two rooms (his 'den' and the drawing room), he carried on with his projects. He was working harder now than he had at thirty, he said, getting in four hours' work – *with my whole mind bent upon it* – before dinner; sometimes, having supped lightly on an egg and a dry rusk, resuming his labours afterwards and carrying on into the night. Outside, the wind might be blowing along the ridges, the great Wellingtonia in the garden would moan and lash, but 'however much tempests may rage before and after, the Hours of ART-WORK MUST BE QUIET HOURS', Palmer told his son. 'When we want a lambent flame we clear the grate getting the noise and dust over for the time. If anything bustles me I am forced to sit still and make an artificial quiet before I can put the right touch.'28

He rarely saw the Ancients in person, now. They were all growing too frail to travel. But they continued to exchange news. Richmond had bought a house in Wiltshire, which he was restoring as a hobby. Palmer was disappointed when, in 1879, he wouldn't accompany him on a seaside holiday: 'Can't you come down and have a social groan over things in general?'[29] he begged. He missed a good grumble with his old friend. Giles kept him abreast of developments in debates of the sort that they had both always loved, dispatching newspaper clippings along with his letters. The interests of deceased Ancients were not neglected. Finch's widow was seventy-two years old when, in 1880, Palmer applied on her behalf for a charitable bequest and secured her £20. Nor was Blake forgotten: when the *Cornhill Magazine* had published an article declaring that the poet had been mad and consigned to an asylum, Palmer had leapt to his defence, penning a letter to say that he remembered Blake 'in the quiet consistency of his daily life, as one of the sanest, if not thoroughly sane men I have ever known'.[30] To the very last years of his life, he remained loyal and when, in 1878, he read that the Quakers, having become proprietors of the church where Blake lay buried, were building over the churchyard, he was outraged. 'They have rummaged the dust of John Bunyan; torn up in gobbets what fleshly remains there were of William Blake,'[31] he wrote.

Palmer's interests, however, were not confined solely to the past. When his godson Willie Richmond was appointed to the illustrious post of Slade Professor of Fine Art, he warmly congratulated him. 'It is kind of you to remember old friends just in the moment of success when people generally forget them,' he wrote in 1879.[32] And he still kept up with Richmond's daughter, Julia, who, in 1881, bought his painting of a bright cloud. Her father had thought well of it too, he told her with delight. He was thrilled to hear that her child Hilda had started learning the violin. It 'demands exactitude of tune which the pianoforte lacks',[33] he enthused, adding 'the value of everything on earth,' as he had always propounded, 'is pretty much in proportion to the difficulty acquiring it'.[34]

Palmer's delight in children never flagged. He followed the progress of all his friends' offspring, inquiring of John Wright's 'dear Earnest' who suffered from fits; sending love and advice to the Stephens's son Holly (short for Holman, after Holman Hunt) and enthusiastically praising the etchings of Hamerton's boy. Sometimes his missives smacked of an old illiberality. A stern letter to Holly's father suggested a bowdlerised edition of Shakespeare, for the boy has been deriving improper amusement from the poet. 'The pagan Juvenal says that PURITY should be inscribed over the door of every house where there is a boy,'[35] Palmer admonished. But for the most part, his affection and generosity shone more brightly with age.

Though his physical strength waned, his mind remained strong. Palmer, even in old age, liked to stay alert to everything from the latest ecclesiastical appointment through news of an earthquake in Quito to the loss of six fowl from a neighbouring farm. 'When old people begin to talk about themselves it is time their families interfered,' he wrote, though the manner of interference, he acknowledged, differed in different nations: 'In some the elders are hunted up into a tree, pelted down with stones and then eaten.'[36] He remained to the end a vivid conversationalist, entertaining his listeners with the passion of his convictions, the coolness of his incredulity, the ingenuity of his defences and the energy of his attacks. He was equally masterful at drawing people out. He would sit quietly while some enthusiastic friend trotted his favourite hobby to and fro before him, said Herbert, agreeing with his companion as far as he thought possible and preferring to overlook blunders rather than pull someone up. He tried hard to sympathise with everyone's stance. And yet, he was maddeningly pig-headed about his own point of view and once he had set off on one of his rants, he would seldom admit defeat. Just when his antagonist felt assured of victory he would suddenly, 'by some ingenious manoeuvre, some energetic confession of faith, or an abrupt retreat into the strongholds of paradox' show that he 'valued the arguments, and the evidence and the authority, not a snap of his fingers, against his own cherished convictions'.[37] It must have been infuriating – particularly when, as Herbert suspected, he didn't necessarily hold to the belief he so pig-headedly espoused.

Palmer continued to read with all his usual passion and prejudice

– though he now needed books printed in larger type – revelling in anything from religious tracts to the old companions of his youth, a pile of which in their ancient leather bindings would always be stacked on his table alongside his drawings and the current volume of his commonplace book. In 1880 he thanked Cope for sending him the latest biography of Milton. It was the sixth he had read in his life, he said, but each had only whetted his appetite for the next. He busily harvested anecdotes from newspapers and periodicals – anything from the tale of a Prussian woman who was pregnant with five children to the story of a cat who travelled 200 miles in four days – for the amusement of Wright who kept a compendium of such peculiarities. Palmer himself was notoriously credulous and could be as entirely persuaded of the capture of a mighty sea serpent at Oban as he was of the actual existence of the devil. In old age he also discovered a fascination for mathematics and, like his father before him, started to carry an algebra book and bag of scribbling paper about with him, keeping it beside his pillow at night. His calculations showed a lamentable want of success and his arithmetic, his son remembered, became something of a family joke.

In 1875 another of the Ancients, Frederick Tatham, became the second of the little band to die. It was he who had done most to help Blake in his frail final years and he had inherited, through his widow whom he had taken in as a housekeeper, many of Blake's late works. He had subsequently fallen under the thrall of a millenarian sect, however, and, persuaded that Blake's ideas were blasphemous, was said to have sold whatever was vendible and consigned the rest of the great visionary's legacy to the fire: plates, blocks, manuscripts, volumes of verse prepared for the press, six or seven epic poems as long as Homer and twenty tragedies as long as Macbeth – all, it was rumoured, went up in smoke. 'A piteous gag had been thrust in to the mouth of Blake's corpse,' declared William Michael Rossetti (brother of the artist). If Frederick Tatham is remembered at all, it is for this act of terrible destruction. It would certainly have clouded his friendship with Palmer, but at the moment of his passing Palmer remembered only the young man he had

once loved. 'I seldom think of Shoreham without recalling his persistent and self-denying kindness to a poor cottager whose sores he daily
dressed with his own hands,'[38] he wrote.

In 1877, John Wright was given the living of the vicar of Newborough
in Staffordshire. Palmer was greatly to miss the 'weekly treat'[39] of a long
Monday evening talk and although the pair continued their lively epistolary exchanges – their good-humoured intimacy is evoked by such
inscrutable lines as 'at next meeting, Remlapacious hopes to tell of the
curious laughing spider stomachial'[40] – they were never to be able to
meet up again regularly for, in 1881, Wright was appointed to his
father-in-law's old Shropshire incumbency, a post in which he would
remain for the rest of his working life. 'If you feel lonely, a shepherd
with a little flock upon a hill,' Palmer told him in 1877, 'think of *my*
loneliness, frozen up and crippled up from the haunts of men, from my
London friends.'[41] He was feeling rather sorry for himself at the time,
having just failed to muster the energy to attend a 'dearly longed-for
Blake exhibition'[42] in the capital. Soon, Palmer was not even keeping
one of his beloved tabbies for company. 'I am not the man I was before
I left off keeping cats,'[43] he mourned in 1879.

Herbert, by this time, was no longer living with his parents. He had
rented a studio in Newman Street, London – a good, light, artist's
workplace of the sort that his father had never had – but he returned to
Furze Hill regularly. It was he who persuaded Palmer to install a printing press in the house. Herbert had been taught how to print by
Frederick Goulding, one of the great copperplate experts of that day,
and now he and his father set to work on producing their own impressions of *The Bellman* and *The Lonely Tower*. From this time on, Palmer's
letters to his son often turned into lists of instructions. Occasionally he
would grow intemperate. 'Pray, throw your brown ink into the dust
hole,' he would cry. Brown ink is 'beastly'.[44] He wanted only black. But
more often, with the help of laboriously precise explanations, father
and son operated harmoniously together. They showed the same meticulous attention to detail. 'The edge of the tree A,' Palmer wrote, marking
out a Scotch pine on an accompanying sketch, 'is at the top a trifle too
light . . . the sucking lamb's bended knee is slightly too light at the

joint . . . perhaps the dark side of the provender trough is too hard wiped.'[45]

Herbert, mastering the art of printing, managed to coax from even the most worn-out plates some of the finest proofs of his father's works. He was paid for his efforts; he needed the money because by then he had met the woman whom he hoped to marry. Yet Palmer was never truly to value his talent with the press and eventually, just at the moment when Herbert felt his prospects were brightest, he was persuaded to give printing up on the grounds that it was less an art than a trade. He had, however, by 1880, managed to save enough to be able to afford to make Helen Margaret Tidbury his wife.

In May 1880, John Giles died. According to one account, he was run over by an omnibus – mown down, quite literally, by the progress that all his life he had fought. Richmond arranged for him – 'the greatest and dearest friend that I had on earth' – to be buried in Highgate Cemetery (where Finch also lay) in the same grave in which he and his family would later be interred. It would not be long before the first of them arrived. Early the next year Richmond's wife, Julia, passed away, just twelve days before their golden wedding anniversary. Richmond was distraught: 'On January 12th I laid the dear and faithful partner of all my joys and sorrows in the grave and my heart is well-nigh broken. My pencil as it were, fell from me and the love of art left me. I wholly gave up professional engagements and spent most of the year wandering in artlessness'.[46]

Palmer tried to comfort his friend. 'Had your affliction befallen *me*,' he wrote, 'I should have been left almost alone upon earth.'[47] But Richmond, he reminded him, had the blessing of a family. He recommended books that could bring comfort – devotional meditations and the works of Pascal – and he wrote to the young Julia, who was going round daily to visit her father, suggesting that she coax him back to 'medicinal'[48] work.

Palmer was now in his mid-seventies. All too aware of the brevity of the time that remained to him, he found comfort in such stories as that of a Bishop Butler who, just a few days before his death, had been strolling in his garden in the company of his chaplain: 'I feel that my feet are upon the rock,'[49] he had said. On warm summer evenings, Palmer too would still wander into the garden and, leaning on his staff, stand gazing at whichever of his wild flowers struggled on. He revelled in his old prints and Shoreham memories, said Herbert. His folio volumes were still kept piled on his table and the contents of his etching cupboard in orderly array. And he still kept on working. He might be found sketching a fine cloudscape or sunset from his windows or pondering one of his pastoral designs. His friends, encouraging him, kept up his hopes. 'I feel like a promising youth with remarkably light hair,'[50] Palmer laughed. And though, to the very end of his life, he suffered from his old disinclination to get on with his tasks, he had at last formed the habit 'of taking the bull by the horns': '[I] always find that after a little grunting he comes along like a lamb,' he said.[51] When instructed by a doctor to lie on a sofa and do nothing, Palmer managed to do so only for a couple of minutes before rising again with an impatient howl.

———

The weather was harsh in Palmer's final winter. Snowstorms swept over the country and he found himself mostly confined to the house. Day after day he would sit in his room, pulling out the pages of an almanac sent to him by Hook. On 18 January 1881, a great blizzard struck, sweeping a white blanket across southern England. Drifts as deep as lamp posts blocked miles of road and track.

Palmer, bundled up in the rough flannel coat of a navvy, retired to the bed in his studio. From there, he worked on the watercolours of his Milton series, completing two paintings – *The Prospect* and *The Eastern Gate* – both images of dawn and both submitted for exhibition that year. Looking at his *Eastern Gate* – a picture of a powerful, bare-chested ploughman guiding his pair of yoked oxen out onto sun-flooded slopes – it is hard not to be moved by a parallel vision of its maker: a little old man bundled up in his bed with the flaring radiance of that glorious dawn breaking like the blare of a trumpet in his head.

As the warmer days of spring approached, Palmer rose and flew to his Virgils. He finished his designs for the second eclogue and, having abandoned it at first attempt, returned with redoubled zest to preparing the tenth. Sometimes working at the washstand that doubled up as a desk, more often remaining in bed, he continued, but the only work that would ever be completed was *Early Morning* (or *Opening the Fold*), which had been published the previous year by the Fine Art Society. This image of the shepherd's penned flock rushing out of the fold with the first rays of new light spoke perhaps of Palmer's own yearning for the dawn of a new world. 'If I were *quite* certain of rejoining my beloved ones, I should chide the slow hours which separated me,'[52] he wrote in April that year. At the beginning of May he was taken ill and by the middle of the month his family had given up hope of him pulling through. Yet he continued to talk cheerfully, his mind ranging freely across familiar pastures, discussing among other things the continuation of his long cherished Virgils. His eyes would brighten with pleasure as he contemplated the difficulties to be overcome.

Palmer's earthly affairs were all sorted. The previous summer – shortly before his son's marriage – he had written his will leaving Hannah modestly provided for, but, knowing that her father would continue to look after her, leaving as much as possible as an annuity to his son. He had suggested that Herbert's fiancée should be given one of the Palmer family bibles and recorded as much as he could remember of his ancestry for a member of the Giles family who had shown an interest. Palmer had few possessions of any financial value to leave. A man who did not even own a watch – what use would he have had of it in his life of peaceful routine? – counted among his most treasured possessions an old shepherd's smock, a huge battered straw hat, a pair of steel-rimmed glasses that had once belonged to his nurse, a few relics of Blake's and a handful of fragmentary casts from the antique. The most precious thing he had ever had was his vision. He had put it down in his pictures. Hannah did not want these to go to auction, Palmer told his son.

The elegant local doctor, in regular attendance at all the most handsome Reigate homes, must have looked a little askance at his latest patient. He would not have thought much of the muddled little room with its makeshift furniture and its cluttered shelves nor of its occupant, the diminutive figure who sat, propped up by pillows, an old cigar box on the table beside him in which were lovingly hoarded a row of densely scratched copperplates. *The Homeward Star* – an image capturing that magical moment when the first star of the evening rises into the night – would regularly have been pulled out of this case. It was probably the very last piece that Palmer worked on before he gave up entirely, only, from then on, from time to time stretching out a frail hand, its seams deeply stained with etcher's ink, to lay it on the cigar box as if its mere presence could offer him comfort in some way.

Palmer suffered the last days of his final illness with the patience that he had been taught by a long and difficult life. He regretted the trouble that he was giving. Hannah sat by his bedside, an attentive figure, for hour after hour, her watch periodically relieved by Richmond who, sitting peacefully by the bedside, must have felt a great loneliness as he watched this companion of his youth slipping slowly away.

On the morning of 24 May 1881, Palmer asked that his son be called into his room. Herbert leaned over his father but he could only guess at the words that were whispered into his ear. A touch of their hands was to be their farewell. Palmer died later that day. When Herbert returned he found Richmond reading prayers by the bedside, his voice broken by grief.

Palmer was not buried beside More, but in what was then a shady corner of Reigate churchyard. It was a fresh showery spring morning of the sort that he would have loved. The leaves of the elm trees cast a dappling shadow and, as the pastor read the words of the liturgy which Palmer had always so loved, a skylark hung singing in the sky far above. Just as the last words of the service faded, it dropped down silently into the grass.

The grave is modest. It is fairly hard to find now. A low and narrow length of local stone, its carved ribs forming a cross, lies amid the long grass. Pale lichens spread across it like opening blossoms. 'He that believeth in me though he were dead yet shall he live,'[53] is inscribed in Gothic script. A church tower presides over the scene. The church had always been the lynchpin of Palmer's world and standing there gazing up at it, it is hard not to recall the lonely tower of his picture. The

etching that he made from this painting is among the finest works in
this medium by any English artist and the bright pinpoint of light that
he picked out from the darkness has become for posterity a symbol of
all that he stood for.

It is this bright speck of shining that inspired the poet William Butler
Yeats. He described it in a poem that he wrote to the moon:

> *The lonely light that Samuel Palmer engraved,*
> *An image of mysterious wisdom won through toil.*[54]

The Legacy

Vision held . . . with such delicate, grave concentration
Geoffrey Grigson, *Samuel Palmer: The Visionary Years*

Linnell outlived his son-in-law by six months. Too fragile to stand at his easel, he passed his time studying his own translation of the Bible and sometimes, on fine days, being pushed around his grounds in an unstable Bath chair. The unappealing picture that his grandson Herbert painted of him is mitigated by the more affectionate account of another descendant who described him roaring with laughter when, tipped out of his wobbly conveyance, he landed feet upwards in a garden bush. Linnell could only write with great difficulty. Even his cashbook entries finally came to a stop, though he still managed to pen a corrective line to his doctor when he found that he had been overcharged on a bill. His last letter was to Hannah, the daughter he had tried for so long to reclaim. 'Why don't you come to see me?' he asked.[1] He knew his time had come. On 20 January 1882, fully conscious to the last, he passed away. He was five months short of his ninetieth birthday.

Linnell was buried in the same Reigate churchyard in which, the previous year, Palmer's coffin had been laid; but this time it was not a small private ceremony. The death of a famous painter was a public event. Shops were shut and a stream of carriages formed part of the cortège. Reigate neighbours were joined by mourners from London until the churchyard was crowded and the little funerary chapel so tightly packed that its doors had to be locked. Linnell, who had disliked the studied dolefulness of conventional mourning and had only rarely attended funerals himself, would not have approved, but the local papers gave voluminous accounts.

Linnell's grave is marked, as befits his character, by a severe upright headstone. He was buried beside his first wife, and his second was to follow in four years' time. His daughter Lizzie, who had never married but remained at Redstone to look after her father, was eventually, when she died in 1903 at the age of eighty-three, to share his burial place. Immediately to the left and right are the graves of other relations. Linnell, in death as in life, gathered his family about him; but Hannah, who died on 27 October 1893, by then no longer in her right mind, was not laid beside her father. She found her last resting place not far off, alongside her husband in his humbler grave.

God, family and art had always been the three most important elements of Linnell's life. The devotion with which he served the first two had had their effect on the last. His paintings varied from the vigorously eye-catching to the merely competent. It is not surprising, given the huge quantity of canvases that he turned out. To the Victorians he had seemed an artist of great talent. 'The most powerful landscape painter since Turner,' *The Times* obituary declared: with his passing 'a glory seems to have faded from the domain of British Art'. And yet, his reputation soon faded. Critical tastes were turning away from descriptive narratives towards the atmospheric innovations of the Impressionists and though in his late works a certain 'impressionism' has sometimes been remarked upon, this stylistic freedom was probably more a result of fading eyesight and faltering hand than a conscious attempt to imitate the innovative French painters who had first burst on to the Parisian art scene in 1874. Superseded by fashion, his oeuvre was soon forgotten. He disappeared into the sort of obscurity that Palmer had long known.

———

Two fellow Ancients still survived. Calvert wrote mournfully to Richmond after Palmer's death: 'You are the only one of our little early band of cherished friends, animated by God-gifted desire to ascend the heavenly slopes of Love – the beautiful ideal of "a kingdom within",' he said.[2] That was in August 1882. Within a year, he too was dead. Only Richmond remained. By then a grand old man of the arts, he had captured many of the most famous faces of his era from Darwin through Charles John Canning (the Governor-General of India during the Mutiny) to Dickens and Charlotte Brontë; but his lively sketches of the Ancients remained as mementos of a high spirited youth: the picture album of a band of fellows he was never to forget. Richmond died in 1896 a few days before his eighty-seventh birthday.

———

Palmer's reputation enjoyed a modest revival after his death. The Fine Art Society, one of the world's earliest private art galleries, had been founded in 1876 and three years later, introduced to the work of Palmer by Valpy, had proposed that it should become the sole agent of his etchings. Palmer, who had gone through the agreement clause by clause with his son and decided that the twig of a tree should become his remarque (the marginal drawing on an engraving or etching which indicates an early state of the plate), had accepted the terms. By the autumn of 1879 he had been sympathising with his poor out-of-place bellman gazing forlornly from the window of a shop in Bond Street.

Shortly before Palmer's death, the Fine Art Society had purchased his *c.*1830 *Yellow Twilight*, among the richest and most luminous of his Shoreham works. 'In few things painted by an English artist is vision held so securely and with such simplicity and such delicate, grave concentration,'[3] Geoffrey Grigson, a later biographer, recorded. Palmer had submitted two of his Milton watercolours – *The Eastern Gate*, in which dawn flares like a vast conflagration across the morning sky, and *The Prospect*, a mellow Italianate panorama in which far-stretching vistas are warmed by a rising sun – to the annual exhibition of the Old Watercolour Society in the last year of his life. He was to be on his deathbed by the time the show opened but the hanging committee accorded his contributions places of high honour. They were praised in reviews. 'Epoch-making pictures,'[4] said his friend Frederick George Stephens and comparisons with Turner were made by two other critics. The sublimity of sunrise had 'never found nobler

expression',[5] declared *The Times*. 'Work of almost unequalled intensity',[6] was the *Spectator*'s opinion. Hannah would probably have read
the reviews out aloud to her husband, watching the smile spreading
across his peaceable old face. The struggle of the painter was 'solitary
and patient, silent and sublime',[7] he had once said. Only at the very
end did he find some reward. It was modest. But by then he had
learnt not to expect too much.

In the autumn of 1881, a few months after his death, the Fine Art
Society staged a memorial show in which more than a hundred of his
works were gathered. In the next year, in a further effort to secure his
reputation, his son Herbert published a memoir which was followed a
little over a decade later by a 'life'. Herbert was a fierce custodian of his
father's legacy, most particularly of his etchings, and when Goulding
produced what he considered to be an inferior impression of the delicate *The Morning of Life* he angrily denounced it as a savage wiping. It
assaulted the viewer, he said, like a slap in the face.

In 1883, Herbert published Palmer's *An English Version of the Eclogues
of Virgil* in a limited edition. Only one of the ten plates – *Opening the
Fold* – had actually been finished. Four others, in various states of
incompletion, had to be brought up to scratch by Herbert who worked,
as far as he was able, in accordance with his father's spoken intentions.
The other five were included as facsimiles after preliminary designs. But
the publication of this volume on which Palmer had lavished so much
thought, time and love went almost unnoticed.

In 1893 his sepias, which had remained closeted away for most of his
lifetime in his Curiosity Portfolio, attracted some attention when they
were exhibited at Burlington House, but still Palmer remained a
marginal figure as far as a wider public was concerned. When people
thought of the great British Romantics they imagined the magnificent
light-flooded dramas of Turner, the passionately naturalistic oils of
Constable, not the tiny luminous squares of some peculiar old visionary who had seldom made anything larger than an open book. Besides,
few of Palmer's pictures ever came up for sale. Although in 1881 the
works which Giles had owned – four little oils and a number of watercolours and drawings – were put on the market, there had been no big

studio sale after the artist's death; and so, apart from the Milton series which Valpy, having waited more than fifteen years for their completion, disposed of within a decade, there were very few Palmer paintings to be bought.

Then, in 1909, Herbert decided to leave England to settle in Canada. Retaining only a few favourite pictures, he sent the remainder of his father's works to auction. The rest of Palmer's legacy – including some twenty clasped pocketbooks – was disposed of in a back garden bonfire that smouldered for several days. 'Knowing that no one would be able to make head or tail of what I burnt, I wished to save it from a more humiliating fate,' Herbert said. Perhaps he was trying to act in accordance with his father's wishes: 'No scraps' had been his 'serious rule'. It was 'seclusion or fire' for 'everything that was not done as well as I could do it at the time'.[8] But it is also likely that Herbert felt awkward about his father's open expressions of emotion. His mental condition was 'in many respects . . . uninviting', he thought; 'neither sufficiently masculine nor sufficiently reticent'.[9] He was discomfited by Palmer's effeminate tendencies and even more so by the unbridled affection that he had shown to his fellow Ancients. When once Richmond had spoken about how Calvert had left the Navy because his 'dearest friend' had been killed, Herbert had remarked: 'There was too much "dearest" about Mr Richmond and sometimes about my father too.'[10] The ardent dreams of a youthful Romantic were probably too remote or too risqué for an ageing Victorian to understand or decode.

It was not until well into the twentieth century that the rehabilitation of Palmer began to take place. His etchings found wider admiration first. They inspired an illustrator, Frederick Griggs, who had originally come across them in a public library as a boy. At about the same time that Herbert was leaving for Canada, Griggs, by then in his mid-thirties, was taking up etching in earnest and, having spent years working on illustrations for a guidebook to the English counties, he particularly appreciated Palmer's feeling for atmospheric landscape. He got in touch with Herbert who, discovering his correspondent to be a

brilliant technician, agreed to part with five of his father's copperplates
so that impressions could be made. Griggs's prints, which he worked on
along with Frank Short, the head of the Royal College of Art's Etching
School, and Martin Hardie, an assistant keeper in the print department
of the V&A (who had himself been in touch with Herbert since 1910),
were of exceptional quality. In 1913 the first catalogue raisonné of
Palmer's etchings was produced.

Palmer's paintings, however, remained little known, though in 1917
the Tate acquired *The Bright Cloud* for its collection and in 1922 a
further group of Shoreham paintings, among them his *Coming from
Evening Church*. Then, in 1925, Laurence Binyon (the writer now best
known for his poem *For the Fallen*, read out every year at Remembrance
Sunday services) published a scholarly volume: *The Followers of William
Blake*. Binyon was not interested in mere imitators of this master. He
wanted to follow a more spiritual line of inspiration and he looked at
how Calvert and Palmer, in particular, had found in Blake's woodcuts a
fresh path that would lead towards the renewal of British art. His book
included examples of their work alongside that of other Ancients.

In 1926, Griggs's prints were published by the Cotswold Gallery. In
the same year Martin Hardie, in collaboration with Herbert (who
wrote an introduction and loaned most of his father's works), mounted
an exhibition: *Drawings, Etchings and Woodcuts by Samuel Palmer and
other Disciples of William Blake*. Opening at the V&A it had a huge and
unpredicted impact. 'The early watercolours in particular are an abso-
lute revelation,'[11] Sir Eric Maclagan, the Director of the V&A wrote. A
year later Hardie gave a lecture to the Print Collectors' Club. Looking
at Palmer's work throughout his long career, he said, 'with its mixture
of research and imagination, of actuality and romance, one feels that it
has the quality of classic poetry . . . It is Gray's *Elegy* in terms of brush
and paint. For it was always of twilight and sunset of which he thought.
For years he turned the pages of the book of sunsets and never tired.'[12]

Interest in Palmer gained momentum. Among his most ardent new
admirers was a band of student printmakers from London's Goldsmiths'
College. Graham Sutherland and Paul Drury were the most prominent, but Edward Bouverie-Hoyton, Alexander Walker and William

Larkins also played a keen part. This group of students had first encountered the work of Palmer a few years earlier when Larkins had stumbled
across his etching, *The Herdsman's Cottage*, in a shop on the Charing
Cross Road. They had been astounded by the detail and density of the
image. Palmer covered the whole of the copperplate in a way that to
them seemed revelatory. They had never before seen, explained
Sutherland, such a complex multiplicity of marks coming together to
create such a luminous tone. It was the complete antithesis of the manner
in which Whistler, for many years the most highly acclaimed master of
the medium, had etched. Sutherland visited the Tate to look at Palmer's
other works. He was entranced by their oddity, by their bold disregard of
convention and their quirkily archaic style, and picked out in particular
a little ink sketch of a peasant girl standing in a ploughed field. 'It seemed
to me wonderful,' he later remembered, 'that a strong emotion such as
Palmer's could change and transform the appearance of things.'[13]

Dressed up in cloaks and wide-brimmed hats, Sutherland and his
friends set off with their sketch pads to Shoreham (and Sutherland,
later renting a house in Farningham, began what was to be a long association with the Darent Valley landscapes). They started, in the late
1920s, to emulate Palmer's style. Drury turned away from the portrai-
ture that had been his primary interest to look at churches and cottages
and dilapidated farmsteads while Sutherland wandered nostalgically
through undulating pastoral views.

For a short while this group flourished. They became known as the
New Pastoralists and their etchings in particular were much in demand.
A tranquil English landscape could hardly have been further in mood
from the up-thrusting Modernism that characterised the then domi-
nant New York markets and there were plenty of buyers who still kept
their conservative tastes. Speculators pushed up the prices of limited
editions. It was boom time for these prints. It is to this brief era that the
phrase 'Come up and see my etchings' dates: to own a collection would
have been a mark of some wealth. But with the 1929 Wall Street Crash
the bottom fell out of a bumped-up etching market and by the early
1930s the New Pastoralists found themselves increasingly sidelined.
Sutherland, needing to make money, pushed himself into closer

alignment with the international Modernist movement: he began moving away from printmaking towards drawing and painting; away from Kentish subjects towards a wider world.

Palmer, however, was not forgotten. Sutherland, along with his contemporaries John Piper and Paul Nash, went on to become part of a grouping which a reviewer, Raymond Mortimer, was subsequently to label 'Neo-Romantic'. They made art that appealed to mystics, he wrote, 'and particularly to pantheists who feel fraternity . . . with all living things' and to those 'with a sense sublime of something far more deeply interfused'.[14] They produced work that showed a deep familiarity with Palmer's Shoreham visions, sharing its shadowy atmospheres, its intensity of feeling and its elaborate techniques.

Appreciation of Palmer gathered pace. Kenneth Clark, as Keeper of the Ashmolean between 1931 and 1933, brought two of his works (his haunting self-portrait was one of them) for the museum and another three paintings (including *Cornfield by Moonlight*) for his own private collection. In 1934 an exhibition of British Art at the Royal Academy showed a dozen Palmer pictures, among them items from the famous Curiosity Portfolio. To eyes by then attuned to the expressive distortions of Modernism, these seemed peculiarly contemporary, even as they spoke of some mystical past. In 1936 the agenda-setting magazine *Apollo* reproduced images of Palmer's sepias for the first time and Grigson, who was to become the artist's biographer, started publishing a number of articles on his work. In 1941, the Ashmolean Museum added the sepias to its Palmer collection.

It was around this time, also, that Palmer cast his spell over a second wave of Neo-Romantic artists. A circle which included among its principal members Keith Vaughan, Michael Ayrton, John Minton, Ivon Hitchens and John Craxton (though the young Lucian Freud and Henry Moore were also loosely associated) looked to his closely wrought vision. To them it seemed to arise from a quintessentially English tradition which they tried in their modernistic work to develop. Nash also renewed his erstwhile interest in Palmer. He wanted to capture what he thought of as the imprisoned spirit of landscape.

In 1947, Grigson's *Samuel Palmer: The Visionary Years* was published, putting the spotlight on Palmer's Shoreham works. These became widely admired as examples of English pastoral, of a peaceful ideal which a world war had put under threat. Soon their influence could be spotted all over the place, from the rural designs of Eric Ravilious through the Utopian drawings of Clifford Harper to the poetic engravings of Laurence Whistler.

Palmer came to have 'almost too pervasive an influence'[15] on English art, Kenneth Clark declared in 1949. Indeed, with the hindsight of history, there seems scarcely a figurative painter in Britain between the 1920s and 1950s who did not look at his work. Anything from the eerie miracles of Stanley Spencer's Cookham canvases to the domestic harmonies of Winifred Nicholson's still lifes were indebted. Palmer's inspiration can be found in the luminous dreams of Cecil Collins, the lyrical patterns of Victor Pasmore's landscapes, the primitive clarity of Cedric Morris's compositions, the shadowy intensities of the engravings of Muirhead Bone. The canvas which still hangs in Palmer's old Shoreham church – it shows the triumphant return from Africa of Lieutenant Verney Lovett Cameron (son of the vicar) having completed the first East–West crossing – was by the artist's old friend Cope. In 1876, when it was painted, the work of this Academician was far preferred to that of the eccentric visionary who had once lived in the village. But, by the middle of the twentieth century, Cope's pictures were being passed off as Palmer's by then extremely popular and hence valuable works.

In the 1950s, however, the baton of Modernism passed from Europe across the Atlantic and, by the end of the decade, artistic trends had undergone a dramatic shift. Painters were looking towards the full-scale abstractions of a New York School that had abandoned descriptions of nature in favour of expressionistic renderings of inner emotional states. Palmer's reputation languished again for a while. He did still continue to find a few cultish followers. His Shoreham visions, with their peculiar magnifications, their mushrooming patterns and their luminous glow, appealed to the tastes of the psychedelic sixties. His *Magic Apple Tree* looked mad as an orchard seen on acid. His proliferating blossoms belonged to some LSD trip. During one druggy binge, Jim Leon, the most important artistic contributor to the magazine *Oz*, had a mystical experience in which he was visited by a divinity called the Goddess of Nature, he said. From then on he devoted his talents to creating paradisiacal visions which can easily be tracked back to the influences of Palmer, as can many of the paintings of Syd Barrett, a founder member of Pink Floyd. But, for the most part, Palmer was forgotten by fashion until, in the 1970s, a faking scandal aroused interest once more.

A cockney, Tom Keating, having returned from a wartime career as a sailor, turned his hand first to picture restoring and then to creating forgeries of, among other paintings, Palmer's Shoreham works. Buying old canvases from junk shops, he would steam the picture from its mount and then paint or draw his own in its place, sprinkling the finished product with vacuum cleaner dust to make it look older, flicking a spoonful of coffee powder to make convincing 'fox marks'. He polished his techniques. Boiled walnuts, he discovered, made a perfect brown bistre for pseudo-Rembrandts and, for Palmer, a layer of gelatine which cracked when warmed was just right for the faking of thickly painted 'frescos'. Keating pulled the unused watermarked pages from an old leather bound diary and then he just waited for the 'the feeling to come over him',[16] he said. Once he made sixteen Palmers in a weekend.

'I'd just sit there whistling softly to myself to help me think, then I'd start to doodle and look at the moon. Dink, donk, dink, tick, tick, tick – it would start to happen. God's honour, I have never drawn a sheep from life, but Palmer's sheep would begin to appear on the paper tick, tick, tick, and there they would be in the guv'nor's "valley of vision" watched over by the good shepherd in the shadow of Shoreham's church. With Sam's permission I sometimes signed them with his own name, but they were his work and not mine. It was his hand that guided the pen.'[17]

With the benefit of hindsight, Keating's pictures present crude amalgams of Palmeresque traits, but in 1976 a prestigious gallery paid £9,400 for what it believed to be an authentic image. Scholars were not convinced. Investigations ensued and *The Times* eventually published an exposé – though ironically, after this widely publicised scandal,

Keating forgeries became sought after in their own right and at least one dealer was subsequently to be duped into buying a fake of the faker's work.

From then on, Palmer's work once again exerted a pervasive power. A painter who could capture the landscape in a manner that was not merely naturalistic, who could infuse it with feeling in a way that escaped the sentimentalism so associated with the Victorians, who could transcend the literal and speak of spiritual forces, directly inspired such artists as those who in 1975 formed the Brotherhood of Ruralists, (a group which, incorporating David Inshaw and Peter Blake, aimed at following a traditional strand of figurative British painting) and found reflections in anything from the hallucinatory landscapes of the Turner Prize-nominated Peter Doig to the computer-scanned drawings of Paul Morrison who, turning the tiniest weed into a wall-sized triffid, plays Palmeresque tricks with scale. In 2009, the Tate staged a show, *The Dark Monarch*, in its St Ives gallery, linking the Romantic legacy of Palmer via the work of a variety of Modernist practitioners to a number of established and upcoming contemporaries, Damien Hirst, Eva Rothschild, Simon Periton and Cerith Wyn Evans among them. Exploring the tensions between progress and tradition, it looked at the meanings – geological, mythical, mystical and magical – that over the course of the twentieth century have been inscribed by British artists into the contours of their landscape.

For a long time it was only the Shoreham paintings that were widely appreciated. The rest of Palmer's career, thanks to the strong critical slant of Grigson's landmark biography, was regarded as little more than a process of sad decline. Only at the very end was he considered to have become interesting again as, withdrawing into the obsessive world of etching, he condensed a lifetime of vision into a few square inches of work. Then in 2005 the British Museum, to mark the bicentenary of Palmer's birth, put on the first major show by this artist in Britain since the V&A's exhibition of almost eighty years earlier. This exhibition, staged in collaboration with the Metropolitan Museum of Art in New York (to which it subsequently travelled), posited that a thread of unique sensibility could be followed from the Shoreham pictures, weaving its way through Palmer's work right to the end of his life. It gave the whole a sparkling coherence. The more commercial works that had until then been dismissed were scanned for sublimations of earlier obsessions, for adumbrations of future concerns. More than 51,000 visitors flocked into the cramped basement gallery – at least double the number that had been predicted. Curators at the British Museum were as astounded as thrilled by the huge popular response.

———————

Kenneth Clark thought of Palmer as the English Van Gogh. There are several similarities between these two eccentric recluses who both believed passionately in the perfect community and set out to establish one: Palmer in Shoreham with the Ancients, Van Gogh with Paul Gauguin in his Studio of the South. They both were profoundly religious and sought to uncover a spiritual presence in nature. And they were both, during their lifetimes, all but completely neglected, considered by all but close friends to have failed.

Van Gogh died before he was forty, having shot himself with a revolver during one of his periodic bouts of insanity. Palmer, however, survived into old age, coming to understand only too well that for those who stand fast to the truth of their convictions – a truth which for him stood 'at a fixed centre, midway between its two antagonists Fact and Phantasm'[18] – the fight will always be tough. 'No one can clear away the brambles without getting thorns into his fingers' he told his son a few months before his death. 'I do not think anyone can get his living without a struggle. The painter's and the poet's struggles are solitary and patient, silent and sublime.'[19]

In comparison with his fellow British Romantics, Turner and Constable, Palmer still has to struggle. His name remains relatively unfamiliar. In part this is because his finest pictures – a scattering of images done in secret by a young idealist in Shoreham and a handful of etchings produced by an ageing recluse who, having lost faith with so many of life's promises, returns to the land of dreams that he had wandered in his youth – are so few. Further to this they are small. They do not ambush the gallery browser like Turner's grand dramas or, like

Constable's canvases, unfurl to lengths of six foot. And yet their very fewness makes them even more precious and, by their very smallness, they become all the more intense.

There is a memorable passage in Emily Brontë's 1847 *Wuthering Heights*, written when Palmer was in middle age, in which the narrator tells of his stay in the house from which the novel takes its title. Coming in from the moor, he unlatches the gate, crosses the garden and is let into the kitchen. From there he gradually progresses inwards, moving through a series of ever more narrowly confined spaces until finally, encased in a box-bed, he lies down to sleep. It is at this moment of physical restriction that his mind flies wide open and imaginative visions are free to flood in. A ghostly Cathy comes clawing at the latticed windowpane. Is it dream or reality? The reader is never quite clear.

Palmer's pictures work in something of the same way. His are not images to be admired from a distance. The visitor has to step closer, to peer inwards as if through the frame of some tiny window to gain an exhilarated glimpse of a painter's private world. Imparted with all the emotion of a passionately held secret, it is capable of holding the imagination transfixed.

The spectator gazes into landscapes as intensely felt in their own way as the passionate canvases of Van Gogh. These little framed boxes, like theatrical sets, their cardboard-cut-out horizons thrown high by the footlights, their moons hanging like lanterns amid foliage unruffled by winds, present a hermetic realm that feels at once far removed from reality and yet, at the same time, full of fresh relevance.

'A preference for the present as a matter of taste is a pretty sure sign of mediocrity,' Palmer told his friend Stephens in 1875. He was not concerned with the merely current. That particular view of genius, he declared, was fit only for 'dogs and cats, which are eminently remarkable for their sympathy with the present'. Rather, he believed along with Samuel Johnson that it is only that which 'makes the past, the distant or the future predominate over the present' which 'advances us in the rank of thinking beings'. 'The best poets and painters appeal to this faculty and instinct within us,'[20] he declared.

Time has proved Palmer to be among that superlative number. This is not simply because his pictures of lost pastoral idylls showed British Modernists a possible way forwards or because, as several reviewers of the British Museum's bicentenary exhibition suggested, his works can still find significance in a contemporary era which, sensing the threat of ecological catastrophe, finds a freshly relevant environmental message in his belief that humanity could live in harmony with nature. It is because Palmer discovered an entirely original way to show us our world anew. This is what lends his most-loved pictures their timeless appeal. We look at our landscapes through the lens of his eye. To see a line of trees silhouetted against the twilight, to watch a harvest moon rising over the fields, to gaze at the evening star shining above a steeple is to remember his images. His mystical visions are entwined with our living experience. His spiritual messages suffuse our surroundings. They deepen and enrich our perceptions, thus advancing us, as Johnson put it, in the rank of thinking beings. An artist cannot hope for any greater accomplishment.

If British tradition had ever encompassed the making of icons, they would not have been so different from Palmer's tiny glowing pastorals. Condensed in the golden patches of his peaceful sepias, in the luminous landscapes of his Shoreham works, in the intricate densities of his tenebrous etchings, is a vision which expands the reaches of the human spirit. 'The soul,' as he always knew he would one day discover, is 'larger than the whole material universe.'[21]

Portrait of Samuel Palmer by Charles West Cope, 1884.

Notes

Chapter 1: The Palmer Family

1   L1023
2   L62

Chapter 2: Early Years

1   L518
2   AHP
3   L63
4   L592
5   L686
6   In his essay 'The Nation of London'
7   Ibid.
8   L871
9   Sketchbook, 1824, p. 81
10 L1015
11 Sketchbook, 1824, p. 7
12 L860
13 L860
14 L899
15 L993
16 L&L4
17 L118
18 Daniel Joseph Kirwan, *Palace and Hovel: Or Phases of London Life*, p. 32
19 L&L5
20 L870
21 L636

22   L581
23   L828
24   L701
25   L49
26   L676

Chapter 3: The Beginnings of an Artist

1   Sketchbook, 1824, p. 75
2   L313
3   L&L99
4   L756
5   L39
6   L795
7   L735
8   L745
9   L876
10   L894
11   L308
12   L&L6
13   Inscribed by the artist on the verso
14   L823
15   L177
16   L982
17   L926
18   William Gilpin, *Essay Upon Prints*, 1768, p. 11
19   L&L15
20   L872
21   Ibid.
22   L651
23   L&L6
24   L516
25   L842
26   As Samuel Johnson described him
27   John Flaxman, *Lectures on Sculpture*, 1829, Lecture VI, 'Composition'
28   L&L7
29   *Examiner*, No. 742, 24 March 1822
30   L677
31   L805
32   L892
33   L&L14
34   Ibid.

Chapter 4: John Linnell

1 Alfred T. Story, *The Life of John Linnell*, Vol. 1, p. 26
2 David Linnell, *Blake, Palmer, Linnell and Co.: The Life of John Linnell*, p. 10
3 Ibid., p. 10
4 Ibid., p. 37
5 Ibid., p. 45
6 Ibid., p. 69
7 *The Times*, 24 January 1882

Chapter 5: The Sketchbook of 1824

1   L&L14
2   Edward Bulwer Lytton, *England and the English*, p. 239
3   C. R. Leslie, *Memoirs of the Life of John Constable*, p. 12
4   L&L13
5   L393
6   L&L15
7   L74
8   L824
9   Ibid.
10 L&L13
11 L&L14
12 L880
13 L706
14 L&L15
15 L&L14
16 1824 Sketchbook, p. 114
17 L217
18 L74
19 Ibid.
20 L836
21 L837
22 F. G. Stephens, *Memorials of William Mulready*, p. 3
23 L&L12
24 Sketchbook, 1824, p. 59
25 L993
26 Sketchbook, 1824, p. 1
27 Ibid., p. 14
28 Ibid., p. 55
29 Ibid., p. 175
30 Ibid., p. 101

31   Ibid., p. 5
32   Ibid., p. 89
33   Ibid., p. 48
34   Ibid., p. 140
35   L&L15
36   L862
37   Sketchbook, 1824, p. 28
38   Ibid., p. 17
39   Ibid., p. 1
40   Ibid., p. 2
41   Ibid., p. 5

Chapter 6: William Blake

1   David V. Erdman (ed.), *The Complete Poetry and Prose of William Blake*, p. 565
2   G. E. Bentley (ed.), *Blake Records*, p. 311
3   Alexander Gilchrist, *The Life of William Blake*, p. 13
4   Peter Ackroyd, *Blake*, p. 39
5   Gilchrist, *The Life of William Blake*, p. 95
6   Bentley (ed.), *Blake Records*, p. 517
7   See William Blake, *The Four Zoas*
8   Erdman (ed.), *The Complete Poetry and Prose of William Blake*, p. 406
9   Blake in *Jerusalem: The Emanation of the Giant Albion*
10   Ackroyd, *Blake*, p. 350
11   Bentley (ed.), *Blake Records*, p. 313
12   Erdman (ed.), *The Complete Poetry and Prose of William Blake*, p. 507
13   Bentley (ed.), *Blake Records*, p. 51
14   Ibid., p. 249
15   Gilchrist, *The Life of William Blake*, p. 52
16   George Cumberland, *Thoughts on Outline*, p. 1
17   Ackroyd, *Blake*, p. 203
18   L509
19   Erdman (ed.), *The Complete Poetry and Prose of William Blake*, p. 325
20   Ibid., p. 231
21   Geoffrey Keynes (ed.), *The Letters of William Blake*, p. 8
22   Ackroyd, *Blake*, p. 336
23   L506
24   Ackroyd, *Blake*, p. 325
25   Erdman (ed.), *The Complete Poetry and Prose of William Blake*, p. 736
26   Ackroyd, *Blake*, p. 312
27   Story, *The Life of John Linnell*, Vol. 1, p. 228

Chapter 7: Palmer Meets Blake

1 L574
2 L&L9
3 L507
4 L824
5 L510
6 Bentley (ed.), *Blake Records Supplement*, p. 290
7 L507
8 L506
9 Ibid.
10 L573
11 L506
12 L595
13 Linnell, *Blake, Palmer, Linnell and Co.*, p. 106
14 Ibid.
15 Linnell, *Blake, Palmer, Linnell and Co.*, p. 104
16 Blake in his poem *London*
17 Hill, Christopher, *The English Revolution*, p. 280
18 L506
19 L508
20 Bentley (ed.), *Blake Records*, p. 13
21 Bentley (ed.), *Blake Records Supplement*, p. 310
22 L506
23 Ibid.
24 Story, *The Life of John Linnell*, p. 149
25 Bentley (ed.), *Blake Records Supplement*, p. 81
26 Ibid., p. 258
27 L663

Chapter 8: The Oxford Sepias

1 L661
2 L&L17
3 L&L15
4 Bentley (ed.), *Blake Records*, p. 318
5 L&L15
6 Ibid.
7 Sketchbook, 1824, p. 81

Chapter 9: The Primitive

1   Ackroyd, *Blake*, p. 40
2   L508
3   L663
4   *London Magazine*, 1820, p. 42
5   Eliot, *Middlemarch*
6   L48
7   Facsimile, p. 7
8   L71

Chapter 10: The Ancients

1   Samuel Calvert, *A Memoir of Edward Calvert*, p. 17
2   Gilchrist, *The Life of William Blake*, p. 299
3   L717
4   Raymond Lister, *George Richmond*, p. 26
5   Calvert, *A Memoir of Edward Calvert*, p. 4
6   A. M. W. Stirling (ed.), *The Richmond Papers*, p. 99
7   L1010
8   Calvert, *A Memoir of Edward Calvert*, p. 53
9   Ibid., p. 18
10 L&L29
11 Calvert, *A Memoir of Edward Calvert*, p. 25
12 Mrs Eliza Finch, *Memorials of the Late Francis Oliver Finch*, p. 7
13 AHP
14 Quoted in Franz Harmann, *The Life and Doctrines of Paracelsus*, p. 172
15 Quoted in ibid., p. 20
16 L59
17 L270
18 L393
19 L233
20 Stirling (ed.), *The Richmond Papers*, p. 114
21 Ibid., p. 14
22 Calvert, *A Memoir of Edward Calvert*, p. 17
23 L508
24 L67

Chapter 11: Shoreham

1   Quoted in Roy Porter, *London, A Social History*, p. 257
2   Jane Austen, *Emma*
3   L970
4   Edmund Spenser, *The Faerie Queene*, Book IV, verse xxix
5   L36
6   L&L40
7   Calvert, *A Memoir of Edward Calvert*, p. 33
8   L183
9   L506
10 L&L131
11 Ibid.
12 L54
13 L17
14 L23
15 Lister, *George Richmond*, p. 16
16 L30 note 1
17 L25 note 1
18 L47
19 L118
20 L824
21 L391
22 L191
23 L678
24 L958
25 L37
26 L175
27 L&L15
28 L247
29 L238
30 L190 note 6
31 L62
32 L16
33 L50
34 L1018
35 L1020
36 L&L40
37 L970
38 L812
39 L666
40 L79
41 L39

42   L204
43   L6
44   L84
45   L37
46   L688
47   L866
48   L58
49   L686
50   L51
51   L79
52   Keynes (ed.), *The Letters of William Blake*, p. 171
53   L510
54   Calvert, *A Memoir of Edward Calvert*, p. 37
55   L67
56   L24
57   L22
58   L32
59   L43
60   L15
61   L84
62   L35
63   L56
64   Finch, *Memorials of the Late Francis Oliver Finch*, p. 79
65   L62
66   L205

Chapter 12: A Work in the Valley of Vision

1   L16
2   L53
3   L8
4   L53
5   L36 note 7
6   L51
7   L9
8   L45
9   L52
10   L42
11   L36
12   Bentley (ed.), *Blake Records*, p. 294
13   L48
14   Ibid.
15   William Gilpin, *Remarks on Forest Scenery 1791*
16   L50

17 L47
18 L51
19 L67
20 L44
21 L53
22 *John Bull*, vol. 5, no. 19, 8 May 1825, p. 150
23 *European Magazine*, Vol. 1, No. 1, September 1825, p. 85
24 *Literary Gazette*, 9 June 1832
25 *Athenaeum*, 10 May 1834
26 L67

Chapter 13: The Pastoral and the Political

1 L63
2 L&L43
3 L64
4 Stirling (ed.), *The Richmond Papers*, p. 18
5 AHP
6 George Eliot, *Adam Bede*
7 George Eliot, *Felix Holt*
8 Sketchbook, 1824, pp. 127–9
9 L&L40
10 L451
11 Eliot, *Adam Bede*
12 Eliot, *Middlemarch*
13 L27
14 *Political Register*, December 1830
15 William Cobbett, *Rural Rides*, p. 184
16 Ibid., from Kensington Across Surrey, October 1825
17 Ibid., p. 136
18 *The Times*, 27 October 1830
19 *The Times*, 30 October 1830
20 *The Times*, 27 October 1830
21 *Political Register*, April 1830
22 *Political Register*, September 1824
23 *The Times*, 27 October 1830
24 L14
25 L451
26 L600
27 L15
28 L958
29 L37
30 In a letter to Hannah Palmer, 30 September 1839

Chapter 14: The Sensual and the Spiritual

1   L938
2   L&L34
3   L724
4   L309
5   L40
6   L207
7   L248
8   L54
9   L15
10 L42
11 L53
12 L&L153
13 L16
14 L17
15 L45
16 L51
17 L183
18 L126
19 L74 note 3
20 L75

Chapter 15: The End of the Dream

1   L34
2   Ibid.
3   Ibid.
4   L248
5   L15
6   L65
7   L23
8   L64
9   L61
10 L63
11 L72
12 Ibid.
13 Ibid.
14 L68
15 L19
16 L23
17 L&L55

18 L65
19 L84
20 L71
21 Ibid.
22 Ibid.
23 L76
24 L84
25 In a letter, 4 August 1836
26 L966
27 L&L55
28 L84
29 Calvert, *Memoir of Edward Calvert*, p. 49
30 Ibid.
31 Ibid., p. 71
32 Lister, *George Richmond*, p. 21
33 L834
34 Finch, *Memorials of the Late Francis Oliver Finch*, p. 32
35 Ibid., p. 225
36 Gilchrist, *The Life of William Blake*, p. 320
37 Letter to Martin Hardie (V&A)
38 L&L37
39 L82
40 L81

Chapter 16 : Honeymoon in Italy

1   L&L59
2   L39
3   L345
4   L&L58
5   L213
6   L230
7   Ibid.
8   L213
9   L232
10 L98
11 L233
12 L215
13 L233
14 Ibid.
15 L150
16 L162
17 L227

18 L385
19 L228
20 L102
21 L133
22 L234
23 L149
24 Ibid.
25 L154
26 L391
27 L88
28 L166
29 L191
30 L174
31 L194 note 3
32 L175
33 L391
34 L219
35 L391
36 L361
37 L168
38 L289
39 L237
40 L103
41 L111
42 L99
43 L113
44 L189
45 L209
46 L179
47 L131
48 AHP
49 L129
50 L304
51 L130
52 Linnell, *Blake, Palmer, Linnell and Co.*, p. 173
53 L175
54 L349
55 L96 note 1
56 L&L62
57 L115
58 L165 note 4
59 L94
60 L339

61   L329
62   L354
63   L405

Chapter 17: Back in England

1   L348
2   L349
3   L380
4   L521
5   L213
6   L190
7   L182
8   L163
9   L182
10   L255
11   L256
12   L392
13   L386
14   L354
15   L234
16   L163
17   *Athenaeum*, 25 May 1833
18   L&L72
19   Ruskin, 'Of Truth', *Modern Painters*, Vol. 1, 1846, p. 402
20   L441
21   L440, note 1
22   L412
23   L429
24   L448
25   Ibid., note 1
26   L464
27   L448
28   L459
29   L479
30   L547
31   L58
32   L&L73
33   AHP
34   L414
35   L407
36   L427
37   L428

38   L835
39   L420
40   AHP
41   L&L68
42   L1064
43   L481
44   L1064
45   L717
46   L717–18
47   Louisa Twining, *Recollections of Life and Work*, p. 133
48   L521
49   L449
50   Ibid.
51   L712
52   L474
53   L761
54   L692
55   L746
56   L544
57   L541
58   L75
59   L&L75
60   L696
61   L446
62   L462
63   L339
64   L445
65   L442
66   L429
67   L430
68   L458
69   L433
70   L435
71   L436
72   L450
73   L429
74   L431
75   L432
76   L434
77   L450
78   Anna Letitia Barbauld, *Lessons for Children*, London 1844, p. 97
79   L435
80   L437

81　Ibid.
82　L451
83　L455
84　Ibid.
85　L456
86　L&L86
87　L451 note 2

Chapter 18: The Years of Disillusion

1　L646
2　L459
3　L646
4　L478
5　L453
6　L453 note 1
7　AHP
8　L464
9　AHP
10　L463
11　Ibid.
12　L466
13　L463
14　L459
15　L&L85
16　L693
17　L&L103
18　'pores and bores' L494
19　L497
20　L&L87
21　L465
22　Charles Dickens, *Dombey and Son*
23　L624
24　L644
25　L156
26　L581
27　L619
28　Ibid.
29　L1074
30　L857
31　L1090
32　L619
33　L&L129

34 L619
35 L766
36 L619
37 L534
38 L547
39 L461
40 Ruskin, *Modern Painters*, Vol,.2, 1848 edition
41 L602
42 L485 note 1
43 L546
44 L523
45 L525
46 L555
47 L495
48 L504
49 Ibid.
50 L502
51 Ibid.
52 L959
53 L481
54 L492
55 L511
56 L499
57 L517
58 L559
59 L538
60 AHP
61 L159
62 L512
63 Linnell, *Palmer, Blake, Linnell and Co.*, p. 285
64 L551
65 Ibid.
66 L1042
67 L587
68 L517
69 L729
70 L581
71 L&L114
72 William Faithorne, *The Art of Graving and Etching.*
73 L&L99
74 Ibid.
75 Ibid.
76 L&L100

77 L189
78 L865
79 Ibid.
80 *Guardian*, 30 April 1856
81 *Critic*, 1 May 1856
82 AHP
83 L529
84 L560
85 Story, *The Life of John Linnell*, Vol. 2, Chapter 4
86 AHP
87 L&L119
88 L871
89 L565
90 L425
91 L556
92 L567
93 L557
94 Ibid.

Chapter 19: A Bitter Blow

1   L530
2   L551
3   L578
4   L609
5   L554
6   L570
7   L577
8   L594
9   L731
10 L602
11 AHP
12 L604
13 AHP
14 L608
15 L614
16 L607
17 L604
18 L609
19 L629
20 L184
21 L675
22 L609

23 Ibid.
24 L613
25 L638
26 L628
27 L607
28 L609
29 L683
30 L642
31 L636
32 L624
33 AHP124
34 L606
35 L618
36 L620
37 L631
38 L&L125
39 L641
40 AHP
41 L624
42 L&L125
43 L642
44 L643
45 L631
46 L642
47 L633
48 L871
49 L730
50 L625
51 L645
52 L681

Chapter 20: Redhill

1   L&L127
2   L1041
3   L648
4   L177
5   L686
6   L755
7   L751
8   L755
9   L654
10 L&L131

11 L650
12 L685
13 Linnell, *Blake, Palmer, Linnell and Co.*, p. 311
14 L772
15 L656
16 L650
17 L674
18 Ibid.
19 L806
20 L&L147
21 L&L148
22 L787
23 L763
24 L752
25 L693
26 L711
27 L665
28 L672
29 L730
30 L720
31 L&L168
32 L653
33 L816
34 L817
35 L&L138
36 L744
37 AHP
38 AHP131
39 L&L132
40 L&L133
41 L&L135
42 L677
43 L750
44 L515
45 L803
46 L&L135
47 L624
48 AHP
49 L675
50 AHP
51 L768
52 L&L129
53 Ibid.

54   L731
55   L&L130
56   Ibid.
57   AHP
58   L810
59   Letter to Martin Hardie (V&A)
60   Ibid.
61   L765
62   L845
63   L850
64   Letter to Martin Hardie (V&A)
65   Ibid.
66   L791
67   L781
68   L679
69   L&L134
70   L&L133
71   L&L130
72   L&L134
73   L759
74   L756
75   L&L128
76   L747
77   L751
78   L747
79   AHP137
80   L&L137
81   L780
82   L874
83   L&L136
84   L897
85   Ibid.
86   L928
87   L&L135
88   L782
89   L&L136
90   L898
91   L&L144
92   L&L22

Chapter 21: The Milton Series

1   L769
2   L&L161
3   L709
4   L809
5   L811
6   L752
7   L&L146
8   L770
9   L777
10 L776
11 L775
12 L797
13 L808
14 L817
15 L818
16 AHP153
17 L658
18 *Art Journal,* 1 June 1866
19 L&L149
20 AHP
21 L&L149
22 L690 note 1
23 L690
24 L698
25 L699
26 L696
27 L970
28 L737
29 L704
30 L&L91
31 L&L152
32 L764
33 L904
34 L913
35 L965
36 Ibid.

Chapter 22: The Lonely Tower

1   L685
2   L&L155
3   Ibid.
4   Ibid.
5   Ibid.
6   L&L157
7   L&L158
8   L970
9   L964
10 L963
11 L820
12 L974
13 L60
14 L974
15 Letter to Martin Hardie (V&A)
16 L&L100
17 Letter to Sir Frank Short, 12 November 1920 (Ashmolean)
18 Linnell, *Blake, Palmer, Linnell and Co.*, p. 345
19 Ibid.
20 AHP
21 L935
22 L939
23 L1015
24 This memoir was published in 1897
25 Philip Gilbert Hamerton, *An Autobiography and a Memoir by his wife*, London 1897, p. 441
26 L928
27 L954
28 L1035
29 L967
30 L919
31 L951
32 L966
33 L1058
34 L664
35 L990
36 L1052
37 L142
38 L956
39 L932
40 L978

41 L941
42 Ibid.
43 L969
44 L1038
45 Ibid.
46 Stirling (ed.), *The Richmond Papers*, p. 88
47 L1055
48 L1058
49 L944
50 L1042
51 L1052
52 L1077
53 John 11:25, the Bible
54 William Butler Yeats, *The Phases of the Moon*

Chapter 23: The Legacy

1 AHP
2 Lister, *Calvert*, p. 58
3 Grigson, *The Visionary Years*, p. 96
4 Stephens in *Athenaeum*, 16 April 1881
5 *The Times*, 13 April 1881
6 *The Spectator*, 16 April 1881
7 L1073
8 L700
9 L&L18
10 Letters to Martin Hardie (V&A)
11 Eric Maclagan in a letter dated 2 November 1926 to A. H. Palmer
12 'Samuel Palmer: Being', a lecture delivered to the Print Collectors' Club on 16 November 1927, Print Collectors' Club, London, 1928, p. 47
13 Quoted in foreword to the catalogue *The English Vision*, an exhibition at William Weston Gallery, London, 1973
14 Malcolm Yorke, *The Spirit of Place*, p. 89
15 Kenneth Clark, *Landscape into Art*, p. 71
16 Tom Keating, *The Fake's Progress*, p. 182
17 Ibid., p. 183
18 L703
19 L1073
20 L923
21 L537

Bibliography

Abbreviations Used in Notes

L Lister, Raymond (ed.), *The Letters of Samuel Palmer*, Vols 1 and 2 (Oxford, 1974)

L&L Palmer, A. H., *The Life and Letters of Samuel Palmer* (London, 1892)

1824 Sketchbook *Samuel Palmer: The Sketchbook of 1824*, edited with an introduction and commentary by Martin Butlin (London, 2005)

AHP A. H. Palmer's unpublished notes, Fitzwilliam Museum, Cambridge

Letters to Martin Hardie Correspondence between A. H. Palmer and Martin Hardie relating to Samuel Palmer, Victoria & Albert Museum, London

Sources

Abley, Mark, *The Parting Light: Selected Writings of Samuel Palmer* (Manchester, 1985)

Ackroyd, Peter, *Blake* (London, 1999)

————*London: The Biography* (London, 2000)

Arts Council, *Samuel Palmer and his Circle: The Shoreham Period* (London, 1956)

Ayrton, Michael, *British Drawings* (London, 1946)

Baskin, Leonard, *Blake and the Youthful Ancients* (Northampton, Mass., 1965)

Bate, Jonathan, *The Song of the Earth* (London, 2000)

Bennett, Shelley M., 'The Blake Followers in the Context of Contemporary English Art', *Huntingdon Library Quarterly*, Vol. 46 (1983)

Bentley, G. E. (ed.), *Blake Records* (Oxford, 1969)

Bindman, David, 'Samuel Palmer's "An Address to the Electors of West Kent",
    1832 Rediscovered', *Blake: An Illustrated Quarterly*, XIX (1985)

Binyon, Laurence, *The Followers of William Blake* (London, 1925)

Blayney Brown, David, *Samuel Palmer 1805–1881: Loan Exhibition from the
    Ashmolean Museum Oxford* (London, 1982)

Bulwer Lytton, Edward, *England and the English* (London, 1833)

Butlin, Martin (ed.), *Samuel Palmer: The Sketchbook of 1824* (London, 2005)

Calvert, Samuel, *A Memoir of Edward Calvert Artist by His Third Son* (London,
    1893)

Cecil, David, *Visionary and Dreamer* (Princeton, 1969)

Clark, Kenneth, *Blake and Visionary Art* (London, 1973)

———*Landscape into Art* (London, 1949)

Cobbett, William, *Rural Rides* (London, 2001)

Crouan, Katherine, *John Linnell – Truth to Nature*, Introduction and Catalogue
    to Martyn Gregory Exhibition (London, 1983)

Cumberland, George, *Thoughts on Outline* (London, 1796)

Dickens, Charles, *Pictures from Italy* (London, 1846)

Drury, Jolyon, *Revelation to Revolution: The Legacy of Samuel Palmer* (Kent,
    2006)

Erdman, David V. (ed.), *The Complete Poetry and Prose of William Blake* (New
    York, 1988)

Evans, Mark, 'Blake Calvert – and Palmer? The Album of Constantine Ionides',
    Burlington Magazine, Vol. 144, September 2002, pp. 539–49

Fenwick, Simon, *The Enchanted River: Two Hundred Years of the Royal Watercolour
    Society* (London, 2004)

Finch, Mrs Eliza, *Memorials of the Late Francis Oliver Finch* (London, 1865)

Flaxman, John, *Lectures on Sculpture* (London, 1829)

Gilchrist, Alexander, *The Life of William Blake* (London, 1863 and 1880)

Gilpin, William, *An Essay Upon Prints* (London, 1768)

———*Remarks on Forest Scenery and Other Woodland Views*, (Edinburgh, 1791)

Goldman, Paul, *Samuel Palmer, Visionary Printmaker: A Loan Exhibition
    from the British Museum, Department of Prints and Drawings* (London,
    1991)

Goodman, Kevis, *Georgic Modernity and British Romanticism: Poetry and the
    Mediation of History* (Cambridge, 2004)

Grigson, Geoffrey, *Samuel Palmer: The Visionary Years* (London, 1947)

Hamerton, Philip Gilbert, *An Autobiography . . . and a Memoir by his Wife*
    (London, 1897)

———*Etching and Etchers* (London, 1869)

Hamilton, James, *Turner: A Life* (London, 1997)

Hardie, Martin, 'The Etched Work of Samuel Palmer', *The Print Collector's Quarterly*, 3/1, 1913

———*Water-Colour Painting In Britain: The Romantic Period* (London, 1967)

Harrison, Colin, 'Treasures of the Ashmolean Museum', *Apollo*, Vol. CXLV (May 1997)

———*Samuel Palmer* (Oxford, 1997)

Herring, Sarah, 'Samuel Palmer's Shoreham Drawings in Indian Ink', *Apollo*, Vol. 148m, I, 441 (November 1998) pp. 37–42

Hill, Christopher, *The English Revolution* (London, 1949)

Hind, A. M., *A Short History of Engraving and Etching* (London, 1911)

Hutchinson, Sidney C., *The History of the Royal Academy* (London, 1968)

Keating, Tom, *The Fake's Progress*, (London, 1977)

Keynes, Geoffrey (ed.), *The Letters of William Blake* (Oxford, 1980)

Keynes, Geoffrey; Fawcus, Arnold; Lister, Raymond; Reynolds, Graham, *Samuel Palmer, a Vision Recaptured*: commemorative handbook for the Palmer exhibition at the Victoria & Albert Museum, 1978–9.

Kirwan, Daniel Joseph, *Palace and Hovel: Or Phases of London Life* (London, 1870)

Leslie, C. R., *Memoirs of the Life of John Constable* (London, 1951)

Linnell, David, *Blake, Palmer, Linnell and Co: The Life of John Linnell* (Sussex, 1994)

Lister, Raymond, *Catalogue Raisonné of Samuel Palmer* (Cambridge, 1988)

———*Edward Calvert* (London, 1962)

———*George Richmond: A Critical Biography* (London, 1981)

———*Samuel Palmer and 'The Ancients'* (Cambridge, 1984)

———*Samuel Palmer and His Etchings* (London, 1969)

———*Studies in the Arts*, ed. Francis Warner, (Oxford, 1968)

———*The Paintings of Samuel Palmer* (Cambridge, 1985)

Malins, Edward, *Samuel Palmer's Italian Honeymoon* (Oxford, 1968)

Matthews, Mike, *Captain Swing in Sussex and Kent: Rural Rebellion in 1830* (Hastings, 2006)

Melville, Robert, *Samuel Palmer* (London, 1956)

Moore, T. Sturge, 'Samuel Palmer's Happiest Designs', *Apollo*, 1936, pp. 329–35

Morgan, D. H., *Harvesters and Harvesting 1840–1900* (London, 1982)

Norman, Frank and Geraldine, *The Fake's Progress: Being the Cautionary History of the Master Painter and Simulator Mr Tom Keating* (London, 1977)

Olson, Roberta J. N., *Fire and Ice: A History of Comets in Art* (New York, 1985)

Olson, Roberta J. N. and Pasachoff, Jay M., *Fire in the Sky: Comets and Meteors, the Decisive Centuries in British Art and Science* (Cambridge, 1998)

Palmer, A. H., 'The Story of an Imaginative Painter', *The Portfolio*, Number 15 (1884), pp. 145–51

Palmer, Samuel, *An English Version of the Eclogues of Virgil*, with illustrations by the author (London, 1883)

Patterson, Annabel, *Pastoral and Ideology: Virgil to Valéry* (Berkeley, 1987)

Payne, Christiana, 'John Linnell and Samuel Palmer in the 1820s', *Burlington Magazine*, Vol. CXXIV, No. 948, March 1982

Peacock, Carlos, *Samuel Palmer: Shoreham and After* (London, 1968)

Porter, Roy, *London: A Social History* (London, 1994)

Pressly, William, 'Samuel Palmer and the Pastoral Convention', *Record of the Art Museum Princeton University*, Vol. XXVIII, No. 2, 1969

Richmond, George, 'Notes on Edward Calvert', *The Athenaeum*, 25 August 1883

Roget, J. L., *History of the Old Water Colour Society* (London 1891, reprinted 1972)

Ruskin, John, *Modern Painters*, 5 vols (London, 1846)

Stephens F. G., *Memorials of William Mulready, RA* (London, 1890)

————*Notes by Mr F. G. Stephens on a Collection of Drawings, Paintings and Etchings by the Late Samuel Palmer* (London, 1881)

Stirling, A. M. W. (ed.), *The Richmond Papers, from the Correspondence and Manuscripts of George Richmond, RA, and his Son Sir William Richmond, RA, KCB* (London, 1926)

Story, Alfred, *The Life of John Linnell*, 2 vols (London, 1893)

Tomory, Peter, *The Life and Art of Henry Fuseli* (London, 1972)

Tromans, Nicholas (ed.), *The Lure of the East: British Orientalist Painting* (London, 2008)

Twining, Louisa, *Recollections of Life and Work; Being the Autobiography of Louisa Twining* (London, 1893)

Vaughan, William, *Art and the Natural World in Nineteenth-Century Britain* (University of Kansas, 1990)

Vaughan, William; Barker, Elizabeth E.; Harrison, Colin, *Samuel Palmer 1805– 1881: Vision and Landscape* (London, 2005)

Warner, Francis (ed.), *Studies in the Arts*, (Oxford, 1968)

White, Malcolm and Saynor, Joy, *Shoreham: A Village in Kent* (Shoreham, 1989)

Wilcox, Timothy, *Samuel Palmer* (London, 2005)

Yorke, Malcolm, *The Spirit of Place: Nine Neo-Romantic Artists and their Times*, (London, 1988)

Acknowledgements

I would like to thank my agent George Capel for her irrepressible enthusiasm, my editor Michael Fishwick for his constant encouragement and a stern ticking-off; Anna Simpson and Alexa von Hirschberg at Bloomsbury for their judicious attention, Laura Brooke for her energetic work in the publicity department and Kate Johnson, the copy editor, for her expertise and thoroughness.

I am enormously grateful to the Royal Society of Literature and the Jerwood Charitable Foundation for the generosity of an award which meant so much more than just the money – though I was delighted enough with that – and to my husband Will for his understanding, patience and undeviating support.

I would like to thank Josh, Alfie and Ella, for keeping me company along the banks of the Darent; my parents for taking care of me like the mad lady in the attic; Anna, Tid and Ben for bearing the brunt of my boring telephone calls; Catherine Milner for always managing to show me the bright side; Alice Miles for her laughter and late nights out drinking; Catherine Goodman for calming walks along the canal; Nancy Durrant at *The Times* for being accommodating; Gordon Cook of the Fine Art Society for his time and advice; and the artists David Inshaw, Emily Patrick and Tom Hammick for their painterly insights. Thank you, too, to the many residents of Shoreham – especially Ken Wilson – who would so kindly point me in the right direction as I poked about in their village; and also to the inhabitants of Palmer's former home in Redhill.

I would particularly like to remember Sebastian whose life ended just before I had ended the book. He wouldn't have read it anyway because it wasn't about him.

I am also thankful to Flea and Bear for staying beside me all through the writing and finally to Katya for coming along right at the end like the last full stop.

Index

A Note on the Type

The text of this book is set Adobe Garamond. It is one of several versions of Garamond based on the designs of Claude Garamond. It is thought that Garamond based his font on Bembo, cut in 1495 by Francesco Griffo in collaboration with the Italian printer Aldus Manutius. Garamond types were first used in books printed in Paris around 1532. Many of the present-day versions of this type are based on the *Typi Academiae* of Jean Jannon cut in Sedan in 1615.

Claude Garamond was born in Paris in 1480. He learned how to cut type from his father and by the age of fifteen he was able to fashion steel punches the size of a pica with great precision. At the age of sixty he was commissioned by King Francis I to design a Greek alphabet, for this he was given the honourable title of royal type founder. He died in 1561.